Adventuring
Along the
Gulf of Mexico

The Sierra Club Adventure Travel Guides

by Donald G. Schueler

Adventuring
Along the
Gulf of Mexico

*The Sierra Club Travel Guide
to the Gulf Coast of the United States and
Mexico from the Florida Keys to Yucatán*

Sierra Club Books   San Francisco

The Sierra Club, founded in 1892 by John Muir, has devoted itself to the study and protection of the earth's scenic and ecological resources—mountains, wetlands, woodlands, wild shores and rivers, deserts and plains. The publishing program of the Sierra Club offers books to the public as a nonprofit educational service in the hope that they may enlarge the public's understanding of the Club's basic concerns. The point of view expressed in each book, however, does not necessarily represent that of the Club. The Sierra Club has some sixty chapters coast to coast, in Canada, Hawaii, and Alaska. For information about how you may participate in its programs to preserve wilderness and the quality of life, please address inquiries to Sierra Club, 730 Polk Street, San Francisco, CA 94109.

Library of Congress Cataloging in Publication Data

Schueler, Donald G.
   Adventuring along the Gulf of Mexico.

   Bibliography: p.
   Includes index.
   1. Outdoor recreation—Mexico, Gulf of. 2. Mexico, Gulf of—Description and travel—Guide-books. I. Title.
   GV191.48.M6S38 1986   790'.09163'64   85-18472
   ISBN 0-87156-756-3

Cover design by Bonnie Smetts

Book design by Paul Quin

Illustrations by Nancy Warner

Composition by Wilsted & Taylor

Printed in the United States of America

10 9 8 7 6 5 4 3 2 1

Contents

Preface

For most vacationing travelers who head for the Gulf Coast each year, the phrase "outdoor recreation" conjures up images of water-skiers, shiny yachts, gaffed marlin, and basking bodies—that world of sun 'n fun that has its fullest flowering at crowded watering holes such as St. Petersburg, Panama City, Galveston, and Cancún. There's nothing wrong with all that, of course, except that such a limited perception tends to ignore most of the real out-of-doors experiences that the Gulf Coast has to offer. The fact is that nowhere on the North American continent has Nature devised a more diverse bounty of landscapes and life forms for the perceptive traveler to enjoy than along the three-and-a-half thousand miles of coast that curve around the Gulf of Mexico from Key West, Florida, to Mexico's Yucatán Peninsula. Despite the pressures of human population and development, there are still vast, wild deltas, tropical rain forests, cypress-shadowed streams, mangrove labyrinths, and unspoiled islands waiting to be explored—not to mention stretches of unsullied beach where the only noisy crowds are composed of gulls and terns.

There are good reasons why the Gulf Coast has not received the attention it deserves even from visitors who love the natural world and want to see as much of it as they can. For one thing, the region has few national forests and, except for the Everglades and two national seashores, no large national parks toward which you can simply point your car, as you can out West. For another, the natural landscapes of the Gulf do not lend themselves, as do mountains, canyons, and deserts, to panoramic overviews. A swamp or marsh or bottomland forest likes to keep its secrets to itself. It turns its back on highways and motorists; and if you invade its privacy without knowing what you're doing, a casual walk may soon become a wade.

Actually, there are many points of access to the Gulf Coast's wild and scenic places—even in Mexico, where public lands are almost nonexistent. The problem is finding out what is where. North of the border, various state agencies publish information about outdoor opportunities in their particular states, but until now there has been no comprehensive regional guide available; indeed, if you wander into a state tourist information center and announce that you want to explore a swamp or canoe an unspoiled river, you may be answered with a bewildered stare.

This book, then, is meant to be useful to anyone, whether Gulf Coast resident or visitor from distant parts, who wants an outdoor experience that goes beyond the much-promoted pursuit of the perfect tan. Whether you are driving a car or an RV, with or without a canoe or motorboat in tow, whether you want a campground with all the facilities or a primitive campsite where the closest neighbors are wood storks and alligators, or whether you prefer to do your traveling vicariously while sitting in your armchair at home, you should find many places in these pages that are exactly to your taste.

The table of contents suggests the book's format. The first chapter provides general information about the Gulf Coast and includes subsections that deal with the special challenges of exploring the out-of-doors in Mexico. But the lion's share of the text is meant to take the reader on a counterclockwise tour around the Gulf, beginning at Key West and ending at Cancún on the Yucatán coast. To actually make this 3500-mile one-way journey in a leisurely fashion, savoring what is to be savored along the way, would take several months. Because most people don't have that kind of time to devote to travel, and also because the Gulf Coast lends itself to a handy if very imprecise divisioning into regions where landscape, climate, and/or human culture have a certain cohesion, I have divided the overall odyssey into ten sections, any one of which would make a worthwhile two- or three-week vacation in the out-of-doors. A chapter is devoted to each section and consists of a brief synopsis of data about access, climate, landscape features, flora and fauna, and prospects for camping, hiking, and boating. This is followed by a hypothetical ideal outdoors tour of the most promising wild areas available—refuges, parks, national and state forests—as well as the most scenic routes along the way.

Obviously, the reader may not wish to follow the travel plan as it is described. (For one thing, he may be heading west to east whereas the ideal tour moves east to west.) But by reading through the chapter on the area of the Gulf that interests you, and consulting the accompanying map, you should have no trouble figuring out a suitable itinerary. Information in the text includes how to get to areas that might interest you and descriptions of what you will find there in the way of natural features and camping and recreational opportunities. An appendix supplements information on public campgrounds in the United States. Inevitably, depending on special interests or time limitations, you may have to choose between alternate routes, especially in the road-happy USA. On the other hand, there are some areas where little choice is possible. This is especially true of Mexico, where, as we shall see, the parks, preserves, and camping facilities that U.S. citizens take for granted in their own country are almost nonexistent.

As already noted, I have tried to accommodate in the text a variety of outdoors preferences, including canoeing and boating, hiking, wildlife viewing, and self-conducted tours along marked nature trails. But the emphasis is always on the Coast, not the wide open waters of the Gulf itself. A considerable literature is already available concerning yachting, sailboating, and deep-sea fishing in the Gulf of Mexico.

Usually, the routes that this tour follows—when a choice is possible—are those that have the fewest billboards, motels, and condominiums along the way. But wherever towns and cities do lie in our path, they will be noted if they are historic or picturesque. In the case of a few exceptional places, notably New Orleans and some Mexican cities, I have pushed the meaning of "outdoors activity" to include descriptions of urban "hikes." In Mexico the sites of notable Indian ruins are also on the agenda, both because they are so remarkable in themselves and because their settings frequently offer the best natural scenery and birding for miles around.

While I am explaining the liberties I have taken with the word "outdoors," I had better forewarn you that, from a geographer's point of view, I have also been a bit free with the term "Gulf Coast." As you will discover, the text sometimes moves pretty far inland when the wonders of the natural world beckon or human exploitation on the Coast repels. Also, in some areas, such as the Florida Everglades and parts of northern Mexico, distance from the Gulf is determined by the only available road.

By way of concluding this introductory note, let me urge you, in approaching the Gulf of Mexico, to adapt your expectations to its special laid-back charms. The world we shall explore is more sensuous than spartan, more hot than cold, more horizontal than vertical, more easeful than urgent. The great trick is to relax and be open. Leave the impatient puritan in you at home to mind the store.

1
General
Information

Climate

Climate on the Gulf Coast ranges from warm temperate-subtropical on the northern shore, to subtropical in southern Florida, southern Texas, and northern Mexico, to tropical from the Tampico area southward. Overall, as millions of refugees from more northerly latitudes will attest, the weather is more often pleasant than otherwise. However, there's no denying that Gulf summers are long and hot. And, the further south you go, the longer and hotter they get, occasionally climbing above 100° F. There are variations within this broad range, however. On the northern shore especially, rains frequently cool things off, and on some mountainous stretches of the Mexican coastline, elevation has the same effect. Then, too, proximity to the open Gulf and its breezes sometimes makes a difference.

Northern Coast winters are variable. Snow is a very great rarity, but there are usually at least one or two hard freezes every year; and there are always some days from mid-December to early March when the temperature is in the thirties or forties and a damp, bone-chilling wind makes the weather seem even colder than it is. But even in January and February, some days may be downright balmy, with no need for the lightest sweater. Most years, most of the time, winter weather between Corpus Christi and Tampa is autumnal, with temperatures ranging from the low fifties to the high seventies. Weeks-long stretches of gray, cold days are pretty rare even on the northern Gulf. Rain on this part of the Coast can fall at any time of year, but least frequently in early autumn. During summers, afternoon showers and thunderstorms occur quite regularly, but they are often very localized.

Although southern Florida and northern Mexico are not immune to winter rain or cold snaps, and even rare freezes, they generally operate on a tropical two-season cycle. And this is always the case for the

1

rest of coastal Mexico: winters are dry and warm; the summers hot and wet. Indeed, on the southern Gulf Coast of Mexico there is only about a ten-degree range between average temperatures during the coolest and hottest months. It is the amount of rain, not the cold, that makes the difference. But tropical precipitation, like northern temperatures, is subject to considerable variation from place to place. During the summer wet season, for example, the rains in most of the state of Tabasco seem endless and torrential, whereas in the western Yucatán they are much lighter and usually occur in midafternoon. Notwithstanding the partial exception of the Yucatán, however, the eastern and southern sectors of the Gulf get a lot more rainfall than northern Mexico and southern Texas at any season of the year.

You will find brief comments about climate in the "At a Glance" section at the beginning of each chapter. As broad guidelines, however, keep the following general rules in mind. The northern Gulf, from Tampa to Galveston, is theoretically suitable for camping and hiking at almost any time of year. Summer has much to recommend it in the way of luxuriant vegetation, langorous evenings, fireflies, and shimmering beaches. But you must be braced for some extremely hot, muggy, buggy days between June and mid-September, plus the occasional drenching rain. As for winter, the weather can shift from one

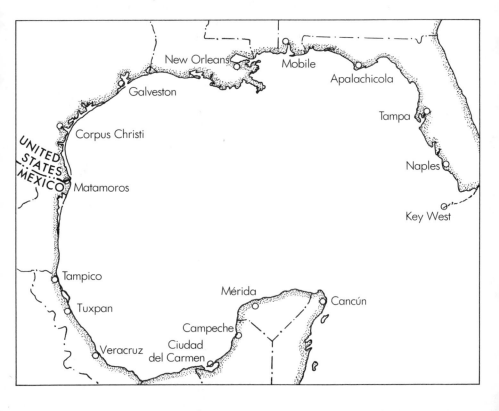

day to the next: from warm and clear to cold and rainy. (During this season you may also have to share the boondocks with hunters.) The best seasons for the northern Gulf are spring (mid-March to early June) and fall (mid-September through November). In southern Florida, December through March is the ideal period. The long summers can be brutal, and the mosquitoes literally overwhelming, except on the Keys. In southern Texas and northern Mexico, spring and fall, as well as many winter days, are just right. Summer is breathlessly hot but fairly dry, and since most of the out-of-doors activity in this region is confined to the bays and beaches, there is always the comfort of the Gulf waters nearby—even if they are lukewarm. In the tropical zone of coastal Mexico, however, only the most heat-resistant Yankees will want to brave summer's torrid temperatures, humidity, and frequent rains. Compared to the states of Veracruz, Tabasco, and Campeche, the northern coast of the state of Yucatán is a bit more tolerable but still awfully hot. In all of this southern half of the Gulf, winter and early spring are the best times to visit, although even then, that ill wind, *El Norte*, can suddenly make the beaches uninhabitable.

The word "hot" has figured prominently in the foregoing comments for good reason. During much of the year, the Gulf Coast swelters and its people sweat. But "hot" is a relative concept, at least on the northern half of the Gulf. Some people are physically designed to take more of the heat, and enjoy it, than others. But it is also a matter of attitude. Even a perfectly scorching day in the out-of-doors can be beautifully enjoyed if you take it on its own terms, not trying to do what it won't allow you to do and, above all, not deciding beforehand that you're going to hate the heat. The only way you can beat it is by realizing that you can't beat it. Dress for the temperature, arm yourself against the bugs, don't push yourself, and have frequent recourse to a good book, ice-cooled liquids, a sweat towel, and available shade. Pretend you're Jungle Jim. Faced with a northern winter, you will remember even the miasmic heat of August on the Gulf with a kind of longing.

A *Note About Hurricanes*   Every stretch of the Gulf Coast has been socked with a hurricane at one time or another, some more often than others. The Galveston area, for instance, gets more than its share, whereas Yucatán's Gulf coastline is rarely hit. These tropical cyclones (by definition, their winds must reach seventy-five miles per hour) are a mostly summer phenomenon, building up force in the Atlantic, the Caribbean, and/or the Gulf of Mexico before coming ashore. Thanks to modern communications systems and weather surveillance, they are no longer the killers that they were earlier in this century. Back then, with much smaller populations on the Coast, a single storm sometimes took the lives of thousands of people. Nowadays, the worst kill hundreds. Even so, those who know about such things warn that if a megahurricane comes into New Orleans's Lake Pontchartrain or Mobile Bay, the death toll may yet compare with that of days of yore, warning systems or not. As it is, ever-expanding property development on the Coast (often in areas where it should not have been permitted) has caused a sky's-the-limit increase in property damage, even when a hurricane is not a record-breaker.

For the purposes of this book, there are two things to remember. First, only people who have not been through a serious hurricane think that it's a Big Thrill. Second, those who die in hurricanes are usually killed by water, not wind. The hundreds of people who lost their lives not all that long ago at places such as Cameron, Louisiana (Audrey), and Long Beach, Mississippi (Camille), just did not believe that tidal waves would reach as far inland as they did. The moral: keep in touch with weather reports during the summer months if you are on or near the Coast; there is usually plenty of advance warning. If you are boating, head for shore; if you are on the shore, head inland to designated areas. Large trailer camper vehicles, by the way, are very vulnerable to high winds. You should definitely not be in one when a hurricane strikes.

A *Note About Heat Exhaustion and Sunburn*   Heat exhaustion is what often happens to compulsive people who don't listen to advice about living with high temperatures. Excessive sweating, followed by headache, wooziness, nausea, irregular pulse, and clammy skin are the usual symptoms. If you just stop, cool off, drink a lot of water with Gatorade powder or salt tablets mixed in, you'll probably be all right in a little while. If you've reached the sunstroke stage, however, which is usually signaled by high fever, cramps, and dry, hot skin, use any means to keep yourself cool and get to a doctor as quickly as you can. En route, keep your feet lower than your head. As for sunburn, it can—and does—ruin vacations for thousands of people every year. All so unnecessary! You are bound to know what your skin can or can't take in the way of solar rays. Just remember that even the easiest-tanning people need to go easy in the blaring light of the Gulf sun. *Never* stay out long on the open water or the beach without bringing protective clothing and a good sunscreen lotion with you.

Geology

During the Jurassic period, some 180 million years ago, the Gulf of Mexico began to take shape as a result of the continental drift that separated the American continents from Europe and Africa. This drift induced the rifting of North America from Central America, which created a closed basin between the two land masses. As the basin was gradually deepened by subsidence, the evaporation of trapped sea-water produced tremendous concentrations of salt. Geologists have named this basinwide salt deposit the Louann.

Some seventy million years ago, during the Cretaceous period, sea levels rose and the Gulf became connected with the Atlantic Ocean. Vast carbonate banks, or reefs, formed in the shallow sea around the perimeters of the Gulf, evolving chemically into the limestone cores of the Florida and Yucatán platforms. During the past sixty-five million years, sediments from the eroding Rockies and Appalachians traveled down the ancestral Mississippi River to fill in and build up the northern Gulf. The weight of these sediments overlying the Louann Salt Deposit forced plugs of salt to move upward, penetrating younger sediments and forming salt domes on the flat coastal plain. A similar process was also in effect in other areas of the Gulf. (Some of these domes, such as those at Avery and Weeks islands in Louisiana and others in the lowlands of southern Veracruz and Tabasco, are presently mined for salt and sulphur.)

The carbonate limestone platforms of Yucatán and Florida continued to grow during this time, gradually exemplifying what the geologists call a "karst topography," one in which the soft limestone is eroded by the action of water to create sinkholes, underground caverns, and subterranean river systems.

Continental drift, technically described as plate tectonics, is a process that continues to move the floor of the Pacific Ocean under the plates of North and South America. The resulting friction causes a buckling upthrust in the earth's surface that creates the mountains and, in some areas, volcanoes that account for the vertical terrain along parts of the Mexican Gulf Coast as far east as the Tuxtlas in southern Veracruz.

During the Pleistocene epoch, comprising a time span from 2 million to 12,000 years before the present, the earth experienced four ice ages, or glacial periods, during which glaciers advanced over much of the surface of North America as well as northern Europe and Asia. These were followed by interglacial periods during which the glaciers retreated in response to the warming of the earth's climate. These advances and retreats inevitably induced radical changes in the levels of the world's oceans. During these periods the continental land mass around the Gulf, as elsewhere, was alternately more exposed or more submerged than it is now. During some interglacial periods, for example, all of eastern Texas and southern Florida were under water, whereas at the zenith of the glacial periods, vast tracts of the Gulf's continental shelf, now submerged, were high and dry. Peninsular Florida was nearly twice as wide as it is now. At the height of the last of these glacial stages, a mere 16,000 years ago, mastodons, sabertoothed tigers, and, quite possibly, man roamed grassy savannahs that now lie anywhere from a few dozen to hundreds of feet beneath the waters of the Gulf. During the glacial periods, rivers carved their way through alluvial sand ridges that marked the highest reach of former seas, creating alluvial valleys that are now submerged bays.

We are presently at some undetermined stage of an interglacial period when the waters of the Gulf—and the world—are neither as high nor as low as they were during the relatively recent Pleistocene epoch. Even for geologists, it is impossible to speculate where we, and the Gulf, will be 16,000 years hence. But there is some evidence that, wherever we are then, it will be, in part, the consequence of the way we are handling the planet now.

History

Pre-Columbian Indian Cultures   Like all Indians in the Americas, the prehistoric peoples who inhabited the Gulf regions were descendants of Asiatic tribes that crossed the long-vanished land bridge across the Bering Strait more than 20,000 years ago. When Spanish explorers arrived in the early sixteenth century, most of the Coast was occupied, though in many places only thinly, by Indian peoples. Among the tribes found along the northern side of the Gulf were the Calusa and Timucuan in southern Florida; the Muskhogean-speaking federations of tribes (Chickasaw, Choctaw, Creek) in northern Florida, Alabama, and Mississippi; the Houma and Cawasha in coastal Louisiana; and the Karankawa along the Texas coast. Although little is known about the pre-Columbian history of these tribes or the earlier peoples who occupied their territories, the discovery of many shell middens and burial mounds has provided considerable information about their relatively primitive lifestyles.

Inevitably, the study of Indian cultures along the northern Gulf Coast has been overshadowed by the research devoted to the vastly more advanced civilizations of Mesoamerica, a region encompassing much of Mexico from the Central Highlands south and east to the Yucatán, as well as Guatemala and Honduras. For the peoples of this region, the successful cultivation of maize, squash, and other crops (c. 2000–1500 B.C.) was the crucial first step toward the evolution of more elaborate social systems. During the so-called Formative Period (1500 B.C.–A.D. 250) the coastal jungles of Tabasco were to become the cradle of the great civilizations of the Classic Period. Here, the still-mysterious mother culture of the Olmecs seems to have had its origins. The Olmec capital at La Venta was violently destroyed circa 600 B.C., but by that time these remarkable people had created distinctive monolithic sculptures, built tall, conical, clay temple mounds, and invented a calendar and vigesimal counting system. Many archeologists theorize that their culture was transmitted to other Mesoamerican Indian peoples during the early Classic Period via the Izapa culture in what is now Guatemala. During the Classic Period (A.D. 250–900), great interrelated city-states evolved in the Valley of Mexico (Teotihuacán), at the Zapotec capital of Monte Alban in Oaxaca, and, on the Gulf Coast, at the Totonic center of El Tajín south of Tuxpan. But it was in the Mayan regions, encompassing Guatemala, Yucatán, and parts of Chiapas and Tabasco, that Mesoamerican civilization reached its highest level of sophistication. By 800 A.D., the Mayans had made advances in astronomical observation, calendar systems, and hieroglyphic writing that would never be surpassed by Indian peoples living in the Post-Classic Period. Their architecture, though not as grandiose as that of cultures in the Valley of Mexico, was remarkable for its sculptured detail, vivid bas-reliefs and frescoes, and the corbeled arch.

By the ninth century, as Europe was slowly emerging from the Dark Ages, Mesoamerica was descending into a dark age of its own. By that time Indian societies had evolved elaborate caste systems ruled by priests and warriors. It is generally thought that the prevalent milpa system of slash-and-burn agriculture, with its capacity for destroying soils, may have been the root cause for the decline of the great city-state cultures of the Classic Period (although more advanced agricultural techniques had evolved in some areas). Food supplies apparently could no longer support ever growing, more concentrated populations. Social structures swiftly disintegrated, and, one by one, the great cities—Teotihuacán, El Tajín, Palenque—were abandoned. Repeated barbarian invasions from northern Mexico and the assimilation of the invaders by the more civilized peoples of the Valley of Mexico led to the ascendance of new cultures. These more militaristic societies—with new, insatiably bloodthirsty gods—would dominate during the Post-Classic Period (900–1521). Prior to the ascendance of the Aztecs in the fourteenth century, the most notable of these cultures was that of the warlike Toltecs (950–1168), who established their capital at Tula in the Valley of Mexico. The invasion of the Yucatán Peninsula by an exiled Toltec warrior—soon to be deified as the Plumed Serpent, Quetzalcoatl—led to a renaissance of Maya-Toltec culture, of which Uxmal and Chichén-Itzá are the major monuments.

The last of the northern tribes to invade and dominate Mesoamerica was the Aztec. By the end of the fifteenth century, this warlike, imperialistic people had built (on the site of present-day Mexico City) the city of Tenochtitlán, the largest and probably the most magnificent metropolis in the world of that time. They were also exacting tribute from conquered tribes throughout nearly all of southern Mexico as far east as Zempoala. The tribute included countless thousands of sacrificial victims for Aztec altars. (Human sacrifice was a common practice in nearly all Mesoamerican cultures; but one of the less happy superlatives that attaches to Tenochtitlán is that its citizens sponsored this particular type of human slaughter on a scale unprecedented in the history of the world.) The exaction of heavy tribute, human and otherwise, was one of the decisive factors that led to the conquest of the Aztecs by the Spaniards. Although modern-day Mexicans often ignore the fact, most of the peoples subjugated by the Aztecs preferred the rule of Cortés to that of Montezuma as the lesser of two evils, and many became the Spaniard's allies. Also, contrary to modern myth, the Spanish friars were a lot more kindly than the literally blood-encrusted Indian priests of yore. Generally, although changes are occurring now (not all for the better), the always-harsh lot of the average rural *indio* has not altered much in the last millennium.

Back on the northern border of the Gulf, the Indian ultimately fared just about as badly, although along some parts of the south Florida and Texas coasts the tribes and their environments were so inhospitable that they kept settlers at bay until well into the 1800s. Before the century was over, however, most of the Gulf tribes, much thinned out by the white man's bullets, liquor, and viruses, had been deported to the West. A few small reservations exist in the coastal South, although the visitor will find little evidence of traditional Indian culture. The notable exception to that rule is the Seminole reservation in the Everglades. However, the word "Seminole" is of relatively recent coinage; it describes a displaced people of mixed tribal ancestry who have acquired their own cultural identity only in this century.

The Spanish Gulf, 1517–1717   In terms of sheer derring-do, nothing in the annals of real-life adventure surpasses the story of the Spanish exploration of the New World. Just a couple of decades after Columbus sailed the ocean blue, Spain had established its presence in the Caribbean, notably Cuba, and the earliest forays onto the mainland were under way. In 1513, more than a hundred years before the Pilgrims arrived at Plymouth Rock, Ponce De León landed, briefly, on Florida's Gulf Coast. (On a return trip eight years later, he would be mortally wounded by an Indian arrow.) In 1517 and 1518, expeditions encountered the Yucatán Peninsula and its unfriendly natives.

The big event came in 1519, when Hernán Cortés, ambitious, brave, and bright, sailed from Cuba without the Spanish governor's permission. He put ashore near the present-day city of Veracruz, which he founded, and ran his ships aground, just in case his several hundred followers had any ideas about backing out of the enterprise. The enterprise, of course, was the conquest of Mexico. The central drama in this incredible saga would occur inland, in the Valley of Mexico; but it was here on the Gulf that the conquistador devised his strategy, impressed Montezuma's emissaries, and cleverly induced the rulers of the Totonac city of Zempoala, north of Veracruz, to imprison a delegation of hated Aztec tax collectors, thereby forcing the Totonacs to burn their bridges and become his first Indian allies. Within a year, the Aztec empire was no more, and Mexico became the Spanish colony that it would remain for three hundred years. During much of that time, it sent to the homeland a wealth of gold, silver, and spices surpassing the wildest imaginings of those who had dreamed of a passage to Cathay. This, despite the fact that much of that treasure was lost to the Gulf's violent storms or to fleets of pirate ships which made all shipping there a chancy enterprise until well into the nineteenth century. In the end, however, Spain had little more to show for the treasure that did reach its shores than it did for the riches, entombed in hundreds of Spanish galleons, that still lie on the bottom of the Gulf.

On the northern Gulf Coast, the most famous of the early Spanish explorations was Hernando de Soto's 4000-mile trek from Tampa Bay (in 1539) to the Mississippi River where he died. But even more fascinating is the earlier expedition led by Panfilo de Narvaez in 1528. This doomed venture was grippingly chronicled by one of its four survivors, Cabeza de Vaca, who, after six years of captivity among the Indians on the Galveston coast, eventually reached the Gulf of California.

Long after the Spanish had implanted themselves on California's coast, the Floridas of the Gulf Coast remained virtually a blank page. Spain, concerned with asserting its influence in European power struggles, was interested only in the New World's mineral wealth. Since de Soto's expedition had demonstrated the absence of gold and silver in the Floridas, the region held little interest for Spanish rulers. By the time a significant Spanish settlement was established on Pensacola Bay in 1696, the French, in the person of the Sieur de La Salle, had already laid claim to the entire Mississippi Valley (1682). At the end of the century, France sent out the brothers Le Moyne, the Sieur d'Iberville and Sieur de Bienville, to establish a colony on the coast. After headquartering first at Biloxi, then Mobile, Bienville selected a site on the Mississippi in 1718 and christened it Nouvelle-Orleans.

The Northern Gulf, 1700–1846   The history of the northern Gulf during the next century and a half sounds like a territorial game of musical chairs—the chairs having nothing to say about who occupied them at any given time. The players, of course, were Spain, France, England, and—the ultimate winner—the United States. For the European powers, decisions were almost invariably determined by continental wars and diplomatic treaties that had little to do with the colonies themselves. To be brief: in 1762, France, after quarreling with Spain for decades about where its Louisiana territory ended and the Spanish Floridas began, ceded Louisiana to Spain. Less than a year later, Spain signed over the Floridas to England, which divided them into East and West Florida. (West Florida extended all the way to the Mississippi River, New Orleans excepted.) In 1783, Spain reacquired the Floridas during a period of renewed national strength. Seventeen years later (1800), during the Napoleonic Wars, it re-ceded the Louisiana territory to France, which, in 1803, sold it to the United States. The United States was beginning to flex its muscles in this new century. It had already claimed Alabama and Mississippi down to the thirty-first parallel, and it now insisted that its Louisiana Purchase included all of the northern Gulf Coast to within a few miles of Pensacola. During the War of 1812, England used Mobile as a base. Annoyed, President Madison cancelled this arrangement by evicting the Spanish governor. In 1817 and 1819 respectively, the states of Mississippi and Alabama were admitted into the Union. By that time, also, General Andrew Jackson, accurately complaining that the Spanish were supporting the Creek Indians in their raids on settlers in Georgia, occupied Pensacola. Spain was too weak to object and, in 1821, ceded all of Florida to the United States.

In two decades, this young country had acquired all of the northern Gulf except the region that is now Texas. Twenty-five years later, it had that also, along with all the American West. Again, to be brief: American settlers were permitted by treaty to settle the unadministered territory during the last years of Spanish rule in Mexico. For a while after the Mexican War of Independence (1810–21) this arrangement continued. However, in 1830, a centralist government in Mexico banned further American immigration and tried to compel settlers already in residence to accept the Catholic faith. The settlers, long accustomed to home rule, opted for independence. Lines on both sides hardened; in the subsequent confrontation, the cruelty of the Mexicans at the Alamo and Goliad confirmed the American determination to rebel and led to the defeat of the corrupt and treacherous General (and once-and-future president of Mexico) Santa Ana at San Jacinto. When Texas was admitted to the Union in 1845, it precipitated a war with Mexico that, dubious in its motivations (on both sides), untidy in its execution, and, by the standards of the day, humane in its conclusion (the United States could have appropriated all of Mexico if it had chosen to), established the national boundaries of the Gulf Coast from that time forward.

The Civil War and Its Aftermath on the Coast   Almost from the day that Bienville founded it, New Orleans was *the* ruling city of the Gulf Coast. It was a major port for seafaring vessels, a terminal for the growing traffic along the great water highway that the Mississippi River had become, and a metropolis for an aristocracy growing rich on sugar cane and cotton. In 1814, its outskirts became the scene of the last and most famous battle of the War of 1812. Neither the ethnic tension between the Creole (French-Spanish) gentry and the newly arrived Americans, nor fires that swept the city, nor malaria and "yellow-jack" (yellow fever) kept it from thriving. By the time the Civil War began, it was the richest city in the nation. To the east, Biloxi, Mobile, and Pensacola had also developed into sizable communities. As for the bayou country west of New Orleans, this had become—and until only a few decades ago would remain—the special domain of a French-speaking people unrelated to the city's Creoles. These, of course, were the Cajuns, descendants of French Acadians who had been cruelly banished from Nova Scotia by the British in the 1750s.

It would be a mistake to imagine most of the American Gulf Coast during this period as other than a subtropical frontier. Except for the rich lowlands of the Mississippi Delta, the Coast was never plantation country. Way down upon the Suwannee River, for example, it was timber, not cotton, that was the money crop. Even into the present century, some stretches of the Florida and Texas Gulf remained much as they had been before the white man came.

Most of the important Civil War battles on the Gulf were naval engagements. New Orleans fell into Union hands in 1862, but Mobile held out until August 1864, when the heaviest naval battle of the war was fought in Mobile Bay. Reconstruction dealt a crippling blow to these cities, along with the rest of the Coast and the South in general. For generations to come, the region would remain the poorest in the country. Only in Texas, where new settlers were pouring into the vast new state, was there a sort of boom. In southern Texas, millions of sheep were turning the fragile grasslands into a mesquite desert. Further north, Galveston was becoming the largest and richest city in the state.

The Coast of Mexico, 1820–1920   If it is difficult to provide a synopsis-history of the northern Gulf Coast during the nineteenth century, it is impossible to summarize events south of the border during roughly the same period. Even lengthy studies leave one with little more than a confused perception of convulsive upheaval and chaos, an unhappy anticipation of the histories of emerging Third World nations in our own time.

By the beginning of the nineteenth century, neither the *creoles* (Mexicans of pure Spanish descent), the increasing *mestizo* (Spanish-Indian) population, or the *indios*, as downtrodden as ever, retained any allegiance to Spain, and after twelve years of gory off-and-on revolution, the Treaty of Córdoba was signed in 1821, confirming Mexican independence. Some of the highlights of the subsequent decades were the rise and fall of the would-be *creole* emperor of Mexico, Augustín Iturbide (executed in 1823); the failure of a small Spanish force that tried to retake Mexico (1829); the rise of the unscrupulous General Santa Ana to his first term as president (1831); the humiliation of Santa Ana and Mexico when the Texans, in effect, won their independence (1838); the brief retaliatory expedition of the French after their nationals had been mistreated (1838); Mexico's declaration of war on the United States when Texas was admitted to the Union (1845); the invasion of Mexico by American troops and the occupation of Mexico City (1847); the ceding of California, Arizona, and New Mexico to the United States (1848); civil war between conservatives and reformists over the reduction of the power of the Church (1858–61) and the triumph of the great Indian reformer, Benito Juárez (1861); military invasion by Spain, England, and France when Mexico failed to meet its foreign debts (1861); the occupation of Mexico City by the French and the short-lived reign of Napoleon III's cousin, Maximilian, as emperor of Mexico (1863–66); the return to power of Juárez (1866) and the execution of the well-meaning but naive Maximilian (1867); the long reign of Porfirio Díaz, which brought stability, solvency, and foreign investment, but at frightful cost to the exploited lower classes (1876–1910); Díaz's expulsion by reformer Francisco Madero with the aid of revolutionaries Pancho Villa and Zapata (1911); the collapse of land-reform efforts and return to chaos and bloody civil wars, out of which emerged the Constitution of Querétaro advocating land redistribution and suppression of the Church (1913–1920).

Busy as the above outline is, it does not even suggest the endless government overthrows and political assassinations, violent regional rebellions, and idealistic intentions gone sour that characterize much of this chaotic and bloody century. The country, cursed by factionalism, corruption, class and regional hatreds, and, above all, a benighted, uneducated populace, could not begin to coalesce into the democratic nation that a few revolutionary leaders wished it to be.

The Gulf Coast, though rarely at the center of events, was often affected, and afflicted, by them. Tampico was the site of Spain's failed effort to retake its former colony. Veracruz cowered under the bombardment of the French during the in-some-ways farcical invasion of 1838; and, nine years later, the city surrendered to American troops who used it as a staging area for a march on Mexico City that rivaled the daring of Cortés's expedition more than three hundred years earlier. During the decades-long War of the Castes (begun in the 1840s), the Indians of Yucatán massacred so many of their *creole* masters that the survivors tried to offer the peninsula to almost any nation that would rescue them. Twenty-five years later, courtesy of the corrupt President Díaz, all of the state of Yucatán would be under the harsh control of a handful of henequen planters. To the west, Veracruz briefly became the seat of government for the great Juárez, Mexico's Lincoln, during the civil war of 1858–61. A decade later, the city witnessed the slave shipments, conducted by Díaz's henchmen, of Sonora's rebellious Yaquis to the Yucatán, where they were sold to planters at sixty-five dollars a head and literally worked to death. From Veracruz, the old dictator Díaz slipped into exile after his forced abdication in 1911.

Mexico: The Modern Period   Compared to the preceding 100 years, Mexico has made considerable progress toward stability in the last half-century, especially in the last two or three decades. The revolutionary Lázaro Cárdenas, who became president in the 1930s, suppressed the Church, distributed vast tracts of expropriated land to peasant cooperatives (*ejidos*), and nationalized the nation's oil industry, which until then had been dominated by foreign companies. Since the 1940s, the revolution has become institutionalized. Democratic forms are officially observed, although in practice, elections are controlled by the Partido Revolucionario Institucional (PRI), people can be imprisoned for their political beliefs, and the president can pass laws by decree. In the area of industrial development, great strides have been made. The vast oil fields discovered along the Gulf Coast have transformed sleepy fishing villages such as Tampico and Coatzacoalcos into boom towns. (Unfortunately, Mexico's too great dependence on this resource during the recent years of worldwide overproduction, compounded by widespread corruption, has played havoc with the nation's economy.) Thousands of miles of new roads have opened up even the most remote regions of the country to settlement. There have been considerable advances in education and especially medical care. The feudal *patrón* system is at an end, at least officially (although in fact it is still prevalent in many areas), and the Indian-Spanish *mestizos* are now the dominant class. All along the northern border, including the coastal area, countless illegal immigrants continue to undertake what Mexicans call the "reconquest of Texas." At the same time, ironically, Mexico's southern border is being crossed by legions of Guatemalans fleeing oppression in their own country.

Mexico properly belongs in the "developing nation" category of Third World countries. But it is a fact that, despite many tangible signs of progress, the nation's problems continue to outdistance efforts to solve them. Countless commentaries have addressed every aspect of these problems, from mismanagement and corruption to the persistence of regional insularity and/or the caste system to the psychological contradictions in the character of the "typical" Mexican, whoever he or she is. But it is clear that none of these problems is as fundamental as the cause-and-effect relationship between a too rapidly growing population and the misuse of natural resources. Most Mexicans are still rural and, by our standards (including the living standards of our minorities), extremely poor. The country's resources—particularly its limited supply of arable land—can scarcely support the present huge population of eighty million. Yet despite government programs encouraging birth control, Mexico's population will double by the end of this century and continue growing for the foreseeable future. The eventual effect of this population pressure on the country's political institutions remains uncertain. But its effect on the environment is already all too apparent: stripped mountains, polluted coasts, vanished forests, eroded soils, extirpated wildlife, and depleted fisheries. These processes are only too evident in the Gulf Coast region from Tampico to Tabasco, precisely because this area is one of the most fertile and productive in Mexico. The one glimmer of hope is that the present administration has at least acknowledged an environmental concern. But as of now, Mexico continues to exploit its natural resources. If that trend continues, Mexico will become much more of a Third World country than it is now, and the consequences, not just for Mexico but for the United States, will be very grave. The next decade or two will tell the story.

The Northern Gulf in Modern Times   In most of the post-Reconstruction Gulf South, the twentieth century didn't start off well, and because of a slump in agricultural prices, things got worse during the twenties, when much of the rest of the country was thriving. (East Texas, where oil was discovered in 1901, was, again, the Coast's prosperous exception.) During the Depression, when everybody was hard hit, the South hit bottom. By the end of the thirties, timber companies had plundered the last of the region's vast stands of virgin pine and cypress. Interestingly, coastal southerners fared a bit better than their inland compatriots because the bounty of the Gulf and the marshes was at their disposal. Many an old-timer, black and white, remembers when waterfowl, crabs, fish, and shrimp—abundant and free for the taking—kept body and soul together.

World War II marked a turning point in the fortunes of the region. Military bases, the expanding oil industry, and the Gulf's port facilities became crucial to the nation's war effort. Despite the bad public relations generated by segregation in the fifties and sixties, the upswing that began in the forties is still underway in a New South that has now become the Sunbelt. In Louisiana and Texas, many other industries have followed where oil led the way. New Orleans has emerged from its long sleep to become one of the nation's major ports and convention cities. Mobile, now that it has that multibillion-dollar boondoggle, the Tombigbee Waterway, to call its own, may soon give the Crescent City a run for its money. From Key West to South Padre Island, wall-to-wall condominiums loom on shiny beaches where, twenty years ago, sea turtles laid their eggs; and prosperous suburbs occupy drained swamps in which moonshiners recently plied their trade. The agony and triumph of the civil-rights movement is already part of a fading past. And coastal cities adapt, like the rest of the nation, to crowded expressways, welfarism, and crime. From every other region of the country, tourists, retirees, and bright young people in search of jobs and the sun arrive here in droves.

For someone who loves the out-of-doors, these recent decades have been in many ways harrowing. Unlike Mexico, the U.S. feels population pressure not at the subsistence level but at the level of affluent wastefulness. The stupendous riches of rivers, swamps, and marshes have been exploited by real-estate developers, the oil industry, mega-agriculture, and the Army Corps of Engineers. But there is good news too: many glorious parks have been established; some wildlife species, such as alligators, eagles, and pelicans, have made a comeback; and many people seem to care more than they used to about saving the wild areas and wild creatures that are left.

Hiking and Primitive Camping

Along most of the U.S. portion of the Gulf Coast there is no lack of natural areas where you can pitch a tent. Federal forests and Everglades National Park, Gulf and Padre national seashores, and all the larger state parks and forests offer sites for primitive camping. For hikers, there are many beautiful trails as well as shorter nature walks in all the parks and refuges. But serious backpackers should not expect the great networks of 100-mile-long hiking paths that can be found in the national forests and wilderness areas of the West. Human development and topography impose limits on how far you can go before you hit pavement—or water.

Following are some points that you may wish to consider. Many apply both to the United States and Mexico, but note also the "Additional Comments" about the latter country.

C*lothing*   Just about everywhere you travel on the Gulf Coast, either in the United States or Mexico, the first word is casual. Of course, some of the larger cities have posh hotels or restaurants where you may feel out of place without a tie, but I assume that an outdoors-oriented reader isn't much interested in that scene anyway. The one significant exception is New Orleans, where the food and night life deserve anyone's attention, and where it is customary to dress up if you are going to a good restaurant or one of the better hotel nightclubs.

The second word is light—lightweight clothing, that is. But there are some important qualifications that apply mostly to the northern part of the Coast—between Corpus Christi and Tampa—between the months of October and March. Winter can sometimes get nasty-cold in this region even though hard freezes are uncommon and snow almost unheard of. Heavy overcoats, snow parkas, and mittens are obviously not in order, but you should definitely take along a warm windproof jacket and sweater. I have known of boaters, inadequately clothed, who tried to travel down a swamp river or across a bay on a freezing evening and ended up with hypothermia. On the other hand, cold spells rarely last very long, and the temperature can turn summer-warm in a matter of hours. The best bet for winter on the northern Gulf is a compromise: take the sort of hiking clothes you would wear in midspring further north, including that jacket and sweater. And check the weather reports before heading for the hiking trails or open water.

The subtropical and tropical sectors of the Gulf—southern Florida, southern Texas, and all of coastal Mexico—usually live up to their hort-sleeve reputation even in December and January. But you can get a real jolt if a cold snap comes along, as it sometimes does. Freezes do hit southern Florida, and even in the Yucatán I've shivered on a winter evening when *El Norte* was blowing. So by all means carry along a warm sweater. At the very least, it may come in handy at an air-conditioned restaurant.

During late spring, summer, and early fall, light wear is the rule everywhere on the Gulf. In a region where saltwater or freshwater is always near at hand, it goes without saying that bathing suits and shorts are essential. But so is some sort of raincoat, even though you may not need it in dry southern Texas or northern Mexico.

Apart from these general considerations, the great thing about the Gulf out-of-doors is that hikers and campers don't need to pack a lot of special apparel. Comfortable walking shoes are a must, of course; but unless you plan to climb one of the steep coastal mountains in the state of Veracruz, or hike cross-country through cactusland, heavy-duty hiking boots are unnecessary. Most people get by with sturdy tennis shoes, although it's mainly a matter of what feels comfortable on your own personal feet. Wading presents a special problem on some swamp trails. If it's simply a matter of soggy ground or inch-deep puddles, ordinary hiking boots will keep you dry. But if a trail is seriously wet, forget it. A water-resistant boot that is truly comfortable has yet to be invented, and most experienced swamp rats prefer tennis shoes because they're light when soggy and dry out quickly. Poisonous snakes are a consideration, of course (see "Snakes and Other Scary or Painful Beasties"), but they are rarely a problem on trails unless you're practically blind. On the other hand, if you plan to make your own trail through southern bottomlands or Mexican scrub or whatever, then by all means wear high boots or leggings just to play it safe.

Again, if you are the type that is always hankering to get off the beaten track, take along heavy jeans, even in summer. The Gulf Coast has its share of burrs and thorns, from blackberry and multiflora rose in the Deep South pinelands to cacti and acacias in the Yucatán scrub. Also, jeans discourage mosquitoes. For the same reasons, have a supply of long-sleeve shirts available in case you need them, even in hot weather. They won't make you feel any warmer than their short-sleeve equivalents and they'll absorb that much more perspiration. Besides, the bug repellent feels better on them than it does on you.

Finally, if you know you're going to be dealing with high temperatures and a lot of sun, take along a hat—any old hat that you feel comfortable wearing—and a supply of large handkerchiefs. The latter, aside from serving as sweat mops, can come in handy as neck protectors if deer flies become a nuisance.

Camping Equipment and Supplies   Backpackers in the Deep South and coastal Mexico do not need the kinds of elaborate camping gear that might come in handy in the High Sierra or someplace like it. Even trails in wilderness areas are not as utterly removed from human habitation as they are in the Rockies or Alaska. And, even if you get lost, the weather is not likely to kill you unless you insist on dying of heat stroke or going boating during a hurricane. Obviously, you need a good sleeping bag that you can get into on a cold winter night and use as a mattress at other times. In some areas of the Mexican outback, or even in swampy U.S. forests where there's a good chance the ground will be both flat and wet, you may want to bring along a net hammock—if you can sleep in one. As for shelter, you won't have snow or subzero weather to worry about, so any respectable lightweight pup tent should do the trick. Naturally, it should be capable of keeping you warm if the temperature drops, but the most basic considerations are good rainproofing and a generous flap of tear-resistant screening that keeps bugs out while letting air in.

For the most part, the essentials that you must carry on any overnight hike are predictable: a compass and, when available, a trail map; a flashlight; bedding and cooking gear; a first-aid kit with antivenom equipment; insect repellent; and, when advisable, water. Even in very wild areas, you should not trust surface water; there is no telling what may have fallen into it and died. Unless you plan to go through the hassle of boiling water or treating it chemically, or (as is usually the case in U.S. parks and government forests) there are water sources at primitive campsites along the way, pack three or four quarts of water per day per person. During warm weather it's a good idea to have a mineral supplement such as powdered Gatorade on hand too.

Concerning food supplies, the same common-sense principles apply along the Gulf Coast that are in effect anywhere else you would go hiking. The difference is that we are rarely dealing with immense tracts of the forest primeval, so you are not likely to be out of reach of a grocery store for more than two or three days at a time, at least in the United States. (As for Mexico, see below.) Even so, bring a bit more than you think you'll require, including the sort of munchies—such as raisins and other dried fruits—that won't induce thirst. As for cooking, much of the area we'll be covering is plentifully supplied with deadwood for campfires, although long stretches of beach or swamp are notable exceptions. In any case, it is always a good idea to have some sort of small, portable stove on hand—a Sterno will do—in case it's raining or you're feeling lazy.

(Speaking of fire, let me add a special emphasis to the standard Smokey the Bear warning. Considering that we are dealing with an environment in which water, either salt, brackish, or fresh, is often a predominant feature of the landscape, it may surprise you to learn how combustible that wet world is. During dry periods, the grassy marshes, piney woods, and scrub country of the western Gulf are all highly flammable. So please take all the Boy Scout precautions when making and putting out a fire.)

One other item: even if you aren't much of a fisherman, find room for some sort of inexpensive collapsible fishing pole and a few lures in your pack. This is great fishing country. Countless streams and cypress-lined ponds teeming with bass, bream, and catfish await you. If you are doing your hiking and camping in the vicinity of coastal inlets, bays, and marshes, there is always the chance of catching flounder, redfish, or pompano from a pier or bridge. And while you're in these estuarine areas, it might also be a good idea to pick up a cheap crab net or two at any hardware store on the Coast.

Additional *Comments About Hiking and Primitive Camping in Mexico*   The big question, of course, is: Should you or shouldn't you? And the small, cop-out answer is: It depends on what kind of experience you are looking for. Following are some comments that should help you make up your mind.

- At the risk of stating the superobvious, you or someone with you should have at least a modest command of Spanish if you plan to spend much time off the beaten track.

- Get used to the idea that the concept of outdoor recreation is virtually nonexistent in Mexico, apart from picnicking on the beach or shooting wildlife at all seasons. The government has designated a number of national parks and reserves, but with few exceptions (mostly important archeological zones), they exist only on paper. Mexico's Gulf Coast is no exception to the rule. Such north-of-the-border conveniences as hiking trails, managed camping sites, and trail maps are almost unheard-of.

- It follows from the foregoing comment that true wilderness is rare in Mexico. Even the most remote-seeming areas usually support some subsistence farmers, ranchers, or fishermen. This is certainly the case along the Gulf. On the other hand, human settlement is less obtrusive than in our country, if only because poverty calls the tune. Farms and villages blend into the landscape as though they belong there. Just think of it—you can travel from the Rio Grande to the Yucatán and never see a trailer home! Also, notwithstanding the human presence, much of the Mexican countryside is wild in the sense of being primitive. You are within easier reach of the amenities of civilization at Everglades National Park, for example, than on some stretches of Mexico's Gulf Coast.

- The question of safety inevitably arises. And the answer is the same as it would be if you pitched a tent for the night at some safe-looking but unsupervised spot along the road in the United States: you are taking your chances. If you aren't willing to do that, forget the whole idea. In Mexico, unlike the United States, you can usually find some frill-less but clean place—not the Ritz, but not a flophouse either—that costs less than the hookup fee at a park campground in the States. But, for what it's worth, I should add that I personally feel safer camping out in rural Mexico than I do in equivalent unsupervised locations in the States. True, there have been some much-publicized bad things happening to Americans lately, mainly in western Mexico, and dope smuggling and big-city crime are certainly on the increase. But when you consider that the average Mexican family is poorer than the poorest welfare mother in our own country, the amazing thing is how comparatively little street crime there is. Bribery and corruption are a way of life, but Mexicans don't assume that the world owes them a living. They tend to be self-reliant, and they support their own families. Unfortunately, it is also true that this is the land of machismo. Women should definitely not wander into the hinterlands on their own. And any traveler should be leery of impromptu camping near one of the oil boom towns, such as Tampico or Coatzacoalcos. Finally, it is worth noting that there is a considerable drug trade going on in the state of Veracruz, both in the mountain boondocks and along some deserted beaches; so ask locally whether it's safe to pitch your tent. Before leaving this dreary subject, let me emphasize that, although there are no guarantees, the great majority of on-their-own hikers and primitive campers in Mexico return from their adventures safe and sound.

■ So then, if you want to do some casual hiking or serious backpacking, how do you go about it? In the travelogue chapters of this book I've made a few suggestions, not recommendations, about likely areas on the Coast. But the real answer is that if you see an area that looks promising, try to get a feel for it by driving around a bit if you can, asking questions, and using your binocs. Then take off. As long as you're not expecting the wilderness primeval, the whole of rural Mexico is walking country and much of it is very beautiful. Of course, if you follow a dirt track or path, you're pretty certain to end up at a village or someone's hut. As for cross-country hiking, novices should warm up with day trips unless they are in the company of an experienced hand. Start out with a compass and a good idea of where you're going, and keep in mind that a lot of Mexican vegetation wears thorns. In some areas—the Yucátan, for instance—the scrub is just plain impenetrable. As long as you're not carrying a gun or crashing through a corn patch, Mexicans are not uptight about trespassing as a rule. When in doubt, it may help to ask a *campesino* about the local custom, even though he'll think you're crazy for wanting to do for fun what he has to do as a way of life.

A special word about maps—namely, that good ones are hard to come by. Even for ordinary motor traveling, if you are contemplating a few side trips off the major highways, it's advisable to have both a standard map distributed by the Mexican consulates and an AAA map. You'll soon notice that a number of secondary roads left out on one map appear on the other. Side roads—or any road, for that matter—may be in much worse condition than either map suggests. For the hiker, it is pretty difficult to find the equivalent of a U.S. Geological Survey map. Trying to figure out cross-country distances from most ordinary maps is, at best, an inexact science.

■ Choosing the right site for primitive tent camping in Mexico is very important, whether you are backpacking or traveling by car. The basic trick is to find a place that isn't too near human habitation or heavily traveled roads. (In some areas, this combination can be surprisingly difficult to find.) If you park within easy walking distance of a farm or hamlet, chances are that you can forget about privacy. Some of the local citizenry, especially kids and drunks, will arrive uninvited and sit around evidencing a harmless but annoying interest in everything you do. As for busy roads, you should camp at a distance from them for safety reasons, as well as to escape the god-awful racket made by Mexican trucks and buses. Driveways leading to *torres de microndas*—microwave towers, of which there are many in Mexico—are likely spots; but any quiet, unfenced pasture or grove will do. Be sure, of course, that your vehicle doesn't block the trail or road. As for beach camping, there are many promising locations along our route; but think twice about choosing an area that seems too deserted. As a rule of thumb, either beaches near fishing villages or uncrowded public beaches are acceptable sites. But ask a local lighthouse keeper or fisherman if it's safe to pitch a tent. Coastal people, in contrast to backcountry campesinos, are usually accustomed to the occasional oddball gringo who likes to rough it. Incidentally, if you occupy a deserted, thatched sun shelter (*palapa*), be prepared to pay some token fee if the proprietor happens to show up.

■ As far as food, supplies, and equipment are concerned, a lot depends on the level of comfort you require. The same general rules that apply along the U.S. sector of the Gulf apply here. The all-important proviso is that, notwithstanding the pervasive human presence, the nearest store where you can buy wine, purified (as opposed to mineral) water, olive oil, or flashlight batteries may be a hundred miles away.

There are a surprising number of young Americans and Europeans, still clinging to a sixties lifestyle, who drift across Mexico for months and even years at a time. They speak Spanish well, don't mind eating tortillas and beans three times a day or sleeping in a hammock, have developed some resistance to amoebiasis, etc. They have their own network, and word of mouth gets them wherever they're going next. But for more orthodox hikers and tent campers who aren't interested in literally bumming it, the sensible thing is not to venture far from the beaten track without a generous supply of the foods and comforts you consider essential to your morale, as well as plenty of purified water. Also, though the problem is much less pervasive than it used to be, some sort of defense against "Montezuma's revenge," such as Minocin, is absolutely essential. Travelers, by the way, are not the only victims. The problem is chronic among Mexicans; so any village pharmacy will have useful remedies. But don't trust folklore preventatives or cures. For example, the widespread notion that you're immune if you eat a lot of yogurt before taking off for Mexico is baloney. The only real preventative is *never* to drink tap water except at luxury hotels where the water is treated, and to avoid all uncooked foods, especially the tempting-looking salads.

To sum up, much of Mexico's Gulf Coast is beautiful country, great for short hikes and long walks; and some of its lovely beaches are perfect for beachcombing. But in a nation where the typical farmer often walks many miles a day, there is no setup for recreational backpacking or primitive camping. If your only experience is with the maintained hiking trails of the Sierra Nevada or Blue Ridge Mountains, you will want to keep that limitation in mind.

Traveling in an RV

RV *Campgrounds* By my definition, an RV is any gypsy wagon you can sleep in lying down, whether a van furnished with ice chest and collapsible cots, a pickup truck with camper attachment, or a Winnebago with all the comforts of home. Along the U.S. Gulf Coast there are hundreds of public and private campgrounds where you can find hookups, showers, barbecue grills, and all the other usual comforts. In state parks and national forests and parks, RV campgrounds are usually located in attractive settings, and the fees are reasonable, ranging from seven to ten dollars per night. During peak seasons, however, campgrounds in the more popular parks are apt to be pretty crowded if not filled up. In southern Texas and, especially, southern Florida, the crunch predictably occurs during the winter season, whereas in summer some parks are practically deserted on weekdays except for the mosquitoes. On the northern Gulf Coast the reverse is the case: the heavy-use season starts in April and runs through the summer. By mid-September the crowds are steadily thinning out even though the weather often remains consistently fine well into November. After that, you can have most parks almost to yourself through March if you don't mind the risk of cold weather and rain.

In the travelogue section of each chapter, I've included occasional comments about timing your visit to a particular park. In general, though, you can assume that inland parks will be less crowded than those offering sand and surf. Even during their most popular seasons, some of the less well known inland campgrounds get heavy use only on weekends, when local folks turn out to picnic or fish. Many state parks accept a limited number of reservations placed a month or two in advance. If you don't want to get involved in that kind of advance planning, try to time your arrival at the more popular parks during the morning hours. If worst comes to worst, as it may during busy seasons, be braced for the possibility that a park campground may be sold out. Gate attendants can usually recommend a private facility that is close by.

P*rovisions and Equipment*   Picking up supplies along the U.S. part of the Gulf should be no problem as long as you consult your road map and note distances between towns. Blue laws are disappearing throughout most of the Deep South, so you should find food stores open along main highways even on Sundays. As far as clothes and equipment are concerned, everything depends on how many home comforts you require and how far away from your RV you intend to stray. If you plan to do a lot of getting back to nature, check the preceding "Hiking and Primitive Camping" section to find out what to take along. You would do well to have a couple of windows screened in case you want to sleep inside your RV on damp or extremely buggy nights; but on fine evenings you should be able to set up around your vehicle and go to sleep with the stars in your eyes. Thick foam-rubber mattresses and/or sleeping bags, a couple of folding chairs, a camp stove, and you're just about furnished. A Coleman lamp comes in handy, too, if moths and other suicidal insects aren't out in force. Inside the van or out, a clip-on Easy Reader Book Lite is perfect for after-dark reading or for locating your midnight munchies without waking anyone else.

RV*ing in Mexico*   The big problem in Mexico, at least for those who want hookups and/or a feeling of security, is finding a campground rather than a campground space. Compared to only a few years ago, the situation has improved, but facilities are still few and far between. In fact, there are none that I know of along the entire northern part of Mexico's Gulf Coast. (This does not mean that Americans don't camp along this coast; many do. But there are no electrical outlets or other conveniences for travelers who want to wire up unless they make arrangements for an extension cord at some hotel.) Tuxpan, south of Tampico, offers the first conventional facility along this route. There is another south of Tecolutla, three or four at Veracruz, another just outside Coatzacoalcos, a couple at Palenque, and two more at Mérida. (All are mentioned in the travelogue sections.) Besides these, there are two or three places, such as the campground near Catemaco, that have a few outlets but are otherwise pretty primitive. All are commercial, of course, but very reasonably priced. They are usually not crowded, and some have pleasant settings. What all this means is that you can, by the hardest, find a decent RV setup most nights if you keep careful track of distances and don't do much detouring. But your journey will seem a lot less schedule-ridden if you accept the prospect of spending some nights at cheap or moderately priced hotels along the way, or arrange with the proprietor to set up in a hotel parking lot. As for doing some unsupervised overnight parking at likely spots along the way, note the preceding remarks about primitive camping in Mexico, as well as comments in the travelogue about particular areas.

This may seem obvious, but I'll say it anyway: it is imperative that any vehicle that you're driving deep into Mexico should be in the best possible shape before you start out. Tires, including the spare, must have a lot of rubber on them. When it comes to repairs, Mexican mechanics are often creative artists; they are, after all, used to dealing with cars that have been terminal cases for years. But "parts is parts." If they have to be ordered, you may spend half your vacation learning the Mexican virtue of patience.

In the way of supplies, pack up all the items mentioned under "Hiking and Primitive Camping" that seem relevant, as well as a couple of five-gallon containers of water. And, for Pete's sake, make sure that you take a large, top-quality ice chest along, which should be kept covered and protected from the sun. The ice machines that we take for granted at every roadside gas station in the States are practically nonexistent in Mexico. In some of the areas where we will be traveling, the only source of ice is the ice plant in a sizable town; so the longer you can make a block last, the better. Mineral water and cold soft drinks, as well as good Mexican beers, are available at any village large enough to have a single store. But you will still want to have some refrigeration for bottles of water and anything else you need to keep cool. Also, bring a lot of nonperishable snacks and canned goods with you. In general, the Mexican versions of ready-made cookies, candies, etc., are not very tasty. The canned and bottled fruit juices aren't so great either—although the same juices are delicious if you can get them fresh, which isn't hard to do south of Tampico. If you like your evening toddy, keep in mind that wide selections of the usual American standbys—vodka, bourbon, scotch—aren't available outside the larger cities. Since you are not supposed to bring more than a bottle or two into the country with you, you may want to consider rum or tequila as an alternate when your supply runs low.

A special word about Winnebago-style travling in Mexico: south of Tampico the terrain is sometimes hilly, and line-ups of gasping trucks and buses are not unusual on steep, uphill grades. In such situations, a large camper vehicle has a tough time passing. Add to that problem the relative narrowness of Mexican highways and streets, the difficulty of maneuvering on unimproved roads that might be interesting to explore, the tendency of fixtures to come unscrewed on bumpy roads, and the aforementioned scarcity of campgrounds with hookups—and what it all means is that driving a motor-home vehicle in Mexico requires special care and patience. Give me a passenger car or a van anytime. And yet, there are many people who drive large campers all the way to the Yucatán and back, parking at suitable scenic spots for days on end, having a grand old time. It's all a matter of knowing what you're getting into.

Canoeing and Boating

It would require a sizable book to deal adequately with the subject of either canoeing or motorboating on or near the Gulf of Mexico. The following comments apply only to getting about either in estuarine areas or on tributary rivers and streams.

S*mall Boats, Canoes, and Rafts*   The Gulf region is an absolute paradise for anyone who knows how to handle a small boat or a canoe. Opportunities for freshwater and saltwater fishing are endless. And the settings are also endless in their variety: mangrove labyrinths; shallow blue bays; green and gold marshes punctuated by hammocks or willow islands; druidical swamps of cypress and tupelo; inlets overlooked by coconut palms; clear, black streams lined with limestone cliffs, pine barrens, or shadowy hardwood bottomlands. It all depends on what you want and where you are.

For the boater who doesn't want the hassle of lugging along a lot of equipment and weight, but who does want to do some fishing and/or some real exploring, the best bet is a twelve-to-fourteen-foot shallow-draft aluminum skiff with outboard motor. The shallow draft is really important, since Gulf rivers have a lot of snags at low water, and marshes and bays are themselves often shallow for a long way out. Your boat should be versatile enough to allow you to either venture pretty far into the open bays and sounds or cover a lot of miles in a short time on rivers and streams.

On the other hand, a canoe is, well, a canoe: easy to tote and put in, able to maneuver through dense swamps and along narrow creeks, and, above all, silent in its passage. If you enjoy becoming as one with the waterscape through which you travel, paddling a canoe is the only way to go. Canoeists, of course, should not expect much in the way of white water. There are a few lively spots on north Gulf Coast waterways and some serious but unexplored rapids on a couple of rivers along the more mountainous sections of Mexico's Coast. But in general, the attraction here has to do with the unearthly beauty of the settings—with transcendental calm rather than roller-coaster thrills. The major problem, apart from not being able to venture far from land, is arranging the take-out if you're touring in a one-car caravan. Fortunately, the current in many Gulf waterways is usually, if not always, mild enough to allow for upstream paddling. Both outboard skiffs and canoes can be rented at a number of parks and private establishments along the Stateside Gulf Coast. In Mexico there are boats and guides for hire at reasonable (negotiated) rates all along the Gulf.

There are, of course, other excellent ways to get yourself afloat depending on the locale, your pleasure, and your expertise: cabin craft, kayaks, sailboats, rowboats, houseboats, even pirogues in Louisiana and dugouts in Mexico. If you are not really compulsive about getting out on the water but would like to do some short-distance exploring from time to time, you might want to consider an inflatable boat. Several small models, with or without motor attachment, are available. Their great virtue is that they take up so little room in a vehicle when they're deflated; and, with the help of a good pump, you can have them unpacked, inflated, and launched in no time at all. They are just right for investigating an intriguing-looking pond or a pretty stretch of stream that can't quite be reached by road or trail. You'd better have a good patch kit along, though. Many southern waterways have more than their share of snags.

The best canoe trails on the U.S. side of the Gulf are to be found between southern Florida and eastern Texas. Most of them receive some mention in the travelogue sections of this book. Those who have an outboard boat in tow can explore nearly all of the same rivers, as well as a smorgasbord of estuarine bays, inlets, tidal marshlands, river deltas, and barrier islands that extend off and on, mostly on, along the entire coast. Indeed, the Gulf's estuarine environment is far and away the largest and most productive in North America, and perhaps the richest in the world.

Time, tide, and low-water seasons wait for no man. I can't emphasize enough the importance of checking out the local scene before getting yourself launched. Boaters who venture out into large bays and sounds need to know how to handle a boat if a storm comes up; and in the Gulf, storms can materialize quickly. Canoeists and boaters alike should be aware that, depending on rainfall, rivers in the Gulf region often vary greatly in terms of their water levels and the force of their currents. Last month's brimming stream, with waters spilling into adjacent forests, may be this month's sluggish creek, barricaded by sandbars and deadwood. This is particularly true in northern Florida, Alabama, and Mississippi, where some of the prettiest canoeing rivers are found. Spring is usually the best season on the northern Gulf Coast, but there is no fixed rule. The wise planner will take advantage of the various park and refuge phone numbers provided in this book to learn in advance about conditions on a particular waterway he or she wants to travel. On request, parks and national forests usually provide maps and other information about rivers and streams within their jurisdiction. Also, a couple of the books mentioned in the bibliography are very useful.

Boating and Canoeing in Mexico   Some of the generalizations that apply to backpacking (see "Hiking and Primitive Camping in Mexico" above) are also true of water travel in Mexico. Although local fishermen know their own territory well, there are no handy guidebooks or maps that can tell you where to go. In fact, published information about Mexican rivers and estuarine areas is practically nonexistent. If you are adventurous enough, simply check out the local scene as best you can and then take off. But for those who do not have the temperament of a conquistador, a few observations are in order. For one thing, much of Mexico's Gulf Coast is not ideal country for canoeists. True, I have often wished I had a canoe available so that, on my own, I could quietly insert myself into an inviting expanse of mangrove swamp or the delta stretch of some alluvial river. But most such expeditions would have to be pretty short. Put-ins and take-outs are hard to arrange, and the availability of overnight camping spots is difficult to determine in advance. In the following chapters I've mentioned a few Mexican rivers that look promising for a daylong trip, and there are unquestionably many other likely prospects, especially in the states of Veracruz and Tabasco. But with scarcely any exceptions, only local people are familiar with these waterways. As far as canoeing is concerned, they are virgin territory, and southern Mexico is a long way to haul a canoe just on the chance that you'll hit it right.

It's also a long way to tow an outboard skiff, even though such a boat offers a faster, more practical way of getting around. On the northern coast of Mexico, many Americans—most of them Texans— bring their own boats to the *lagunas* to fish and shoot ducks. A few even come as far south as the Laguna Tamiahua, between Tampico and Tuxpan. Usually such people are old hands who know exactly what they're doing and where they want to go. For less experienced persons, the alternative is simple and convenient: when you feel the urge to get on water, hire a boat and guide. (You can't do one without the other in Mexico, since boats are a big investment and no sensible fisherman is going to trust some stranger with the source of his livelihood.) At some of the bigger towns, such as Tampico, Tuxpan, Veracruz, Ciudad del Carmen, and Campeche, there are charter boats (usually carrying a maximum of four passengers) available for fishing trips. Smaller places with some sort of resort facilities, such as La Pesca, Barra del Tordo, Tecolutla, and Champotón (all mentioned in the travelogue sections) are also accustomed to providing the traveler with a fascinating boat trip out into the lagoons, up a tidal river, or both. But if you want to explore unexplored mangrove streams or isolate yourself on some sun-bleached barrier island, the best way to do it is to haggle with a local fisherman. If you're determined to make it on your own, just remember that you really will be exactly that: on your own.

Wildlife

Birding   In the travelogue sections of this book I make frequent reference to birding opportunties along the Coast. For good reason. Nowhere else in North America will you find such a variety and abundance of bird species, or so many that are of surpassing beauty. The diverse habitats of the Coast breed their own specialties—from mangrove cuckoos and great white herons in the Keys to flamingos and toucans in the Yucatán. And during winter it sometimes seems that half the avian population of the rest of the continent has made the

Gulf region its home. Every locale has its spectacles: the all-season flocks of lovely wading birds, the great winter rafts of ducks and geese, the whooping cranes arriving at Aransas, the pelicans and frigatebirds along the coasts of Florida and Tabasco, the jewellike warblers and rare cockaded woodpeckers in the piney woods, and the brilliant mot-mots and parrots of eastern Mexico. Not just serious birders, but any-one who is capable of being moved by the natural scene, will be en-tranced by this ornithological bounty. If you go a step further and try to identify the species that you see, you will add a whole new dimen-sion to the pleasures of your trip. So by all means take along a pair of binoculars and a field guide.

A*ll About Alligators* The Gulf Coast is home to several crocodilians: the American crocodile, which survives at the southern tip of Florida and in a few mangrove swamps in Mexico; the Morelet's crocodile and the Central American caiman, which also hang on, just barely, in parts of coastal Mexico; and the American alligator, the only one of these species that you are likely to see on your travels. Until fairly recently it, too, was endangered; but conservation efforts during the last few decades have enabled it to make a successful comeback—so success-ful, in fact, that in some areas of Florida and Louisiana it is the star attraction at parks and refuges. The alligator is capable of great speed both in the water and, for short distances, on land. But when you see him he will probably be loafing on a log or mud bank, motionless as a rock. No matter; the sight of this prehistoric fellow lying out there in front of God and everybody without a cage around him is bound to thrill you. 'Gators are the premier inhabitants of the southern wet-lands, and it is a joy to have them around again. They are useful crea-tures, too, digging large holes in the marshlands that become watery oases for other wildlife during periods of extended drought. The fe-males even have a maternal sensibility that is very rare in reptiles. They guard their solar-heated nests to keep marauding raccoons away and, when the chirruping babies have hatched, gently dig them out and carry them safely to water in their toothy jaws. Thereafter, the six-inch youngsters often take the sun on their mother's knobby back.

Inevitably, of course, the question arises: How dangerous are these formidable reptiles to people? The answer is: Not very. In Florida there have been a few bad scenes in recent years, with people getting mauled and even, on a couple of occasions, killed by alligators. But almost invariably these incidents have occurred at the edge of ponds or canals where the animals have been fed by anglers so consistently that they have lost their fear of people. In spite of the warning signs, I have seen people throwing food to 'gators in almost every coastal park in Florida. The great wonder is that attacks are so extremely rare. The canoeist who sees a ten-footer swimming nearby, for example, has lit-tle to fear. And anglers often wade within yards of even the largest specimens. Still, use a little common sense in your dealings with these reptiles. Don't feed them. And don't let your little kid scramble along the banks in areas where alligators are present. Oh, yes; and if you value your doggie (who is supposed to be on a leash anyway if you are in a park or refuge), don't let him cavort in or near alligator-occupied waters. 'Gators are not really programmed to attack people, but Rover is fair game.

O*ther Critters*   Birds and alligators are the big wildlife shows in the Gulf States, but there are a wondrous lot of other creatures to be found in the region's rich ecosystems. Obviously, your best chance of seeing some of them is in the larger protected parks. Myakka in southern Florida and Aransas in Texas are special favorites of mine. Wherever your are, early morning and late evening are the best times to spot white-tailed deer, raccoons, opossums, armadillos, and perhaps a bobcat or Brer Fox, all in a wide variety of habitats. Gray squirrels and the nocturnal flying squirrel are abundant in the bottomland hardwoods, whereas fox squirrels prefer the piney woods. In the marshes you have a good chance of seeing nutria as well as muskrat and possibly an otter or mink. One of the most famous citizens of the Keys is the easy-to-see Key deer, a diminutive subspecies of the whitetail. Southern Florida has a lot of wild hogs and the southern Texas refuges are home to the piggy javalina. You don't have much chance of glimpsing the southern black bear in its few remaining haunts in Florida and Louisiana, or the handful of panthers—a southern version of the cougar—in the Everglades, but it's nice to know that they're around. None of these animals, including bears and panthers, poses a serious threat to people. If there are exceptions, they must be the skunks and raccoons in some of the Florida parks. These animals have been made bold by handouts, but they're still wild; so don't try to pet or feed them.

In Mexico, the chances of seeing wild mammals are much slimmer than in the United States. There is too much unregulated hunting, too much abuse of natural ecosystems, and no meaningfully protected preserves at all. All larger animals are vanishing from one area after another, and some are headed for extinction. Yet even so, if you spend enough time on back roads and trails, you'll see something exciting sooner or later: a coyote in the northern mesquite country; a coati mundi on a hilly curve; an anteater in the Yucatán scrub; even, perhaps, a black howler monkey in the remnant jungles at Palenque or Cóba.

For purposes of consistency, fish and other kinds of aquatic life deserve a paragraph too. After all, they are wildlife. But the subject, I confess, defeats me; it's like trying to discuss the universe in a paragraph. Suffice it to say that the Gulf and its vast tributary network of rivers, swamps, marshes, and bays support a cornucopia of freshwater and saltwater fish species, as well as an endless list of other marine fauna: shrimp, oysters, crabs, clams, octopodes, jellyfish, corals, anemones, sponges, snails, and so on. The fishing here is still the finest in the Western Hemisphere despite the stresses that people have placed on this rich resource. Even folks who are not ordinarily turned on by the sport should bring some sort of hook and line along, just in case they get tired of seeing everybody else get into the act. Crabbing is also fabulous, and crab nets are cheap and simple to use. As for shelling, many of the Gulf beaches, especially after a storm, are a collector's paradise.

Snakes and Other Scary or Painful Beasties It's been said over and over again by every knowledgeable naturalist until he's blue in the face: most snakes are not only harmless to humans but useful to them (as extremely efficient rodent controllers). Moreover, in their special, scaly way, snakes are really quite beautiful. And the Gulf region has an impressive variety to marvel at. But still, the Adam in most of us will never forgive snakes for moving around without feet. All I can say is that the naturalists are right. You should not harm any snake—even a venomous one—if, as will almost certainly be the case, it has not harmed you. In my experience, rattlesnakes (excepting the pigmy rattler) are becoming pretty rare in the coastal South, outside a few refuges and parks. As for the fabled coral snakes, it is true that it manufactures a serious venom, but its fangs are so small that they would probably not break your skin unless you held the creature between your fingers or toes while it gummed you. The pale brown and beige southern copperhead is a potentially more serious customer and fairly common in a wide variety of damp to dry habitats. But like other species, it will do its best to get away from you if it can. In the lowland South, particularly in swamp country, the main fellow to look out for is the cottonmouth, a rather thick-bodied member of the pit viper family with the usual triangular head and, most often, a dullish gunmetal black coloration. (Don't confuse him with the very common, harmless black racer.) I've never heard of anyone being bitten by a cottonmouth while in the water; the main risk comes when someone is stepping over a log or mucking about in a boggy place without looking where he's putting his feet. I've done a lot of that myself and have come within inches of stepping on a cottonmouth at least a dozen times, with no worse result than a case of nerves on both sides.

Still, the danger is there, and people do get bitten by poisonous snakes occasionally. Should that happen to you, the crucial thing is not to panic. Follow the directions on a snake-bite kit if you have one with you, or apply a homemade tourniquet to the affected limb if you don't (remembering not to cut off circulation for long periods at a time). Then walk—don't run—to your car and head for the nearest hospital. If you're alone and beginning to feel ill, ask someone at a filling station or a country store to drive you, but not at a speed that will kill you both. Meanwhile, keep reminding yourself of this cheery fact: most people (in the United States) are capable of recovering from snake bite even without any medical assistance at all. As for those of us who haven't been bitten, the chances are that we never will be even if we slog our way through all the swamps that are left to slog through. However, special care should be taken in Mexico. Tropical climates make life easier for snakes, and a couple of Mexico's poisonous snake species are potentially more dangerous than anything we have to offer. The obvious moral is that, if you decide to leave the trail and wander in the bush, you should wear leggings or boots and watch your step. Once again, however, the risk should be kept in proportion. Between 100 and 150 Mexicans die of snake bite each year, not very many when you consider that tens of millions of sandaled or barefooted campesinos are traipsing around in snake country every day of their lives. And I have never heard of an American who has been killed by a snake in Mexico.

Ironically, the most frequent injuries inflicted by Gulf wildlife occur, not in the steamy swamps or shadowy forests, but on the open, sunlit coasts. The villains are not slithery snakes, panting panthers, or aggressive 'gators, but spiny sea urchins, Portuguese man-of-wars and other jellyfish, or stingrays half buried in the underwater sand. None of these are likely to do you in, assuming you don't have some super-allergy or a weak heart; but they inflict a really nasty sting that may cause pain for hours or even days. A lot of home-grown remedies have been proposed, from lime juice to meat tenderizer, but the best bet is probably soap and warm water and hydrogen peroxide, or, better, a visit to a doctor. Stingray and urchin wounds should be treated as punctures. The best cure, of course, is prevention. Keep your eyes alert when wading in the shallows. All of these hazards are easy to spot except the stingray, which looks like a flounder hiding in the sand. Shuffling along, rather than lifting your feet, is the best way to keep from stepping on one of these fellows.

Sharks are a big, bad bugaboo in the imaginations of many people. Actually, attacks are very rare on the north side of the Gulf, although they have occurred here as on almost every coast of every continent. In Mexico, there have been a number of attacks along the coastline of the state of Veracruz. The whole subject boils down to a matter of paranoia versus perspective. Wherever you are, you are much more likely to be clobbered by another car while driving to the beach than being gobbled up by Jaws once you get there. For what consolation that is worth.

Finally, we come to crabs. Crabs? you ask. They aren't a hazard, are they? The answer, of course, is no. Unless, that is, you're camping on the beach and some quite harmless little fiddler or other beach crab decides to climb over you while you're sleeping—and you have a heart attack before you're fully awake. Seriously, for the uninitiated, it can be downright alarming to wake up to that sort of experience. So be prepared. Before you sack out, you should be able to notice whether there are a lot of beach crabs in the vicinity. If you're not sleeping in a secure tent and don't relish the idea of having these curious fellows scuttling around you in the dark, you may want to consider sleeping somewhere else. The more sensible solution, of course, is to make pets of them in your mind.

Insidious Insects   Ah! Here we get to the real hazards. But before we deal with them one by one, keep in mind that tropical and subtropical bugs are, in most instances, no worse than their counterparts in less balmy climes. During summer, Canadian and Alaskan mosquitoes compare unfavorably with almost anything the Deep South has to offer. Deer flies are as much a plague in the temperate forests of upstate New York as in the hardwood forests of the South. As for ticks, I've picked up more of them hiking through the Colorado sagebrush than ever I have in the Southern boonies. The real problem with Gulf Coast bugs is that they are around longer—the price we pay for escaping the snow and sleet and freezing cold of northen regions.

Mosquitoes: These are probably the most notorious insect nuisance, but in most circumstances, they are also one of the easiest to deal with. A good repellent (preferably sprayed on one's clothes rather than oneself); muted, light-colored clothing; and a tight screening or netting for bedtime use are the best safeguards. Interestingly, mosquitoes are usually not a terrific problem in deep tupelo and cypress swamps, where the tannic acid in the water seems to keep their numbers down. In the piney hills behind the northern Gulf Coast they are rarely a serious nuisance at all. On the other hand, if you are in or near the marshes or, most especially, the mangrove swamps in warm weather, have the spray at the ready! In the Everglades and wetland stretches of the Mexican Gulf Coast, there may be at least a few mosquitoes around even in winter if the wind isn't blowing. I've often wondered how, in the old days, southern Florida residents could stand those humming clouds, even with the use of smudge fires, before window screens and, later, repellents were invented. Or, for that matter, how poor people along the Mexican Gulf still get by with their coconutshell fires. Old hands argue that a certain immunity develops from prolonged exposure. I've tried this out myself and found it to be sort of true. That is, I have become so used to being bitten that I've forgotten about being itchy. Incidentally, malaria and the other ills that certain species of mosquitoes (there are many varieties) used to inflict on Gulf Coast residents are pretty much under control now, even in tropical Mexico.

Ticks: Anytime you walk through the woods or scrub during warm seasons of the year, you run the risk of picking up a few ticks, especially if you're not following an open path. In my experience, mesquite thickets and the unburned gallberry scrub in piney woods are favorite habitats for these pesky bloodsuckers. But there's no telling.

One year they'll be all over the place; the next year not. Once they get their heads under your skin, the standard remedy is to cover them with a suffocating substance such as nail polish or petroleum jelly, forcing them to withdraw. Most of the time, though, experienced wood walkers can feel the ever-so-light crawl of a tick on their skin before it burrows in.

Chiggers (redbugs): Unfortunately, there's no detecting this minute nuisance before it goes to work on you. Contrary to popular belief, the mite itself doesn't burrow into your skin. Instead, by emitting a secretion, it creates a sort of tube that penetrates the epidermis. Your body's reaction to this foreign "tube" causes the red, itchy spot that can last for days. Chiggers are at their worst during the late spring and summer. Clothes and repellents deter them somewhat, but you are very likely to get a dose of them if you lounge on a bed of dead leaves or walk through same in bare or sandaled feet. It helps to wash your feet and legs with hot water and soap after a woodland walk. Once they've worked you over, which may involve anywhere from one to a dozen bites, there's not much you can do except apply an anti-itch antiseptic. Personally, I don't consider chiggers all that big a problem. When ah itches, ah scratches (which you're not really supposed to do). But some people seem more sensitive to them than others.

Fire ants: These pestiferous invaders from South America build their hills anywhere in the South where the land is sufficiently dry, especially in pine barrens, wild meadows, and pastures. A while back the U.S. Department of Agriculture waged a multimillion-dollar insecticide war against the fire ant, which had the predictable effect of killing a lot of birds and poisoning ecosystems without doing the ants much damage. Now the South is learning to live with these pests. The fact is that they aren't a significant problem unless you are careless enough to stand, sit, or pitch your tent on one of their usually very visible hills. If you do, you'll quickly see wherefrom they get their name! In which case, the trick is to move fast. (Some people can't quite believe all those firey pinpricks are happening to them until scores of ants are climbing up their legs.) Forget modesty and the churlish laughter of your companions; hop out of your jeans or pants in a hurry. Rub your hands up and down your legs, hard, until all the ants are done for. Normally, the pain will subside in a few minutes, although itchy, white "pimples" may mark the bites for days. Naturally, people who are seriously allergic to insect stings must be extremely careful when hiking in fire-ant country. And young children, in particular, should be taught to beware of fire-ant hills. For most of us, even if we are careless, the discomfort is brief and, once the initial Saint Vitus dance is over, no big deal.

Deer flies, black flies, and no-see-ums: As far as I'm concerned, any one of these wretches, when out in full force, is a greater bane than snakes, ticks, chiggers, and mosquitoes combined. Deer flies can be somewhat deterred by heavy applications of repellent and/or long-sleeve shirts. When I'm hiking through heavily shaded woods (the deer flies' favorite hangout) during June and July, I also wear a large kerchief that covers their preferred targets: my chin and neck. Only two good things can be said about these stinging fiends: they usually don't attack unless you're moving, and their kamikaze instincts make them satisfyingly easy to kill (though you're apt to slap yourself silly in the process). As for beach-loving black flies and no-see-ums, there's nothing good to be said about them except that their presence is erratic and a light breeze is enough to blow them away.

Scorpions: These creepy-crawlers are found now and then in southern Florida and more often in southern Texas, but their main Gulf homeland is Mexico. Because of their spooky appearance and their occasional penchant for showing up in the closets or shower stalls of the cheaper Mexican hotels, inexperienced travelers tend to rate them as one of the most frightening of tropical hazards. Actually, their sting, though painful, is almost never fatal to healthy persons, although you should certainly see a doctor. If you don't stick your hand into dark holes or corners, or go running around in your bare feet at night, the chances of being stung are pretty remote.

O*ther Wildlife*   I refuse to end this chapter on a scary note. Quite apart from the spectacular birdlife, the alligators, and the interesting mammals, the Gulf ecosystems brim with an amazing variety of less noticed and quite harmless life forms, some very common, others specialized and rare, which, even for the amateur naturalist, are exciting to see. These include a wide range of turtles and amphibians that make themselves at home in every creek and stream; the endangered dune mice of Florida's barrier islands, the galaxies of butterflies in the Yucatán's forests, the iguanas of the tropical beaches, and on and on. Tuning in to an awareness of some of these fascinating creatures, and learning a bit about them, are sure-fire ways of making your travels even more exciting.

2
The Florida Keys

At a glance

Access   Regularly scheduled flights are available from Miami to Marathon (in the central Keys) and Key West. Hwy 1 is the only road access.

Climate   Winter is the ideal season in the Keys. The weather is balmy and sunny, the nights often cool. In this subtropical climate, spring and fall are not sharply defined. Summer temperatures are high, often in the nineties, but modified by ocean breezes and rains.

Topography and Landscape Features   The Keys, a chain of islands 180 miles long, are the last outcroppings of peninsular Florida. The lower Keys, laid out on a roughly north-south axis, are composed of the same Miami oolite limestone that forms the mainland. The upper Keys, lying along a northeast-southwest axis, have as their backbone the fossilized remains of an ancient coral reef. Extensive live coral reefs lie offshore on the seaward side of Key Largo and several other islands in the chain. Natural sand beaches are few and narrow. More typically, the shoreline is characterized by limestone ledges and mud and sand flats.

Flora and Fauna   Because the Keys are the southernmost part of the United States, they are a biological treasure house, even though most species found here have their counterparts on the southern side of the Gulf. Mangroves are the most noticeable vegetation, but forests of Jamaican hardwoods—mastic, gumbo limbo, poisonwood, mahogany—survive on some of the islands. Hurricanes and soil salinity keep these trees from becoming very tall. A great variety of tropical exotics have also been introduced, including most of the many species of palms. The island fauna is very striking. A number of endemic subtropical birds can easily be seen here, along with a great number of more widely distributed species. Many keys in Florida Bay are rookery sites for spectacular numbers of waders. Pine Key is the home of the tiny Key deer. And the endangered American crocodile survives in the mangrove swamps at Key Largo.

Camping   There are public campgrounds with hookups and other facilities for RV campers and tent campers at three state parks—on Bahia Hondo, Long Key, and Key Largo. Commercial campgrounds are also available. The public campgrounds are always crowded during the winter season.

H*iking, Canoeing, Boating, Etc.*   Nature walks have been set up at the state parks, the Key Deer Wildlife Refuge, and the Lignumvitae Key State Botanical Site. However, as you might guess, there is no room on the small, heavily developed Keys for serious hiking. Nor are the Keys really suited for canoeing, although there is an interesting canoe trail through the mangroves at Coral Reef State Park. Boating is the strong suit; the Keys are paradise for anyone who owns or can rent a fourteen-to-sixteen-foot outboard motorboat. There are marinas and boat ramps aplenty. Once launched, what you get are brilliantly clear Gulf Stream waters, the whole of Florida Bay and its scores of mangrove islets to explore, and great fishing. Under the "Etc." heading, skin diving and snorkeling are the most notable activities, with miles of coral gardens waiting to astound you. Birding is also fantastic.

O*utdoors Highlights*   Key West; the Dry Tortugas; Key Deer Wildlife Refuge on Big Pine Key; Lignumvitae Key State Botanical Site; the coral reefs at John Pennekamp State Park.

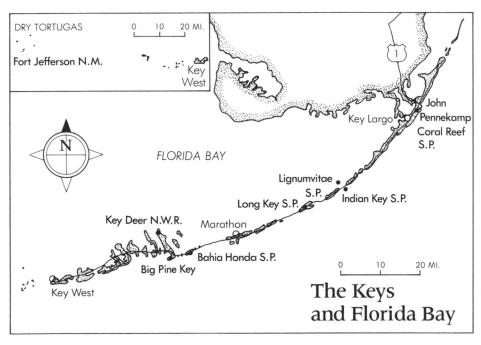

The Keys and Florida Bay

I t is fun to think of metaphors that describe the way the Florida Keys trail out from the mainland far into the blue Gulf. A broken string of beads. The tail of a kite. The vertebrae of a prehistoric beast.

The word "keys" comes from the Spanish *cayos* for "little islands"; and, indeed, most of the Keys are very small and fragile looking. It's doubtful that anyone has ever decided how many of them there are. Should we count all the tough little clumps of red mangrove that, at high tide, haven't a square foot of dry land to show for themselves? Are the scattered islets in Florida Bay part of the tally? What is certain is that there are a lot of Keys out there, and nobody has visited every one of them.

Until recently, human habitation on these beautiful but bleached, harsh islands has been pretty sparse. The Calusa Indians, the domi-nant tribe along Florida's Gulf Coast when the Spaniards came, have left behind the traces of a few villages and middens. But during the white man's term there were few efforts to permanently colonize the Keys—with the notable exception of Key West—until after the Civil War. The Spaniards maintained only a few missions and salvage out-posts. From the sixteenth century to the beginning of the nineteenth, pirates were the most notable, if transient, inhabitants of the islands, using them to hide, ambush ships, replenish stores, and, yes, bury treasure. In the nineteenth century they were superseded by the more legitimate wrecking industry, headquartered at Key West. The wreck-ers were intrepid souls who salvaged cargoes, and sometimes people, from the many ships that came to a bad end on reefs and shoals while passing through the Straits of Florida. They were largely responsible for making Key West the most prosperous town in Florida during much of the nineteenth century. On the few other keys that were in-habited at all, settlers made a hard living by exploiting the seemingly limitless resources of sea and bay. Fish, sponges, and shellfish were the staples; but less prolific creatures—manatees, alligators, crocodiles, Key deer, several kinds of sea turtle, and various species of wading birds (whose plumage was in demand for ladies' hats)—were also har-vested relentlessly, so much so that all of them were on the verge of extinction by the turn of the century. The turtles, the manatee, and the crocodile never have made a real comeback in spite of decades of protection.

Although the Florida East Coast Railroad reached Key West in 1912, and the Overseas Highway was completed in 1938, the really serious human invasion of the Keys did not get under way until World War II, when various military establishments revived the economy. Since then, tourism has been the major industry, along with an on-going boom in the construction of houses and condominiums and all that goes with them. The Keys have become a Shangri-la for any-one who is in love with small boats, saltwater fishing, the blue sky, and blue—impossibly blue—clear water. Tens of thousands of those in-love people have now made this or that little Key their home, and millions more come to visit every year. Driving along the Overseas Highway, you may well wonder how many more people can be accommodated on these little fragments of coral and limestone before they vanish under the weight of asphalt and cement.

But there is something nicer to wonder at: if you scout around, you will discover that quite a bit of the unspoiled Keys still survives, after all.

On that cheerful note, let us begin our tour.

Key West and the Dry Tortugas

You may not think of Key West, the southernmost town in the United States, as a gateway to a wilderness, but that is what it is. Not the least of its attractions is the palpable sense that it is, very literally, the end of the line. For those who are lured on by the pure blue and white and gold of the essential Gulf, pared down to its most basic ingredients, this is the last lodging, the last place where terrestrial creatures, man included, can make themselves at home. The old part of the town, at the island's southern tip, still retains vestiges of its past. On some streets the handsomely galleried nineteenth-century architecture and the palmy ambiance are downright Bahamian, not least of all because quite a few Bahamians came to these parts during the last century, attracted by Key West's flourishing economy. Wrecking, salt making, sponge gathering, fishing, cigar making (an art brought to the Keys by refugees from Spanish Cuba), and shipping made the town a lively, raffish sort of place in the old days; and even now the motels, subdivisions, and tourist shops that take up most of the island have not wholly obliterated that free-wheeling atmosphere. People who settle here have always been prepared to take their chances, with hurricanes, hidden reefs, and sudden storms; and, sometimes, with risky enterprises, from wrecking and rum running to, more recently, hustling and smuggling dope.

Between the World Wars, Key West endured hard times. But since World War II, the Navy and, especially, tourism—inadvertently aided and abetted by the example of various celebrities—have kept the town booming. Although Ernest Hemingway or Harry Truman or Tennessee Williams would hardly recognize their hideaway now, it is still an enjoyable place (albeit an expensive one, especially during the winter season). There is a lot to see, including Hemingway's home, the aquarium, and the interesting exhibits at the East Martello Gallery and Museum. The nicest part of all, though, is just moseying around, walking those too-few streets that have a real West Indian charm, admiring the wonderful plants in the Peggy Mills Garden, checking out the shrimping fleet at the Key West Bight, and rubbing shoulders with locals, beach bums, and fellow tourists during the evening ritual of watching the sun go down at land's end.

Beyond Key West lies the wilderness mentioned earlier. If it were just open water, it wouldn't count, even though the term ought arguably to apply to the sea, which is still the least spoiled of the planet's biospheres. But for our purposes, what matters is that there are small archipelagoes of land out there, scattered out against the blue like bread crumbs on a glass table. From a plane, what first strikes you is the transparency of it all. It is like looking into an immense aquarium in which most of the fish are too small to see. The follow-up impression is of color: of islets, yellow-white and black-green, changing to pale jade or swimming-pool blue as their slopes submerge, stained in places by the variegated texture of reefs or blue-black meadows of sea grass. Further out are the inky blues and bottle greens of the greater depths. Not that the greater depths are all that deep. Compared to the western Gulf, the waters off the Florida Gulf Coast stay shallow for a long way out. The immense expanse of Florida Bay, for example, never gets more than nine feet deep; and even forty or fifty miles out from the Coast, the water is only fifty or sixty feet in depth. Toylike yachts and fishing boats cast easy-to-see shadows on the underwater hills and dales.

But the most lasting impression, at least for me, is of the wonderful redundancy of natural forms: a child playing on a beach can see these same whorled shapes and contours repeated, in miniature, in the tidal shallows at his feet.

The last outposts of the Florida Keys are a half-dozen tiny islands known collectively as the Dry Tortugas. Protected now, they and their adjoining waters are part of the **Fort Jefferson National Monument**. They are seventy miles west of Key West, which is where you can hire a charter boat to visit them if you have the time and money. Aside from doing some fishing, and experiencing the pure, brilliant blueness of the Gulf en route, there are three good reasons why you might want to make the trip: the reefs, the birds, and the fort.

Even from the railing of a boat, coral reefs are something to see. If you can arrange to do some scuba diving, so much the better. The coral beds in the Dry Tortugas are the southernmost extension of the great string of reefs that extend off and on along the eastern flank of the Keys. Here they are not nearly as extensive as they are off Key Largo, in the Coral Reef National Marine Sanctuary and the John Pennekamp State Park. But they are every bit as beautiful, and you are more likely to have them to yourself. They are rightly called gardens, yet they have no relation to anything that grows in soil. Here the plants and flowers are composed of the secreted limey skeletons of quintrillions of organisms called polyps—nearly a hundred different kinds of them, all tiny. Out of its living self, each kind and colony creates its own sculptured form, growing on the hard core of its previous generations like fungi on deadwood. Those forms are suggested by the different names: star, lettuce, gorgonian, elkhorn, staghorn; but it is a fact that no words or even photographs can adequately describe their bizarre, unearthly beauty. In nature, far more than in human architecture, form is supposed to follow function. But it is hard to believe that coral really has to assume such fantastic shapes and hues just to fill some ecological niche. As biologists are only beginning to discover, Nature has produced a greater variety of life forms than is actually necessary to fill the earth's available environments. Which is another way of saying that Nature is more imaginative and whimsical than she has to be. Coral reefs are a case in point.

Nevertheless, the form-follows-function rule does apply to the totality of a coral reef if not to the riotous fantasy of its parts. For one thing, reefs protect shorelines from the eroding force of storms and hurricanes. For another, pulverized coral skeletons produce amazing quantities of sand, which in its turn produces essential habitat for all sorts of crustaceans, mollusks, and fishes. (The process is helped along by fish species, such as the parrotbill, that browse the coral and grind it in their jaws.) And, most interesting of all to browsing humans, the reefs offer sanctuary to a host of marine creatures. Of fish alone, there are more than four hundred species, with names such as butterfly fish, beau gregories, rock beauties, and porkfish, many of them gorgeously colored. Among other residents, there are sea urchins, spidery crabs, and tentacled anemones that are as imaginatively designed as the coral itself. In viewing them, the undersea explorer should move with care, however—not just for his or her own sake, but the reef's. Coral protuberances are brittle, easy to break or scratch. Sometimes, before the coral can regenerate itself, algae infest the wound and, like a cancer, destroy the whole colony. Anchors, by the way, are an even greater menace than divers. The captain of your charter boat will probably know better than to drop anchor on a reef; but if he doesn't, mutiny.

Even more than the coral gardens, it is the birdlife that brings visitors to the Dry Tortugas. A few bleak, sandy acres on Bush Key are the only nesting ground in North America of the sooty tern. The birds are virtually never seen on the mainland except when a hurricane drives them there. Yet on this tiny island great numbers of them pack themselves together and then quarrel acrimoniously over the invisible boundary lines that separate their nesting territories. Overhead glide those avian pirates, the frigatebirds, biding their time. They intercept the sooties as they bring fish home to their young, harassing them until they drop their catch. Meanwhile, in the nearby bushes that give the key its name, the colony of another tern that is rarely seen on the mainland, the brown noddy, has also set up housekeeping. There are roseate terns here too. And in summer, blue-faced and brown boobies—handsomer birds than their names suggest—dive for fish or pose on channel markers, no doubt waiting for some happy birder to add them to his life list. The blue-faced booby, especially, is almost never seen anywhere in the United States except in the Dry Tortugas.

Garden Key is just a little to the west of Bush Key. It would be interesting to accompany someone out here who hadn't been fore-warned about Fort Jefferson, just to see the look of disbelief on his or her face. The fort rises from the great emptiness of the Gulf like a pon-derous mirage. Although its brick, hexagonal structure is much like that of other nineteenth-century forts on the Gulf Coast, it is far and away the largest of them all. The thick brick walls rise fifty feet above the moat, are half a mile around, and enclose most of the island. But the really extraordinary thing about the place is simply that it is there at all. Like a Sherman tank in a glass palace.

The fort was meant to be a U.S. Gibraltar, guarding the Straits of Florida, when construction was begun in 1846. But before it was ever finished, the invention of masonry-piercing artillery cannon had made it obsolete. During and after the Civil War it was used as a pris-on. During subsequent wars it served as a staging area for naval ships, a seaplane base, and an observation post. In the decades between, al-though officially declared a national monument in 1936, its visitors were mostly rum runners and vandals. Now, however, the place has been tidied up, and National Park personnel are in residence. You can camp on the island overnight if you get permission from the Ever-glades National Park superintendent in Homestead and take every-thing, including water, with you. Whether you would want to do that depends on your temperament. Fort Jefferson is the most isolated na-tional monument in the United States south of northern Alaska. There are the resplendent tropical skies, the coral reefs, the terns. There is also the terrific sense of aloneness, even if one isn't by oneself. One thinks of Dr. Samuel Mudd, the good samaritan who was imprisoned here because he set John Wilkes Booth's broken leg. One wonders what he thought about, gazing at these same skies, these same screaming birds. (Fort Jefferson National Monument, c/o Superinten-dent, Everglades National Park, Homestead, Florida 33030; 305/247–6211.)

Even if there were not the Dry Tortugas and their rare terns, the Florida Keys would still be a great place for anyone even mildly inter-ested in birdlife. Almost anywhere that the Overseas Highway crosses a shallow inlet or sideswipes a mangrove thicket, you are likely to spot at least some gulls, terns, shorebirds and/or waders. Apart from boast-ing a unique and, in some cases, flashy collection of species that are year-round residents, the Keys attract many birds during the winter months for much the same reasons that they attract people. But for the serious birder, the best of all possible times is the spring. Then the Keys are host not only to full-time and winter-only species, but also to a host of tired migrants that put down here to rest after a long, hard flight across the Gulf.

Brown pelican. *Photo by Florida Division of Tourism.*

Even before you leave crowded Key West, you should get out the binocs and look around. Frigatebirds are usually riding thermals above the docks, and lugubrious pelicans—always one of the most endearing of birds to watch—are posted on the piers. The city cemetery is a great birding spot, especially for migrant songbirds, and has been the scene of some rare and unusual sightings. But probably the best area for general viewing is along South Roosevelt Drive en route to the East Martello Tower Museum, which you will want to visit anyway. The shallow saltponds on the left are a wonderful place to see assorted plovers, sandpipers, sanderlings, gulls, royal terns, and ducks in winter and spring. During summer you may see clapper rail, the attenuated black-necked stilt, and one of southern Florida's specialties, the smooth-billed ani, which looks like a grackle in need of a nose job.

Stock Island, just east of Key West, is also a good spot for some easily accessible birding—which is surprising when you consider that this is one of the most brutally developed Keys in the whole chain, nearly all of it jammed with trailer parks, businesses, and industrial sites that have spilled over from Key West. Yet north of the highway lies the Key West Botanical Gardens, a fascinating tangle of native and exotic shrubs and trees, much overgrown, where you have a good chance of seeing birds unique to the area, such as white-crowned pigeon, gray kingbird, black-whiskered vireo, ani, and mangrove cuckoo. (To get to the Gardens, take the first left turn after crossing the channel from Key West, pass some Monroe County service buildings, and turn right at the Mosquito Control building.)

Heading east through the lower Keys you travel across a number of islands given over to the military, intensive real-estate development, or low-lying mangrove thickets. There are several picnic areas along the road and many spots where you can pull over and glass the scene for birds. This is not surf-and-swim country, however. Boca Chica Key has a beach area that is pleasant for a picnic, but the water is shallow for a long way out. The wading, however, is a delight, offering an opportunity to study the rich marine life in the brilliantly clear water. (Just keep in mind that sun rays reflecting off all that bright water will fry you even faster than they would on a white-sand beach.)

The Central Keys

Thirty miles north of Key West, the Overseas Highway arrives at Pine Key and its adjacent islands, easily the most exciting land areas in the Keys from an ecologist's point of view. This, despite the fact that the islands actually traversed by the highway—the Torch Keys and Big Pine itself—are already heavily developed in some areas, and the bulldozers are still at work. The saving grace is that sizable tracts on these Keys, as well as several smaller, less accessible islands north of them, are part of the Key Deer Refuge and/or the overlapping Great White Heron National Refuge.

The most famous citizen of these islands is the Key deer, a highly specialized version of the Eastern whitetail. Over the centuries it has adapted to life on the Keys by shrinking itself to about the size of an Irish setter. That way, it requires less sustenance from its harsh environment and has a better chance of finding whatever food is available. In its search for mangrove seeds and the like, the little creature rushes into mangrove tangles where an ordinary-size whitetail would fear to tread. Unfortunately, its adaptability didn't encompass the wiles and stratagems of our own species. Not so long ago, islanders were still hounding it to the brink of extinction. (Literally hounding it, since dogs were used to drive the hapless animals into the water, where hunters could blast away at them.) Older conservationists will still remember the nationwide crusade in the late forties that finally browbeat a reluctant Congress into creating a national refuge. Since those days, the deer have increased from about forty to four hundred, as many as their diminished habitat can support. Now the main predator is the automobile, which kills dozens of them each year.

To reach **Key Deer Wildlife Refuge**, head north on Key Deer Boulevard (County Road 940) and take a left on Watson Boulevard. At the refuge headquarters some of the deer are on display in pens, but it is not too difficult to have the more exhilarating experience of seeing them in the wild. Refuge personnel can give you directions to roads and trails where, early in the morning and at evening, the animals are likely to be seen. They also show up in more developed areas on No Name Key or in Big Pine Key's subdivisions, where some well-meaning residents unwisely feed them. (Key Deer Refuge, P.O. Box 510, Big Pine Key, Florida 33043; 305/872–2239.)

Marvelous as these deer are, they are by no means the only reason for exploring Big Pine and the adjacent islands. Here land areas are oftentimes sheltered and extensive enough to support a remarkable subtropical vegetation. The inevitable mangrove fringe gives way on higher ground to a weird, scrawny forest in which slash pine, the only ones on the lower Keys, grow in close association with various palms. In much of this area the living, biologically speaking, is hard; the trees, like the deer, have dwarfed themselves in order to get by. Yet there are places where the scene becomes markedly more luxuriant. One such place is Watson Hammock. To reach it, continue on Key Deer Boulevard past the refuge headquarters turnoff for a little more than a mile; then take the road on the left, just below a sizable lake. Park when the road becomes impassable and continue on foot, heading left when the trail forks. The hammock that surrounds you is straight out of the West Indies, a wonderfully gargoyle world in which the trees blossom with bromeliads and orchids. Strangler fig, torch-

Key deer. *Photo by Florida Division of Tourism.*

wood (which burns when green), mahogany, guava, poisonwood (which, when touched, has an effect similar to poison ivy), and the rare manicheel (which is more poisonous even than poisonwood) all grow to heights exceptional in the Keys. Since there is no hunting here, you may possibly see a representative of Pine Key's special tribe of raccoons: their fur is pale yellow, and the rings on their tails are sometimes barely visible. This is also a splendid place for birding. The Keys' specialties—white-crowned pigeons, black-whiskered vireos, mangrove cuckoos—frequent the area, as well as birds of prey (including the bald eagle) and, in season, a lot of migrant songbirds.

Just before you leave Big Pine Key, heading east, there is another area worth investigating. This is the southern peninsula of the island, from which the highway takes off for Bahia Honda. Just before reaching a private camping area at mile marker 33, a paved road turns off to the right. Follow this for about a third of a mile. On the right is a barricaded dirt road, bordered by a cactus hammock and saltpools. The hammock is remarkable for a species of tree cactus and a type of prickly pear that, like the Key deer, can be found nowhere else in the world. While you are here, or anywhere else in the Keys where saltwater flats are in view, be on the lookout for the rare reddish egret and the white form of the great blue heron. The former is an amusingly undignified bird that tends to rush its prey in awkward lunges rather than stalking it as a proper heron should, and the latter is one of the largest and loveliest of the American waders. Formerly known as the great white heron, it is the namesake of the refuge that begins at the northern end of Pine Key. Like the Key deer, this heron was hunted to the verge of extinction. Now there are about two thousand—still no great number—in Florida Bay and the Keys. They look like giant cousins of the far more common great egret but are actually a form of the great blue heron. They do not move about in flocks, so you must count yourself lucky if you see even a few of these stately creatures during your travels in the Keys.

The only public campground in the lower Keys is at **Bahia Honda State Park**, which lies just east of Big Pine. The park has camping sites on both sides of the island. Those convenient to the marina and the old trestle bridge are less shady and secluded than the ones situated a little further off in a hammock setting. The beach here, lined with coconut palms and Australian pines, is the best in the Keys. There is also a nature trail, featuring rare little silver palms as well as views of the island's hammocks and mangroves. The inlet north of the highway is a favorite place for wading birds, including, at times, roseate spoonbills, reddish egrets, and yellow-crowned night herons.

Be forewarned, though: like the two other state parks in the Keys, Bahia Honda is very popular. In winter you should have a reservation or arrive very early in the morning. There is, by the way, a private campground on little Ohio Key, right next door. It's not as scenic as

Bahia Honda, but it's a good place for birding. (Bahia Honda State Park, Route 1, Box 782, Big Pine Key, Florida 33043; 305/872–2353.)

Beyond Seven Mile Bridge, almost all of the inhabitable portions of the Keys have been given over to end-to-end development. Usually there isn't even a view of open water except when you cross connecting bridges. There are, however, a few places where remnants of the natural world have been preserved. One of these is the **Long Key State Recreation Area**. The beach here is somewhat steeper and narrower than the one at Bahia Honda, and, as usual in the Keys, the water is better suited for wading than swimming. As at Bahia Honda, the camping sites that line the shore are in great demand, especially between Christmas and Easter; so you should make reservations well in advance or expect to be turned away. For all this heavy use, however, and the audible traffic on the nearby highway, the park is a nice place to be. As always in the Keys, there are the incomparable skies and iridescent water, so different in their tropical coloring and translucence even from those no further north than Miami. And anyone interested in nature will enjoy the park trails that lead you behind the camping area into the Key's narrow interior. The park offers a short boardwalk trail and observation tower, but the best bet is a longer, 1½-mile loop that takes you through dense, low, tropical hammocks and mangroves to a stretch of beach at the southeastern end of the island that usually hosts numerous shore birds at low tide. A footbridge crosses a lagoon often frequented by wading birds. (Long Key State Recreation Area, P.O. Box 776, Long Key, Florida 33001; 305/664–4815.)

The best thing about Long Key, however, is that it makes an ideal place to camp for a day or two while you visit **Lignumvitae Key State Botanical Site**, a nature preserve, and also, perhaps, **Indian Key**, a state historical site, both just a few miles to the east. These islands, the former small and the latter minuscule, lie, respectively, north and south of the eastern tip of Lower Matecumbe Key. They can be seen from the Indian Key Picnic Area (not to be confused with Indian Key itself) between Lower and Upper Matecumbe, but both are safely out of the highway's reach. It's easy to visit them, either in your own boat or one hired at Lower Matecumbe or Long Key, and there is good fishing in the channels en route.

Indian Key, with its palms and mangroves, is a little boy's dream of Treasure Island. There are places to picnic and watch the pelicans cruising by, and shells can be found in the sandy marl. Nearby are superb coral reefs lying just offshore from both Upper and Lower Matecumbe Keys. But Indian Key's strong suit is history. From the sixteenth to the early nineteenth century, Spanish, French, English, and American sailing ships passing through the dangerous Florida Straits were wrecked along these coasts with dismaying regularity. There is still a lot of sunken treasure out there, covered by sand and coral. During the early days, survivors of shipwrecks who came ashore here—including, according to one eighteenth-century account, several hundred Frenchmen at one time—were apt to be massacred or burned alive by the fierce Calusa Indians. Eventually, the Calusas were themselves killed off by white men's guns and diseases or amalgamated by Creek Indians infiltrating from northern Florida. In 1825, an enterprising if rascally fellow named Jacob Houseman set up houses and wharves on the Key, then convinced the state government to declare his little settlement the county seat of newly created Dade County. Here he was joined by a brilliant, far-sighted botanist, Dr. Henry Perrine, who dreamed of using the area for the study and propagation of tropical plants from around the globe. These dreams were never realized, however. Perrine and six other people were killed on the Key by raiding Indians in 1840. Houseman managed to escape, but he died in an accident a year later and is buried on the island. Since then, most calamities have been the work of Nature, particularly the terrible hurricane of 1935. If you look to the east, you will see Upper Matecumbe Key, where hundreds of World War I veterans, working on the Overseas Highway, were swept away by tidal waves, along with the train that was coming to their rescue. Among residents of the Keys, the toll was even higher. Throughout all of this area, including Indian Key, skeletons were still being recovered from mangrove jungles a decade later.

On that grisly note, let us turn to Lignumvitae Key, where the history is chiefly natural. If one must choose between which of the two Keys to visit, then this one wins hands down. Except for a single house, a walking trail, and a stone wall that may mark a trading post built here circa 1700, the island is as much a wilderness as it was before the first white man ever saw it. As always in the Keys, you must not expect wilderness to mean towering forests. Yet this is a genuine tropical jungle, where not even the slash pines of Big Pine Key, much less the imported Australian pines that are everywhere present on the developed Keys, have ever taken hold. On this small island there are about a hundred tree species deriving from the Florida mainland and the Caribbean that were carried here by tidal currents. Mahogany, mastic, strangler fig, gumbo limbo, poisonwood, and paradise tree, not to mention the Key's namesake with its tiny, blue flowers and chalky bark, grow in a dense profusion that makes a tunnel of the trail. It is also a haven for birds, including all the Keys' specialties and, in winter and spring, a host of migrant species. Also, twenty-six species of butterflies flourish here (along with mosquitoes, alas) because the island is not sprayed.

We are very lucky to have this little gem of a Key. If the Nature Conservancy, an outfit devoted to saving unique ecological areas, hadn't bought the island in the late 1960s and held it until the state could take it over, it would be shore-to-shore subdivision by now. Because it cannot stand much human wear and tear, the trail is open only for ranger-guided tours: a two-hour walk beginning at 9:00 A.M. and one-hour walks at 1:00 P.M. and 3:00 P.M. There is, of course, no camping.

The Upper Keys

At Tavernier on Plantation Key, turn left (heading east) at mile marker 89. The second house on the left is a research station for the National Audubon Society, a good place to pick up birding information for the area. Audubon has a sanctuary, Cowpens Key, on Florida Bay nearby. It is one of the most important of the several rookeries on the bay, the others being within the boundaries of Everglades National Park. During the nesting season, the mangroves are aswarm with roseate spoonbills, egrets, great white herons, reddish egrets, and other waders all caught up in the serious business of raising their young. At any time of day, the comings and goings of all these large, beautiful birds creates an astonishing spectacle; at evening, when the birds are heading homeward against the incomparable backdrop of the Keys' sky— billowing cumulus clouds edged with the same pinks and golds and lavenders that tint the birds' wings—the sight will stun you with its beauty. It hardly needs to be said that you must view the rookery, when it is active, from offshore. Boats can be hired at Tavernier for this purpose, as well as to view the wildlife in other areas of Florida Bay. Again, check at the Audubon station.

The third of the state parks in the Keys where camping is available is at **John Pennekamp Coral Reef State Park** on Key Largo. This place is even more crowded and intensively managed for recreation than the other Keys parks. There is a beach, a nature trail through the mangroves, an observation tower, camping and picnic sites, a boat launch and boat rentals, a concession store—in short, the works. One of the most pleasant things you can do here is to explore the nearby mangrove forests in your own, or a rented, canoe, guided by a ranger who leads daily tours. Another important attraction is a nature center with first-rate exhibits. (At the time of this writing it had been heavily damaged by fire, but will probably be reopened by publication date.)

Although the park is well planned and well managed, the crowds and the intensive use are not to everyone's taste, especially if you want a camping site and are turned away—which is very likely to happen if you do not have a reservation made well in advance. However, the offshore coral reefs are all the justification that the park needs. These are by far the most extensive reefs in the Keys. The park provides convenient access to them in the form of glass-bottomed-boat tours and snorkeling trips that require no experience on your part. A couple of cautionary remarks are in order, however. During winter, when most people are visiting the park, the water is not always as clear as it is during the summer months. Also, you should think twice about visiting the reefs on your own unless you are an old hand at boating. The reefs are five miles offshore and can be tricky to maneuver. You would not be the first person that they have run aground.

One way or another, however, you must see the coral reefs if you come to the Keys. Not to do so would be like visiting Athens without seeing the Parthenon.

Highway 1 departs the Florida Keys midway on Key Largo. Except for private resort developments at its northernmost tip, much of the upper Key is still densely mantled with hammock and mangrove as I write this. Unfortunately, that will soon change. The area has escaped development this long only because, until fairly recently, the water mains to the Keys bypassed it. Now, due to some questionable political and bureaucratic finagling, the tap has been turned on. The only remaining debates are over how many tens of thousands of people will be packed on the Atlantic side of the island and how much the pollution caused by their presence will damage the coral reef at their front doors.

But at least much of upper Key Largo's backyard will remain the mangrove jungle it is now, thanks to the federal government, which is acquiring the area as a crocodile refuge. Few of the millions of tourists who pour across the Lake Surprise Causeway are aware that crocodiles, not just alligators, reside in the United States. Even fewer realize that the causeway bisects the heartland of this endangered reptile's range. Only two or three hundred of them survive, but here in the vicinity of Lake Surprise their numbers seem to have stabilized, at least for the present. You are not likely to get a look at one, since they are shy, retiring fellows; and besides, their breeding grounds in Everglades National Park and the federal refuge are off-limits to people. But as you drive across Lake Surprise, it's pleasant to reflect that a couple of crocs may be basking within yards of the bumper-to-bumper traffic. Give them a wave and wish them well. While you're at it, wave goodbye to the Keys and wish them well too.

3
The Everglades and the Big Cypress Country

At a glance

Access   Miami is the eastern point of entry for airborne visitors, with direct flights from most major American cities. There are also regularly scheduled flights to airports at Naples and Fort Meyers. People on wheels who are arriving from Florida's east coast have their choice of several highways funneling into the Homestead area. From the west coast, travelers can choose between Hwy 84 ("Alligator Alley," soon to become part of I-75) or, further south, Hwy 41 (the Tamiami Trail). Both traverse some beautiful country but the latter provides a more intimate view. Hwy 29, on the western edge of the Big Cypress Preserve, is the only improved road that cuts north-south through a part of this region.

Climate   Here in southern Florida, a tropical weather cycle prevails. There are only two seasons: winter, which is pleasantly warm and dry as a rule, and summer (beginning in May), which is hot, humid, and often wet. Mosquitoes, even more than high temperatures, make the latter season off-limits to all but the most masochistic campers.

Topography and Landscape Features   Southern Florida is built on the submerged foothills of the Appalachians. The base is limestone, created by the compressed and cemented shells and skeletons of myriad sea creatures during the various epochs when this landscape was covered by prehistoric seas. Limestone is very susceptible to acidic erosion, caused by the mix of decaying vegetation and rainwater. As a result, the surface is pocked and pitted, and the nether regions are riddled by subterranean caves and tunnels. Peat soils are rich but very thin. The flatness of the terrain accounts for the phenomenon of the Everglades, a river of grass that is many miles wide and only inches deep—about which you'll find more in the following travelogue.

Flora and Fauna   In this country, elevations that can be measured in inches account for astonishing differences in vegetation. Among the more notable ecosystems—often intersecting—are vast mangrove swamps; freshwater prairies, sloughs, and sawgrass-covered "everglades"; the hammocks of tropical and subtropical hardwoods (gumbo limbo, strangler fig, royal and sabal palms, etc.) that appear as islands in the aforementioned ecosystems; the pine forests and palmetto that colonize limestone ridges; and the cypress, which can be found in rounded domes or in scattered, stunted stands. The fauna is equally fabulous. Nowhere else in the United States will you encounter such a wealth of wading birds or so many extroverted alligators. Among the endangered species, the main ones you have a decent chance of seeing are the snail kite, the bald eagle, and (maybe) the Cape Sable seaside sparrow. The Florida black bear and the extremely rare Florida panther, not to mention the Everglades mink and the round-tailed muskrat, still hold out here. Deer, bobcat, wild turkeys, and small game species are abundant in some areas.

Camping   There are two large RV campgrounds (without hookups) in Everglades National Park and another small campground (Chekika State Recreation Area) north of Homestead. On the western edge of this region, Collier-Seminole State Park (see Chapter 4) also has a large RV campground. Along the Tamiami Trail there are a couple of privately owned facilities, one at Ochopee and another at Everglades City. A number of primitve campsites are available in the parks, although some can only be reached by water. Primitive campsites for hikers are also located along the Big Cypress segment of the Florida Trail.

Hiking, Canoeing, Boating, Etc.   There are several lengthy hiking trails in Everglades National Park, as well as many shorter nature walks; to the north, a long north-south segment of the Florida Trail traverses the Big Cypress Preserve. Canoeists can try one of the shorter water trails in the Flamingo area of Everglades National Park or tackle the long mangrove wilderness journey between Flamingo and Everglades City. Small-boaters can also explore the bays and trails in this mangrove country or gain access to Florida Bay from Flamingo. Saltwater fishing in the bays is great. Birders and nature lovers will be in paradise anywhere in this region, but the sun-and-swim set will find slim pickings, except perhaps at hard-to-reach Cape Sable.

Outdoors Highlights   Anhinga Trail is the single most popular draw at Everglades National Park, but the whole park is a highlight, including Shark Valley on the northern boundary. In the Big Cypress country, the Loop Road (Hwy 94) and the Fakahatchee Strand State Preserve are the main attractions for the nonhiker, although the former presents problems for the motorist, as noted in the travelogue.

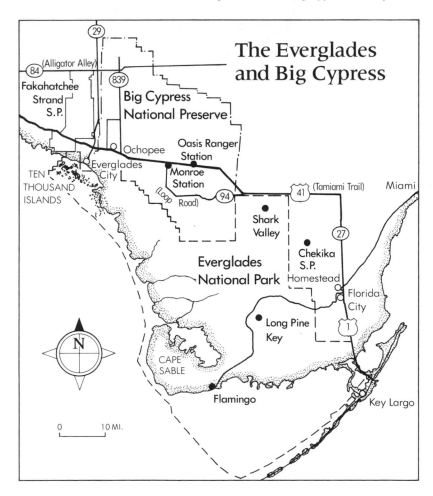

The Everglades
and Big Cypress

(29)

(Alligator Alley)
(84)
(839)

Fakahatchee
Strand
S.P.

**Big Cypress
National Preserve**

Ochopee

Oasis Ranger
Station

TEN
THOUSAND
ISLANDS

Everglades
City

Monroe
Station

(Loop
Road)

(94)

(41) (Tamiami Trail)   Miami

Shark
Valley

Everglades
National Park

Chekika
S.P.

(27)

Homestead

Florida
City

Long Pine
Key

(1)

N

CAPE
SABLE

Flamingo

Key Largo

0   10 MI.

Twenty-one miles north of Key Largo, Hwys 1 and 27 meet. Before heading for Everglades National Park on Hwy 27, you may want to fill the tank and stock up on provisions; it's almost fifty miles to Flamingo with no services along the way, and when you get there, you'll find that groceries cost a bit more than at Florida City or Homestead.

The Everglades

Of all the wild places on our Gulf Coast itinerary, **Everglades National Park** is the one most written about and visited. Yet for many people it remains an enigma, even after they have been here. It is so unlike any other large wilderness area in the nation, and so absolutely the antithesis of the more familiar mountain and desert parks, that it sometimes sabotages the expectations of travelers coming here for the first time, even when they think they are prepared.

Understanding is all. Even people who really couldn't care less about nature can appreciate, at some surface level, the purple mountain's majesty and all that. But the Everglades do not offer that kind of accessibility when viewed from a car doing fifty-five miles per hour. You need to take your time and know, at least in an amateur way, what you're looking at.

Much of the basic information can be acquired at the Visitor Center, situated amid royal palms, live oaks, and mahoganies, at the entrance to the park. Here there are pamphlets, books, a nice map, and a short film. After that, an ideal tour would include at least one day, preferably two, spent in the Long Pine Key area, where one of the park's two campgrounds is located. It operates on a first-come, first-served basis, which in winter means getting there as early in the day as you can. There are no hookups.

Long Pine Key has the highest elevation in the park, and despite its inland location it is rightly named a Key. This limestone outcropping is at the southernmost end of a low ridge that runs down the Atlantic Coast from Fort Lauderdale. Just a few thousand years ago, an eyeblink in geological time, the surrounding freshwater prairies were a shallow sea, much like Florida Bay is now. Long Key itself must have looked somewhat the way the lower Keys would look today if they weren't covered with concrete and people. Since the seas receded, the periodic sweep of fire has made this relatively dry ridge a suitable habitat for such fire-tolerant species as the Florida slash pine and the saw-palmetto. Nowadays, various parts of the Key are regularly burned by park personnel in a simulation of natural cycles. Otherwise, hardwood hammocks, which already share some of this dry ground with the pines, would take over all of it.

Despite the open, rather uniform look of the pine forest, there are many plants in this community, including the palmetto and coontie (a small, palmlike cycad with roots from which Indians used to make flour). They survive fires by keeping their roots tucked away in damp solution holes in the limestone. Soon after the flames have swept through, they poke up new green leaves. Around them, the blackened peat is quickly covered by flowering vines and legumes such as moonvine and tamarind.

The Park Service has created a self-guided nature trail that takes you through the pinelands north of the park road. But the best way to experience this terrain is on the much longer series of linked trails (about seven miles) that start at the campground and wind through the center of Long Pine Key. In the evenings you may see deer and raccoons; and in summer, along with the mosquitoes, there are often twilight conventions of fireflies. Unquestionably, however, the most glamorous inhabitant of Long Pine Key is the Florida panther. A half-dozen of this all-but-vanished southeastern subspecies of the mountain lion survive here. They're not likely to let themselves be seen; but it is a great thrill just to know that one of these shy, harmless beauties may have recently crossed the path you're walking on.

Taylor Slough at the eastern end of Long Pine Key is a more famous attraction than Long Pine itself. No wonder! The Anhinga Trail, which extends out over the slough, is one of the most accessible and dependable places in the park to see wildlife. If you have time, the spot is definitely worth several visits. Early morning is the best time of day, and winter and spring are the best seasons; but there is likely to be a good show going on at any hour, any time of year. Taylor Slough is a shallow depression in the limestone that extends from Long Pine Key to Florida Bay. The Anhinga Trail crosses a stretch of sawgrass marsh and thickets of willow, custard apples, and groundsel as well as the dark, clear waters of the slough itself. Along the way, you will certainly see alligators, herons, turtles, and the strange snake-necked bird, the anhinga, for the which the trail is named. The anhinga swims underwater, spears fish, and, like the cormorants to which it is related, spreads its wings out to dry. Like most of the wildlife along Taylor Slough, it is unafraid of people and obligingly raises its young and poses for pictures within yards of the boardwalk.

At the water's edge there will probably be great egrets and green-backed, little blue, and tricolored herons, as well, perhaps, as white ibises or limpkins. If you have sharp eyes, you may see a Cape Sable seaside sparrow, a rather ordinary-looking bird, but a very rare and cherished addition to any birder's list. In the water, coots and common or purple gallinules are usually puttering around within a few feet of languid alligators. (Not that the 'gators are always languid: come here at dawn in late winter and the boardwalk sometimes vibrates with their amorous grunts and bellowings.) The reason the Slough is so popular with wildlife is that it dependably retains water, even during the worst droughts. To people, the place is a natural aquarium, but to birds and alligators it is a cafeteria, loaded with bream, bass, long-nosed gar, and turtles, all clearly visible beneath the surface.

The Anhinga Trail is so spectacular that visitors sometimes ignore the more specialized attraction of the Gumbo Limbo Trail, which begins at the same parking lot but heads the other way, into one of the hammocks at the edge of Long Pine Key. (The traveler in southern Florida has the opportunity to become a connoisseur of hammocks, which come in many shapes and sizes. Strictly speaking, the term refers to dense clusters of hardwoods on slightly elevated islands of peat in fresh or brackish marsh. But the word is often used to describe any clump of trees or shrubs that breaks the horizontal stretch of the water prairies, including cypress "heads," which require peat-filled depressions, rather than elevations, to exist in this flat world.) Anyway, the hammock traversed by the Gumbo Limbo Trail is a magical little place. After the wide sky and broad sweep of the sawgrass, it is like coming inside a shuttered house jammed with trees instead of furniture. This

Great egret. *Photo by Florida Division of Tourism.*

is a low hammock, and most of the trees are small. Unobtrusive labels introduce you to pigeon plum, pigmy live oak, wild coffee, paradise tree, strangler fig, and, of course, the gumbo limbo, easy to spot with its smooth, bright red-brown trunk. Everywhere there are epiphytes—air plants—and resurrection ferns, a garden within a garden. All told, seventy-five different kinds of trees and plants can be found along this one little trail, a number that would be unimaginable in a comparable area of northern forest.

Once we leave Long Pine Key and Taylor Slough behind, the park road takes a sharp turn southward. It is important to pause at this turning, though, and walk the short trail to the Pa-hay-okee Observation Tower. Of all the several detours off the main road that are set up to display the Everglades' attractions, this one, and its counterpart at Shark Valley on the northern perimeter of the park, are probably the most important. Why? Because here you have the opportunity, rare in this flat land, to look far out over the thing itself: the great, lonesome river of grass, the real Everglades, sweeping by in a broad, invisible current.

The Everglades is one of the weirdest rivers in the world: a hundred miles long, fifty miles wide, and six inches deep! Its headwaters are at Lake Okeechobee, which serves as a catchbasin for the Kissimmee River drainage to the north. The overflow from the drainage seeps southward in a wide, shallow sheet. Since the slope that the river descends may drop only an inch or two in a mile, its current is imperceptible to the eye. Yet this shallow, slow-moving flow influences the existence of everything in its path; and its path covers most of southern Florida. During the wet season it brings life to an elaborate web of dependent ecosystems: freshwater prairies, sloughs, coastal marshes, hammocks, and mangrove swamps, not to mention the teeming waters of Florida Bay. And because the flow is so gradual, the Everglades can remain wet for months after the summer rains have ended. It is this capacity to retain slow-moving water that accounts, more than any other factor, for the region's ecological wealth. Eventually, especially during extended periods of drought, much of the river of grass dries up, except where there are sloughs and 'gator holes. In the old days, this was the time when fires swept the Glades. In the natural scheme of checks and balances, these fires had their role to play, forestalling the encroachment of hammock vegetation on the open prairies and limestone ridges.

Now, however, that ancient cycle has been radically altered by— guess who? Man's short-sighted manipulation of the Everglades began about sixty years ago with a flood protection plan, in response to a devastating hurricane that killed thousands of people at Lake Okeechobee. Eventually it grew into a series of epic drainage schemes. These projects had the effect of short-stopping the flow of Everglades water, diverting it to Miami and the vast truck-farming operations on

Florida's east coast. Immense, leveed conservation areas—actually shallow reservoirs—were created below Lake Okeechobee. When the water wasn't needed in wet years, it was simply dumped into the Atlantic. Meanwhile the Everglades died of thirst. Millions of its creatures were burned in horrific unnatural fires that swept the region, and southern Florida's underground aquifer, deprived of infusions of Glades water, was invaded by saltwater that rendered many wells in the Miami area unusable. The upshot is that 44 percent of the former Everglades is now given over to agribusiness and subdivisions, and 49 percent is allocated to conservation-area impoundments (which at least retain some natural features). Of the original Everglades, only 7 percent is preserved in the national park. And even now, that 7 percent must wait its turn for allocations of water during dry years.

Meanwhile, southern Florida's human population continues to grow at a runaway rate, and water tables in the limestone aquifer, which the Everglades used to recharge, get lower and lower. But to the naturalist's eye, the birdlife of the area is perhaps the most poignant indicator of the long-term damage. Old-time residents remember when the usual way to calculate the abundance of wading birds was to count the number of acres they blanketed when they settled down. Those days are over now, and the decline continues.

Lest we be too glum, however, we should remind ourselves that there are still enough birds on hand to gladden the hearts of all but the most jaded wildlife viewers. And, even more important in the long run, the state of Florida is at last beginning to devise a series of truly enlightened conservation measures to protect the Glades. If they are implemented, they will undo much of the ecological harm that has been done in the past.

Meantime, here at Pa-hay-okee, you can get some feel for the majestic sweep of this improbable river. Everything in the wide view ties together: the dark blue-green of the hammocks, the gray-blue of the cypress heads, the many green-yellow textures of grass, reeds, and sedge. And, over all, the brilliant tropical sky, with perhaps a flight of egrets or a circling hawk to make it all too perfect.

Between Pa-hay-okee and Flamingo, there are several notable turnoffs. Probably the most interesting is Mahogany Hammock. The mahogany is a tropical tree, and long ago timber cutters almost eliminated it throughout its limited range in southern Florida. But along this boardwalk trail you can see a number of these handsome trees. There are also rare paurotis palms, some mammoth strangler figs, satinleaf, and enormous leather ferns. The atmosphere is totally different from that of Gumbo Limbo Hammock: the trees are taller and less crowded; there is more light filtering through the canopy; branches and vines are heavier. A sign along the path directs your attention to the inch-deep moat that the hammock has made for itself. The acidic interaction of rainwater and the hammock's own decaying vegetation have etched a shallow depression in the soft limestone. Thus, these vulnerable hardwoods protect themselves to some extent from the threat of fire.

The road southward continues for a while through sawgrass prairies punctuated by hammocks and small cypress. Then it plunges into mangrove country, the dense foliage closing in on the road like a hedge. For years after Hurricane Donna tore through the park in 1960, this same stretch of road was a graveyard of dead mangroves, a million blasted roots and branches lying like skeletons in the marl. Even the park botanists wondered if the trees would ever come back. But hurricanes, unlike bulldozers, are something that the tough mangroves can cope with. Now it is difficult to realize that a monster hurricane ever passed this way.

Flamingo has a large campground (no reservations, no hookups), as well as a motel, fancy restaurant, grocery store, boat and canoe rentals, and a sizable marina that can handle boats up to sixty feet. (Some facilities are closed between June and November.) A fee for using the campground is charged only from November through April, which tells you something about camping conditions during the warm months. Even in winter the mosquitoes sometimes make a mild nuisance of themselves. By May they behave like winged piranhas. If a breeze isn't blowing, you better get used to the idea of bathing in repellent, which, of course, will not necessarily discourage the sand-

Everglades. *Photo by Florida Division of Tourism.*

flies. There are some lunatics and masochists, myself among them, who do not much mind these summer miseries when equipped with a screened camper or bugproof tent; but no one should try braving the Everglades' summer bugs in an undefended sleeping bag.

For normal people, winter is the time for Flamingo. Then it is a glorious place, offering much to see and do. Most of the possibilities involve a boat or canoe, but by no means all. There are several hiking trails—actually service roads for the most part—that range in length from two to fourteen miles. The landscapes they traverse are subtle and interesting rather than spectacular. You will see forests of red, white, and black mangroves steadily advancing across the mud flats and oyster bars, building land inch by inch out of the vegetative debris caught by their spidery roots. There are "wet" prairies where the sawgrass ripples and waves; "dry" prairies supporting a surprising number of desert plants—agave, cactus, yucca; occasional stunted hammocks; and water, water everywhere in canals, limestone lakes, and bays. This southern part of the park is a brackish zone where salt-water and freshwater meet, absolutely vital to a host of marine organisms, including baby shrimp, on which the region's entire chain of life depends. The neat thing is to notice details: the small but edible coon oysters attached to roots; the salt crystals purged from the black mangrove (the most salt-tolerant of trees) through the undersides of its leaves; the rough edges that give the sawgrass (really a sedge) its name and remind you that it is one of the world's oldest growing things; the small, often very beautiful snails that, in the best Darwinian tradition, develop their own different patterns depending on which hammock they call home. Alligators are usually on hand, and it is just possible that you may see a Florida bobcat. There is a considerable population of these handsome creatures in this unlikely habitat. They show themselves fairly regularly in the vicinity of the bridge that crosses Buttonwood Canal.

The birds, of course, are the Everglades' most spectacular attraction. Along any of the hiking trails they will be part of the scenery. Bear Lake, at the end of a two-mile walk, is a favorite haunt of wading birds, and in winter white pelicans are often seen there. Indeed, during the winter months you can often see astonishing congregations of birds without budging from Flamingo. Swarms of brown pelicans, gulls, terns, and cormorants frequent the marina, and from the campground area the view of Florida Bay may include egrets, great white herons, roseate spoonbills, various shorebirds, white ibis, and quite possibly a bald eagle or osprey.

Still, this is a world best seen afloat. In a small skiff on shallow Florida Bay you can fish in some of the nation's finest estuarine waters, where pompano, redfish, snook, mackeral, or sea trout might or might not take your bait. While waiting for them to make up their minds, you can hobnob with pelicans, porpoises, stingrays, and sharks, or glass—but not land on—the hundred-odd islets scattered 'round. Some of them will be capped by huge stick nests to which ospreys and eagles return each year.

For the inland waters, a canoe is best. There are several marked canoe trails ranging from three to twelve miles in the Flamingo area. Any one of them will take you into a world that is still pure wilderness. My favorite is the Bear Lake Canoe Trail to Cape Sable. Along the way you will see mangrove jungles, low hammocks of sabal palms, wild fig, buttonwood, Jamaican dogwood, and marl ridges sprouting cacti and yucca. Your destination, Cape Sable, is one of the very few sizable stretches of wild beach left in southern Florida. The Park Service should be congratulated for resisting—so far—the temptation to build a road to this isolated place. The narrow beach, composed of finely ground shells, is overlooked by coconut palms that either were planted by early settlers or carried as nut seeds across the Gulf from the Caribbean. In summer the beach becomes the nesting place of the vanishing loggerhead turtle. These enormous sea creatures have lost so many other nesting places to humans that park rangers must take special measures to protect their nests from raccoons, who will, by the way, help themselves to any food you leave around at night. There are primitive campsites, but you must carry all supplies with you, including water.

The same rule about supplies holds for the long, north-south canoe journey that the park affords those adventurous souls with stamina enough to attempt it. This is the 100-mile inland water trail from Flamingo to Everglades City at the northwestern end of the park. It is accessible to both small craft with outboard motors (eighteen feet maximum) and canoes. The former can make the one-way trip in six or seven hours, the latter in as many days. The route is well marked, but if you are careless you can get stuck in places with picturesque names such as "The Nightmare." A detailed guide to the waterway is available at the Visitor Center, but it is still important to register with the park rangers before starting this adventure. In the old days people got lost in this wilderness and died. Times have changed, but people still get lost. In any case, canoeists must register in order to use the camping sites. There is so little solid ground that most of these places are manmade platforms (chickees) holding no more than eight people overnight.

The route traverses both wide bays and creeks so narrow that the mangroves form a tunnel overhead. Rivers lead to places few people ever see: small lonely beaches, coastal prairies, oyster banks, and open bays. Along the way there may be pelicans, wood storks, raccoons, alligators, bottle-nosed dolphins, possibly a rare manatee. Always, around you, beside you, sometimes over you, there is the mangrove labyrinth. If the continuing prospect of that labyrinth attracts you, and if you have the time and energy, this journey will be an unforgettable experience. If you get easily bored by mangrove labyrinths, forget the whole idea. In any case, do not think of making this trip in summer.

(Everglades National Park, Homestead, Florida 33030; 305/247–6211.)

For the majority who do not plan to exit the Everglades via northbound canoe, it is now time to get back in the car or camper and hit the road, savoring, one last time, the loop trails and other stops as one leaves the park.

Homestead is the last sizable town between you and the western end of the Tamiami Trail—a tidy place, old-fashioned in a 1940s way with its clean, pink, stuccoed storefronts. It is best praised by noting what it is not—namely, a long, strung-out smear of parking lots, billboards, and motels, of which Florida has more than its share.

North along Hwy 27 there is one public campground, the last one before you reach Collier-Seminole State Park on the other side of the state. This is **Chekika State Recreation Area**. It can be reached by turning left on 168th Street, actually a county road, about sixteen miles north of Homestead. Head inland for another seven or eight miles through vast, irrigated truck farms that were once part of the Everglades. Chekika is a small park and takes a lot of wear and tear. During January and February it is sometimes crowded with young people who can't get into the parks on the Keys, and on weekends throughout the year it gets a lot of daytime use from youth groups and families of migrant workers. But most of the time the campground, carved out of a dense hammock, is uncrowded at night. The hammock itself is pretty—cabbage palms, live oaks, and some West Indian trees—growing much taller here than further south in the national park and the Keys. There are also a couple of limestone ponds, one of them available for swimming, and a modest trail crossing a bit of sawgrass marsh and a slough. But the main attraction to stopping here, other than finding a home for the night, is the palpable sense of being at a crucial, sharply drawn boundary. There is no transition. At one's back are all those boring fields of vegetables. Ahead lies the mysterious presence of a great wilderness, more sensed than seen. (Chekika State Recreation Area, P.O. Box 1313, Homestead, Florida 33030; 305/253–0950.)

After you hit the Tamiami Trail and head west, the next important stop is **Shark Valley**, the northern entrance to **Everglades National Park**. There are no camping facilities there, and it is no longer permissible to drive your car along the loop road that leads to the observation tower deep in the Shark River slough. Instead, you may take one of the park's informative tram tours or make the trip afoot or by bicycle, always assuming that high water in late spring or summer has not closed the road. Round trip, the loop is about fourteen miles.

Even though you have been to the southern part of the park, this visit to its northern reaches is a rewarding way to spend a few hours. It is here that the sawgrass ecosystem is best seen and understood. Narrow footpaths lead off the road, tunneling into yet another kind of hammock, a bayhead. Here, redbay, cocoplum, wax myrtle, and a profusion of royal and leather ferns build a little fortress of shadow besieged on all sides by the sun-swept openness of the water prairies. Rivulets flow through the bayhead during the wet months, drowning the path; but if you take off your shoes and press on, you may encounter, as I have, baby alligators chirruping in the clear, tannic water. If it is dry season, you will certainly see their larger brethren in the canal that accompanies the road, as well as turtles (terrapins, red-bellied sliders, perhaps soft-shell), and schools of killifish, minnows, and gambusi. Though you might not guess it in summer, these millions of little fish keep the fifteen local species of mosquitoes from being even more numerous than they are. In their turn, they provide full-course meals for larger fish as well as the egrets and ibis that patrol the canal and nearby sloughs.

The plant life along the trail seems at first glance to blur into a green monotony, but in fact it is amazingly various. Along with the ever-present sawgrass there are alligator flag, muhly grass, beardgrass, cattail, arrowhead, water lily, spike rush, and on and on. Even for someone who is not a botanist, it becomes a pleasant game to pick out some of the species with the help of a field guide or the roadside signs.

As at Pa-hay-okee, fourteen miles to the south, the observation tower at the end of the Shark Valley loop affords a glorious view of the sawgrass Glades. On a dry spring day you just may be looking at more wild alligators here than you will ever see anywhere else at one time. If you scan the sawgrass prairie with your binoculars, chances are good that there will be some Florida sandhill cranes out there along with the usual waders. But, for wildlife lovers, the most exciting possibility is that a very rare snail kite may be in view either at the tower or somewhere along the road. (In spring, a pair of these dark, beautiful birds are regularly seen flying over the marsh or perching in the low hammocks east of the road, just a hundred yards from the Visitor Center.) This creature is a masterpiece of evolutionary specialization. Its curved beak is exactly designed to fit the whorls of the shell of the apple (pomacea) snail, and the kite is absolutely dependent on this single food source for its survival. The snail, in turn, is dependent on year-round flooded marshes. In a healthy marsh ecosystem such as the Usumacinta Delta, across the Gulf in southern Mexico, this same kite is one of the most common raptors that can be found anywhere. It is a measure of how badly we have screwed up the Everglades that this bird should be so rare in our own country. But at least we are doing better than we were in the 1950s, when there were only twenty snail kites left. Now there are a few hundred. However, come another drought, if the choice boils down to Miami's lawn sprinklers or the survival of the kite—a possibility not at all far-fetched—the bird may disappear forever. (Information about Shark Valley can be obtained from the Everglades National Park office in Homestead; see above.)

The Big Cypress Country

As you keep moving along the Tamiami Trail, you will notice that a few miles beyond the Shark Valley Visitor Center the landscape begins rather swiftly, though not dramatically, to change. Instead of sawgrass marsh and impoundment levees lined with Australian pines, there are now vistas in which open prairie begins to yield to small, scattered cypress, then cypress heads and mixed hammocks of cabbage palm and hardwoods that crowd close to the road. Almost before you know it, you are well within the precincts of the **Big Cypress National Preserve**.

In some respects, the Big Cypress is a continuation of the Everglades, since it shelters most of the same plant and animal species—which means that it is a fabulous place. Unlike the Glades, however, it is less shallow river than shallow basin. It relies on seasonal rains rather than Lake Okeechobee for its watery well-being. Some of its slow-moving runoff helps water the Everglades, but most of it drains westward to the Gulf in the Ten Thousand Islands region. As in the Everglades there is an abundance of freshwater prairie and lovely palm and hardwood hammocks. But here there are more limestone ridges dry enough to support thin-looking forests of slash pine. Most characteristic of the area, however, are the cypress.

The Big Cypress got its name, not because the cypress are so tall—most aren't—but because they cover such a vast area. They come in "heads" or "domes" or "strands," or in spindly forests scattered across the limestone prairie. The domelike effect of some groupings is created because the taller trees are standing in the middle of concavities in the limestone where water and peat are deepest. Naturally, the ones on the outer edges must make do with fewer nutrients and therefore grow more slowly. As for the strands, they are narrow forests of cypress growing along the shallow sloughs, often intermixed with other hardwoods wherever the ground gets high enough to form hammocks. But it's those little, runty fellows scattered all over the place that are the real oddities: they have taken root in the limestone wherever the surface is pitted and wet enough to offer them a skimpy living. They are so stunted that some people suppose that they are a different species altogether from the ones found in domes and strands. Actually, almost all these trees are pondcypress, a somewhat smaller subspecies than the mighty baldcypress that were cut down by the timber companies years ago. Some of these little fellows out on the prairie are actually centuries older than their taller brethren in the domes, but they just don't have the wherewithal to grow big and strong. Nowhere else in the world will you see cypress growing under these peculiar conditions.

The Big Cypress area has had more than its share of exploitation. Lumbering, cattle ranching, sugar-cane plantations, oil exploration—this region has seen them all. It was the land speculators, though, who almost finished off this unique ecosystem for good. Vast areas were drained, sloughs were gutted, and thousands of gullible people were sold lots that turned out to be underwater half the year. Joyfully, there was a last-minute change in this grim and familiar scenario. A lot of people on the western coast were getting worried that they would soon be having the same problems with the Big Cypress aquifer that the eastern coast was experiencing with the Everglades. To make a long story short, in 1974 more than half a million acres of the Big Cypress were set aside as a national preserve. The designation allows for many human uses to continue in the area, but it prevents the outright destruction of wild lands. The Big Cypress National Preserve is the best thing that has happened to Florida in a long time.

Depending on the condition of your car and/or your feet, you may wish to take a detour off the beaten track along the Loop Road that leaves the Tamiami Trail at the eastern edge of the preserve. This is county highway 94, a highway in name only. It heads due west for fourteen miles, then turns north for another ten miles to link up again with Hwy 41 at the scarcely perceivable community of Monroe Station. This Loop Road offers a terrific opportunity to see the Big Cypress close-up. But be forewarned! Once you pass the Everglades–Big Cypress Environmental Center about ten miles in, the road begins to look as though it had been shelled by mortars. If you plan to drive the rest of the route—the part worth seeing—in a passenger car, either stay below ten miles per hour or prepare to pay for a front-end realignment when you reach civilization again. Along the way, there are a few pull-over spots in the swamp where I suppose you could camp overnight if you want free lodgings, but I'm not recommending it. Some of the good ole local boys obviously make use of these places in and out of season, judging from the shotgun shell casings and other unlovely forms of litter. A more pleasant arrangement, if you don't have four-wheel drive or a car that can move for miles in first and second, is to hike from the Environmental Center early in the morning and have someone pick you up at Monroe Station late in the afternoon.

For all I know, this road may be repaved by the time this book is published; but, personally, I hope it always stays as awful as it is. Heavy traffic needs to be discouraged here. One of the perverse delights of being in this area is knowing that you aren't in a park. The Big Cypress, even though it's a preserve, is open to intensive commercial and recreational use. There are still hunting camps in here (usually surrounded by garbage), even though the proprietors made lucrative deals with the federal government years ago to vacate the area by now. And during the hunting season (not the best time for your hike) hunters and ORVs are lined up like firing squads. But in a weird way, that is part of the Loop Road's charm. Not, of course, the litter and the camps, which mercifully peter out two or three miles beyond the Environmental Center, but the fact that here the natural world manages to hold its own in spite of all the use and abuse that still goes on. I don't know of too many places in Florida, outside the parks, where you can walk a road in springtime and find an honest-to-God eight-foot alligator basking on the pocked tarmac. Or rouse a half-dozen shaggy woods hogs from their noonday siesta. Or surprise a doe crossing in front of you—at midday. Or politely step around a sizable cottonmouth peacefully basking atop a culvert. Yet I have seen all of these sights on this road during a three-hour walk. More: this is a fine place for birding. I am convinced that all the great crested flycatchers in the South gather right here for their annual convention. At any time of year there is the likelihood that a flock of great egrets or white ibis will wheel up ahead of you through the cypress strands, or that the scream of a red-shouldered hawk will break the silence.

The north-south stretch of this road is the best part, unquestionably because it is the most horrendous to drive. The old canal is choked with cypress and cocoplum. At intervals the divided halves of a tall hammock throw the road into deep shadow. It is like being in the Florida of fifty years ago, the sort of Florida where man had already made his presence felt, but where a black bear might still amble across the road ahead of you.

For the adventurous, the Big Cypress offers a thirty-eight-mile hike over the southernmost segment of the unfinished Florida Trail. The latest eight-mile addition, just opened, begins on the Loop Road (check at the Environmental Center for the starting point) and ends at the **Oasis Ranger Station** on the Tamiami Trail, located about seventeen miles west of the Shark Valley Visitor Center at Everglades National Park. The main leg of the hiking trail starts at the ranger station. If you wish to take a relatively short (sixteen miles round trip) hike, or don't have someone to pick you up at the other end, there is a loop that will bring you back to the ranger station. On this loop, there's an overnight primitive campsite, with pump water, along the way. However, if you want to make the whole trek from the Tamiami Trail to Alligator Alley (Hwy 84), you should make preparations well in advance by contacting the Big Cypress National Preserve staff at the Oasis Ranger Station or the Florida Trail Association (see Bibliography). Meantime, you need to realize that: (1) In wet years, some parts of the trail near Alligator Alley will be under shallow water even during the dry winter season, so you may need to do some wading. (2) February and March are the best months for the hike because most hunting seasons are over, the weather is dry, and bugs aren't out in force yet. (3) You cannot leave your car for long at the roadside park at the northern terminus of the trail. Sadly, the possibility of vandalism or theft is real. (4) The trail can be hiked in two days, but if you are to savor the Big Cypress, a three-day hike is preferable. Besides, the two permanent primitive campsites are spaced for a three-day trip. (5) Some of the trail follows dirt-marl roads where hunters' ORVs have left their scars.

This country is wild enough to suit almost any taste, but it is not untouched wilderness.

Nowhere else in the course of our tour will you see a landscape quite like this one. Much of the prospect is relatively open, savannah-like. Depending on variations in elevation that can be measured in inches, stunted cypress and slash pine take turns as the predominant vegetation, growing in gritty marl or peat soils that often do not succeed in covering the raw limestone crust. This is a world of striking contradictions. With its hard rock and wiry grasses and dwarfed trees it looks almost arid; but then again, with all those marshy ponds, forested sloughs, and palm-crowded hammocks, it seems anything but. The most lasting impression, however, is of the ancientness of this landscape, human imprints notwithstanding. Dinosaurs might feel at home here. It seems fitting that the omnipresent cypress and sawgrass are among the oldest of growing things. And then there are the air plants, which give to all the trees, but especially the wizened cypress, a weirdly tufted, druidlike look. Only a few species, such as the stiff-leaved wildpine and the butterfly orchid, take to living in the open sunlight. Most require the gloom of the hammocks, where each species develops its own strategies for survival. Some have tough skins that prevent transpiration; others cleverly shape their leaves into pockets that hold water; still others have bulblike stems that act like sponges. Sadly, many of the bromeliads and orchids of the Big Cypress are now extinct or nearly so. The ravages inflicted on the ecosystem by drainage and cutting have been compounded in these latter days by the illegal depredations of collectors, some of them prepared to hunt down the last of a species precisely because it is so rare.

Wildlife in this hard country is not exactly abundant, but there is quite a bit of it around. Whether you see much of it depends on the quietness of your progress, time of day, time of year, and the presence of water. Plus luck. In the dry season, be especially on the lookout near sloughs and ponds adjoining hammocks and cypress domes. Here you should find many of the same species associated with the Everglades. On the piney ridges, deer may show themselves or possibly a flock of wild turkeys—almost always running, not flying, away. There is also a good chance of seeing the American swallow-tailed kite. This exquisite bird, stark black and white, is not as rare as the snail kite, but it is nevertheless very uncommon almost everywhere except in the Big Cypress. Here, it is not only visible but surprisingly bold. I have watched it zooming in and out among the cypress only yards from where I was standing. (Oasis Ranger Station, 813/695–4111 or Big Cypress National Preserve, P.O. Box 1247, Naples, Fla. 33939; 813/262–1066.)

If you would like to take a short walk into the Big Cypress just to get the feel of it, you might consider detouring onto the County Road (839) that heads north a few miles east of Ochopee. Three-and-a-half miles above the Tamiami Trail, be on the lookout for a scruffy gas station on your left. Just beyond, on the right, an old concrete bridge crosses a canal where cormorants often fish. Follow the track a short distance to the second of two small limestone quarries and park. From there, a number of ORV trails lead into the cypress prairie and across pine and palmetto ridges. After the initial ugly tangle of trails thins out, the natural scene takes over. Careful, though! There is a sameness to this landscape, and if you start switching from one trail to another you can easily get lost. Take a compass, or scratch pointers in the marl at junctions.

Before we get too far west along the Tamiami Trail, a couple of brief comments should be made about lodging in this area. As yet, there are no public campgrounds in the Big Cypress Preserve. However, a privately owned campground with hookups is located at Ochopee, as well as the area's lone motel. Beyond that, the nearest facilities are at Everglades City or Collier-Seminole State Park. But for those who are low on funds or who don't want to head west just to find a place for the night, there is an alternative if you aren't too fussy. This is Monument Lake, which you won't find on your road map. It's about a mile west of Monroe Station (where one exits the previously described Loop Road) on the Tamiami Trail. There is no sign, only a dirt road turning off through a barely noticeable break in the metal guardrail on the north side of the highway. The real landmark is a microwave tower looming above the trees a ways back from the road. Near it are a small limestone pond and a row of Australian pines. There are no facilities, and the place is not too tidy or scenic; but it will do. Probably local hunters use it during hunting season, but when I was there in early spring it was deserted except for a few mosquitoes.

In terms of amenities, Everglades City is your best bet while on the Tamiami Trail. It is gateway to both the Big Cypress and the northwestern part of Everglades National Park. It has private campgrounds, a marina, a small Visitor Center, boat and canoe rentals, good birding, and tours of the Ten Thousand Islands, that maze of tiny mangrove islands that make up the northern portion of the park's vast mangrove wilderness. The town is neat and pretty, with houses high on piers and some picturesque frame buildings that retain the ambiance of an old Gulf fishing village. It looks tame now, but not so many years ago this was the alligator poaching capital of the world. While opening beers with their skinning knives, patrons of the local pub would brag openly about the number of alligators they had poached the night before in the neighboring park. But fortunately, those good ole bad days seem to be over. (For information on wildlife tours, contact the Everglades National Park headquarters, Homestead, Florida 33030; 305/247–6211, or Everglades National Park Boat Tours, P.O. Box 119, Everglades City, Florida 33929.)

The Fakahatchee Strand is the largest drainage slough in the southwestern sector of the Big Cypress and is vital to the well-being

Big Cypress National Preserve. *Photo by Florida Division of Tourism.*

of the great mangrove wilderness to the south. The northern part, above Alligator Alley, is in private hands. The southern part is protected in the 60,000-acre **Fakahatchee Strand State Preserve**, which lies to the west of the Big Cypress National Preserve. Though under separate management, the two preserves are ecologically dependent on each other. The Fakahatchee just may be the most important natural area in the state of Florida. Superlatives abound: the hammocks in this swamp boast our largest native stand of royal palms, trees that deserve their grand-sounding name even if their lumpy trunks do look as though they were made with silly putty; the Strand contains the most abundant and diverse collection of orchids and other air plants in the United States; and rare Florida black bears, mangrove fox squirrels, and Everglades mink are in residence. Most important of all, however, the Fakahatchee harbors the largest concentration of Florida panthers—more than a dozen animals—that survives in the world. But there is some irony in this fact: most of the remaining panthers make their home in the privately owned portion of the Strand north of Alligator Alley, not in the preserve to the south. Apparently the discrepancy can be explained by differences in deer populations. On the private lands there is a lot of second-growth forest, only light hunting, and therefore plenty of deer; whereas in the preserve, maturing hammock forests (which reduce deer habitat) and heavy hunting have caused deer numbers to decline. As a result, only two or three panthers still frequent the state-owned part of the tract, and they are not successfully rearing young. The state of Florida has officially committed itself to saving the panther. But in order to do so, it will evidently have to devise a means of increasing the deer population (and decreasing the hunter population) in this vital southern sector of the Fakahatchee.

Although plans for campgrounds are reportedly in the works, the Strand has not yet been developed for heavy tourist use, which is just as well, considering how desperately some of its wild inhabitants need to be left alone. But there is a boardwalk trail located behind Indian Village Bend on the Tamiami Trail, seven miles west of the intersection with Hwy 29. Here you can obtain an impressive glimpse of the shadowy interior of the Strand, with its majestic baldcypress festooned with air plants. An even better bet, however, is to drive along the Janes Scenic Road, which begins a few miles north on Hwy 29 at the eyeblink town of Copeland. For ten miles a jungle of struggling trees presses up against the road. The royal palms, despite their abundance, are overshadowed by the presence of cypress, water oaks, and other hardwoods that crowd around them. On this road I remember seeing one of those stunning juxtapositions that Nature sometimes arranges for the delighted eye: a large, mixed flock of black vultures and white egrets rising together among the trees in an almost too allegorical combination.

Near the end of this stretch, the road crosses three or four tiny culverts spanning a slough. You might want to pause here for a moment. On the right is a small limestone pool where you may spot an alligator or two. On the left, if it is still the dry season, you can walk a short way into the lovely forests of the Strand (but be careful of rusted barbed wire from defunct fences). Here the baldcypress, not the smaller pondcypress, reign. They can be seen in conjunction with sweet gum and red maple, an intimation of swamp forests further to the north.

The official federal map of the Big Cypress indicates that the road beyond the Fakahatchee Strand State Preserve is not recommended for vehicular travel. This may seem strange since it is in better shape than the road in the preserve. In any case, it is instructive to proceed further, even though you may not like what you see. You are entering upon a real-estate developer's thwarted dream, a conservationist's redeemed nightmare. If a movie director were shooting a film about what the world will look like a hundred years after a nuclear war, he would be well advised to consider this landscape as the set. A vast grid of paved and unpaved roads and arrow-straight canals slices up a quarter of a million acres of the Big Cypress wilderness like a cheese. You drive through a strange silence, with these ugly roads, ugly canals, ugly spoil banks laid out mile after mile against the billowing green of trisected, brutalized forests. But for once, Nature has defeated the greedy dreams of the spoilers. Despite the drainage canals and ditches, seasonal flooding in the Big Cypress has drowned the intended lawns of all the thousands of tract houses that were never built here.

It is pleasant to think that an occasional panther still leaves its pawprint in the area. It is even more satisfying to think that some day the bulldozers that cleared the way for these roads may return to destroy them. There is talk now that this whole huge segment of the Big Cypress should be set aside to help protect Florida's diminishing water resource. Anyone who cares at all about the environment must hope that someday soon the talk will translate into action. (Fakahatchee Strand State Preserve, P.O. Box 548, Copeland, Florida 33962; 813/695−4593.)

4
Florida's South-Central Coast

At a glance

Access Tampa is the major regional air terminal, but Fort Meyers and Naples are also easily reached by scheduled flights. The major coastal road is I-75, paralleled by heavily built-up Hwy 41. Further inland, there is no one through-highway traversing this entire region, although Hwy 29 covers much of it. Alternate routes through this area are discussed in the travelogue.

Climate As far north as Tampa, the dry winter–wet summer cycle is still the general rule. Winters are usually mild, although the chance of cold snaps or even an occasional freeze increases with every north-bound mile. The hot summers are generally bearable on the beaches. Inland areas, though not quite so buggy and steamy as the Big Cypress and Everglades, are not designed for energetic outdoors activities during summer (May through October). Boating and stream fishing, however, go on all year.

Topography and Landscape Features Inland, peninsular Florida's limestone terrace imperceptibly gains a bit more elevation. Low sand ridges mark former beaches of prehistoric seas. In contrast to the broad, shallow sloughs further south, rivers have definable banks. On the coast, a long chain of barrier islands composed of alluvial river soils has been built by the northward-moving Gulf current. These islands have wide, heavily developed beaches, fronting the Gulf. On the landward side they shelter extensive mangrove-lined bays.

Flora and Fauna Plant communities are diverse. Hammocks with some West Indian hardwoods persist at least as far north as Charlotte Harbor, and many air plants remain abundant throughout the area. However, oak and cabbage palm hammocks predominate as one moves north, along with pine flatwoods, sand pine scrub (on infertile sand ridges), cypress domes, and dry prairies covered by saw palmetto scrub. There are opportunities for seeing the threatened wood stork and countless other bird species, including osprey, bald eagle, and

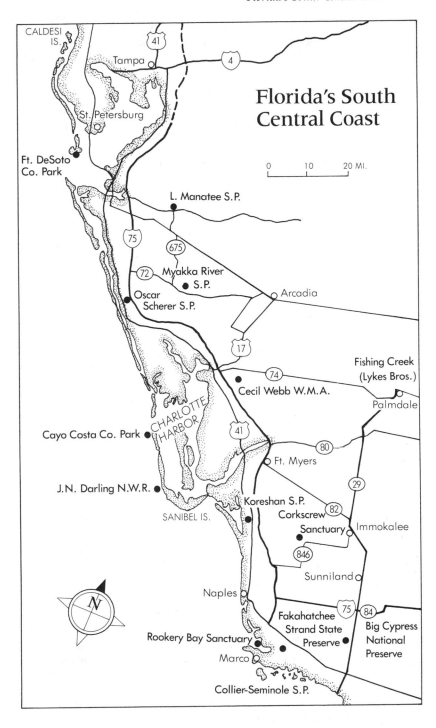

Florida's South Central Coast

CALDESI IS.

Tampa

41

4

St. Petersburg

Ft. DeSoto Co. Park

0   10   20 MI.

L. Manatee S.P.

75

675

72   Myakka River S.P.

Oscar Scherer S.P.

Arcadia

17

Fishing Creek (Lykes Bros.)

74   Cecil Webb W.M.A.

Palmdale

CHARLOTTE HARBOR

Cayo Costa Co. Park

41

80

Ft. Myers

29

J.N. Darling N.W.R.

Koreshan S.P.

82

Corkscrew Sanctuary

Immokalee

SANIBEL IS.

846

Sunniland

N

Naples

Fakahatchee Strand State Preserve

75   84

Big Cypress National Preserve

Rookery Bay Sanctuary

Marco

Collier-Seminole S.P.

American swallow-tailed kite. The rare manatee frequents coastal rivers. Deer, wild hogs, and alligators are abundant. The area south of Sunniland supports most of the few Florida panthers that still survive in the world.

C*amping*   Collier-Seminole and Myakka state parks are the largest public campgrounds for RVers in search of hookups, showers, etc., but Koreshan and Oscar Scherer state parks are also likely prospects. In Tampa–St. Petersburg, Fort DeSoto gets a lot of year-round use. Inland, the best bet is privately owned Fisheating Creek Campground. Primitive camping—away from it all—is best at Myakka, although Fisheating Creek is also good. And Cayo Costa is great if you have a boat. Also note travelogue comments about the Cecil M. Webb Wildlife Management Area.

H*iking, Canoeing, Boating, Etc.*   There are self-guiding nature trails at all the parks, but for the serious hiker Myakka, with its miles of beautiful hiking trails, is far and away the best prospect. Canoeists have many wonderful options, among them the mangrove wilderness of Collier-Seminole, beautiful Fisheating Creek, the Myakka River and its lakes, or some segment of the Peace River. Numerous shorter trips are possible, including the water trails at Koreshan, Oscar Scherer, and Ding Darling Refuge. As for outboard boaters, the only problem—as usual on the Gulf Coast—is which area to choose when there are so many alternatives. Charlotte Harbor, the Peace River, and Blackwater River in Collier-Seminole are all renowned for their fishing, but there are many other prospects. However, outboard motors are banned at Myakka. The shelling on Marco and Sanibel islands is famous worldwide. At the latter island, so is the birding.

O*utdoors Highlights*   Collier-Seminole State Park; Ding Darling National Wildlife Refuge; Corkscrew Swamp Sanctuary; Fisheating Creek Campground; Myakka State Park.

If you plan a round-trip journey through southern Florida, you have the pleasant option of seeing different parts of the region coming and going, since you can follow a coastal route when heading one way and an inland route when going the other.

The Gulf Coast route leads to Collier-Seminole State Park and the Ding Darling National Wildlife Refuge on Sanibel Island, but it also involves either driving through the development-choked Gulfside strip between Naples and Tampa or using I-75, with its typical Interstate detachment from the surrounding landscape. On the other hand, Hwy 29 allows a more intimate look at the terrain of southwestern Florida while avoiding much of the development uglies on the Coast. But it also bypasses the aforementioned parks. Fortunately, both routes take you equally close to the Corkscrew Swamp Sanctuary, about which, more presently.

The Coastal Route via Naples

The drive west along the Tamiami Trail passes through some of the most beautiful sections of the Big Cypress National Preserve and the Fakahatchee Strand. However, in this section it is easy to see how the highway itself has messed up the area's natural drainage: north of the highway the landscape is thick with palm hammocks and cypress strands, whereas southward, where the flow of freshwater is impeded, the mangroves and brackish coastal prairies take over.

Fortunately, this problem has been left behind by the time we reach **Collier-Seminole State Park**. This beautiful place is a microcosm of the larger ecosystem in the western part of the Big Cypress. Whether for that reason, or because it's a handy stopover at the end of the Tamiami Trail, the campground is often sold out during the winter months.

Most of the park's 6500 acres is a mangrove wilderness, an officially designated one; but there are also cypress swamps, saltwater marshes, and a string of hammocks that support the second-largest native stand (after the Fakahatchee's) of royal palms in the nation. The

Fishing pier, Naples, Florida. *Photo by Florida Division of Tourism.*

hammock that borders the campground would make Tarzan feel at home. A nature trail leads you through a jungle of West Indian hardwoods, the trees impressively tall despite the fact that this area, like the lower Glades, was ripped apart by Hurricane Donna in 1960. The scene is ripe with a nice vegetable decadence. Large, coarse strap ferns grow from rotting mastic trunks; strangler figs strangle this or that; and a rather sinister vinelike tree, appropriately called Devil's Claw, wraps thick tendrils covered with crude thorns around its statically horrified neighbors. As in all hammocks, the air is thick with the aroma of damp-scented leaves and decaying mulch. But here—all hammocks are different, remember—instead of the usual sudden break between the wall of hardwoods and its surrounding prairie, there is a transition zone where buttonwoods and mangroves gradually take over. In all, this is one of the loveliest tropical hammocks that can be conveniently visited in southern Florida. For anyone heading north, it is also one of the last.

But aside from visiting the hammock and checking out a replica of a log blockhouse used in this area during the Seminole War, there isn't that much for landlubbers to do at Collier-Seminole. This is a place where the boater and the canoeist have a decided edge. For them there is a sizable boat basin opening onto saltwater marshes, mangrove swamps, and the Blackwater River. The canoeist can follow a thirteen-and-a-half-mile trail leading through a watery maze of tidal creeks, bays, and mangroves, mangroves, mangroves. Those who wish to prolong the wilderness experience will find an overnight primitive campsite on a speck of dry land called Grocery Place. En route, the tidal flats will usually be decked with the stunning array of roseate spoonbills, herons, white ibis, and egrets that only southern Florida can take for granted. If you know what you are looking for, you may also spot the mangrove cuckoo, the small mangrove terrapin, or the orange mangrove water snake, all of which require (in case you hadn't guessed) a mangrove habitat to survive. The fishing in the Blackwater River is renowned, and pelicans and osprey will be on hand to show how it is done. The river also offers the remote but exciting possibility that a manatee might break its surface. For all its walrus size, this enchantingly homely creature is totally harmless, which is more than can be said for the propellers of speeding motorboats, which kill or maim scores of these rare animals every year.

Canoeists may not have to worry about manatees, or motorboat propellers for that matter, but there is a risk of getting lost. The water trails are marked; but if you are careless and go astray, there are few landmarks in the mangrove wilderness—and just about every year someone loses his way. A compass and map are essential equipment. It is also necessary to register at park headquarters when beginning and ending your trip. Aside from considerations of safety, there is a limit (thirty) on the number of canoes that can use the trail each day. (Collier-Seminole State Park, Marco, Florida 33937; 813/394–3397.)

After leaving Collier-Seminole, you may feel like heading for Marco Island. If you take Hwy 951 coming or going (there's a toll bridge on this route), you will want to stop at the Nature Conservancy's Briggs Nature Center, an important bird refuge on Rookery Bay. It offers some of the same experiences—birding, canoeing, and boardwalk tours—as Collier-Seminole but without the campgrounds. At Marco Island itself, there is still public access to the shining white beach. However, for crotchety people like myself who remember when this was the last great wild beach on the peninsula between Cape Sable and the Panhandle, that isn't much consolation. In those not-so-long-ago days, large numbers of loggerhead turtles came ashore to nest, and collectors scouted miles of lonely sands searching for rare seashells. The state had the chance to save the island, but didn't. Now, when you come driving out of the mangroves and over the bridge, you may be shocked by the sudden miles-long wall of condominiums that confronts you. In fairness, though, there is still good shelling, and the tamed beach is a great place to get a tan.

Also in fairness, the exploitation of Marco Island is downright tasteful compared to what has happened to the coastline further north. Even miles inland, this part of Florida is now gripped by a delirium of development. Trailers and little concrete-block houses line up in last year's cattle pastures under the broiling summer sun. Dirt roads leading off into cutover scrubland have names such as 5th Avenue and Garden Lane. Evidently some folks must hate the northern cold a lot to trade in everything else for the sake of warm winters. For many of them, there isn't even a beach within twenty miles.

You will not be able to avoid some views of this terminal developmentitis in the Naples area while heading for Hwy 846 and the Corkscrew Swamp Sanctuary. But never mind. The swamp itself is all the compensation you will need. However, there are no camping facilities or food supplies (except vending machines) at the sanctuary; so you may wish to take advantage of all that spreading development I've been grumbling about to pack up a picnic lunch before you start out. That way, you can spend a whole day at the swamp if you wish. Also, you should be aware that the place is well known nowadays. Especially in the winter months, you will have to share it with all the other people like yourself who are wishing they didn't have to share it with you. In late spring and summer there are fewer visitors, but there is also less wildlife in view. However, during these months the swamp itself is more exuberantly beautiful than at any other time. And—good news—the warm-weather mosquitoes here are not quite as bad as they are in the prairies and mangroves a little to the south and west.

The **Corkscrew Swamp Sanctuary** is the most famous of the National Audubon Society's refuges and one of the most important natural preserves in the nation. Its 10,000-plus acres lie at the northernmost rim of the Big Cypress, just where the piney flatlands of central Florida begin. It is a cypress strand, situated, like others in the Big Cypress country, along a relatively narrow depression in the limestone plain. However, it differs from those others in two important respects: it is exceptionally large, and it has never felt the blow of an axe. Here grows the last great stand of virgin baldcypress in the state, and, for that matter, in the nation. There are not too many places on the Gulf Coast, or anywhere else in the United States, where you can know that you are looking at a scene that has not changed in the last thousand years. Indeed, some of the trees around you have been alive during most of that time.

One approaches the swamp across a small prairie that separates it from the surrounding pinelands. This openness allows the wall of cypress to assert itself, to announce the separateness of the country you are about to enter. In fact, though themselves very venerable, these cypress in the outer perimeter are pondcypress; the real biggies, the baldcypress, are still to come.

The boardwalk leading through the swamp is one of the longest of its kind anywhere, nearly two miles. During its looping course, there are numbers along the way that match those in a well-done guide pamphlet; so, if you take your time, you can learn a lot about the extraordinary land-and-waterscape you are passing through. But information, though necessary, is secondary here to the visual impressions that unfold, and these are always dominated by the cypress themselves. What *is* it about cypress? Why is it that so many people, myself included, consider them among the most movingly beautiful forms in nature? The combination of strength with delicacy? The fluted, tapering contours? The primeval association with water rather than dry land? The potential (and here accomplished) antiquity both of individual trees and their ancestral line? All of that, I suppose. But in the end, as with all such enthusiasms, one's response is more than the specific explanations can account for.

There is nowhere else that I know of where you can walk so far into a cypress wilderness and still keep your feet dry. Along the way you will see southern Florida's amazing displays of orchids and other air plants, including the swarms of resurrection fern that coat boughs like fur, drying up in dry weather but turning green in wet. There are open sloughs and ponds—open, that is, as far as the cypress are concerned, but crowded with water lettuce, arrowhead, pickerelweed. In these sunlit spaces there is almost always something to notice: an alligator half submerged in what looks like tossed salad; a sentinel egret; a red-shouldered hawk crying its wild keee-kee as it flies to its nest in the trees right behind you; or perhaps a brown limpkin, a sizable but secretive bird that the pedestrian has an excellent chance of seeing here.

Stepping back into the cypress again is like reentering a cathedral; yet despite the green, ferny lushness of the place, you may sense that it is not, after all, really tropical. The air plants are everywhere, a few strangler figs are in sight, but most of the West Indian trees seem to be in short supply. Instead there are a lot of red maple, sweet bay, and wax myrtle—adaptable trees that do well in more temperate zones.

Cypress, like mangroves, produce a lot of tannin, so the water passing beneath the boardwalk is wine dark and clear. I remember being startled to see a large, black shape swimming in this shallow water right under the place where I was standing. It took me several seconds to realize that I had seen an anhinga busily trying to spear a fish. The abundance of birdlife in the swamp depends on the season and on whether the year has been dry or wet. If you come in late winter, and if nesting conditions are right, you are certain to see a spectacle that, of itself, would make the trip to Corkscrew unforgettable. The swamp is the site of the largest remaining rookery of wood storks in the nation. Thousands of these large, striking birds, tastefully attired in white with black trim, gather here to raise their young. At such times, the wide prairie that flanks the swamp (overlooked by an observation tower) is alive with their comings and goings, and the trees nearby are heavy with them. But wood storks are highly specialized creatures. They cannot raise a brood unless water conditions are just so—receding enough to crowd small fish into the drying ponds where they can be caught by the birds' thick, probing beaks, but not diminishing so rapidly that water and fish are gone before the nestlings are fledged. Even under wholly natural conditions, wood storks probably had some nesting failures. Now, since man has been manipulating the water regimen in southern Florida, those failures have increased and the population has radically declined. The Audubon Society's effort to augment the birds' food supply by constructing artificial impoundments has had only limited success. The long-term future of the species is still in serious doubt. So, if you are lucky enough to be at Corkscrew when the storks are nesting, and are making a success of it, rejoice in the fact that they have had another reprieve. (Corkscrew Swamp Sanctuary, Route 6, Box 1875–A, Naples, Florida 33942; 813/657–3771.)

After Corkscrew, the next major natural area on this alternate coastal route is the Ding Darling Wildlife Refuge at Sanibel Island. Backtrack to I-75 and head north. If you plan to go directly to Sanibel, exit at Fort Meyers on Daniels Road. There are no public campgrounds on the island, however, so if you are looking for a place to camp for the night, **Koreshan State Historical Park** near Estero is a nice possibility. This little park preserves the attractive settlement of one of those communal religious sects that were a common phenomenon in nineteenth-century America. The pleasant campgrounds are alongside the Estero River, a lovely little stream that is perfect for a short canoe trip. (Koreshan State Historic Park, P.O. Box 7, Estero, Florida 33928; 813/992–0311.)

Whichever way you approach Sanibel Island, you will have to drive through miles of subdivisionland. But the detour should be worth your while. For seashell collectors the island's Gulf beach is one of the happiest hunting grounds in the United States (especially after storms), and there are lots of people who come here just for that purpose. There are usually many shorebirds on hand also. However, for someone who delights in seeing wildlife, the bay side of the island is the main draw. The minute you have crossed the toll bridge you realize that real estate is big business in Sanibel; it has been ever since the bridge was built in 1964. But residents of the island deserve three cheers for their exceptional concern for the environment. Much emphasis is given to planting native vegetation (although the exotic Australian pine is still everywhere in evidence), and the islanders have pioneered in using natural methods of mosquito control. Most important of all, they supported the establishment of a wildlife sanctuary, now nearly five thousand acres, on the island's bayside coast as part of the **J.N. Ding Darling National Wildlife Refuge**, one of the finest places for birds, and birders, on Florida's west coast. The refuge is named for a resident of Sanibel who was famous as both a cartoonist and conservationist. (Darling's savage, widely circulated cartoon depicting the slaughter of Key deer was a decisive factor in the last-minute rescue of that species.)

The refuge is nicely set up for touring by car, although there is often so much to see that you spend more time outside your vehicle than in it. The solar-powered Visitor Center has excellent exhibits, and even the road you drive on has a special interest: it is actually a dike separating the tidal saltwater on the right side (bay side) of the road from brackish impoundments on the left. The impoundments provide stable water levels that impede the reproduction of saltwater mosquitoes and encourage the presence of tiny killifish, which feed upon mosquito larvae while themselves providing dinner for fish-eating birds. Ergo, people get mosquito control on an island that once held the world record for mosquito densities. At the same time, the wildlife benefits from an increased variety of habitats and food sources! After seeing the way development has proceeded elsewhere in Florida, it is a delight just to be in such a sanely managed place.

If you have been canoeing in the Everglades or Collier-Seminole, it is possible that you may be a little jaded about the mangrove prospect along the refuge road. But you will not be bored by the birds that can be found here in abundance. Alongside the dike, or in the bays, the mangrove thickets, or the sky overhead, there is almost always something to see. Wading birds are here year-round—various herons, egrets, perhaps spoonbills or wood storks—as well as pelicans, gallinules, cormorants, and anhingas. On the tidal flats to your right, willets and black-necked stilts probe the mud, and on the left, in the impoundments, there is always an alligator or two peering out from among the mangrove roots. In spring you should see ospreys feeding their young in nests built on manmade platforms. Come winter, all these birds are joined by thousands of migrating waterfowl: scaups, green- and blue-winged teal, shovelers, pintails, and wigeons.

As a pleasing conclusion to this tour, there is a half-mile boardwalk trail leading through and across a hammock that is—once again—different from others you may have visited. The West Indian vegetation is relatively low, more like the Everglades' Gumbo Limbo Hammock than the one at Collier-Seminole; and the trail itself is often a narrow tunnel. But much of the ground you traverse is composed of a shell midden built up by the long-vanished Calusa Indians as a site for their rituals. If legend is correct—and the killjoy historians say it isn't—it was also used as a hideout by a pirate whose soda-pop-sounding name, Gasparilla, has been given to the trail. Here can be found a crowded mix of trees and plants: sea grape, bamboo, wild coffee, gumbo limbo, limes, and bromeliads, some of them approaching the northern limit of their range. In winter especially, there are many songbirds on the premises.

Those who want to take a more private look at the refuge can follow a short canoe trail on the edge of Tarpon Bay. Other canoeing opportunities are available on the Buck Key tract at the island's western tip. Check at the Visitor Center for information. As noted above, no camping is permitted in the refuge. (Ding Darling National Wildlife Refuge, P.O. Drawer B, Sanibel, Florida 33957.)

If you would like to have a go at some primitive camping in this area, and you have your own outboard boat along or access to a rented one, you should definitely consider **Cayo Costa Reservation**, a Lee County park on a few hundred acres of unspoiled barrier island north of Sanibel and Captiva islands. It lies at the mouth of Charlotte Harbor and can be reached from Captiva, Pineland, or Bokeelia. Primitive campsites are on the southern end of the island. You need to take along everything, including water, with you. What you get for your trouble are miles of wide, white beach without a development in sight, and bayside woodlands and mangroves. Adjacent to the county park is a state preserve with more of the same unblemished beachscape. Shelling and surf fishing on the beach side, and birding on the bay side, compare with Sanibel—only here there is no background of condos. If you plan to camp overnight, register with the custodian. (Cayo Costa Preserve, P.O. Box 7, Estero, Florida 33928; 813/992–0311. Lee County Recreation Department, Box 398, Fort Myers, Florida 33902; 813/332–0808.)

One final spot needs to be mentioned on this coastal route: the **Oscar Scherer State Recreation Area** just off I-75, a few miles south of Osprey. The park is small but it contains a fine mix of natural habitats—pine forests, marshes, hammocks, and, as the centerpiece, a clear, dark tidal stream winding to the Gulf, perfect for a day's canoeing. The park also has a sizable campground. If you have called ahead to Myakka and learned that the campground there is full, this may be an ideal alternate site, especially if you arrive on a weekday. (Oscar Scherer State Recreation Area, P.O. Box 398, Osprey, Florida 33559; 813/966–3154.)

The Alternate Inland Route

At this point, while the traveler on the coastal circuit drives back to I-75 and heads north toward Oscar Scherer and Myakka state parks, let us backtrack about seventy miles and consider the inland route that begins at Ochopee. The drawback here is that there are no state-owned refuges or campgrounds along the way. On the other hand, the roadside scenery is interesting, there is a privately owned campground of exceptional quality, and, best of all, the subdivisions and trailer parks are few and far between.

After taking the scenic drive through the Fakahatchee Strand (described in Chapter 3), head north along Hwy 29. Here there are three signs in succession that you are unlikely to see anywhere else in the United States: "Panther habitat," "Less than 30 left," and "Please drive carefully." That last is good advice, unfortunately ignored too often. Hwy 29 and nearby stretches of the Tamiami Trail and Alligator Alley (better named Slaughter Alley) have taken a dreadful toll not only of the panthers, but of the vanishing Florida black bear and legions of other wild creatures as well. However, this grim note is somewhat balanced by the happy scene that greets you as you drive along. The canal on your right borders the Big Cypress National Preserve, and, especially during dry season, it is full of alligators, huge turtles, and great blue herons. Between Ochopee and Sunniland I've counted as many as forty or fifty 'gators sunning on the banks, a tribute to conservation efforts that have brought this grinning saurian back from near extinction during the last two decades. How much more exciting to see them here, wild, than stacked like logs in some "Gator Farm"! (The trick, of course, is to spot them while keeping your eyes on the road.)

Immokalee, the next stop north of Sunniland, is geologically interesting because it is located on what was once an island in the prehistoric Pamlico Sea. It also has a certain sociological interest because it belongs to the "other Florida" that tourists rarely see: a storage and processing center for the vast truck farms that surround it, with a large population of Hispanics and blacks. The town is not scenic, but not ugly either. Here the traveler following this alternate route will want to turn off and head for the magnificent Corkscrew Swamp Sanctuary fourteen miles to the west on Hwy 846 (see above).

North of Immokalee, the fields of vegetables gradually yield to cattle country, the openness pleasingly relieved by cypress and cabbage palms standing alone or in heads and hammocks, with perhaps a foraging wood stork circling for a landing in a canal or slough. Beyond La Belle, a pretty town with live oaks shading tidy streets, lies Palmdale, the most inland point on our roundabout route.

The great attraction in this area is Fisheating Creek, a stream so beautiful that, once you have seen it, you are not likely ever to forget it. There are no state parks hereabouts, but Lykes Brothers, Inc., which owns a huge chunk of real estate in the area, operates the **Fisheating Creek Campground**—three campgrounds, actually—on Hwy 27 a mile north of its junction with Hwy 29. The main campground, west of the highway, is a clean, well-managed place in a pretty riverside setting, with hookups, laundromat, tennis courts, grocery store—the whole shebang—at rates higher than those at state campgrounds but still very moderate. On the east side of the road there is a very large "wilderness" campground (as well as a motorbike campground, mercifully segregated in its own four hundred acres). Check at the main campground to find out how to get there, since the entrance route isn't clearly marked. The area made available for primitive camping ranges in size from one thousand to two thousand acres depending on the number of users. Unfortunately, a maze of random tracks crisscrosses through the woods, and in wet weather it's easy for a passenger car to get stuck. But the price is right, the river view is lovely, and on weekdays you will have the place almost to yourself. At both campgrounds there are large areas in which to enjoy pleasant walks (when it isn't too wet) through riverine forests dominated by cypress, palms, and oaks draped in Spanish moss. At the main campground there is also horseback riding through the "western wilderness."

But the great attraction is canoeing on Fisheating Creek. Reservations are necessary. Canoes are for rent if you don't have your own, and in either case the management, for a fee, provides transportation to primitive campsites on the river at stages that allow for a leisurely one- or two-day trip. The transition to the river, after the miles of Florida highways and the tidy, civilized campground, is startling. Once embarked, you will drift through a world that seems never to have been touched by humans before. Cypress rear up from the still surface; boughs draped with moss and air plants lean overhead; the trunks of fallen trees support sunning alligators, turtles, and herons; small ponds cover themselves with lilies; water grasses of exquisite delicacy cluster among the cypress knees; otters occasionally allow themselves to be seen.

In short, this water journey is a perfect way to spend a day or two, especially for those who have little experience with southern rivers and have not brought along their own canoe. The fishing, for perch and maybe bass, is good; so have your gear and license with you. (Lykes Fisheating Creek Campgrounds, P.O. Box 100, Palmdale, Florida, 33944; 813/675–1852.)

From Fisheating Creek, we head due west on arrow-straight Hwy 74. I have always liked this drive through the cattle country of south-central Florida, not least of all because you can go for mile after mile without seeing a billboard or even a house. The country is board flat, with long stretches of saw palmetto scrub gradually yielding to pine plantations. Herds of handsome Brahma cattle, each accompanied by its entourage of cattle egrets, graze the prairies. Be sure to be on the lookout for Florida sandhill cranes on the scrub flats, and if it is evening, watch for deer in openings in the piney woods.

Since our next destination is Myakka State Park, we can either turn north on Hwy 31 after driving twenty-nine miles on Hwy 74, and travel to Arcadia through cattle and farm country, or keep heading west on Hwy 74. The latter route passes along the northern boundary of the Cecil M. Webb Wildlife Management Area. Most of the terrain is heavily managed as pine plantation and is only moderately scenic; but if you happen to be passing this way on a weekend sometime between March 4 and October 28, and you would like a primitive camping site, the management area offers a welcome break. In that event, when Hwy 74 meets with I-10, head south on the interstate a few miles and take the next exit, which puts you right at the entrance checkpoint. You will be in an area of grassy lakes, prairie, and cutover pines. Roads in the campground are in good shape but elsewhere they are pretty rough, especially in wet weather. And remember, except for a few holidays, it's weekends-only between the dates already mentioned. During late fall and winter, this is strictly hunter heaven. (Game and Freshwater Fish Commission, 620 South Meridian Street, Tallahassee, Florida 32301.)

After, or without, the pause at Cecil M. Webb, our tour heads north. I-75 is the convenient way, but if you aren't in a hurry, you may enjoy taking the backdoor route along Hwy 72 via Hwys 17 and 761. Hwy 17 has nothing much to offer except real-estate mania, but once you cross the beautiful Peace River onto Hwy 761 the landscape is pleasantly rural again, at least for the next few years, with citrus groves and cattle pastures. Once on Hwy 72, the landscape assumes the daydreaming look of backcountry Florida: wet, open grasslands that are half pasture, half prairie, punctuated either by piney islands or hammocks that are sometimes composed entirely of cabbage palms, sometimes of mixed stands of palms and live oaks. The latter are my favorites in this area. There is something about the rounded, shaggy outlines of the oaks in combination with the rather spiky shapes of the palms that is very satisfying.

After a while the hammocks close in on the road. Small marshes appear, each with its egret-on-duty. We are at Myakka.

Myakka State Park is one of Florida's finest. It should not be missed. However, the general rule that applies to all southern Florida parks deserves special emphasis here: if you plan to do some camping during the winter months, make reservations in advance. By March the crowds have begun to thin out, but even in summer, on weekends when it isn't rainy, there are often quite a few local people in the park. Unlike Everglades, Collier-Seminole, and other parks further to the south, Myakka is a year-round place to visit, even for those who are not fond of toughing it out. As late as May, I have camped here without being much bothered by mosquitoes, and although they certainly start ganging up in subsequent months, they are usually tolerable if you come prepared.

The Myakka River and its two large lakes are fed entirely by local rains. Upper Myakka Lake, north of Hwy 72, is the site of campgrounds and facilities and is inevitably the most utilized section of the park. Yet even here the relative lack of privacy does not take away from a pleasure in the setting itself, nor does it seem to disturb the wild creatures that are always on display. Though we are still in that flat, wet world we have been traveling through all along, the landscape has begun noticeably to change. The large hammocks, once entered, prove to be surprisingly open at ground level. They are dominated by live and laurel oaks and cabbage palms, with saw palmetto, as always, demarcating subtle lifts in elevation. The heavy branches of the oaks wear gardens of air plants, "water pots," butterfly orchids, and serpent ferns; but the tangle of West Indian trees to the south is absent. More surprisingly, there do not seem to be any cypress in view along the edges of the lake. Instead, there are scores of small marshes filled with maiden cane and clumps of pop ash, the nesting haunts of sandhill cranes.

The southern shore of Upper Myakka Lake is accessible for its entire length by road. The northern side can be reached by means of the "world's largest airboat," which departs from the concessionaire's dock four times a day. It is noisy, but the alligators, ibis, and herons don't seem to mind, and the accompanying nature talk is interesting and instructive. There is also a tram that will carry you seven miles into the marshes, where an observation tower affords a wonderful view not only of the interwoven patterns of forest and open prairie, but also of a large rookery packed, in season, with white ibis. At sunset, the open expanses of the lake become an intense Prussian blue under skies of orange-gold, while close to shore the grasses and lilies merge into long, purple streaks. Transferred to a picture calendar, the effect would be gorgeously vulgar. Here it is merely gorgeous.

Lower Myakka Lake, in the southern sector of the park, is every bit as beautiful, but much less looked at. It is part of a 7500-acre wil-

derness area and can be visited by a limited number of hikers or canoeists daily. Myakka is, in fact, a wonderful place for both activities.
A segment of the Florida Trail winds through many miles of hammocks and pine flatwoods in the park and is available for serious backpacking. But even those who are less ambitious should have no trouble getting away from the madding crowd simply by following one of
the dirt trails that lead away from the lake through deep groves of oaks
and across openings crowded with dense brush. In the evening or early morning you will probably see deer and wild turkey, which are almost tame here. And you will certainly hear wild hogs rooting in the
palmettos, sounding alarmingly like a convention of bears. These
bristly descendants of domestic swine are a real problem at Myakka
since they eat up acorns and other foods that could be better used by
the native wildlife. It is easy to understand why wildlife managers are
obliged to control them. But it would be sad if they were altogether
eliminated. Their visible presence adds a certain glamor to Myakka's
beautiful forests. European boars they're not; but they look like them.
Glimpsing their dark shapes in the green shadows is like seeing a medieval tapestry spring to life.

Travel by water at Myakka depends on muscle power, which is
good news for canoeists but not for motorboat enthusiasts. Park
waters are plagued by hydrilla, an underwater plant pest that chokes
out more desirable aquatic vegetation. The stuff spreads by fragmen-
tation; so outboards are banned because the chopping action contrib-
utes to the problem. For the canoeist, however, the Myakka River is a
dream come true. There is an almost landscaped look to the scenery
unfolding along the shores—the massive oaks and the grassy prairies
that look like uncut meadows. But away from the campgrounds and
picnic tables, this is the Florida of a thousand years ago. Just so you
don't forget that, a ten-foot alligator will cruise past in the clean, dark
water, or flocks of wood storks, ibis, and snowy and great egrets, perhaps with great and little blue herons mixed in, will be feeding in the
shallows as you drift by. After some miles of paddling through this flat,
watery world, your only complaint will be that there has to be an end
to it. You will wish, as I have, that this grand wilderness was even larger than it is. (Myakka State Park, Route 1, Box 72, Sarasota, Florida
33577; 813/924–1027.)

Moving north, you can head directly for I-75 on Hwy 72 (with a
stop at Sarasota and the marvels of the Ringling Museum) or leave
Myakka by the back door, via Hwy 675, traveling through cattle country that looks pretty much like the landscape east of the park. Imperceptibly, however, the topography is changing. You are not all that far
from the western edge of Florida's central highlands, the elevated
ridge that runs halfway down the center of the state. The highlands
stayed dry during some of the periods when all the land you have been
traversing was under water. Hwy 675 crosses the ancient marine ter-

races that marked the advance and retreat of those prehistoric seas. You can take a close look at the sandy flatlands that are characteristic of the area if you stop off at Lake Manatee, a small state park that you will pass on Hwy 64 as you head for I-75. The scenery is pleasant but unspectacular—just open palmetto prairie, scrub pine, and dense thickets near the manmade lake. There is no campground, but the lake is said to have good fishing for bass and perch.

Ahead lies Tampa–St. Petersburg.

The segment of I-75 adjacent to Tampa should be just about completed by the time this book goes to press, in which case you will have the option of bypassing the metropolitan area if you wish—something not easily done heretofore. If you do visit these linked cities, particularly St. Petersburg, I would advise that you avoid the coastal route, Hwy 19, when you are ready to leave—unless, of course, you want to drive seventy miles without ever being out of sight of billboards and drive-in everythings.

Tampa–St. Petersburg

Tampa is the major port and industrial center on Florida's Gulf Coast, as well as the adopted home of a great multitude of refugees who have fled the northern winter. The huge, sheltered bay that separates the city from St. Petersburg may or may not have been first discovered by Juan Ponce de León in 1513. In any case, the great explorer was mortally wounded by an Indian arrow here while trying to establish a colony in 1521. Soon after the United States acquired Florida in 1821, what is now downtown Tampa became the locale of Fort Brooke, an outpost during the Seminole War. But the real history of Tampa begins in 1884 with the ambitious dream of a wealthy businessman, Henry Bradly Plant, who decided he would be the Gulf Coast's answer to Henry Flager, the developer of Florida's east coast. Among other things, he attempted, unsuccessfully, to attract wealthy tourists by creating a Moorish fantasy of a hotel, minarets and all. Even by Floridian standards of exuberant excess, the building is still something to see, though now University of Tampa students, rather than millionaires, walk its echoing halls. Cuban exiles who moved their cigar industry here from Key West in the 1880s had more luck with their enterprise. For years, Ybor City, now an enclave in downtown Tampa, was cigar maker to the world.

As for St. Petersburg, it is a relatively new city that began to boom as a tourist center—with a special appeal to the elderly—in 1924, when a bridge was built linking the Pinellas Peninsula with Tampa. The completion of the Sunshine Skyway in 1954 opened the city to traffic moving north and south and also, some would say, to terminal development. St. Pete's fine island beaches are now backed by an unbroken string of condos, marinas, and suburban homes that all seem to have screened swimming pools and boat channels in their backyards. The shiny yachts and red sails in the sunset make a pretty picture, but someone in search of unspoiled Florida had better look elsewhere. Birders, it is true, can stay busy for hours just glassing the spoil banks and mud flats spanned by the causeways. Thanks to a number of mangrove refuges in the bay, flocks of sophisticated shorebirds and waders conduct their lives within yards of heavy traffic.

At the tip of the peninsula is **Fort Desoto County Park**. It is very developed; but the crowded campground is tastefully designed, and there are bicycle paths, boat ramps, an old fort, and miles of beach, as well as a nature trail where you can pretend that you are in the presence of a virginal innocence that does not, in fact, exist. (Fort Desoto Park, 407 South Garden Avenue, Clearwater, Florida 33516; 813/866–2662.)

If it's ecological virginity you want, you must go up to Dunedin at the other end of the peninsula, and from there, by boat or ferry, to **Caladesi Island State Park**. The contrast between this small barrier island and the nearby crowds and traffic takes some getting used to. Sea, sand, dunes, and—that final perfect touch—a background of trees instead of condos combine here to create the ideal picture of a Gulf shoreline. The gleaming white beach is the most obvious attraction, but the interior of the island, with its narrow forests of pine, live oaks, cabbage palms, and palmetto, is at least as beautiful—and more private. On the bay side is a dense belt of mangroves, a haven for egrets, herons, and pelicans, which shuts out sight and sound of the teeming mainland a couple of miles to the east. If you get far enough away from the ferry landing, it is sometimes possible to feel that you have the whole place to yourself. Enjoy the feeling while you can during the course of a too-short day. Unlike Cayo Costa to the south— which this island much resembles—there is no overnight camping, and between here and Apalachicola Bay, two hundred miles to the north, there is not another barrier island so accessible and unspoiled. (Caladesi Island State Park, P.O. Box B, Dunedin, Florida 33528; 813/443–5903.)

5
Florida's North-Central Coast and Big Bend Country

At a glance

Access Tampa and Tallahassee have the main airports in this area, but Ocala and Gainesville are also handy. In the southern sector of this region, I-75 and Hwy 19 are the major roadways. (The latter is heavily built up from St. Petersburg to Homosassa Springs.) In the northern sector, Hwy 98/19 is the only route that stays anywhere near the Gulf Coast. Side roads heading both inland and to the Coast are described in the travelogue.

Climate Moving north, the climate shades from subtropical into southern temperate. The four seasons of the temperate zone are more sharply defined. Rain falls at any time of year—still most frequently in summer, least often in fall. Winter weather is erratic, ranging from the eighties to (rarely) 25°F or lower, and cold spells occasionally continue unbroken for days or even weeks. Summer, not winter, is the time when people hit the beach.

Topography and Landscape Features In this region, Florida's central highlands encroach upon the narrowing coastal plain. Rivers, some very short, cut deeper into elevated limestone ridges. They are fed by underground springs welling up from the porous limestone aquifer. Although the rivers create productive estuarine deltas, large bays and barrier islands are uncommon on this part of the Coast except in the Apalachicola area.

Flora and Fauna Ecological communities are very diverse: cypress swamps, freshwater prairies, oak and cabbage palm hammocks, bottomland forests of deciduous hardwoods, salt and brackish marshes, and vast pine and palmetto flatwoods interspersed with oak or titi hammocks. Great numbers of migrant birds—waterfowl, songbirds, hawks—gather at refuges and parks. Waders and alligators, though

not quite as abundant as in southern Florida, are still common. Apalachicola National Forest and nearby parks contain the nation's largest
remaining populations of the rare red-cockaded woodpecker. A few
black bears also survive in the national forest.

Camping   Public campgrounds in this area tend the be concentrated
in the southern and northernmost sectors. Hillsborough State Park
and Withlacoochee State Forest are excellent bets for RV campers, and
the latter is also fine for primitive camping. In the north, the Apalachicola National Forest and Ochlockonee and St. Joseph Peninsula state
parks offer a wide variety of camping possibilities. There are also some
opportunities for primitive camping at St. George Island State Park. In
the midsection of this coast, small public campgrounds are located

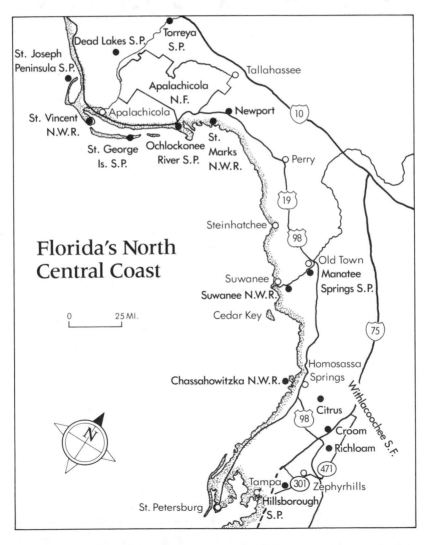

near St. Marks National Wildlife Refuge and at Old Town, but the only sizable facility with hookups is at Manatee Springs State Park. Fishing towns on the Coast have some private RV facilities. Also, isolated dirt roads in the backcountry near the Coast offer possibilities for do-it-yourself primitive camping if you want to take your chances.

Hiking, Canoeing, Boating, Etc.   If you are a hiker, you will really come into your own in this region, with a wide range of habitats to walk (or, if you prefer, wade) through. Long segments of the Florida Trail traverse each of the three sections of Withlacoochee State Forest as well as wilderness areas in St. Marks National Wildlife Refuge and Apalachicola National Forest. Or you can tramp through the barrier-island forests of St. Joseph Peninsula State Park or St. Vincent National Wildlife Refuge. The canoeist is also faced with a choice of riches. One fine canoeing river after another presents itself along this stretch of the Coast. This is, in fact, probably the best region for canoeing on the entire Gulf, provided water levels are right. Some of the more promising opportunities are discussed in the travelogue. Boaters can take a crack at most of the same waterways, but a majority will probably prefer the fine fishing in the coastal marshes near towns such as Suwannee or Steinhatchee or the tidal inlets of Apalachicola Bay.

Outdoors Highlights   Richloam (hiking) and Croom (camping) sectors of Withlacoochee State Forest; *all* the national wildlife refuges (Chassahowitzka, Suwanee, St. Marks, St. Vincent); Cedar Key and other coastal fishing towns; Apalachicola National Forest; St. Joseph Peninsula State Park.

W hen the I-75 bypass is finished, it will put you almost at the doorstep of **Hillsborough River State Park** on Hwy 301. This may be a mixed blessing, since ready access will make this beautiful place even more popular than it already is, and unlike Myakka, the crowds on a busy weekend are not so easy to escape. Still, you should consider making this detour. As of now, most of the heavy use is daytime, local, and concentrated at the picnic area and out-of-place swimming pool. Weekdays, even in summer, there will usually be attractive campsites available, and during early mornings and evenings you will have the trails along the river almost to yourself.

Though quite small, the park is fascinating both in terms of its natural beauty and historical interest. For the first time, you fully realize that southern Florida is behind you. There are still plenty of cabbage palms in evidence, as there will be for many miles to come. But essentially the riverine forests here are those you will encounter along the northern edge of the gulf. Here are the live and water oaks, the sweet gum, magnolia, red maple, and cypress draped heavily in webs of Spanish moss. On the entrance road, stands of very tall pines grow on the higher ground. But the river itself, rising in the Green Swamp to the north, is the most strikingly different part of the picture, especially when compared, say, to the Myakka, or the Estero, or Fisheating Creek. For much of its inland course, the Hillsborough cuts between limestone banks that at low-water stages rise ten or fifteen feet above the river surface. Immense baldcypress, normally associated with still water and swampy silences, wrap roots around solid rock and stand in swirling currents. Where the river crosses limestone outcrops, it actually forms modest rapids—an uncommon sight on our journey!

For the walker, the nature trails afford a more lengthy look at a southern stream than that available in most state parks. For the canoeist, there is the option of putting in at Crystal Springs (on Hwy 39, which branches off Hwy 301 a few miles north of the park) or embarking at the park boat dock (where canoes may be rented) and traveling four miles downstream into the large cypress swamp at Flint Creek County Park. Either way, the Hillsborough offers you some magically beautiful views of itself. But as usual, check with the park staff first for on-the-scene advice.

Anyone even mildly interested in history will enjoy visiting the park's exact replica of Fort Foster, one of the log forts used by U.S. troops during the Seminole War in the 1830s. Not too many Americans are aware that this Indian uprising really was an honest-to-God war. On an early nineteenth-century scale, it was as costly to the United States—economically, psychologically, and militarily—as Vietnam. The fort, complete with uniformed soldiers, brings that largely forgotten chapter in the nation's past to life. However, the excellent van tours—the only way to see the fort—are available only Fridays through Sundays and on holidays. (Hillsborough River State Park, Route 4, Box 250-L, Zephyrhills, Florida 33599; 813/986–1020.)

The Green Swamp and the Withlacoochee State Forest

The next stop on the itinerary is the 113,000-acre **Withlacoochee State Forest**—forests, really, since it is composed of three separate tracts: Richloam, Croom, and Citrus. For someone who prefers to visit the forest headquarters right off the bat and pick up information about recreational opportunities—good idea, of course—the best bet is to take I-75 to Hwy 98, cross over to Brooksville, and head north a few miles on Hwy 41 to the headquarters building. But those eccentrics who wish to stick with our ideal tour have a more roundabout course to follow. After leaving Hillsborough, our aim is to travel north for a while via Hwy 471, avoiding the more trafficky and developed scene along Hwy 301. To do this, cross over on Hwy 54 at the trailer park town of Zephyrhills. (Note: when you reach the junction with Hwy 98 you must turn south a couple of miles on 98 in order to link up with 471, a fact not clearly indicated on most road maps.) Hwy 471 will take you through a part of the Green Swamp, which until recently was a more truly impenetrable wilderness than any other in the state with the arguable exception of the mangrove swamps south of Naples. Even now, with timber and oil companies working it over, developers chewing away at its edges, and armies of hunters on the prowl in it each winter, there are still places in its depths where hardly anyone has ever been since the days when this whole region was the stronghold of the Seminole Indians and their famous chief, Osceola. You should pause for a few moments where the highway crosses the lovely Withlacoochee River and gaze about you. The waterway traverses the great blank space on early maps where the Seminoles held out for years before being driven south to their final refuge in the Everglades. This entire stretch of road passes through a hauntingly beautiful yet secretive landscape of cypress heads and strands interspersed with prairies and small ponds. After the first ten miles or so, hardwoods and pine flatlands begin to predominate. Here there are dirt roads leading into the Richloam sector of the Withlacoochee State Forest. But this section of it isn't campers' country: you can get stuck when it's wet if you don't have four-wheel drive; and, if it's dry, oil and lumber trucks will coat you with gritty dust.

When you hit Hwy 50 at the nice little eyeblink hamlet of Tarrytown, head east through more pine flatlands on your way to campgrounds in the Croom sector of the Withlacoochee State Forest. Those of you who want to do some hiking should note, however, that about five-and-a-half or six miles below Tarrytown there is a hard-surfaced road turning off on your left. After half a mile, it brings you to the Richloam Fire Tower, the starting point for a twenty-five-mile hiking trail that circles around the eastern half of the Richloam tract. There are other trails in the Croom and Citrus sections of the state forest that are notably hillier and drier; so it all depends on your preferences. But this particular trail affords the only opportunity I know of to penetrate a portion of the Green Swamp on foot. Richloam is a working forest; therefore, much of the path leads through flat pinelands managed for timber production. But there are many stretches that weave in and out among moss-clouded hammocks and cypress strands on the wilderness banks of the Withlacoochee and Little rivers. Here you can come to terms with what this magnificent swamp is all about. Primitive campsites are available; but if you haven't time to hike the entire trail, you can use crossover forest roads as shortcuts. The path can get wet in rainy months, so you should phone the forest headquarters (see below) about conditions if you don't plan to stop there first.

The Croom tract is the part of the forest that is most set up for recreational use, with several improved campsites, boat ramps, and so on. To get there from the Richloam area, just keep heading west on Hwy 50. A couple of miles after you cross Hwy 35, you will see a sign indicating the road to the Silver Lake campgrounds. (If you hit I-75, you've gone a mile too far.) The lake itself is a beauty, and the campgrounds are very pleasant. But unless you need an electrical hookup, you would do well to skip the first of them (Silver Lake) and set up in one of the other two (Cypress Glen or Crooked River) since they are more removed from the traffic on I-75. Or, you can skip this whole campground complex and stay on the access road, heading for one of the campgrounds north of I-75. (Old Iron Bridge Campground, located in a beautiful hammock overlooking the Withlacoochee River, is the most developed of these.) All of the campgrounds get some heavy use in summer and during the hunting season, but there are nearly always sites available.

The Citrus sector of the forest, a few miles northwest of Brooksville and the forest headquarters, also has improved campgrounds, but the natural surroundings are not quite as scenic as those at Croom.

There are hiking trails at both Croom and Citrus, each with a maximum course of more than twenty miles. Neither offers the extensive swamp landscapes available at Richloam, although there are damp stretches on the Croom trail at times. By Florida standards, much of Croom and Citrus, especially the latter, are decidedly hilly—hot work when the weather is warm. There are hardwood hammocks and pine plantations, but also upland stretches of scrub oak and sand pine. Croom boasts deep ravines and abandoned mines; Citrus, limestone caves and rocky hammocks. The Croom trail begins at the Silver Lake Recreation Area, where you can also pick up a map and other information. The forest headquarters, which is on your way to the Citrus tract, will provide the same information for that trail. (Withlacoochee State Forest, 7255 U.S. 41 North, Brooksville, Florida 33512; 904/796–4958.)

For those who prefer being afloat to being afoot, Silver Lake and the Withlacoochee River offer almost limitless possibilities. The river widens and narrows as it twists in and out of cypress swamps, sloughs, small lakes, and freshwater prairies; and there are more than a hundred miles of it available for exploration. Some sections such as the detour into Jumper Creek Swamp—an ecological reserve—admit you to a surreal cypress-shadowed world so deeply hidden that you wonder if even the alligators know their way around. You can rent a canoe and all equipment, arrange for take-outs, and otherwise plan for trips ranging from two hours to eight days at the Canoe Outpost, Nobleton, just north of the Croom tract. Rentals are not exactly cheap, but the hours or days on the river are worth the price. It's a good idea to make reservations at least a few days in advance. (Canoe Outpost, Box 188, Nobleton, Florida 33554; 904/796–4343.)

Suwanee River Country

You could easily spend weeks in and around the Withlacoochee State Forest, but for us it is time now to get back to the Coast. At the point where Hwy 98 links up with Hwy 19, you will be safely north of the worst sleaze on the latter highway. As if to celebrate this cheerful fact, there lies immediately to the west one of the most wonderful, if hard-to-pronounce, wild areas on the Florida Gulf Coast. This is the **Chas-sahowitzka National Wildlife Refuge**, a more-than-30,000-acre maze of marshes, bays, hardwood swamps, mangroves, and clear-water creeks, most of it wilderness, and all of it teeming with wildlife. Although the refuge is not exactly a well-kept secret—35,000 persons visit it each year—the majority of users are fishermen and duck hunt-ers. Most out-of-staters, even those eager to experience the natural scene in Florida, are likely to pass the place by. Part of the problem concerns access. There are proposed plans for a road that will take vis-itors to the edge of the marshes, but for the immediate future the only entry is by water. However, even if you haven't got a boat or canoe in tow, arrangements can be made.

The first thing to do is to head for the refuge headquarters on the west side of Hwy 19, about a mile north of the junction with Hwy 98. There you can pick up information about regulations, natural history, weather, and water routes, and also walk the nature trail nearby. Then go back a mile to the little community of Chassahowitzka on the easy-to-miss side road west of the Hwy 98 junction. Here you will find a Lykes Brothers Campground, less elaborate than the one at Fisheating Creek but nevertheless very serviceable, at the headwaters of the Chassahowitzka River. Camping facilities (there are none in the ref-uge), ready access to the refuge, and boat and canoe rentals are all available here. During winter and on weekends reservations are ad-visable, but if the placc is filled up there are other campgrounds nearby.

The refuge is an estuarine complex in which millions of gallons of water, welling up from underground springs every day, are carried by the Chassahowitzka and other short creeks and streams to the marshes downstream, where they blend with the Gulf's salt tides. The visitor first paddles (or putt-putts) through a belt of marsh-fringed hardwood swamp and jungly hammock dominated by cypress, live and water oaks, southern red cedar, and sweet gum. Below Potter's Creek, this landscape gradually yields to another that is equally lovely but very different. Here tidal bays and winding waterways intermesh in a crazy-quilt pattern with great expanses of marsh grass. According to species, season, and time of day, these long reams of grasses change their hues: gold, green, mauve, beige. On every side, in dramatic con-trast to the prevailing horizontal lines, cabbage palms present them-selves singly, in small clumps, or in large, dense gatherings that look more like oases than island hammocks. While keeping the Chassa-howitzka as your main route, you may wish to detour into the swamp wilderness to the south, along Crawford or Johnson creeks. Or, if you are an experienced boater and have a nautical map and compass along, you can explore some part of the labyrinth to the northwest, always keeping in mind that when the tide is out around here, it's out, and you can easily end up stranded on a mud flat if you stray far from the channels. The novice should not even think of wandering from the main waterways; it is all too easy to get lost. And, of course, both pro and amateur should check with the refuge staff for guidance before starting out.

Given those precautions, your day or days in the refuge will be a memorable experience. The birdlife is prodigiously abundant. In winter as many as twenty thousand waterfowl are on hand, representing some fifteen different species; and in the swamps and hammocks scores of migrant songbirds, including many warblers, can be found. Winter is also the time of the manatee or sea cow; these endangered creatures must move into the rivers to escape the killing chill of open waters. At such times they are heartbreakingly vulnerable to the propeller blades of speeding motorboats—so much so that this one stupid cause alone may ultimately bring about their extinction. So, if you explore the refuge in a motorboat, please do be careful. Besides, the refuge staff are very hard-nosed about speeding violations.

Though you may not spot a manatee, there is still more than enough to see. Bald eagles, as well as some forty pairs of ospreys, nest on the refuge. Coots are so numerous at times that they blacken the water, and wading birds and cormorants nest on the outer mangrove islands by the thousands. The wonderful thing is that you can look not only around and up, but down! The water is usually so clear that you can see to amazing depths. Where springs well up at the stream heads, fish gather in great numbers, apparently just to enjoy themselves since they do not seem to feed. And where saltwater and freshwater intermingle, you may have the rare chance to hook fish from both sea and stream at the same spot. Whether they are biting or not, you can certainly see them—redfish, bass, speckled trout, mackeral, bream—swimming around below you. Better still, the channel at the mouth of the Chassahowitzka is perhaps the best place on the entire Gulf to observe rare green and loggerhead turtles feeding in their watery realm. For someone whose idea of a turtle is a red slider sunning on a log, the sight of these enormous creatures swimming below the boat can seem unreal.

The best seasons for viewing wildlife at the refuge are winter and spring, but there is a lot to see at any season. Keep in mind that the subtropics are behind us. In winter it can get pretty nippy. (Chassahowitzka Wildlife Refuge, Route 2, Box 44, Homosassa, Florida 32646; 904/628–2201.)

Before leaving this immediate area, you may want to have a quick look at Homosassa Springs and Old Homosassa, which are just up the road from Chassahowitzka. This was a quiet, very pretty area not all that long ago. Now it's Touristville incarnate. Still, there are boat tours and lodgings. Also, if you have kids along, it might be worth visiting the famous springs here. There has been an effort to present the attractions in a tasteful way, and children will enjoy the walk-through cages where native and exotic fauna intermix and where captive manatees are on view. The springs themselves are clear and beautiful. Swarms of fish can be seen from an underwater chamber, and wading birds, unalarmed by the crowds, come visiting from the wilds. If you can find your way through the new subdivisions to Old Homosassa, drive along the older streets that tunnel through the greenery. There are still a few vestiges of the sleepy little fishing village that once was here. Even at the tourist pier, with its fish food dispensers and spider monkeys on a mini-island, there is the wonderful sight of pelicans boldly swooping above the boats and herons waiting around to snitch a fish from the bait traps. Across the channel stands a handsome two-storied house from an earlier era. By its mere presence, it rebukes what the developers have done to this part of contemporary Florida.

The Big Bend Country

Beyond Homosassa Springs we are approaching Florida's Big Bend country. It is difficult to summarize the abundant recreational possibilities of this region because there is no specific focus for any one large area. Except for Manatee Springs State Park, there are no parks or large public campgrounds available along these next 150 miles of Highway 19/98. Moreover, everything worth seeing requires a considerable detour off the main highway. These detours are usually at right angles to the coastline, sometimes requiring the traveler to head back to Hwy 98 without making much of an advance in the general direction he or she is going. There is, in fact, no coastal highway of any sort—that is, one that offers views of the Gulf—for the good reason that in this area the sandy beaches of the Naples-to-Tampa area have given way to the less touristy but more pristine world of marshes, swamps, and tidal flats that we glimpsed at Chassahowitzka. To see that world at its best you really need to take along a boat or rent one. Also, since virtually all the land in the area is private, camping opportunities are limited; so you should be prepared to stay in motels or private, not-very-parklike campgrounds. None of these problems alter the fact that this is wonderful country to explore.

One of the most promising locales includes Manatee Springs, Cedar Key, and the new Suwannee River National Wildlife Refuge. **Manatee Springs State Park** takes its name from the 117 million gallons of water per day that come welling out of the limestone here to augment the flow of the lower Suwannee, and also from the manatees that used to frequent this spot but don't much anymore. It is a sleepily beautiful setting, with a very pleasant campground situated in the deep shade of the riverine forest—an ideal spot to use as headquarters while exploring the whole area between the Waccasassa and Suwanee rivers. Swimming in the springs is a fantastic experience: the water is as clear as that in any swimming pool, but with limestone ledges instead of blue plastic lining surrounding you. If you can prove that you are an experienced diver, the flooded underground caverns are yours to explore. And for those who prefer to do their exploring on the water rather than in it, there are boats and canoes for hire. Park staff can advise you on how much of the lower Suwannee can be conveniently navigated. Way down upon those lower reaches there are no plantations to long for, and the only old folks at home are likely to be fishing from their motorboats; but never mind these petty discrepancies. With its majestic forests mantled in green and gray, and its generous sweep (three hundred yards wide near the coast), the river lives up to its legendary reputation. In high-water years, however, its current can get pretty strong—no problem for the motorboat set, but hard work for canoeists paddling upsteam. As for the hiker, there is not only a self-guided nature trail, but also miles of woodland track leading through the 2000-acre park, with views pleasantly alternating between dense lowland hammocks of oaks, hickories, and magnolias, and the drier, sunlit pinelands. (Manatee Springs State Park, Route 2, Box 362, Chiefland, Florida 32626; 904/493-4288.)

If you haven't been aware of it already, you will begin to notice now that a natural phenomenon has appeared that you had forgotten all about in southern Florida—to wit, hills! Modest hills, to be sure, but real ups and downs nonetheless. You will especially notice these when you explore the new 50,000-acre **Suwanee National Wildlife Refuge** downriver from Manatee Springs State Park. As is too often the case with federal refuges, hunters, not plain old nature lovers, have the right-of-way. And, as usual, there will be no camping (which is just as well, from the wildlife's point of view). But even now, the place is wonderful to visit on foot. Once you find it, that is. Not all the county roads show on the road maps. At Manatee Springs, ask directions about how to cross from 320 to County Roads 330/347 without going back to the main highway. Then head south past the small riverside community of Fowler Bluff. A few miles beyond lies the new refuge. Cypress heads, small ponds and reedy sloughs, and thick hardwood forests of oaks, red maples, ash, and sweet gum alternate with stretches of pinelands on the gently undulating landscape, precisely arranged in relation to degrees of wet or dry. Little blue herons, egrets, and rural blacks with cane poles fish the roadside ditches. At too frequent intervals there are dirt roads leading into the tract, heading for the river. When I was there, all were closed to vehicular traffic, but there was nothing to stop a person from taking a walk through the lovely woods. Northern parulas, pileated and red-bellied woodpeckers, cardinals, and nuthatches flickered through the undergrowth. The dirt roads were stapled with the prints of deer—a lot of deer—as well as wild turkey, raccoons, and armadillo.

It is a real joy just to know that this splendid forest, on the banks of this noble river, is now protected from development. With the right kind of light-handed management, it should soon be an exciting but, one hopes, not-too-accessible place to visit.

On the coast nearby is Cedar Key, one of those Florida towns that you wish some good fairy would put into a trance or something, so that it could go on sleeping until the right kind of Prince Charming developer came along and kissed it into wakefulness. Even now, although there are more Pelican Realty signs than pelicans on hand, it still manages to hold on to the literally weather-beaten charm that made it such a pleasure to visit in the recent past. In the nineteenth century it was a busy, rowdy seaport, variously abused by Civil War troops, railroad tycoons, hurricanes, and fires. Now, after generations of being no worse than a quiet fishing village, it is under assault again. Cinder-block motels, trailer camps, and chic modern dwellings vie for footholds on its few dry acres. Yet for all that, the town is still a wonderful place to be. It is perched on a surprisingly steep, high little island—several of them actually—with a wide expanse of marsh and hammock in its backyard and the Gulf of Mexico at its front door. There are still some nice old frame houses with tin-sheeted roofs, friendly porches, and the occasional bit of gingerbread frill—a vaguely Bahamian architecture that has a local rightness to it. Cabbage palms, cedars, and loopy, storm-twisted oaks line the streets. On the beach a little park is available for picnicking. And there is a good little museum—housed, unfortunately, in an out-of-place modern box.

A few miles offshore lies the Cedar Key National Wildlife Refuge, a collection of eight island remnants of a huge sand dune that formed on the coastal plateau thousands of years ago. The islands range in size from six to 165 acres. The highest of them has an amazing elevation—by Gulf Coast standards—of more than fifty feet. More important, though, they harbor one of the largest wading-bird rookeries in the nation, with an average of 50,000 egrets, herons, and ibis nesting there in a single year, as well as thousands of cormorants and pelicans. For obvious reasons, the islands are off-limits to people during the breeding season, January through June. You can visit them during the rest of the year, but you may not want to. They are surrounded by wide mud flats that make them hard to get to, especially at low tide. Even more discouraging, they are acrawl with the highest concentration of cottonmouth snakes known to exist in the nation. If that puts you off, console yourself with the thought that most of the bird species can be seen in the marshes right around Cedar Key.

On your way to or from either Hwy 19/98 or Manatee Springs, note the Cedar Key Scrub Preserve along the roadside, an interesting if not exactly beautiful fragment of the red cedar thicket that once covered much of this part of the coast. Further on, you may want to try Hwy 345 instead of Hwy 24. It is a much prettier road, with flooded hardwood forests and pine flatlands near the coast and, a little further inland, a beautiful harmony of pasture and hammock. In spring, wild iris and other flowers bloom in the roadside ditches.

On the north side of the Suwannee River, just south of Old Town, is a small county park, New Pine Landing, with thirty campsites and

Cedar Key. *Photo by Florida Division of Tourism.*

a boat ramp. This is the last public campground of any kind between here and Newport. Beyond Old Town, you can pay your money and take your choice about which of the roads leading to the coast you would like to follow. Birding is excellent in most seasons; and the further you get away from Highway 19/98, the more interesting the scenery becomes, in spite of being roughed up at frequent intervals by the timber companies.

The little towns at the ends of these roads do not have the calming sense of a colorful past that still lingers at Cedar Key, but if you do not expect of them what they are not, they are totally likable. And they can be a lot of fun. Each is different, but they have many traits in common. To begin with, commercial and sport fishing are the only reason any of them exist. The town of Suwannee is a fair example of the general type. (When you drive down to visit, by the way, don't expect any views of the nearby famous river along the road; instead, there are long, pleasant stretches of pinelands, swamps, and bays.) As always, the few shell-paved streets dead-end at the water's edge. Bungalows with screened porches, trailers, boat sheds, and houses lifted high on piers are all scattered casually along the waterways. A drowsy quietness is the rule, broken only when a boat, its decks well below the sandy lawns on either side, chugs up the canal. There are boat lifts and ramps. Gulls, and maybe pelicans and cormorants, hang around. Oysters are for sale. The good smell of salt and fish and marsh encourages the appetite. And always there is at least one unfancy local restaurant with synthetic wood paneling and artificial flowers where you can get excellent fried fish fresh from the Gulf. These places are usually packed on weekend nights. The waitresses are friendly, the helpings large. Some tables are occupied by whole families, others by good ole boys. Most of the customers—resident fishermen, blue-collar retirees, and vacationing regulars—know each other, and a loud, good-natured camaraderie prevails.

If you decide to take the Hwy 361/51 loop further to the north, Steinhatchee is the biggest of the little towns along the way, and Ray's Restaurant is locally celebrated. While you are here, take an evening drive along the last ten miles of Hwy 361 to where the road dead-ends in the marsh. The blacktop passes through the typical mix of coastal woodlands in this area: heavily managed pine forests (often looking scorched in spring as a result of controlled burning), red oak scrub, hardwood hammocks packed with sweet gum, and small cypress strands. But the best is saved for last: during the final mile or two of its existence, the road crosses over the marshes amid imposing stands of cabbage palms and straggling islands of pines. This is one of the few places left in Florida where the no-fence law still prevails; so you will probably be greeted by the old-fashioned spectacle of cattle lounging all over the road. (There are also wild hogs around; so for their sake and your own, drive slowly! Hitting one is the equivalent of colliding with a tree.) Finally, you are at your destination, which is nowhere— nothing but open marsh, palm hammock, inlets, egrets, and the encompassing sky. And out there just beyond view, the Gulf. If you haven't had the chance to explore this world by boat, here at least you can get the feel of what you're missing.

Incidentally, an unimproved road a few miles back connects this dead-end with a parallel highway leading to Horseshoe Beach. But it can be dusty or boggy, depending. Check at Jena, across the river from Steinhatchee, for directions. Horseshoe Beach is another of those tiny communities that is worth a visit, and there are some fine coastal swamps and hammocks along the way.

Before leaving this general area, the reader might want to keep in mind that, some eighty road miles to the north, the Suwannee River has its origins in the Okefenokee Swamp, easily one of the largest, most splendid wilderness ecosystems surviving in the Deep South or anywhere else. It lies outside the province of this book; but if you want to experience a cypress swamp that looks like Creation on the fifth day, one that seems to go on forever, then the foray into Georgia would certainly be worth your while. As for the Suwannee itself, in its upper reaches it contains long stretches that are superb for boating. Occasionally canoeists with a lot of energy and time to spare have traveled all of its 250 meandering miles. There are impressive swamp forests along its course, but also high limestone cliffs, sand hills, a couple of tricky stretches of shoals, some development, and odorous sulphur springs.

Perry, where Hwys 19 and 98 part company, is an unlovely melange of motels and filling stations strung out along the highway; but
lodging and food are reasonable. Also, this is a good place to stock up
on supplies if you plan to camp out north of St. Marks Refuge or do
some canoeing along the stretch of Hwy 98 that lies ahead.

These next forty miles of Hwy 98, like most of Big Bend Florida,
belong to the lumber companies. Given the development alternatives,
one must be glad that this is so, even though modern silvacultural
techniques now make it possible to pare back the swamps and hammocks more and more ruthlessly, replacing hardwood forest with
rows of monotonous but profitable pines. So far, thank heaven, a lot
of that junglelike hardwood forest still survives, which explains why
this stretch of the highway is particularly beautiful in its sodden sort
of way. We can forget the rolling hills for a while. In wet years, the
spring floods come right up to the edge of the road, holding the bulldozers and tree crushers at bay for a long time after. If you would like
to take a dry-footed look at this area, keep an eye open for the Aucilla
Wildlife Management Area on the south side of the road, just east of
Econfina River. The road into the management area leads to an impoundment much used by migratory waterfowl and wading birds.

Canoeing in Big Bend Country   Between Perry and the Apalachicola National Forest, Hwy 98 crosses several rivers, and even from the
bridges one can get a sense of their special magic. In some places, the
cypress stand in sober ranks, while elsewhere a static avalanche of
dense, green foliage, laced with Spanish moss, leans right into the river as though to drink. In one place the banks are well defined; in another, or in a wetter season, there are no banks at all—only flooded
forests thick with shadows.

Canoeing in such places is like no other experience in the world.
But as always when traveling on any stream in unfamiliar territory,
there are provisos attached. If you just want to get your canoe wet, it
is generally okay to put in wherever it's convenient and paddle half a
mile or so, after checking the current to take into account the return
trip. But if you are more ambitious, don't rely on your road map for a
river's layout. Water levels can vary greatly, underwater snags are
sometimes a problem, especially in dry seasons, and on a couple of
these rivers there are unexpected shoals. For people traveling in a single vehicle, there is, of course, the whole problem of the turn-around
(getting the car from where you want to put in to where you want to
take out and then getting yourself back to the put-in spot again) to
consider. Note the comments on canoeing in Chapter 1 and, even
more importantly, check locally concerning river conditions. You may
also want to consult the *Downriver Canoeing* booklet listed in the bibliography. The following remarks are not at all a definitive guide, but
they will suggest some of the possibilities.

Econfina River: This is a perfect example of a southern lowland stream. It should not present problems even if you are a beginner, unless you positively insist on getting lost in the swamp forest that lines the way. The distance to the take-out is four easy miles. Put in at Hwy 98; then drive to County Road 14 two miles to the west. Follow it south for five and a half miles. Turn left at a wide limestone road and drive the short distance to where a bridge crosses the river. If there is only one car, a round trip of a mile or two should not be strenuous work. But put in from County Road 14 and do the upstream paddling first.

The Wacissa and the lower Aucilla rivers: Both of these rivers are excellent for canoeing, but—not to belabor the point—they should be checked out first. The Wacissa is a wide, easygoing river, excellent for beginners, with a put-in at the small recreation park just south of the town of Wacissa. Many northern Florida canoe enthusiasts consider it the prize among rivers in the area. The current is not strong, allowing you to paddle upstream as well as down. The crystal-clear springs feeding into the river invite exploration, so you can have a wonderful time without heading more than two or three miles downstream. However, if you want to make a real trip of it, you will need more detailed information, especially if you plan to travel the entire fourteen-mile stretch to the take-out ramp at Hwy 98. In order to reach the ramp you must navigate the junction with the Aucilla, via an easy-to-miss channel. It is possible to lose your way if you don't follow directions carefully.

The lower Aucilla is also a superb canoeing river. But it is narrower than the Wacissa, the current is somewhat stronger, and there are some rock shoals. On one stretch there is even that rare phenomenon in these parts, a sequence of two rapids running over limestone rocks! If you don't want to run them (they should in any case be checked out before you do), the portage is an easy one. Here, too, the scenery is lovely, and there are well-defined banks where you can stretch your legs, picnic, and admire a "dry" river forest of oaks, hickories, holly, and pines. The put-in is at a wooden bridge just above the point where County Road 14, heading north from Hwy 98, meets Hwy 257. The take-out is at a road branching off 14 that leads to an abandoned bridge. Ask locally for exact directions. You won't get lost on the Aucilla, but you may get lost trying to get to it!

St. Marks and Wakulla rivers: These two rivers are of special interest because they are so convenient to St. Marks National Wildlife Refuge, about which, more in a moment. Both are exceedingly beautiful spring-fed rivers, fairly wide, with gentle currents that allow for upstream paddling. Both get some motorboat use, especially on weekends, and the St. Marks in particular has some development on the upper west bank for a couple of miles. These intrusions on your own intrusion are quickly canceled out, however, by the sheer magnificence of the river views. In places, majestic stands of baldcypress or tupelo dominate the flooded banks, while elsewhere a jungle of Carolina willow, red maple, swamp rose, and buttonbush crowds the shore. On the St. Marks, limestone banks sometimes climb quite high above the water. Limpkins search among the arrowhead and swamp lilies for apple snails. Alligators drape themselves on logs or banks, and herons and egrets preside over their own reflections. The water, though sometimes clouded by heavy run-off, is usually dark and clear. It is possible to make a round-trip journey of a few miles on either river from Hwy 98. The Wakulla also lends itself to an easy turn-around, with the put-in at the bridge on Hwy 365 and the take-out either at Hwy 98 (four miles) or the municipal park at the town of St. Marks (six miles). The Wakulla is the more swampy of the two rivers; in contrast to the St. Marks, there are hardly any dry banks where you can get out and walk around.

St. Marks National Wildlife Refuge is the largest and most accessible of the federal refuges on Florida's Gulf Coast—and definitely a place you should not pass up. Camping is not allowed on the refuge, but there is a small first-come, first-served state forest campground on Hwy 98 at Newport, right on the banks of the St. Marks. During much of the year the place is surprisingly uncrowded, but you can forget about it between November and late January, when the hunting seasons on parts of the refuge and the adjoining state management area are in full swing. There is another campground at **Ochlockonee River State Park**, just off Hwy 319 south of Sopchoppy, at the western edge of St. Marks, where the same general rule about camping opportunities applies. This latter camping site offers a very pretty riverside setting amid tall flatland pines and live oaks. The maturity of the pine forest is confirmed by the presence of the highly specialized red-cockaded woodpecker, which must have large stands of decayed and aging pines in order to survive. Also be on the lookout for the fox squirrels in this area, which wear a particularly beautiful shade of silvery fur. There is a boat ramp here, and the area is ideal for motorboating; but for that reason, as well as the nearness of Ochlockonee Bay and the incoming tides from the Gulf, it is not suitable for more than short canoe trips. There are better opportunities for canoeists further upstream on the Ochlockonee River that will be mentioned when we get to the Apalachicola National Forest. (Ochlockonee River State Park, Box 5, Sopchoppy, Florida 32358; 904/962–2771.)

The main entrance to St. Marks Refuge is on Hwy 59. You will have no problem recognizing the refuge boundaries: after passing through the heavily cutover forests of the Aucilla Wildlife Management Area, a powerful wall of pine flatlands is waiting there to meet you. A mile further on is a handsome Visitor Center. The ramp overlooks a typical coastal pond where you may spot an alligator among the water hyacinth. Not to worry if you don't, however. Unless it is midwinter, when they're dormant, they will be all over the place a mile or two down the road. That is where a series of large, shallow impoundments have been built, an arrangement that pleases not only 'gators but hordes of wading birds and migrant waterfowl. The fastidious visitor who wants his or her wilderness straight may quibble a bit about the managed look of things along the road. The dikes and the windbreak cedars do not exactly evoke the marsh primeval. But why be picky when there are tricolored herons, egrets, ibis, coots, and gallinules all around you, and maybe an osprey or a red-tailed hawk overhead? The resident and migrant birds that use the refuge (272 species) are a Who's Who of avian America. In a couple of hours at the observation platform next to the historic, very beautiful lighthouse tower, you can glass anywhere from twenty to fifty species of birds—from red-winged blackbirds and marsh wrens to wood storks, mallards, pintails, and bald eagles—depending on weather and season. Also available are views of the "real" marsh, most of it a designated wilderness, thick with needlegrass and laced by channels.

Serious hikers will be interested in knowing that a long stretch of the Florida Trail passes through almost the entire length of the refuge. However, it isn't necessary to undertake such an ambitious pilgrimage in order to explore the refuge's varied ecosystems. Check at the Visitor Center for information about the various trails and the distances involved. The best, and the longest, is the twelve-mile Deep Creek Trail, which can easily take all day if you make the whole loop. You will stroll through piney flatwoods, gaze out at the wilderness marsh, pass reedy ponds, choose—if you wish—a "wet" trail (which is a wade during wet seasons) through a magnificent stretch of hardwood hammock and swamp, and traverse the impoundment dikes. If you have the stamina and want to prolong the hike—in which case you better start out at the crack of dawn—you can add the additional three miles that take you to the Pinhook River with its wooden bridge, limestone formations, and junglelike forest. The woods will most likely be alive with birds: chickadees, warblers (pine, yellow-throated, northern parula, prothonotary, etc.), kinglets, and towhees. Just possibly you may see the rare red-cockaded woodpecker, which nests on the refuge, or a flock of wild turkeys. And in the ponds and swamps, be on the lookout for wood ducks and limpkins. Of course, if warm weather has set in, mosquitoes and deer flies will be among the more abundant wildlife on hand; so take along the bug juice. (St. Marks National Wildlife Refuge, Box 68, St. Marks, Florida, 32355; 904/925–6121.)

After leaving the refuge, the problem of alternate routes once again confronts us. The trick is to figure out the best way to see the most of the big bend in Florida's northern coast that lies ahead. This time it isn't a matter of whether or not to avoid the development uglies, but whether you prefer your out-of-doors amid shadowy inland forests and swamps or on the sunny dunes and beaches. With a certain amount of crisscrossing north and south, you can, in fact, have some of both. So, rather than prescribe specific alternate routes, I will simply mention, first, the places most worth seeing inland and then those worth visiting on the Coast.

An Inland Route Through the Big Bend

It wouldn't be right to describe the inland circuit without noting the existence of **Wakulla Springs and Lodge**, west of Wakulla on Hwy 61. Probably no other private resort in Florida, or, for that matter, on the whole Gulf Coast, deserves so much praise for its sensitivity to the environment surrounding it. The comfortable lodge, built in the Spanish mission style much in vogue in the 1930s, is surrounded by 4000 acres of pristine woodlands. In its front yard is the incredible spring that is the source both of the Wakulla River and the resort's quiet fame: a huge limestone cavity pumping out 600,000 gallons of water per minute. The water is so glass-clear that you can normally see the deepest point, 185 feet below the surface, without any difficulty. The effect is mesmerizing: alligators, gar, bass, and turtles swim among grottoes and underwater gardens like goldfish in a crystal bowl. In the final analysis, though, it is the totality of the place that is most deeply satisfying. Here at its origin, the river is as beautiful as anything in Florida. The banks teem with unfrightened wild creatures: ospreys nest at aeries continuously occupied for generations; cormorants and anhingas dry out their wings; wood ducks paddle among the cypress knees. An excellent trail leads through alternating habitats in which pines, hardwood bottomlands, or cypress swamp predominates. At evening and early in the morning, deer cross your path unalarmed. In early spring, the woods are radiant with flowering dogwood.

It is quite a scene—but not a place for the fidgety who don't know how to entertain themselves. There are glass-bottomed boats and a "jungle cruise," swimming, walking, peace and quiet, and a nice dining room; but no bar or television sets. People come back here year after year, especially in the spring, so reservations need to be made well in advance. (Wakulla Springs and Lodge, Wakulla Springs, Florida, 32305; 904/222–5950 or 640–7011.)

The next stop, if you can call about a half-million acres a stop, is the **Apalachicola National Forest**, one of only two national forests that lie close to the Gulf. Before exploring this area you should pick up information concerning your special outdoors interests at the National Forest Service headquarters in Crawfordville, on the eastern edge of the forest (or, if coming from the west, at Bristol on Hwy 20). If you just drive into the area without having some idea of what you want to see and do, you may wind up feeling frustrated.

Like all national forests—and more so than some—the Apalachicola is managed for multiple use. There is a big business in logging going on all around you here, and you will see plenty of evidence of it: recently cutover boondocks, controlled burns, and so many logging roads that you could grow another large forest on the ground they take up. That many roads may be necessary for an efficient timber operation, but you wish that a lot of them were closed to general traffic, especially in late fall and early winter, when the forest is aswarm with hunters. Truth is, the public doesn't need that much access. This excess of access is a particular threat to the forest's bears, which may not sound like a matter of earth-shaking importance until you consider that this is one of the few places along the Gulf where a reputedly stable population of Deep South black bears still survives. But they can stand only so much pressure from people. Obviously, all the four-wheel-drive traffic and whizzing bullets can't be very good for their nerves. Or for the nerves of Thoreauvian campers either. So unless you're into all that yourself, I would suggest steering clear of the forest during hunting season (November through January) even though there are some designated "safe" areas.

The rest of the year, the Apalachicola is a wonderful place to be. The predominant aspect of the forest is pine flatland in various stages of growth, with a thick groundcover of gallberry and saw palmetto. But this linear landscape is relieved of any threat of monotony by the constant presence of thousands of rounded bayheads—dense, shrubby, swamp thickets of titi—large and small, background and foreground, lurking like kept secrets among the nothing-to-hide rows of pines. On drier ground in the northeast sector, the longleaf pines have an understory of scrub or turkey oak, and along the bluffs of the Apalachicola and Ochlockonee rivers there are deep hardwood forests. Each of the little creeks and branches that drain the forest has its own private swamp of cypress and tupelo intermixed with titi. In short, there are some really lovely places to explore, as long as you know what you are doing and where you are going. Keep in mind that some wet places really are impenetrable; also, that timber rattlesnakes are occasionally encountered in the pinelands and that cottonmouths are rather abundant in the swamps.

Easily the most challenging place to hike in the Apalachicola is its one certified wilderness area, the 24,000-acre Bradwell Bay Swamp in the eastern sector. But the term "hike" is used loosely here. "Wade" or "slog" would be more exact—or "dog-paddle" if the water is really high and your legs are short. A segment of the Florida Trail is being planned through this wilderness, and the rewards of venturing into it are undeniable: on higher "islands" there are stands of pine so inaccessible that they have never felt the axe, and in the heart of the area, ringed by massed walls of titi, there is a virginal tupelo swamp in which a dinosaur might feel at home. But it is easy to get lost in this beautifully inhospitable wilderness enclave. Titi thickets, like mangrove islands, tend to look alike. Even the intrepid should check with the forest staff first. In truth, I almost wish that the Florida Trail would be rerouted, or the wilderness area enlarged. There ought to be one part of this great forest that is inviolate. At the least, since the area is an important denning area for bears, it should be off-limits during the cubbing season.

There are other, less demanding places that can be reached by a short walk or wade, in particular the oak forests of Morrison Hammock Scenic Area (off Hwy 309, a few miles southwest of Sopchoppy); and, if your car can take it, there is a pretty but rutted ride along Forest Road 13 in both the eastern and western halves of the forest. Highway 65 also offers a pleasant and much easier drive, with little development along the way.

Canoeing in the Apalachicola is usually done on the Sopchoppy or the Ochlockonee. (The Apalachicola River, though fine for boating, is too wide and the current too strong to make a good canoe trail.) The Ochlockonee is itself a good-size river below the Tarquin Dam at the northern edge of the forest, but its water levels are very variable, depending on rains and water releases from Lake Tarquin to the north. Although currents can sometimes be tricky, especially after a water release, the canoeing is usually easy; and there is no shortage of campgrounds and boat ramps along the river's sixty-seven-mile course. Some canoeists may be bothered by the presence of motorboats, in which case the best, most private moments may involve short side trips into the canopied sloughs and creeks that feed the main stream. Everywhere, though, the riverine scenery is lovely, with cypress and hardwood flood plains alternating with high, piney bluffs. The fishing for bass, perch, and catfish is great. In very dry spells, usually in fall but also sometimes in March and April, some portage may be necessary, and stumps and snags can be a problem for canoes and motorboats alike.

The Sopchoppy in the eastern sector of the forest is a wonderful little stream for canoeing, and the higher up you can put in, the wilder it is. But check out the situation with the Forest Service staff. In highwater periods, you can start out at Forest Road 13, but amateurs may not want to try this since the course of the stream is apt to lose itself in the swamp for a short distance, and the vegetation crowds in really close before you reach a stretch of defined banks and pine forest. Better to put in ten miles further down at the bridge on Forest Road 329. There are some lovely cypress and hardwood forests through here as well as pine flatwoods. You should see fox squirrels and perhaps an alligator or two, and birdlife abounds. Keep your eye out especially for the red-cockaded woodpecker, one of the "Most Wanted" on the birder's list. The Apalachicola National Forest has more breeding pairs of this very rare bird than any other place in the nation.

There are about a dozen campgrounds located in the forest, some offering just the basic facilities, others well developed. The most elaborate of them is Silver Lake in the northeastern corner of the tract. This relatively small lake is lined with pines and cypress, and there is a sandy beach area where you can swim. Considering that it is right at

Tallahassee's back door, it isn't surprising that it's packed on holidays and summer weekends. The real surprise is that at most other times and seasons you will have no trouble finding a place to camp.

Almost all the other campgrounds are attractively located either on or near the Ochlockonee River, or in the southwestern part of the forest. Most have boat ramps allowing access to either the Ochlockonee or Apalachicola river. Someone planning to take I-10 or Hwy 20 through Florida's Panhandle should consider the very pleasant and rarely busy Camel Lake campground in the northwestern corner of the forest. It is about two miles off Hwy 12 on Forest Road 105. Swimming (unsupervised) is allowed in the pretty lake. (West Apalachicola National Forest, Box 578, Bristol, Florida 32321; 904/643−2477. East Apalachicola National Forest, Box 68, Crawfordville, Florida 32327; 904/926−3561.)

An even more attractive campground can be found at **Torreya State Park** about twenty miles further north, off Hwy 12 via County Road 270 or 271. Not for the first time, we are straying quite a distance away from the Coast; but this place really deserves your attention if you are anywhere in the vicinity. Briefly, the park is located on an astonishingly high (150 feet!) steep bluff, overlooking the Apalachicola River. Travelers homesick for a bit of vertical topography can do no better than to stop here. The verticality applies to ecosystems as well as topography. The powerful river has cut through one layered life zone after another as though it were a knife. Cypress swamps yield to hardwood bottomlands, and these give way to narrow ravines, loud with rushing water, and steep slopes thick with hickories, ash, beech, and oakleaf hydrangea, all climbing to the highest crests crowned by magnolias and tall pines. Each of these life zones can be seen along the excellent seven-mile hiking trail that encircles the park. The naturalist will be fascinated by the presence of the Torreya yew, an unpretentious little tree (otherwise known, rather unkindly, as "stinking cedar" because of the odor of its leaves) that is unique to this area.The forests here are said to have much the same composition as those in the Appalachian chain that ends 250 miles further north. In the fall there is a brilliant coloration that would almost do credit to New England. And at any season you will probably have plenty of elbow room in this lightly visited park. (Torreya State Park, Star Route, Bristol, Florida 32321; 904/643−2674.)

While we are traveling through this inland section of northern Florida, canoeists should take note of the Chipola River and **Dead Lakes State Recreation Area** just west of the Apalachicola River and its namesake forest. If you are a canoeist, you can put in on the Chipola north of I-10 at Florida Caverns State Park on Hwy 166, or the public boat ramp at Hwy 167, or the Merritts Mill Pond dam at Hwy 90. A one-day trip will take you as far as Hwy 274 or the rest area on Hwy 20. A two-day trip will enable you to reach Dead Lakes State Recreation Area. The canoeing is easy, and there usually aren't too many motorboats on the river. However, the banks along the upper reaches are generally high, so there isn't much swamp scenery; and fields and pastures often come right down to the water's edge. If your destination is Dead Lakes, however, you will find swamps aplenty. Be alert when you get there: this is a very extensive flooded area in which a deep forest of young cypress is growing out of the ruins of an older one that was evidently killed by natural changes in river water levels. Even at this immature stage the cypress create the majestic effect so peculiar to their species. However, this flooded forest can seem like a hall of mirrors if you drift too far into it, and you may become temporarily lost. Since most local people only come here on day visits to fish, the campground at Dead Lakes State Recreation Area on the western edge of the lakes is usually not crowded. (Dead Lakes State Recreation Area, Box 989, Wewahitchka, Florida 32465; 904/639–2702.)

The Coastal Route Along Apalachicola Bay

During the entire journey along Florida's Gulf Coast, we have only encountered a couple of uncondominiumized beaches since leaving Everglades National Park about eight hundred miles ago. Marshes and swamps, of course, are the ecological equivalent of Ali Baba's cave. But still, it would be pleasant to have a chance to rediscover what an unspoiled Florida beach is like. And here at last, on the state's northern coast, we find a few places where we can do just that.

The town of Apalachicola is the handiest jumping-off place for these local expeditions. Besides, in its own right, it is an appealing place to pause. Its only claim to fame—a considerable one—is the fact that a local physician, Dr. John Gorrie, invented the first artificial refrigeration here while trying to devise a primitive air-conditioning unit to make his patients comfortable. That was 140 years ago. It would take about a century before the air-conditioning part of his idea became a household item. But air-conditioning aside, Dr. Gorrie's town is a comfortable place to be. I wish there were more coastal towns like this. Nary a highrise or huge shopping mall in sight—just neat, modest homes on quiet, shady streets, with live cattle egrets rather than plaster ducks on the lawns. And an old-fashioned downtown with some wooden storefronts left and streets that all seem to lead to views of fishing boats and the Gulf. There are also some excellent, unfancy seafood restaurants in this vicinity; so ask around.

The first of the beaches we want to visit lies just offshore on St. George Island. The toll bridge at Eastpoint, completed in 1965—by which time Floridians should have known better than to build it—has opened much of this fragile island to heavy development that will inevitably do it lasting harm. The good thing about the bridge is that it provides visitors with a panoramic view of why this barrier island and others like it should be left alone. The vast expanse of Apalachicola

Bay, cradled by St. George's slender arm, lies all around us. These shallow waters, enriched by the Apalachicola River's hampered but still nutritive flow, are the nursery ground for an inconceivable wealth of marine life, which supports the most important fishery in the eastern Gulf. In season, there are hundreds of oystermen out here in their skiffs, raking up oysters with handheld tongs. The birds are here in force too: great blue herons, cormorants, pelicans, terns, gulls, all getting their share of the bounty spilling from this estuarine cornucopia. For now, at least, it is a gladdening scene.

St. George Island State Park happily protects the eastern end of this vulnerable island. Here there is a nine-mile reach of sand and dunes and (usually) moderate surf, interrupted only twice by the shelters and restrooms of beach-use areas. One of the very best things about this park is that, except for summer weekends when it does get crowded, there are more crows and mooching red-winged blackbirds at the picnic tables than there are people. Almost anywhere, you have the beach practically to yourself.

The great thing about this place is that everything is so absolutely pared down. After the byzantine richness of the bottomlands and marshes, the spaces and textures here seem almost spartan in their clean simplicity. In this respect, St. George differs even from the beachscapes at St. Vincent and St. Joseph, which we'll get to shortly. Here nothing is immoderate, except when a tropical storm rams the surf halfway across the island. The beach is narrow. The dunes directly behind it are often almost low enough to look over. On the bay side, the slash pines are pretty straight and close together in the vicinity of East Cove, but they never get impressively tall. Further east they thin out, dwindling to two or three little stands holding on for dear life at the island's end. All the modest vegetation out here—sea oats, yaupon holly, rosemary, woody goldenrod—is doing the same thing: holding on, and, in the process, holding the island together. Sometimes it doesn't work. The most imposing sight is of the inland dunes moving steadily bayward in the midsection of the park. They are as white as snowbanks and reach considerable heights. Sticking out of them are the tops of pine trees that are being buried alive. A couple of boardwalk trails lead you carefully over these too-volatile sands and take you through the pines to the bay, where oystercatchers, black-bellied plovers, willets, and dunlins make a living in the sandy shallows. Once, in the sparse grass, I was lucky enough to see the rare Gulf salt marsh snake that makes its home here.

There is an attractive, if sometimes buggy, primitive campsite on East Cove at the end of a three-mile trail. As yet the park has no developed campground, but I am told that one is being contemplated. Much as I would like to use it myself, I hope it never materializes—partly because the dunes can stand only so much recreational use, but also because there is an elegant simplicity to this place that is easily destroyed by too many human voices. This is a park that needs to be more-or-less left alone. It should be mostly left to people who need to feel left alone for a while. (St. George Island State Park, Box 62, East-point, Florida 32328; 904/670–2111.)

St. Joseph Peninsula State Park, just around the horn of Flor-ida's Big Bend, sticks out into the Gulf like the arm of a ninety-eight-pound weakling who is trying to flex his muscle. It is like St. George the way two brothers are often alike: there's a family resemblance, they're both loved, but they don't have much in common. When I first visited St. Joseph about twenty years ago, almost the entire peninsula was uninhabited. I remember the pervasive sour-sweet odor, not un-like that of fermenting malt or an overripe corpse, that emanated from the huge St. Joe Paper Mill across the bay. I also remember being grateful for that smell, thinking that it would keep this corner of Flor-ida safe from the developers as long as the mill endured. Well, the mill is still there, and so is the aroma when the wind is coming from the north; but developers are a hardy breed, and this was, after all, the last privately owned beach on the Florida Gulf Coast that was innocent of A-frames and condos. So now it has lost its innocence. All the more reason, then, to hold our nose and be grateful that 2500 incredibly lovely acres at the end of the peninsula still exist.

There are two sizable campgrounds here, one beside a pretty pond and the other in a dense stand of cabbage palms and pines that allows for privacy. Both are very popular in late spring and summer, when people come here to fish, swim, go crabbing, collect shells, and sun themselves; so you should make reservations well in advance. There are also a considerable number of rentable cabins being built on St. Joseph Bay, part of a legislative policy that encourages the state park system to pay its own way. To all this human bustle must be added the after-dark comings and goings of large numbers of raccoons and skunks. The animals understandably delight most campers; but they are confirmed shoplifters and will carry off a T-bone or a loaf of bread in a second if it's left unguarded. To add insult to injury, they may keep you awake for an hour—if the transistor radio in the tent next-door does not—while they bicker over their loot in the nearby bushes.

But never mind! Belive me, St. Joseph is worth these daunting pioneer perils, and the occasional bug bite as well. The people, camp-grounds, cabins, and marauding beasties, plus boat ramp and marina, are all located at the southernmost end of the park. Beyond lie miles of some of the most splendid coastal scenery on the Gulf, much of it an official wilderness. The scale here is much grander than at St. George. The dunes are enormous, and the white beach has a fine, wide berm. There is a real interior to this island, too, albeit a narrow one. It is crowded with slash pines and pine scrub, watered by small freshwater ponds, and frequented by deer, deer flies, and the occa-sional fox or bobcat. On the bay side are sand banks, marshes, palm hammocks, and pine flatlands. Either shore makes for pretty easy walking, but inland hiking is hard work because of the deep, dry sand. Hikers who wish to explore the last five miles of the island, the wilderness area, must register before starting out. Primitive camping is permitted, but the number of users at one time is necessarily restricted.

Whether roughing it or not. your best time to be at St. Joseph is in fall or early spring. True, you stand a better chance of catching the aroma from the St. Joe Paper Mill, but the crowds will have thinned out. And in fall (late September and all of October) there is a special attraction: the peninsula is a focal point for eastern hawks on their annual migration. Since the birds fly around the Gulf rather than across it on their southward journey, St. Joseph is the natural funneling point where they must turn to head west. In the wake of a cold front, more than a thousand buteos and accipiters may congregate at the peninsula in a single day. Sharp-shinned and Cooper's hawks, which under other circumstances are not easily seen, are the most abundant species here; but there are also good numbers of kestrels, northern harriers, and red-tailed and red-shouldered hawks. Most thrilling of all is the possibility of seeing the endangered peregrine falcon, which is sighted at least a few times every fall. With or without that bonus, though, the gathering of large numbers of migrating hawks is one of the most remarkable shows that Nature puts on, an exalting sight for wildlife lovers in general and birders in particular. If you're here at the right season, be sure to check with the park staff

St. Joseph Peninsula. *Photo by Florida Division of Tourism.*

about weather conditions and the best observation posts. (St. Joseph Peninsula State Park, Box 909, Port St. Joe, Florida 32456; 904/227–1327.)

Our last stop in the Apalachicola area is also the least accessible, and for that reason among others, perhaps the best of all. This is **St. Vincent National Wildlife Refuge**. It is a blocky, 12,000-acre wedge at the western end of Apalachicola Bay. Exploring it is like wandering through some grand house in which each room is furnished in a different way. Where to begin? There are the beaches, of course, about fourteen unspoiled miles of them mostly on the Gulf side. Driftwood, shells, expired horseshoe crabs, delicious coon oysters, and assorted flotsam and jetsam lend themselves to beachcombing; pelicans cruise the surf; shorebirds and terns move in as the tide moves out. In summer, the heavy, scuffled track of a loggerhead may lead beyond the high-tide mark to the spot (which you must not disturb, of course) where she has buried her eggs. Where the beach ends, the dunes begin, an undulant swath two hundred yards wide that finally comes to a halt against a twenty-foot-high ridge lined with a lovely, if battered, forest of live oaks. Behind it the sandy slope descends to the pine flatlands and palmetto thickets. In this quiet world the sad, sweet call of the white-throated sparrow or the ebullient song of the Carolina wren sounds with a startling clarity. So does the startled rush of a wild hog or a deer. If you've glimpsed the latter, by the way, it may or may not have been a native whitetail. There are also Indian sambur deer on the island, naturalized citizens left over from the days when this was a private hunting preserve. They and the other game species, including resident flocks of wild turkey, are pretty wary, since they are legally hunted in the fall (to keep them from eating themselves out of house and home) and illegally poached year-round. But if you move quietly, you should see several of their vanishing backsides in any lengthy exploration of St. Vincent.

You may see a snake or two, since the island has an abundance of them. They will most likely be harmless rat snakes, black racers, or water snakes; but there are also quite a few rattlesnakes and cottonmouths on hand. You should have no problem as long as you stick to the grid of jeep trails that crisscrosses the island. Especially in the eastern and northern sections, these tracks will lead you to that incomparably beautiful combination of freshwater ponds, salt marsh, and cabbage palm hammock that is such a characteristic part of Florida's coastal scene. At the eastern end of the island, this combination is made more perfect by the presence of a narrow "Tahitian" beach, regrettably eroding, which is backed by tall palms instead of dunes.

For all its beauty and ecological fascination, St. Vincent is not set up for visitors. It is a refuge, after all, not a park. You can pick up information at the refuge headquarters on Hwy 30 directly across from the island's western tip; but you should know in advance that only

St. Vincent Island. *Photo by Florida Division of Tourism.*

day use is ordinarily permitted, that facilities, including drinking water, are nonexistent, and that transportation to the island is not provided. You will need to supply your own boat or hire one at Indian Pass or somewhere else nearby. And, last but not least, you should expect a welcoming committee of mosquitoes and biting flies during warm-weather months. A day at St. Vincent is more than worth all of these inconveniences, but it helps to be prepared for them. (St. Vincent National Wildlife Refuge, Box 447, Apalachicola, Florida 32320; 904/653–8808.)

Unless you're in the mood for a Coney Island atmosphere, you will probably want to give Panama City a wide berth by heading north on Hwy 65 or Hwy 71. If you have time, you can find a pleasant campground in Apalachicola National Forest or at Dead Lakes State Recreation Area and explore the surrounding area (see above). When you are ready to move on, head west on Hwy 20. The miles of commercial pine forests along this road may not qualify as the most exciting scenery in the world, but they beat the heavy traffic and billboards on Hwy 98 or the beachy funk along Alt. 98, Panama City's "scenic" route.

6

From Florida's Panhandle to New Orleans

At a glance

Access   Major air terminals on this part of the Gulf Coast are at Tallahassee, Mobile, and New Orleans. Other cities, notably Pensacola and Gulfport, can also be conveniently reached by air. The main east-west highway is I-10. Hwy 98, which hugs the Coast, takes much longer to travel but offers a more varied scene. In the Panhandle, Hwy 20 is a handy means of skirting the Panama City area.

Climate   Along the northern Gulf Coast, fall and especially spring are gorgeous, although don't expect much autumn coloration. Winter is iffy, with hard freezes or heavy rains a possibility; but the chilly season rarely starts before December, and even then there are usually a lot of nice days too. Summer is hot, with temperatures often in the nineties, but it only lasts about four months (June through September).

Topography and Landscape Features   On most of this part of the Gulf the land mass of the continent has more elevation to it, so the coastal plain is relatively narrow. At their high-water marks, prehistoric seas built up massive dune ridges, now pine-covered hills, that begin not far inland. In other periods, when the ancient seas were lower than they are now, rivers gouged out deep valleys that have become the great bays at Mobile and Pensacola. Alluvial deposits from these rivers have provided the building materials for a vital string of barrier islands with wide, white beaches.

Flora and Fauna   Wherever the ground is high and dry enough, great forests of slash and longleaf pine, growing both in natural woodlands and plantations, dominate this region, usually in association with understories of dogwood, yaupon, and wax myrtle. However,

115

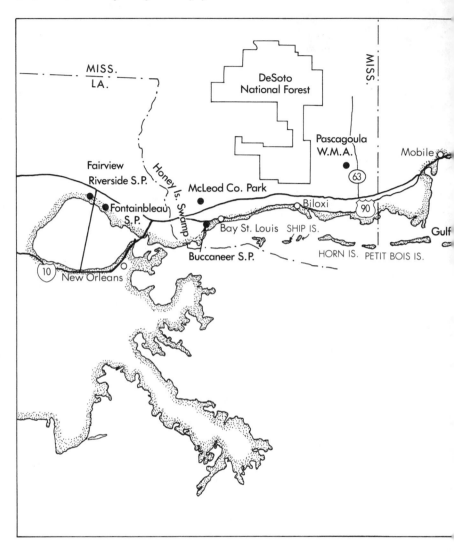

thousands of waterways, from tiny creeks to large rivers, create over-flow zones ranging from a few yards to a few miles wide. In these damp "bottomlands," hardwood forests flourish. Oaks, magnolia, sweet gum, red maples, and hickories predominate where the season-al overflows are not very frequent or long-lasting. In low-lying swamps, cypress and tupelo take over. The bottomland forests are ide-al habitat for many wildlife species, including bobcat, gray fox, deer, gray squirrel, and a great variety of resident and migrant songbirds. The piney woods are home to bobwhite quail, fox squirrels, armadil-los, and the rare gopher tortoise. Where the waterways meet the Gulf, estuarine marshes and bays—protected by barrier islands—have cre-ated a vital nursery for marine life. This entire northern coast of the

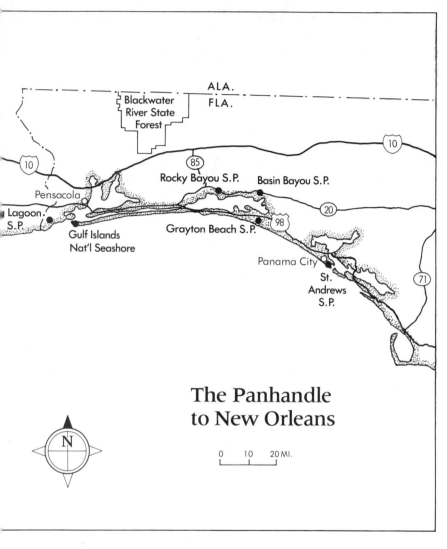

ALA.
FLA.

Blackwater
River State
Forest

Rocky Bayou S.P.   Basin Bayou S.P.

Pensacola

Lagoon.
S.P.

Gulf Islands
Nat'l Seashore

Grayton Beach S.P.

Panama City

St.
Andrews
S.P.

The Panhandle to New Orleans

N

0   10   20 MI.

Gulf, from Apalachicola Bay westward, is called the "fertile crescent" because of its productive fisheries.

Camping   There are many public facilities for RV and primitive campers on this part of the Coast. The largest RV campgrounds located right on the Gulf are at the Fort Pickens sector of the Gulf Islands National Seashore and Alabama's Gulf State Park. Both are crowded during warm months. However, there are a number of smaller state parks on the back bays that are not quite so heavily used. Inland, Blackwater River State Forest (Florida) and De Soto National Forest (Mississippi) are likely camping prospects. So is the Pascagoula Wildlife Management Area in Mississippi when hunting season isn't under way. In western Mississippi and eastern Louisiana, respectively, Buccaneer and Fountainbleau state parks are good stopovers. For primitive campers, Horn and Petit Bois islands offer an exceptional experience.

Hiking, Canoeing, Boating, Etc.   Although there are wonderful nature trails at some of the parks on the Gulf, and miles of sand for beachcombers, serious hikers will prefer the long trails in the Blackwater River and De Soto forests, or the more haphazard rambling along maintenance lanes in the Pascagoula bottomlands. For canoeists, the Blackwater and its tributaries (Florida), the Perdido (Florida-Alabama), the Escatawpa (Alabama-Mississippi), and Black Creek (Mississippi) are some of the better-known canoe trails. The Pascagoula and Honey Island swamps are ideal for canoeists who are also swamp freaks, but heed the advice in the travelogue. For boaters, as usual, "the water's the limit"—lots of rivers, swamps, bays, and islands to explore.

Outdoors Highlights   The Santa Rosa Island section of Gulf Islands National Seashore; Horn, Petit Bois, and East Ship islands; Big Lagoon State Park; Blackwater River State Forest; De Soto National Forest; Pascagoula Wildlife Management Area; Honey Island Swamp.

If you follow Hwy 20 west, or I-10 for that matter, prepare to feel pleasantly indecisive about the wealth of unpublicized outdoors opportunities that lies ahead. Once again, there are coastal or inland routes to consider. And, again, much depends on your preferences. Inland lie the rolling, piney hills and clear, sandy streams—great for canoeing and hiking—that characterize the Blackwater River State Forest. On the Coast are protected stretches of unspoiled beach, several small but biologically interesting parks, more old forts than you will probably have time to visit, and bays, ramps, and fish enough to keep the most addicted boater happy. In either direction there are a number of public campgrounds to choose from.

If you want to spend an easeful day weighing the options, either the **Basin Bayou** or **Rocky Bayou State Recreation Area** is at your disposal—unless, of course, both are filled up. They lie near one another on Hwy 20 as it follows the edge of Choctawatchee Bay. Basin Bayou is a good place to launch a small boat, splash around in the shallow water, and set up camp for the night under low but shady oaks. While cooking the fish you just may have caught, you can admire the view of the great bay and, in the distance, the barrier beach that shields it from the Gulf. The only trouble with this tiny park is that, notwithstanding a short nature trail in the pine woods, there really isn't much room to move around. (Basin Bayou State Recreation Area, P.O. Box 278, Freeport, Florida 32439; 904/835–3761.)

Rocky Bayou is the more interesting of the two parks. It lacks the bayside view, but the camping area faces the pleasing if less spacious prospect of Rocky Bayou itself (actually a bay within a bay). Along with a boat ramp that gives access to both freshwater and saltwater fishing, and a pretty picnic and swimming area, the park has enough space to allow for a bit of exploring. Three different nature trails lead through a complex little ecosystem in which the vegetation changes character each time you pass over a sand ridge, descend into a swale, or walk at water's edge. Southern red cedar and sand pine, that runty, hard-living species peculiar to Florida, have an advantage in these poor soils, but turkey oak, longleaf pine, and yucca also hold their own. Wherever the soil gets a bit richer, live oaks, magnolia, and holly assert themselves. In fact, the trail leading to the bayou passes through a forest that, with its ferns and moss and lichen, suggests those of the great hardwood bottomlands awaiting us a little further to the west. The longest and most interesting of the trails, however, is the one that leads along Puddin Head Lake, a manmade impoundment that doesn't look manmade. The woodlands here were heavily damaged by a hurricane in 1975, but, except for a certain openness in the canopy, you wouldn't guess that now.

I think you will like this friendly back-bay park. There is nothing here that is very spectacular, but this is what the sandy country behind the great dunes and bays of the Florida Panhandle really looks like: bright green in the bough, tough at the root. If there is one complaint it is that wildlife is not much in evidence here, except for cardinals, towhees, and some of the other more familiar songbirds. Alligators are supposed to be in residence at Puddin Head Lake, but they and any wading birds in the vicinity were keeping out of sight when I was there. On the other hand, the fishing is usually good enough to inspire anglers to come back for more. (Rocky Bayou State Recreation Area, P.O. Box 597, Niceville, Florida 32578; 904/897–3222.)

Inland to Blackwater River State Forest

Blackwater River State Forest is one of Florida's better-kept secrets, at least as far as out-of-staters are concerned. Millions of vacationers zip through the Panhandle along I-10 without knowing that its 180,000 acres lie just a few miles away.

The forest spans a (for Florida) high, relatively hilly region where sandy loam topsoils cover reddish or orange clays—an intimation of the bright red clays that predominate further to the north. This is the land of the longleaf pine. Although the state forest is managed to accommodate the faster growing slash pine as well as the longleaf, there are innumerable views of the longleaf barrens that once blanketed all of the Deep South's hill country. As in the case of most southern pines, fire is and always has been the great arbiter in the longleaf's life cycle, clearing out the hardwood understories that would otherwise overwhelm it. Even the youngest longleaf, knee high to a rabbit, has an exceptional capacity to withstand the flames. You will see many of these scorched but alive little pines if you visit the forest in late winter after the season of controlled burns. However, you may not recognize them for what they are. Longleafs, unlike other pines, grow as a single, branchless stalk for their first few years while they establish a root system. In their infancy they are often mistaken for tufts of wire grass; a little later, the only thing they resemble is an endearing but very hairy green hobbit. Yet when they grow up, they are the noblest of southern pines: long-needled and with boughs that lift up like menorahs, supporting in the spring eight-inch buds that look like candles. A great unencumbered stand of them, straight as grenadiers, with needles shining in the sunlight as though sheathed in ice, comes as close as the vegetable world ever gets to looking like a Marine regiment on parade.

One other thing about the character of longleaf pines before I let the subject drop: some afternoon, if there is a halfway decent breeze blowing, listen to them. The soughing of the wind in their branches is one of the most disturbingly lovely sounds in nature.

It would not do if the Blackwater River State Forest were populated exclusively with slash and longleaf pines. Most wildlife require a diversified habitat, and fortunately there is enough of that to go around here. In between burns, wax myrtle, gallberry, huckleberry, and yaupon, as well as many wildflowers, form a low understory amid the pines—the favored haunt of quail, pine warblers, pileated woodpeckers, armadillos, and the increasingly rare gopher tortoise. Walking through the forest, you will probably notice evidence of the armadillo, one of the few wild creatures that has actually expanded its range in recent decades. Demolished fire-ant hills testify to its fondness for ant eggs, and small holes in the path indicate where it has rooted for worms or grubs. You may even see the animal itself hustling around in its suit of armor. Armadillos are usually nocturnal, but occasionally they emerge from their burrows in broad daylight, especially during a drought when they have to work long hours to make a living. If one does cross your path, don't be surprised by its seeming boldness. The truth is that this comical-looking little creature is not very bright. (Incidentally, any burrow that you come upon in the piney hills is likely to have been dug by an armadillo, but double-check to be sure. If the entrance looks better suited to admit a salad bowl than a football, you have probably discovered the home of the shy gopher tortoise, who should not, of course, be disturbed.)

It will surprise no one that the Blackwater River State Forest boasts a river named Blackwater River. But all the other major streams in and near the forest—Sweetwater, Juniper Creek, Coldwater, Perdido—could answer to the same name. In fact, in Alabama and Mississippi, several rivers do. They all have in common waters that are clear but darkly stained by the tannin from cypress and other trees along their banks. In itself, this would be no news to us; in our tour we have already encountered many rivers the color of strong tea. The difference here is that the rivers are not traveling between limestone ridges or through deep swamps. Instead, they run mile after mile across beds of white sand—sand that also forms berms along their shores. The contrast between dark water and white banks is very striking, very beautiful. And it is intensified by the hues of the accompanying forest: blue-green in summer, but shot through with vermillion (sweet gum and red maple) and gold (yellow poplar) in late autumn. There are some cypress and tupelo along the way, as well as pure stands of water-loving white cedar (locally called juniper), but this is not swamp country; you can climb ashore almost anywhere, and there are many sandbars on which to picnic and camp. Except for the occasional little blue or great blue heron, the wading birds are regrettably absent and alligators are scarce. But songbirds abound, and wild turkey, raccoons, and deer are sometimes glimpsed at the water's edge. Bass, perch, and catfish are present in these rivers, but the angler will have better luck at the forest's three stocked lakes—Bear, Karick, and Hurricane—where boating (electric motors only) is permitted.

As you might guess, this is superb hiking and canoeing country. A twenty-one-mile segment of the Florida Trail crosses the forest diagonally. It follows the Andrew Jackson Red Ground Trail, which was one of the earliest trade routes for Indians and settlers in western Florida. There are primitive campsites along the way and many places where you can peel off your clothes and take a refreshing dip. A four-and-a-half-mile trail begins at the Krul Campground and intersects with the Red Ground Trail. The canoeing, when it's good, is very, very good, but when it's bad—during serious dry spells—it can be anything but, at least in places. The Blackwater River and the other waterways in this area are undredged, unspoiled; they must be treasured on that account alone. But their naturalness implies dealing with a fair measure of snags and fallen trees during low-water periods, usually in summer and fall. By all means check at the state forest headquarters at Munson; or in Milton or Bagdad, both just north of I-10, where there are canoe rental and transportation services. In either of those little towns you can also rent inner tubes and spend a glorious afternoon floating downstream on your fanny.

There is no lack of camping opportunities in the forest, although the developed recreational sites can get crowded in summer. Three campgrounds have electric hookups: Coldwater, which is reached via a marked turnoff from Hwy 191 several miles south of Munson; Blackwater River, in the small state park located in the southwestern corner of the forest; and Krul, just off Hwy 4 a few miles east of Munson. There are five other comfortable campgrounds that have showers, flush toilets, and other home comforts. Four of these are located in the northeastern part of the forest. The fifth, Bear Lake, is centrally located on Hwy 4, a couple of miles east of the Krul Campground.

Besides these developed campgrounds, there are several primitive campsites that can be reached by car, as well as a couple along the Red Ground Trail. (Blackwater River State Forest, Route 1, Box 77, Milton, Florida 32570; 904/957−4111.)

The Seashore Route in West Florida and Alabama

West Florida   In a quest for unspoiled beach on Florida's Panhandle, you can pretty much forget about the shoreline east of Navarre, which we have bypassed. It gets a lot of traffic, and most of it is being intensively exploited. True, there are fine beaches at St. Andrews and Grayton Beach state parks that you may want to be aware of, but campsites are hopelessly packed during the warm months, especially at St. Andrews, where the early summer use compares with the winter congestion at parks in the Florida Keys. Not that campsites and hookups are always a cinch to find in the parks to our west, but there is less hassle getting to them, and they usually boast more miles of beach where the Robinson Crusoe in us can have free rein.

Florida's part of **Gulf Islands National Seashore** is the major case in point. About four million people visit one part of the seashore or another each year; but there are parts of the beach that are almost always deserted, though you may have to do some walking to reach them. The easternmost part of the seashore, on Santa Rosa Island, is a good example. (If you are on Hwy 20, take Hwy 85 south to Hwy 98, then head west until you reach Navarre, where you can cross the causeway to the beach. If you are traveling on I-10, follow Hwy 87 to the causeway.) At Navarre Beach, take Hwy 399 west (after picking up what you need for a picnic if you plan to stop during the next ten or fifteen miles). Within a few minutes you will have traded the beachfront developments for a world of white dunes, sea oats, laughing gulls, long sloping beaches with tidal sandbars, a moderate surf, and all the Gulf sea and sky you could ever want. For most of these first miles, there is not that visual complication—which I, for one, miss— of an attendant forest, or even a sizable marsh, in the bayside background; the planes are all horizontal, unless you want to count the sometimes impressive rise of the frontal dunes. In this world there are few shadows and no shade.

There are also no legal pull-overs until you reach an authorized parking space some miles past the entry point. The dunes are simply too vulnerable to stand the random pitter-patter of droves of tourist feet. Speaking of which—this is a good place to pause and contemplate the sea oat, not least of all because there isn't much around in the way of other vegetation for us to contemplate. This modest yellow grain is a hero among growing things, if also something of a masochist. Unlike nearly all other plants on the northern Gulf Coast, it does not mind being doused with salt spray or scorched by the sun or buried in drifting sand. Though pretty sparse-looking above ground, it has an amazing root system that spreads for yards around it. When it is buried, it simply grows more roots near the new surface of the dune, creating a veritable net that holds the sand in place. In time, the anchored dune becomes a wall behind which other courageous plants such as bayberry and beach pea can find shelter, and eventually even trees can take root. The system is hardly perfect, of course; storms and littoral drift often have their way with barrier islands. But without the stabilizing effect of the humble sea oat, there would be no dunes and therefore no islands at all. And without them, there would not be productive estuarine sounds like the one behind us, or any hurricane protection for the towns and cities on the mainland shore. No wonder that Floridians take a protective view of this protective plant. Leave it to the red-winged blackbirds to spread the seed around. If you so much as pick a stalk, you will have not only your ecological conscience to deal with, but the chance of a five-hundred-dollar fine.

Beyond this Santa Rosa stretch of wilderness beach lies, for contrast, touristy Pensacola Beach, connected to its namesake city by a long causeway. Except for a small historic area, Pensacola is not what you would call picturesque, but it has the easy virtue of an interesting past. Once the resort of pirates, prostitutes, and other riffraff, the town has probably been burned, pillaged, and traded back and forth by more nations than any other community in the United States. Some uncharitable visitors have expressed regret that those processes were ever discontinued. Yet we have Pensacola and its former city fathers to thank for the preservation of the western end of Santa Rosa Island, a move that made its eventual inclusion in the Gulf Islands National Seashore possible.

This Fort Pickens sector of the Seashore, to the west of Pensacola Beach, gets a lot of use, but then, there is a lot of beach to go around. The first five miles past the entrance station cover a dune terrain much like that of the stretch between Navarre and Pensacola Beach. There are a couple of places to park and get to the beach, and even at the height of the summer season you can have a lot of beach to yourself if you're willing to walk far enough to find it. Most of the time, though, a hike isn't necessary. The swimming and tanning are all you could ask for, and there are usually interesting shells to pick up, or black skimmers, willets, and terns to admire, or the comically busy little sanderling to laugh at. The damp sand is satisfactory for castle building.

At the western tip, where the island quadruples its average width, you will find on the bay side that lovely mix of marshes, weathered live oaks, and stands of slash pine that I, for one, find as irresistible as the beach itself. There is a fine nature trail through these interlocking life zones that allows you a close look at how they were shaped by the interaction of land and sea. In the spartina grass marshes, great blue herons and egrets go about their ancient business, and raccoon tracks mark the sand.

The visitor with a feel for history will also love Fort Pickens, one of the most renovated of the forts along the Gulf Coast. It has the distinction of being the only federal fort north of the Keys to successfully resist capture by the Confederates during the Civil War. A couple of decades later, it housed as prisoners the famed Geronimo and his followers.

Along with all that, there are more amenities than any reasonable person could ask for: fishing jetties, bicycle trail, concessionaire and laundromat, scuba diving, etc. There is only one problem: finding a campsite. No reservations are accepted; so during warm-weather months you may have to get there very early in the day if you hope to find a spot. (Gulf Islands National Seashore, P.O. Box 100, Gulf Breeze, Florida 32561; 904/932–5302.)

Wonderful as Gulf Islands is, the western side of Pensacola Bay is far and away the better bet for misanthropes, introverts, primitive campers, or people who just want a no-fuss place to set up for the night. Those who desire the basic campground comforts will like **Big Lagoon State Park**, on the sound behind Perdido Key. The park is far enough off the beaten track to escape all but summer weekend and holiday crowds, and even then, you can usually squeeze in. You have to keep alert to get there, though, since road maps are not detailed enough to straighten out the tangle of county roads in the area. The simplest procedure is to take Hwy 98 west from Panama City, turn south on Hwy 293, and keep going. Or you can follow County Road 292 to its junction with County Road 297 and then turn east on the latter road.

When you reach the park, the austerity of the terrain may at first surprise you. This is what Rocky Bayou would look like if that park had been sandblasted. The basic behind-the-lagoon ecosystem is the same, but here the ridges were more recently sand dunes, and the whole area is still exposed to the tantrums of the Gulf. As a result, the sand pines and scrub oaks look exceptionally oppressed: stunted and twisted by wind and wave. But they have the severe bonsai beauty that goes with that kind of treatment. Indeed, there are whole areas that look like Japanese sand gardens. Not that all of the park is like that. Where the ridges offer some protection, groves of trees grow fairly tall. The campsites are not very shaded but are otherwise okay, and there are swimming areas, a boat ramp, and an observation tower that overlooks Big Lagoon and the barrier island, Perdido Key, that shelters it somewhat from the Gulf. (Big Lagoon State Recreation Area, Route 1, Box 350, Pensacola, Florida 32507; 904/492–1595.)

If you just want peace and quiet, sun and sand, and the opportunity to do some primitive camping, you should consider the **Perdido Key** part of the Gulf Islands National Seashore. The simplest way of getting there is from Hwy 98, via Hwy 293. When Hwy 293 joins 292, follow the latter road. If you are coming east from Gulf Shores, follow Alabama State Road 182. Park at Johnson Beach, where there are picnic grounds and restrooms, and then head east along the shore, carrying all supplies, including water and sun shade, with you. There are six or seven miles of nothing but sand and surf ahead, and you can cover as much of it as you wish. The landscape here is oddly level, without even much in the way of dunes to break the flatness. There is good reason for this. In 1979, Perdido took a terrific beating from a hurricane while defending the mainland just behind it. A six-foot-high storm surge swept across the island's width. Presumably, with time and a little help from the sea oats, Perdido will build its once tall dunes anew. Meanwhile, the poor island looks a bit bland and featureless. But no matter; there is always the bright, changeful edge of the Gulf itself, offering all the beachcombing and swimming you could wish for. (For information, contact the Gulf Islands National Seashore, address above.)

Alabama   The same hurricane that flattened Perdido Key in 1979 made a mess of Alabama's Gulf Shores, crunching beach houses, snapping trees in half, and kicking mobile homes around as though they were tin cans. Far from discouraging development on this vulnerable coast, however, the hurricane seems to have stimulated it. Apparently, the logic is that hurricanes never strike twice in the same place, which actually is no more true of hurricanes than it is of lightning. Anyway, as you drive along the coast (Hwy 182) between Gulf Beach and Gulf Shores, a growing number of condominiums—some not bad-looking—rise between you and the open Gulf. So much for sea oats, dune protection, and sane land zoning. Midway in this advancing tide of construction, however, comes a welcome break: for two-and-a-half miles, the beach, as well as several thousand acres of real estate behind it, belong to the state of Alabama.

We are at **Gulf State Park**. Alabama, of course, does not have much frontage on the Gulf Coast, so this large recreation area is the state's one-shot effort to outclass the dozen-odd well-run parks along Florida's Panhandle. And if the measure of success is the diversity of entertainments and facilities, Alabama wins hands down. You could almost hold the Democratic Convention here if delegates brought along their Winnebagos. There are nearly five hundred improved campsites, one large motel complex, a convention center, rustic cabins, an eighteen-hole golf course, three lakes, two pavilions, and no doubt a partridge in a pine tree. In the vicinity of the campgrounds you can follow several short, connecting nature trails through groves of live oaks, pines, and palmetto or along marshy lake edges where alligators can sometimes be observed. Also, canoes (summer only) and rowboats can be rented and used to commute between three sizable lakes behind the dunes. But despite these pleasant activities, and because of them, this is definitely not a park for anyone who wants to get away from it all. By way of compensation for so much intensive development, park officials have wisely set aside a large preservation area to the east of the campgrounds. Here the vulnerable secondary and interior dune systems, with their forests and thickets of slash and sand pine, oaks, yaupon, and titi, are necessarily closed to the public. There is just too much "public" on hand, and this type of country cannot stand a lot of trampling.

Gulf State Park's strong suit is its beautiful public beach. The beach area can't quite escape the development that parenthesizes it at either end; but there is plenty of room to move around, and the sand is as white here as sand ever gets. At the western end, an 825-foot fishing pier offers you the chance to try your luck with rod and reel, or even a cane pole. (Gulf State Park, Route 2, Box 9, Gulf Shores, Alabama 36542; 205/968–6353.)

Gulf State Park, Alabama.

At the western tip of Gulf Shores, well beyond the community itself and the development that encroaches further and further along Bon Secour Bay, lies **Fort Morgan State Park**. The fort has seen more action than most of its coastal brethren; its strategic position, and that of Fort Gaines across the channel, kept the port of Mobile in Confederate hands until the last months of the Civil War. Although the layout is star-shaped, its aspect is much like that of other Gulf Coast forts—massive, red-brick walls with large, arched tunnels leading to the sunlit parade ground at its center. A nice natural touch has lent itself: colonies of barn swallows, not very common on the Coast, nest in these medieval-looking passageways. Their wheeling, dipping flight in spring makes a delicate contrast with all the brick heaviness roundabout.

You can swim and fish here, and a boat ramp is being planned. But this is a very small park, and there is no camping. For me, the major attractions are the handsome, rambling, nineteenth-century wooden buildings outside the fort, only one of them restored; and the bayside clusters of oaks, pines, wax myrtle, and palmetto, which, in spring especially, are aswarm with birds—indigo buntings, pine warblers, cardinals, nuthatches, and many others.

Mobile: If you're in a hurry, I-10 will get you across the northern reaches of immense Mobile Bay, and through Mobile itself, in no time at all. But the city is worth your attention. The Spanish (twice), the French, and the British have all possessed her, and even after she was claimed by the United States, she gave herself to the secessionist Independent State of Alabama in 1861 and, soon after, to the Confederacy. Like New Orleans, with which she has more in common than, say, Birmingham, she has seen a lot of high and low living in her long life. Ironically, her greatest tragedy was to fall into the hands, not of generals, but of government planners who controlled the urban-renewal programs of the recent past. Those programs have ripped the urban hearts out of scores of America's older cities; Mobile's special misfortune was that she had more heart to lose than most. I still fondly remember her downtown neighborhoods, rich in elegant if somewhat shabby nineteenth-century dwellings, before most of them were bulldozed away. Now the city, growing more prosperous every day, is trying to preserve what is left. There is still enough—several blocks on and near Government Street, and a few more in the vicinity of reconstructed Fort Conde—to enable you to recreate in your imagination the charming coastal city that Mobile was only a generation ago.

There is, by the way, a heavily developed but nicer-than-average campground called **Chickasabogue Park** on Mobile's northern outskirts. Take I-65 to exit 13 and head west on Hwy 158 to Shelton Beach Road (Hwy 213). Turn left, then left again at Whistler Street. A final left at Aldock Road will take you to the park entrance. A big chunk of the park's 1000 acres is given over to picnic grounds, playing fields, and full-service campsites. But considerable acreage remains as unspoiled bottomland hardwood forest. There is a three-mile nature trail, a primitive tenting area, a pretty creek, and canoes for rent. Just don't expect the wilderness primeval. (Chickasabogue Park, 760 Aldock Road, Mobile, Alabama 36613; 205/452–8496.)

Canoeists in search of a more serious outdoors experience will be interested to know that there are several rivers and streams in southern Alabama that rival those in Florida. Among them are the Perdido, on the Alabama-Florida line, and the Escatawpa, which crosses from Alabama into Mississippi. Check the Canoe Trails Outdoor Shop in Mobile for information. You can also inquire about the possibility of exploring the delta of the Mobile and Tensaw rivers. Few travelers are aware that this swamp wilderness exists at the headwaters of Mobile Bay, a vast (and unprotected) maze of marshland, flooded forests, and winding creeks. Nearby bottomlands and swamps have been sacrificed—along with tens of thousands of wetland acres further north—to the multibillion-dollar Tennessee-Tombigbee Barge Canal, one of the most expensive boondoggles in the history of the Army Corps of Engineers, which is saying a lot. But the good news is that a great deal of wild country still remains in the Mobile-Tensaw Delta. The problem (a welcome problem, really, given the unprotected status of the area) is that access is limited, and there are not many on-the-scene camping opportunities.

Mississippi

One can only hope that someday Alabama will exhibit the same concern for the Mobile-Tensaw Delta that Mississippi has already shown for its most important river swamp, the Pascagoula. The story of its preservation is one of the most dramatic in our nation's conservation history. Responding to a campaign masterminded by the Nature Conservancy, state wildlife officials and thousands of ordinary citizens convinced the state legislature during the 1970s to buy and set aside 35,000 acres of magnificent bottomland forest as the **Pascagoula Wildlife Management Area**. The feat was truly remarkable when you consider that Mississippi is our poorest state; its people had never before demonstrated a serious concern for the natural environment; and the land was paid for without a dime of federal money.

Here in the Pascagoula River Basin, we are entering the great bottomland forests of the central South. If you head north on Hwy 63, past the crossroads town of Wade, you will presently discover that you are driving along the edge of a high bluff. To your left, the land drops away into a great trench, five or six miles wide and seventy miles long, its floor covered with an unbroken blue-green pelt of forest. This is the river valley through which the Pascagoula winds and twists, cutting corners, perpetually changing course. Frequently, the erosive pressure of the current breaks through one of the river's countless serpentine loops, creating a shorter route for itself in its journey to the Gulf. The abandoned loop then becomes one of the scores of oxbow lakes scattered throughout the swamp. This ecological complex—a changeful river, a web of crescent lakes formed by its abandoned beds, a great alluvial forest that floods when the river rises and dries out when it recedes—is what makes the Pascagoula Swamp so special. Elsewhere in the central South, rivers of this size have almost all been brutally channelized. Their bottomland forests have been drained (at taxpayer expense), cut, and turned into soybean fields for the benefit of agribusiness. Of hundreds of thousands of acres of such forests that once covered Mississippi's alluvial plains, the Pascagoula is the only large tract that survives.

Like all southern woodlands, this one has been worked over by the timber cutters. Nevertheless, for long stretches, the bottomlands suggest what this area must have looked like before the white man came: the very air is stained with an encompassing greenness; on the higher ridges where floods rarely reach, spruce pine, red oak, hickory, and wild pecan intermix, forming a canopy a hundred feet above your head. Swamp maple, water oaks, and sweet bay take over at lower elevations, their boughs heavy with resurrection fern, Spanish moss, trumpet vines, cat briar, and lichens—even full-size palmettos growing in the crotches where branches join. At the water's edge are the black tupelo, willows, and cypress standing in their own reflections.

The Pascagoula is a notable fishing river, rich in bass, catfish, perch, and even the occasional rare river sturgeon. But it is rather wide and muddy, with a strong spring current; it is better suited for small, shallow-draft motorboats—"john boats"—than canoes. The canoeist will be more at home on Black Creek, which joins the Pascagoula north of the county road linking Wade and Vancleave. Black Creek offers a superb canoe trip that begins many miles to the northwest in De Soto National Forest—about which, more when we get there by road. But the canoeist can put in closer to the Pascagoula Wildlife Management Area at either Hwy 57 or 26. He will also find the quiet oxbow lakes much to his liking, as well as the flooded springtime forests that give access to them.

In late spring, summer, and early autumn—before the hunters and their hounds take over—these same forests can be peacefully explored on foot, though not too deeply unless you are following an access lane. There are many miles of such lanes leading across sloughs and through mighty stands of bottomland hardwoods. At times you can walk among cypress whose trunks have been worked like clay by the river's strong current. More often, though, the banks rise well above the water. River-edge trees are constantly having the earth pulled out from under them. For a while they hang on, roots exposed. Then they topple into the drink, where they inconvenience boaters and provide welcome sunning platforms for turtles, including the Pascagoula yellow-blotched sawback, a subspecies found nowhere else in the world.

The swamp possesses an impressive fauna, including deer, bobcat, wild turkey, beavers (which adapt to fluctuating water levels by digging summertime burrows in the banks and winter lodges atop them), and more gray squirrels than anywhere south of Manhattan's Central Park. This is also the only place where I have had the heart-lifting experience of seeing six exquisite swallow-tailed kites in view at one time. In the sloughs, herons ply their trade, pileated woodpeckers (locally called Indian hens) hammer away, and prothonotary warblers, like motes of golden light, flicker through the underbrush. However, wildlife in the Pascagoula Swamp is more wary than it is along most of Florida's rivers. Hunting in the management area is better controlled now than it used to be, but a lot of shooting still goes on, legal and otherwise. Alligators, which should be all over the place, are only occasionally seen.

Local folks are not always conscientious about picking up their litter, so some spots where boats are launched are a bit cruddy-looking. But despite such small shortcomings, the Pascagoula is one of the premier bottomland forests surviving in the Gulf Coast area, and its miles of massive forests and winding waterways afford plenty of room in which to escape the uglier influences of your fellow man.

As in the case of most large wild areas, especially swamps, the Pascagoula Wildlife Management Area is not the sort of place you just wander into. Check out the scene before doing anything else. There are two headquarters offices. One is at Parker Lake, a mile east of the river (three miles west of Hwy 63) on the county road connecting Vancleave and Wade. The other is off Hwy 26, six miles west of Lucedale. At either location you can get maps and detailed information about hiking, canoeing, boating, and fishing. There are roads leading to ten of the oxbow lakes, and there are about a dozen boat ramps with shady camping sites in the nearby woods. None of the campgrounds has hookups and most fall into the primitive category. Almost always there is plenty of room for privacy; but be aware that some years, during April and May, the Pascagoula floods these camping areas. (Detailed information about hiking, boating, etc., should be picked up at the headquarters offices, where you can explain your special interests. Those interested in an extended canoe trip on Black or Red Creek can write to the Department of Wildlife Conservation, P.O. Box 451, Jackson, Mississippi 39205.)

The **De Soto National Forest** is linked to the Pascagoula **Wildlife Management Area** by general proximity and, in particular, by Black Creek, probably the best canoeing trail in southern Mississippi and certainly the most popular. Too popular, some people may feel, especially on summer weekends, when it gets its heaviest use. However, since there are some ninety miles of river suitable for canoeing, most stretches have more than a sufficiency of peace and quiet in which to enjoy the loveliness around you. Some canoeists go the whole route, from Big Creek Landing, just west of Hwy 49, along the entire course of Black Creek and then down the Pascagoula to the river marshes below I-10. But for most of us, Black Creek divides into "upper" and "lower" sections, each of which allows for trips of varying length. The upper section is almost entirely within the De Soto National Forest. Here Black Creek is relatively narrow, walled in by unbroken forests of pine and mixed hardwoods. The clay banks are fairly steep in places, and there are many sandbars, stapled with the tracks of deer, on which to camp and picnic. Even narrower is Beaverdam Creek, a tributary stream that offers eight miles of backcountry canoeing before reaching Black Creek. Here especially the towering trees on either side lean out across the water, almost touching branches above your head.

As for those of you who would like to see something of the Pascagoula Swamp, you may wish to start your journey further downstream, although more small motorboat traffic may be encountered here. This lower stretch allows for an exploration of beautiful Red Creek, which joins the Black not long before their combined flow reaches the Pascagoula River. There are few sandbars in this lower stretch, but plenty of dry banks on which to camp, even in spring, when high water moves into the surrounding forest, allowing you to move with it if you wish. Snags and downed trees are commonplace, which is as it should be on an unspoiled river; but it does mean that you have to stay alert. Depending upon your pleasure, there are a number of options about where to put in and take out, but finding the appropriate landings in the crisscross of forest roads can get complicated. Fortunately, the two national forest headquarters, where you can get maps and directions, are handily located: take Hwy 49 north from I-10 or (if you have already been exploring the Pascagoula Swamp) Hwy 26 west from Lucedale. One office is on the west side of 49 at the tiny town of McHenry, the other on the service road just east of 49 at the Wiggens exit.

At either of these headquarters you can also pick up information about the forest's two hiking trails, the Tuxachanie (seventeen miles) in the southern sector and the Black Creek (forty miles) in the Wiggens area. These trails are among the prettiest in the South, with the Black Creek Trail having perhaps a slight edge, partly because it follows the old pathway of Indians and pioneers, but mostly because it traverses larger areas of unspoiled forest. One section has been granted wilderness status. Not that any forest in the region has, strictly speaking, kept its virginity intact. The nice thing about the Deep South,

De Soto National Forest, Mississippi. *Photo by Jim Grice.*

though, is that trees grow fast. Now the forests along the trail look much as they did in the old days, with mighty longleaf pines, loblollies, and red oaks towering above dense understories of dogwood, yaupon, sassafras, wax myrtle, or, in more open stands, palmetto and gallberry. Everywhere, there is the clean fragrance of pines and leafy mold. (In summer, alas, there is also the hum of deer flies.) And often along the trail, a creek or pond comes into view—or a southern bog.

It is worth pausing for a paragraph to marvel at the southern bog, a specialized life zone within the larger ecosystem of the southern piney woods. These bogs—or savannahs—are squishy, water-logged patches found either at the bottom of slopes or in shallow depressions in the pine flatwoods. They are the home of yellow and parrot pitcher plants, easily recognized by their gaudy, tubular bodies (actually leaves), flapped lids, and downward-looking, waxy blooms. If you gently lift the flap of one of them, you will see small insects at the bottom of the funnel leaf that are in the process of being vegetably devoured. The pitcher plant's veiny red coloration, as well as its nectar glands, lures hapless bugs into the leaf; then slippery, downward-pointing hairs drop them into a vat of digestive enzymes at the bottom. The whole process is pretty creepy in its miniature way. You aren't sure whether to be glad that people aren't as small as flies, or that pitcher plants aren't as big as trees. The pitcher plants are not unique in their gruesome little habits. There is a dismaying amount of plant carnivory going on in these piney-woods bogs. Bladderworts, for example, have tiny chambers on their leaves that close up when a small insect enters them. Or consider the tentacled sundew—a tiny, red plant that grows flat to the ground on sandy mud. The lilliputian sunburst of its leaves is covered with flexible spines, each topped with a sticky drop of "dew." When a little bug gets stuck on one spine, others nearby reach over and help to hold it while it is consumed.

But let us not dwell on these horrors. There are many other more conventional plants in piney-woods bogs for us to contemplate. Indeed, such places become veritable gardens of wildflowers in the summer, with leopard lilies, sunflowers, meadow beauty, yellow-fringed orchids, grass pink, and little white hardheads (which look as though someone had picked all their petals) respectably getting their nutrients in the good old-fashioned way, from the soil itself.

You can camp wherever you wish along either the hiking or canoeing trails in the forest. As for established campgrounds, the more-or-less primitive sites such as Cypress Creek or Fairly Bridge Landing are the most attractive spots. The more accessible places—particularly the Big Biloxi on Hwy 49, midway between I-10 and McHenry—sometimes attract local people who have lost the best of their country manners in recent years. (De Soto National Forest, Route 1, Box 62, McHenry, Mississippi 39561; 601/928–5291. Or Box 248, Wiggens, Mississippi 39577; 601/928–4422.)

The best bet for travelers who would like hookups and other conveniences is the **Flint Creek Water Park**, a privately run recreation area just a mile north of Wiggens on Hwy 29. The recreation area is heavily developed, with a large, manmade lake suitable for boating, fishing, water skiing, swimming, even water slides. But the camping areas are pretty and decently secluded from all the other stuff. Except for some summer weekends and holidays, the place is not too crowded. (Flint Creek Water Park, Route 3, Box 309, Wiggens, Mississippi 39577; 601/928–3051.)

It would be very wrong to leave this back-of-the-Gulf ecosystem of piney woods and boggy savannahs without noting the **Mississippi Sandhill Crane National Wildlife Refuge** that lies athwart I-10 between Pascagoula and Biloxi. Actually, this 17,000-acre preserve would be worth much more than a mere mention if it were set up for the public. Quite rightly, it isn't. There is a Visitor Center and a short nature trail; but this refuge is one of the relatively few in the federal system that exists solely to protect a very endangered species or, more exactly, a subspecies: the Mississippi sandhill crane. This large, splendid-looking bird differs from other sandhills in its darker coloration, its less sociable, non-migratory lifestyle, and its extreme rarity. Only about fifty wild birds survive, all of them here on this single protected tract. There is little chance that you will see them if you do visit the refuge (although you just may hear their beautiful rattling calls from some distant savannah). Nevertheless, a visit is well worth your while, especially since the Visitor Center and nature trail are only three-quarters of a mile north of the Gautier/Vancleave exit of I-10. Exhibits at the center illustrate the natural history of the unique and threatened savannah-pine flatwoods ecosystem; and the beautiful one-half-mile trail threads its way between a swampy bayou and a series of pitcher plant bogs. (Mississippi Sandhill Crane National Wildlife Refuge, P.O. Box 6999, Gautier, Mississippi 39553; 601/497–6322.)

The Gold Coast   Whether or not you decide to explore the Pascagoula Swamp and/or the De Soto National Forest, you should dip down to Hwy 90 and take in at least part of Mississippi's Gulf Coast. There is the fact that the most glorious barrier islands on the Gulf of Mexico are out there waiting for you. But even aside from that best part, which we shall come to shortly, the Coast hereabouts has a lot to recommend it as long as you don't expect it to be what it is not— Hwy 1 in northern California, for instance.

Heading west, the first public access to the Mississippi Gulf Coast is at **Davis Bayou Campground, Gulf Islands National Seashore**. If you are on I-10, turn south to Hwy 90 at the Vancleave exit. As you near Ocean Springs on 90, watch for the sign directing you to the National Seashore. This mainland parcel is less than a mile square and is squeezed between housing developments, but it is an attractive, well-managed place with views of tidal creeks, marshy inlets, small ponds, and coastal forests. The Visitor Center boasts a stunning collection of wood sculptures of local wildlife as well as an interesting film on coastal ecology. There is a nature trail, a boat ramp, and a pleasantly laid-out campground with about fifty first-come, first-served sites, all with electrical hookups. During warm months they get pretty heavy use, so it's a good idea to arrive fairly early in the day. Once you are set up, Davis Bayou makes a wonderful home base from which to explore much of coastal Mississippi. It is also the departure point for a summer weekend shuttle to Horn Island, discussed below. (Davis Bayou Campground, Gulf Islands National Seashore, 3500 Park Road, Ocean Springs, Mississippi 39564; 601/875–3962 or 601/875–9057.)

Ocean Springs, next door to the park, deserves a brief drive-around. This was the first permanent European settlement in Mississippi, where the Sieur d'Iberville established a fort in 1699. Not much in the way of historical artifacts remains, but the town is a pretty place to look at. Streets gently dip and rise, wandering through neighborhoods made handsome by the abundance of magnolias, oaks, azaleas, and pines. A bridge crosses a quiet tidal inlet where small boats anchor and egrets fish. Several homes were designed by Frank Lloyd Wright or his precursor, Louis Sullivan. But the real genius of this place was Walter Anderson, whose brilliant, vaguely van Gogh–esque paintings of the Gulf Coast's natural scene are only now beginning to receive the attention that rightfully belongs to them. The Ocean Springs Community Center wears on its walls a mural he painted for a dollar. At Shearwater Pottery, where his relatives produce and sell pottery, you can visit the little house he lived in and decorated with his paintings. More than any other person, he expresses what is most beautiful and true about the Gulf's northern coast.

Just across Biloxi Bay from Ocean Springs is the **Gulf Marine State Park**. As soon as you cross the bridge on Hwy 90, coming into Biloxi, take a left onto the service road where the tiny park and its aquarium are located. The aquarium is a must for anyone with even an amateur interest in marine biology. It is totally different from the usual Marine Wonderlands where seals jump through hoops and porpoises kiss their keepers. This exhibit, both beautiful and instructive, affords realistic views of the variety of marine life to be found in coastal environments, from freshwater streams to open Gulf.

Inspired by this piscine bounty, you may then wish to adjourn to the park's nearby fishing pier. If you've brought along your fishing pole, you can try your luck at catching some of the redfish, black drum, flounder, sheepshead, and speckled trout that have just been eyeballing you through panes of glass. The pier, located right at the mouth of Biloxi Bay, is a fine spot to get your line wet, especially in spring and fall; but fishing is always a gambler's game, so don't be cast down if you don't get a bite. On the other hand, you just may have the incredible luck to be on the Coast during a "jubilee." A jubilee occurs when a pool of oxygen-deficient water is pushed to shore ahead of a rising tide, while at the same time offshore winds are driving surface water out into the Gulf. Under such conditions, which can occur anywhere from three or four times a year to not at all, crabs and flounder practically run themselves aground, and jubilant Coast residents catch them by the bushel. But even on an ordinary summer night, if you drive along the Coast you will often see propane lamps beautifully shining far out in the shallow waters of Mississippi Sound, announcing the location of waders gigging flounders or catching soft-shell crabs when the tide is coming in.

There are, let's face it, sizable stretches of Mississippi's Gold Coast that are pretty tarnished-looking. Hurricane Camille, which slammed ashore here in 1968, did not exactly help matters. In terms of wind velocity and tidal surge, the storm was the worst ever to strike the U.S. mainland, the hurricane equivalent of Sherman's march through Georgia. The measure of Camille's ferocity is that, for once, the developers have been relatively cautious about rebuilding. Even now, you can drive past low-lying beachfront property, especially in the vicinity of Long Beach, and see only weedy lots where plush subdivisions once stood. Unfortunately, the commercial rebuilding that has taken place, particularly between Biloxi and Gulfport, is no better than it should be. Never mind, though. On the Gulf side of the highway, you will have mile after mile of wide, flat, white beach (much of it manmade) and blue water to look at. There are any number of places where you can pull over to get some sun and take a dip. However, since this is a sound, separated from the Gulf by the aforementioned barrier islands, you will have to wade pretty far out to reach a depth suitable for swimming.

Even on its landward side, despite frequent lapses into architectural vulgarity, the Mississippi Coast still boasts an impressive collection of fine old residences, many of them reborn from the gutted hulls left by Camille. Some are in the area between Gulfport and Biloxi, including Jefferson Davis's magnificent home, Beauvoir. But most are at Pass Christian. Here wealthy New Orleanians built antebellum summer "cottages" in the old days, and scores of them survive, elegantly nestled among shaggy oaks on a three-mile ridge above the Gulf. You have to keep your eye out, though, since the homes are barely visible from Hwy 90. Soon after you reach the corporate limits of Pass Christian, be on the alert for an unmarked side road that starts paralleling Hwy 90 along the tree-lined ridge, just when the ridge itself becomes noticeable. Within seconds, you will be in another world, passing one architectural gem after another. These homes, in striking contrast to most modern dwellings, "belong" to their environmental setting and the local cultural traditions that shaped their construction. They are not pretentious houses for the most part, but they keep a nice balance between comfort and decorum. A lot of pleasant, civilized hours must have been spent on their graceful porches. It's a good thing that their carefully chosen location atop this ridge has saved most—not all—of them from being literally gone with the wind.

The Barrier Islands

As you cross the bridge between Ocean Springs and Biloxi and begin the drive along the Coast, you will notice a low-lying island almost within swimming distance of the shore, the thin grid of pine trees along its bay side plainly silhouetted against the Gulf sky. This is Deer Island, which guards the productive marshes of Biloxi Bay. Conservationists and developers are presently battling over its fate; but even if the conservationists win, there will still be some uncertainty about how it will be used in terms of public access. I mention it here because, if you find it beautiful to look at—and you will—then you will have an intimation, but only that, of the chain of magical islands that lies ten miles further out in the Gulf, beyond eye's reach. These are Dauphin (in Alabama), Cat, **Petit Bois**, **Horn**, and **East** and **West Ship Islands**. The latter four are of special interest to us. As part of Gulf Islands National Seashore, they are the most protected and unspoiled, and, at the same time, the most available to the traveler who loves wild and isolated places.

We have visited barrier islands before this—from Sanibel and Caladesi to St. George and Santa Rosa—and there are others to come. They, and all other islands, have their special magic, as generations of imaginative kids, lyric poets, and rapacious developers can confirm. But the ones we are considering now are arguably the loveliest in the Gulf, the *crème de la crème*, the golden isles. One of their ardent admirers, incidentally, was the aforementioned Ocean Springs artist, Walter Anderson, who used to row out to Horn Island in the moonlight (something you are not advised to do) and claim it as his hermitage and studio for weeks at a time.

Part of the appeal of these particular barrier islands is undoubtedly the fact that they are more isolated and undeveloped than almost any others along the Gulf Coast. Even their origin has been something of a mystery, or at any rate, a subject of learned debate. In recent years, however, there has been a growing consensus among marine geologists that they are built out of sedimentary sands derived from Mobile Bay and, ultimately, the Appalachian highlands. The westerly drift of littoral currents has steadily moved the islands westward with it, eroding their eastern edges and adding to their western tips. The process has been almost unnervingly rapid. Much of Petit Bois, for example, used to belong to Alabama two hundred years ago. Now all of it is in Mississippi. But the great uncertainty is whether any of these ancient processes will be able to continue for much longer. The dams on southern rivers and the ship channel dredged in Mobile Bay now deflect the sedimentary sands that the islands require to rebuild themselves. If they disappear, the loss will not be of the islands only. They are not called barriers for nothing. Without them, Mississippi Sound would be doomed as well. With it would vanish a vital link in the "fertile crescent" of estuaries that make the northern Gulf Coast, from Apalachicola to Galveston, the most productive fishery in the world.

West Ship Island is, of all the Mississippi islands, the most heavily visited. Regularly scheduled commercial tour boats leave from Gulfport and Biloxi during all but the winter months, with both morning and afternoon round trips available in summer. During the fall, only weekend trips are available. (The Gulfport boat leaves from the easy-to-find Gulfport Small Craft Harbor [601/864–1014 or 436–6010]; the Biloxi boat takes off from the Pan American Boat Dock at the Buena Vista Motel, just east of the unmissable Biloxi Lighthouse standing in the middle of Hwy 90 [601/432-2197].)

West Ship Island acquired the "West" in its name quite recently. In 1946 a hurricane cut Ship Island neatly in two; but in fairly short order, tidal action replaced its missing middle. But then Camille's storm surge bisected the island again, and thus far Nature has not spliced the eastern and western halves back together. West Ship Island differs from its sisters in that it has a very nice fort; it offers some amenities, such as bathhouses, showers, and a concession stand; and it has no trees. Fort Massachusetts is possibly my present favorite among forts on the U.S. section of the Coast, mainly because it is small enough to seem downright cozy compared to most of the others, but also because it looks like half a doughnut. It got its name, apparently, when Confederate soldiers who had occupied the fort exchanged cannon fire with the Union ship *Massachusetts*—without either side doing much damage to the other. Once you have seen the fort and reflected on other aspects of the island's history (for example, during the War of 1812, British ships rendezvoused here before their unsuccessful attack on New Orleans), you can give yourself up to the grand white beach, the sun, and the surf—a perceivable surf out here, in contrast to the mild little waves that ordinarily lap the mainland shores.

But it is the other three islands—East Ship, Petit Bois, and Horn—that are the favorites of most people who know them all. They have less history than West Ship Island and no old forts or modern facilities; but they have a wilderness solitude where time and history hardly seem to matter and beaches where human footprints are few and far between. And they have trees—although, as the name would imply, Petit Bois does not have too many of them. The great wonder is that there are any here at all, so far out in the empty Gulf, on long strips of land rarely half a mile wide that are often lashed by storms and hurricanes and the eroding influence of the tides. One of the most glorious of all natural settings is that where woodlands come down to meet the sea. And here, on these narrow, delicate islands, that combination has a special, oddly poignant beauty. Horn Island is the crown jewel of the chain because it brings that combination together so perfectly (although East Ship runs a close second and Petit Bois a close third). There is, moving south to north, the great blue emptiness of the Gulf; then the shell-sprinkled beach composed of sand ground fine as sugar; after that, the dunes with their brave colonies of sea oats, seaside rosemary, goldenrod, and panic grass; next, the sudden forests of pines, live oaks, and yaupon; behind them, the small, freshwater pools thick with pickerelweed and arrowhead, or brackish lagoons edged by spartina; and, finally, the narrow bayside beach with its coarser sands and tamely lapping wavelets.

If there were nothing else to recommend Horn Island—and there is everything else—the place would be special because of its importance to birds of prey. I saw my first peregrine falcon here fifteen years ago, screaming its wild, crazy cry as it flew above the pines. This, remember, was during the DDT days, when it seemed very likely that pesticides would finish off the beautiful peregrine, as well as many other bird species, once and for all. I can still hear my companions whooping, "It's immature! It's immature!"—meaning that there was still hope: there might still be enough peregrines reproducing to allow concerned citizens the time they needed to save the birds—and people—from an increasingly poisoned environment. Now it is fairly commonplace to see peregrines at Horn Island during their winter migration. Just as wonderfully, the island is a nesting haven for another erstwhile victim of pesticides, the osprey. Thanks to the island's isolation, the nesting colony here was able to raise young successfully long after DDT had killed off their mainland kindred. The island still contains one of the highest concentrations of breeding osprey pairs on the Gulf Coast.

Horn Island also supports a herd of wild hogs, dumped here long ago by mainland settlers as a handy source of protein. You will see their tracks and wallows on the beach, where they scavenge at night, but you will almost certainly not see the animals themselves. Considering the limits of their domain, they are extraordinarily successful at keeping out of human sight. Like wolves on Isle Royal, the hogs seem to control their own fertility, although no doubt the alligators in the brackish lagoons help them out occasionally by dining on piglet. They do keep the groundcover on Horn a lot more cropped-looking than it is on hog-free Petit Bois or East Ship Island, but apparently the animals are not as much of a problem here as they are in areas where they compete with native species such as deer and turkey.

For people, the main problems are deer flies in the island woods and black flies on the beach. Also mosquitoes. The black flies, which do not seem to be much repelled by repellents, are usually at their worst during late summer. But in the case of all these insect pests, much depends on wind, temperature, amount of rainfall, and so on. Sometimes they're a plague; sometimes, even in summer, they're not. You should come prepared, psychologically as well as with repellents and long-sleeve shirts. And don't forget to protect yourself from the sun. Fair-skinned people can get a bad burn just in the hour or so that it takes to reach the islands.

Only primitive camping is available on Horn, East Ship, and Petit Bois. For those without their own boat, Horn Island can be reached by means of a shuttle that leaves from the dock at the Davis Bayou section of Gulf Islands National Seashore, described above. The service operates only during the summer (through September). The boat leaves Friday afternoons at 4:00 P.M. and returns to collect passengers on Sunday evenings. However, you can make arrangements to stay an entire week. Campers must carry everything with them (sixty-pound limit), including water, although there is an emergency water source at the ranger station. The number of campers who can use the island is strictly limited. On weekends when there is an overflow, the shuttle also takes campers to a primitive site on East Ship. Petit Bois can only be reached by private boat. Persons who have their own boats—a minimum length of sixteen feet is recommended—are free to find their own way to the islands. However, only experienced boaters should make the trip. Late-afternoon squalls occur rather frequently during summer, and northers can make for rough going in winter. Even old hands at boating should get advice at Davis Bayou or the excursion docks before starting out. Among other considerations, there is the fact that the islands can only be walked across conveniently at a very few places (among them, the ranger station in the middle of Horn Island); so the visitor will want to know where to park his or her boat. (William M. Colmer Visitor Center, Gulf Islands National Seashore, 3500 Park Road, Ocean Springs, Mississippi 39564; 601/875–9057 or 601/875–3962.)

Beyond Pass Christian, Hwy 90 moves inland. However, if you take a left immediately after crossing the Bay St. Louis Bridge, the road will take you a bit further along the Coast. Bay St. Louis is a nice little town that has been somewhat bypassed by all the Gold Coast action. It was not bypassed by Hurricane Camille, however. Some of the fine, old homes that lined its waterfront are gone. Still, this is a pretty drive, providing a very intimate, close-up look at the shoreline. Even by Gulf standards, the water is very shallow here: at low tide, children thirty yards out from the narrow beach seem to be walking on water, and occasional sunbathers lounge on sandbars surrounded by sheets of water a couple of inches deep. Nor are sunbathers the only ones using these sandbars. Large concentrations of shorebirds, egrets, and great blue herons gather along here during summer, apparently getting a little R & R after the hassle of raising the annual family.

If you proceed for some miles along this road you will come to **Buccaneer State Park** (also reached from Hwy 90 at Waveland). The park is small, but it has a sizable developed campground—about 150 sites with hookups—as well as a primitive camping area nearby. The campground is nice enough, and not too crowded except on height-of-summer weekends, though it is somewhat short on shade and privacy. There is also a "wave pool" on the premises that features the "live wave action" that is generally lacking on the Coast itself. It costs to get in, but kids love it. For the nature lover, though, the park offers little of interest except for the bird-haunted shallows and beach at its front door. Avoid the picnic area on the beach—a pretty enough site much used and abused by locals. Also skip the Old Hickory Nature Trail. When I walked it the only things to look at were discarded beer cans and paper plates. (Buccaneer State Park, Box 180, Waveland, Mississippi 39576; 601/467-3822.)

Directly north of state-run Buccaneer is a smaller but in many ways prettier county park, **McLeod Water Park**. To reach it, head north on Hwy 43 from Waveland (about ten miles) or from the Kiln exit of I-10 (about four miles) and turn left at the sign. The park has about twenty-four shady hookup sites and an extensive area for primitive camping. There are also showers, fishing piers, a boat launch, a well-maintained picnic ground, etc. The great attraction is the Jourdan River, a short but lovely tidal stream that winds through coastal forests and swamps until it empties into the Bay of St. Louis. The riverine woods are a beautiful mix of pines, magnolias, and live oaks with understories of yaupon, dogwood, and wild azalea. In low spots, tupelo and cypress take over. This is a fine place to camp for a night or to launch a day trip in a boat or canoe. Fishing for bass, catfish, and perch is good. On nice weekends the place gets a lot of local use, but during the week it is rarely crowded. (McLeod Water Park, Route 3, Box 973, Bay St. Louis, Mississippi 39520; 601/467-1894.)

Louisiana

At the Mississippi-Louisiana border, the Interstate crosses a high bridge that offers an impressive overview of the Pearl River and the **Honey Island Swamp** through which it wanders. Actually, there are three branches of the Pearl on this last lap of its journey to the Gulf. Since they flood frequently in winter and early spring, they have managed to preserve the great swamp along their borders from the development boom in nearby Slidell (if not from the Army Corps of Engineers). Large areas of the swamp are now managed by state or federal agencies, and there are still places in it that are as wild as wild can get. In some respects, Honey Island is like that other great Mississippi swamp, the Pascagoula, on the eastern side of the state. But whereas large expanses of Pascagoula forest remain high and dry during all but the wettest years, most of the Honey Island Swamp takes some flooding every spring. The current is pretty muddy, and there are few sandbars at the river bends. Also, the lumber companies have worked this swamp harder than they did the Pascagoula—a real hatchet job. Although it is certainly very beautiful, its forests have not yet recovered their once majestic scale.

Even if you don't have a boat in tow, you can still get some feel for the area by heading about five miles north on Hwy 59, which intersects with I-10 on the west side of the Pearl. After crossing the West Pearl at the Mississippi line, take the Honey Island exit and follow a narrow road into the **Pearl River Management Area**. (Take it easy when you approach each of a dozen little bridges that are flooded during high water; the potholes, if they haven't been recently filled for the hundredth time, will put your head through the roof of your car.) After a couple of miles, a sign will direct you to a nature trail leading into one of the drier corners of the swamp. The path burrows through what seems to be, in warm months, a greenhouse thick with the steamy scents of leafy growth and decay. Red and gray lichens stain the black tree trunks. Toadstools erupt from the mulch so swiftly that dead leaves and twigs rest on their heads like caps. This second-growth forest is a characteristic "dry" bottomlands mix: beech, water oak, holly, magnolia, sycamore, black gum, sweet bay, and the ubiquitous sweet gum. It has just about transcended its adolescence: dominant trees are gaining girth, and the understory, dense a few years ago, is thinning

Honey Island Swamp, Louisiana. *Photo by Jim Grice.*

out, making it tempting to stray from the trail. Gray squirrels and gray fox are at home here, as well as raccoons, deer, bobcat, and opossum. All around you the shimmering screen of leaves is alive with hard-to-see birds: prothonotary, hooded, Kentucky, and northern parula warblers; Acadian flycatchers, titmice, wood thrushes, great crested flycatchers, and scores of others. Barred owls are abundant here; so it is quite possible that you may rouse one of these large, silent-winged birds from its afternoon nap. The path's destination is a pretty little swamp pond at the river's edge.

Incidentally, the gravel side road from which the nature trail departs offers a pleasant two-mile drive into the bottomland forest. On evenings in late winter and spring, there is always the chance that an armadillo or perhaps a deer will cross the road.

There are several places at which to enter the waterways of the lower Pearl. All three of the main branches are available to boaters, but canoeists should probably stick to the West and Middle Pearl. A commercial campground and, nearby, a boat ramp and canoe rentals are available to travelers where Hwy 59 crosses the Pearl River, a short distance from the spur road leading to the just-mentioned nature trail. At a public ramp below the Hwy 59 bridge, canoeists can gain access to the (unmarked) Porter's River Canoe Trail. This and another excellent Honey Island canoe trail (Peach Lake) are described in detail in *Trail Guide to the Delta Country* (see the bibliography). If you're traveling on I-10 and have brought your own boat or canoe with you, there is a "secret" way of getting launched into the swamp with an absolute minimum of fuss: simply pull in at the Louisiana Welcome Center, just west of the swamp, and drive around to the back on the trash-disposal road. As soon as you pass through the gateless fence you will be at a warden's home office, adjoined by a tiny primitive campground (not very scenic, but okay if it's getting late and you need someplace to pitch your tent) and a very large boat ramp on the West Pearl. If the current is not too strong, the canoeist may want to paddle about a mile and a half upstream to reach the junction with the Middle Pearl; but the West Pearl is just about as scenic, though a bit wider. (On either stream you can take out at Hwy 90.) The prettiest parts of the Honey Island Swamp are to be found, as you might expect, along some of the little sloughs or bayous that wander off from the main waterways; but before you get too carried away in following them, it is essential to know what you're doing. The swamp, after all, covers about 250 square miles. Also, currents sometimes have a misleading way of flowing out of the main channels instead of into them. And they can be strong. So don't be shy about asking local fishermen at boat ramps or on the river itself for advice. (Pearl River Management Area, Louisiana Department of Wildlife and Fisheries, Box 14526, Baton Rouge, Louisiana 70898; 504/342–5875.)

If you don't have your own boat and don't feel like renting one, but still want to experience at least a couple of hours of being waterborne in the swamp, an informative Honey Island Swamp Tour can be arranged. The tours begin at Indian Village Landing (from Slidell, head south on Hwy 190 for about three miles and turn left on Indian Village Road). Check in advance, however. (Dr. Paul Wagner, 106 Holly Ridge Drive, Slidell, Louisiana 70458; 504/641–1769.)

Ambitious souls who yearn to take a lengthy canoe trip in this beautiful area should consider starting out on the lovely Bogue Chitto River at a point above the **Bogue Chitto National Wildlife Refuge**. The river corridor winds in and out among flooded forests that are, according to "upriver" canoeists, even more lovely and intimately viewable than those in the state management area further south. In either sector there are good opportunities for seeing wildlife if you are reasonably quiet. Alligators are becoming numerous in the Pearl River Basin, but they are wary, as are minks, beavers, and otters. Wading birds and the exquisite wood duck are abundant; and in winter, small oxbow lakes and flooded woodlands support great rafts of waterfowl. (For advice concerning put-ins, take-outs, and rentals, contact the Canoe and Trail Shop, 624 Moss Avenue, New Orleans, Louisiana 70124; 504/488–8528. There are also canoe and boat rentals in Slidell.)

State parks with public campgrounds are not at all as numerous in southern Louisiana as they are in Florida. However, there is a very pleasant one, **Fountainbleau State Park**, located on Hwy 190 just south of Mandeville, with both developed and primitive campsites. The park fronts on Lake Pontchartrain, and the setting is attractive, with the ruins of an old plantation sugar mill looking picturesque in a frame of huge live oaks and pines. This is a fairly large park, 2700 acres, and it adjoins a small wildlife refuge. So, even though there is considerable development—swimming pool, bathhouses, and so forth—it is possible to follow miles of nature trails into the peace and quiet of the surrounding forest. Birding here is excellent, with a nice mix of shore and woodland species. However, the place gets crowded on holidays. (Fountainbleau State Park, Mandeville, Louisiana 70448; 504/626–8052.)

Just a few miles beyond, on Hwy 22 east of Madisonville, is **Fairview State Park**, a much smaller campground than Fountainbleau (about eighty developed sites) that is located on the shady banks of the Tchefuncte River. The setting really does offer a fair view of the lovely river, and there are boating and fishing opportunities. But the chief attraction of the place is that it makes a convenient headquarters if you plan to explore Louisiana's "Florida Parishes" north of Lake Pontchartrain. I guess that someone on a budget might even consider the park as a possible home base for visits to New Orleans, although the city's downtown is a thirty-five-mile drive away across the Pontchartrain Causeway. (Fairview State Park, Madisonville, Louisiana 70447; 504/845–3318.)

7

New Orleans and the Louisiana Coast

At a glance

Access   New Orleans is the destination for direct flights from all parts of the United States. Lafayette and Lake Charles and Baton Rouge also have regular airline service. Interstate 10 crosses the northern edge of the coastal region, offering access to the northern portions of the Atchafalaya Basin Swamp. To the south, Hwys 90 and 82 wind through the coastal bayou and marsh country. However, as noted in the travelogue, this is an area where traveling the side roads is half the fun.

Climate   Temperatures and rainfall are much the same as those along other sections of the northern Gulf Coast, with winter temperatures ranging from the low eighties to, occasionally, the low twenties. Spring, usually under way by the second week of March, is a fine season, as is fall. The hot summers—often humid, with frequent afternoon rains—discourage outdoor activities in the buggy marshes, other than boating, between June and September. There is often a difference of several degrees between temperatures on the northern and southern shores of Lake Pontchartrain.

Topography and Landscape Features   Virtually all of the southern coast of Louisiana—many thousands of square miles—is a vast deltic plain created by the Mississippi River. Over the centuries it has shifted its outlet to the Gulf numerous times, building new deltas composed of alluvial soils washed from the land surface of more than half the nation. This process can occur fairly swiftly. For example, most of the river's present delta below New Orleans is less than eight hundred years old. Largely because of levees built along the Mississippi in this century, the river is no longer able to change course or recharge the marshes with alluvial silt. As a result, existing deltas, especially in the eastern part of the state, are rapidly disappearing (see "The Marsh Ref-

uges" in the travelogue). The terrain of southern Louisiana is characterized by a complex estuarine ecosystem of interlocking freshwater,
brackish, and saltwater marshes. Unusual geological features are large
salt domes (massive plugs of salt forced up to the surface from deep
within the earth) and "cheniers" (stranded sand ridges surrounded by
miles of open marsh). Bayous, the former beds of the Mississippi and
its tributaries, traverse the region. So do thousands of miles of oil-
company canals. In the east-central sector, the river basin of the Atchafalaya River has created the largest overflow bottomland swamp in
the United States.

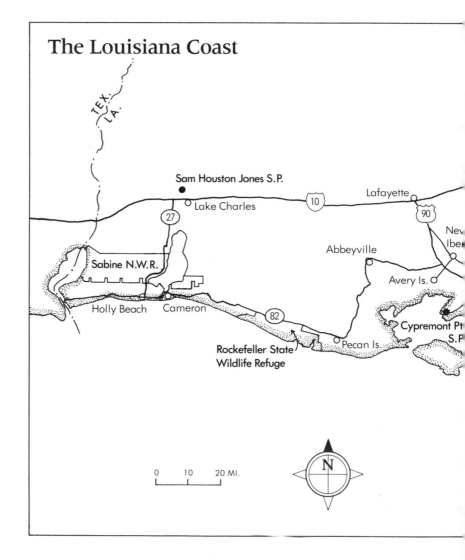

The Louisiana Coast

F*lora and Fauna*   The Atchafalaya Basin and many bayou ecosystems harbor large stands of bottomland and swamp trees—sweet gum, red maple, water oak, tupelo, cypress, and black willow. Waterways are often choked with water hyacinth. Cajun country is famous for its magnificent live oaks. Marsh vegetation is composed of a wide array of marsh grasses and sedges, pickerelweed, alligatorweed, and many other water plants. Dense stands of willows grow on levees and mud flats. The marshes and bottomlands support an abundant fauna. Winter congregations of waterfowl are among the largest in the world, and millions of migrant songbirds descend on the cheniers each

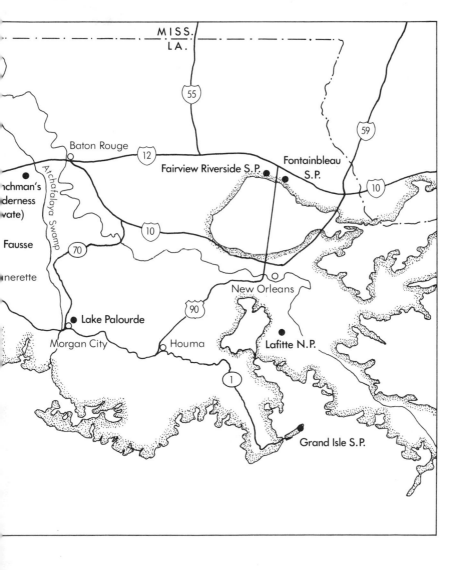

Cypress Swamp, Southern Louisiana. *Photo by U. S. Forest Service.*

spring. The area also supports the highest concentrations of fur-bearers—nutria, muskrat, mink, and otter—in the nation, as well as many alligators and wading birds. A few black bears survive in the Atchafalaya drainage.

Camping   Except for Fountainbleau and a couple of smaller state parks near New Orleans, and Grand Isle State Park southeast of Houma, sizable public campgrounds are scarce in southern Louisiana. There are a couple of municipal campgrounds mentioned in the travelogue. Also, just northwest of Lake Charles, which is pretty far inland, Sam Houston Jones State Park offers camping facilities. But in much of the coastal area, RV campers will have to obtain hookups, etc., at motels or private campgrounds. Of the latter, the best is probably Frenchman's Wilderness, just off I-10 on the west side of the Atchafalaya Basin.

Hiking, Canoeing, Boating, Etc.   There are longish nature walks at Fountainbleau State Park, the Honey Island Swamp, and Jean Lafitte National Historical Park in the eastern part of the state, and, to the southwest, in the huge federal refuges. Atchafalaya Basin levees are also available for long hikes. But southern Louisiana is best suited for the waterborne. Both boating and canoeing in the Honey Island and, especially, the Atchafalaya Basin swamps offer incomparable experiences. And Jean Lafitte National Historical Park has a pretty canoe trail. Boaters have an almost limitless choice of marshland bays, inlets, and bayous where they can mosey around and fish. Privately run swamp tours are also available. Other activities include visiting plantations, sampling Cajun cooking and festivals, crabbing, and, in early spring, enjoying perhaps the most fantastic birding in the nation.

Outdoors Highlights   "Hiking" through New Orleans; plantations in bayou country; Jean Lafitte National Historical Park; Atchafalaya Basin Swamp; Rockefeller Refuge; Sabine National Wildlife Refuge; Avery Island.

New Orleans

The Crescent City is far and away the Gulf's grandest city, one that connoisseurs of cities speak of in the same breath with San Francisco and New York. Houston-Galveston is bigger and richer, Mobile shares much the same history, Veracruz is as colorful, and Tampa–St. Pete has nicer winters. But New Orleans is, well, New Orleans. Once you have penetrated through the Great American Everywhere of its suburbs, the city has a presence, insular but sophisticated, that is utterly its own.

For one thing, the city is very old; for another, it wears its age well. It was founded in 1718 by the great French explorer-statesman, the Sieur de Bienville, who named it in honor of the Duc d'Orleans. Without so much as a by-your-leave, the French ceded the colony to the Spanish in 1762. In 1800, by which time the citizens were at least reconciled to Spanish rule, it was handed back to France; but then, before anyone could get used to that idea, the United States acquired it as part of the Louisiana Purchase in 1803, to the considerable outrage of its residents. For a long time afterward a quite startling animosity existed between the native Creoles and the newly arrived Yankees. (In the traditional New Orleans context, by the way, "Creole" denotes natives of French and/or Spanish descent, not those of mixed white and black ancestry.) Despite the hard feelings, as well as such other little drawbacks as epidemic yellow fever, malaria, and fires that burned down the city, New Orleans prospered. Sugar cane, cotton, and especially the city's strategic position at the mouth of the young nation's greatest trading route, the Mississippi River, made it the richest city in the United States. Its lively planter aristocracy supported a less-than-puritan lifestyle in which gambling, duels, quadroon ballrooms, and a love of theater and the opera were notable features.

The Civil War and Reconstruction put an end to the city's high living, although not, ultimately, to its spirit of fun. It always was, and still is, an essentially Mediterranean town, despite a moderating Anglo-Saxon influence. In some ways, it is a lucky thing that for almost a century New Orleans, along with the rest of the Deep South, did not share in the nation's love affair with progress. Its backwater status preserved its past. Now, of course, the city is booming: it has the first or second largest port in the nation, depending upon how such things are measured; a huge tourist industry; lots of banking and petrochemical business; and—lest we stray entirely from the ecological scene— a vital fish and shellfish industry. In the last ten years a brand new skyline has become the symbol of the city's growth.

But the great thing is that the city has not demolished its past— or, almost as bad, mummified it—in its belated pursuit of progress. Even the new highrise skyline looks sort of dramatic in its dynamic contrast with the much older but still vital sections of the city.

Everyone has heard of the tourist's New Orleans: the justly famous restaurants, the bacchanalian Mardi Gras season, the jazz and Dixieland, and the razzmatazz of Bourbon Street. But the emphasis here is on the New Orleans that can simply be looked at, on the assumption that the reader who takes pleasure in natural landscapes may also enjoy cityscapes when, as occasionally happens, they, too, delight the eye. The fact is that New Orleans has far and away the finest *toute ensemble* of historic architecture in the nation. There are literally thousands of nineteenth-century residential and commercial buildings, almost limitless in their variety, always distinctive in their regional nuances, and usually quite beautiful. The French Quarter, of course, is famous on this score, and for good reason. But not everyone is aware that there is a long belt of old faubourgs, or neighborhoods— and most really are neighborhoods in the old-fashioned urban meaning of the word—that follow the curving course of the river for miles, from downtown Bywater to uptown Carrollton. Along with the many variations on Creole styles, there are narrow shotgun houses, raised plantation mansions, Italianate neoclassical town houses, Victorian chalets, and on and on. For the architecture or history buff, or anyone who is visually oriented, New Orleans is an inexhaustible feast for the eyes. Some of the old neighborhoods, such as the Garden District, Uptown St. Charles, and the Audubon Park area, have never lost their cachet. Others are still slummy. And many others—three cheers for gentrification!—have been or are being rediscovered, recovered, and renovated.

For those of you who might like an urban hike for a change, I herewith proffer a few suggestions. Before you start out, though, you might want to pick up a guide to local architecture at a bookstore.

Lower Bourbon Street, in the French Quarter, is the most famous of New Orleans thoroughfares, but from an aesthetic point of view it is the one ugly street in the Vieux Carre. In general, the further away from Canal Street you get, the prettier and quieter the Quarter gets. Do not miss the lovely side streets on the downtown side of Jackson Square. Some of the very nicest are St. Philip, Ursuline, and Governor Nicholls between Decatur and Rampart. And by all means walk along Esplanade Avenue, the oak-shaded "Fifth Avenue" of one-time Creole society. While you are on Esplanade, pause at the corner of Royal Street to take in the stunning perspective of cast- and wrought-iron balconies narrowing like an arrowhead pointed at the heart of the towering business district.

The downtown side of Esplanade—the Faubourg Marigny and beyond—is where all the artists, waiters, professors, and yuppies have settled now that the Quarter has become too touristy and expensive. Though grandiose Creole mansions become scarce here, all the other charms of the Quarter are present, without the commercialism. Indeed, you can follow Bourbon and Royal for dozens of blocks, admiring hundreds of Creole and Victorian cottages and the city's famous shotgun houses. These last evolved, apparently, from a mixture of Acadian/Nova Scotian and Caribbean architectural styles, with a dash of Victorian gingerbread thrown in for good measure. The name derives from their railroad layout: hypothetically (the owners might object to the actuality), you could shoot a gun at the front door and the pellets would exit at the rear without hitting an intervening wall. A lot of renovation has been going on in these old faubourgs, but you still sense the lingering ambiance of a *Streetcar Named Desire* sort of scene.

On the business district side of the Quarter, Canal Street is, for my money, the grandest Main Street in the United States, with its famous Custom House and many baroque and Victorian business buildings still intact. Best of all, it remains wonderfully alive long after dark, rather than becoming a nocturnal no man's land like the central business districts of so many American cities.

While you're in this neighborhood, take a look at the revitalized Warehouse District on the river side of Camp Street. Here, long rows of handsome nineteenth-century warehouses, recently restored, comfortably coexist with the new office buildings and hotels along Poydras Street and the riverfront.

The real Uptown lies beyond Lee Circle and the Mississippi Bridge. It is comprised of a long chain of attractive old neighborhoods that roughly parallel the city's great uptown avenue, St. Charles. The oldest and finest of these is the Garden District, between Jackson and Louisiana. This area was, and to some extent still is, the bastion of the city's "American," as opposed to its Creole, aristocracy, the New Orleanian equivalent of Beacon Street or Nob Hill—only more intact and visually exciting. The area is packed with splendid town houses, raised plantation cottages, neoclassical mansions, and gingerbread shotguns.

Coliseum Street, which runs through the district between Jackson and Louisiana, just may be the most lovely urban residential street in the nation, though Uptown St. Charles runs a close second. Even the occasional little 1920s and 1940s uglies that have crept in here and there only intensify the beauty that surrounds them. Beyond Napoleon Avenue lies the "uptown" Uptown—a wonderful assortment of neighborhoods such as Audubon Park, University, and Carrolton—where comfortable Victorian and Edwardian homes line up under massive live oaks.

Even an experienced hiker could wear his or her feet down to the ankles before seeing all of New Orleans's architectural treasures. For someone with limited energy and/or time, the Uptown area is best seen with the help of the St. Charles streetcar, which is a delight in its own right (except at rush hours). After exploring the Warehouse District, catch the streetcar on St. Charles Avenue and get off at First Street, just beyond Jackson. (The Avenue will have become abruptly residential.) The Garden District lies to your left as you face Uptown, on the river side of St. Charles. Walk over to Coliseum and turn right. At Coliseum and Washington, you may want to have lunch at Commander's Palace, one of the city's better restaurants both in terms of cuisine and decor. Afterward, when you've seen enough of the District, hop back on the streetcar and travel up to State Street. The neighborhood on both sides of St. Charles hereabouts is surpassingly beautiful, but the best bet is to head again for the river. After a few blocks of looking around, walk uptown to Audubon Park, a large, very pretty urban park. There, if you're in the mood, you can ask your way to the Audubon Zoo, one of the best small zoos in the nation. Among its attractions is a Louisiana swamp exhibit that will set you up for the real thing. If, after all that, you are too tired to walk back to St. Charles to catch the streetcar, you can hop aboard the bus on Magazine Street and take in that thoroughfare's motley mixture of the charming and the flaky as you head downtown.

In recommending New Orleans's marvelous neighborhoods to the pedestrian stranger, I would be remiss if I didn't add a note of caution. The plague of crime that has cursed all of urban America during the last twenty-five years came relatively late to this amiable city; but it now has its share. As is always the case, some areas are less safe than others. Below Canal Street, stay on the river side of Rampart Street. Uptown, unless you have a local guide, confine your wanderings to the areas between St. Charles and Magazine, at least until you get past Jefferson Avenue. You will miss some wonderful neighborhoods by doing so, but you'll still have more to see than you can take in in a month. In general, just use your common sense; the indications that an area might be risky are the same here as anywhere else. But unlike anywhere else, this town is an enchantress. Take it easy, and enjoy her!

Perhaps because New Orleans is such a ready-made tourist gold mine, the state of Louisiana has never felt obliged to develop—or protect—the many other assets that would encourage travelers to remain in the state after they have done the French Quarter. At any rate, Louisiana—specifically southern Louisiana—has only recently begun to make some effort to accommodate nonnatives who would like to see its really remarkable natural scene. There are packaged excursions to plantation country, it is true, and local tours of Cajunland. And there is certainly no lack of boating and fishing opportunities for those who bring boats with them. But except for a couple of municipal campgrounds and one hard-to-reach state park way out on Grand Isle, there are no public camping facilities south or southwest of the City of Light. There *are* some of the greatest marsh refuges in the world down here, as well as the nation's largest river basin swamp, several wildlife management areas, and many scenic bayous. But nearly all the users are natives whose interests are consumer-oriented—hunters, trappers, commercial and sports fishermen. For the most part, despite the former slogan on the state's license plates, few people outside Louisiana know it is a sportsman's paradise. This is too bad—not just because of the pleasure this lovely country could offer travelers, or the economic boost they could offer it, but because a bit more nonconsumptive nature appreciation on the part of outsiders might—who knows?—encourage folks down here to treat their rich natural heritage with more respect than they do.

Be that as it may, travelers in this glorious area have, for the time being, the special pleasure of investigating wild areas that are somewhat off the beaten track. You will love this country; but don't expect to find the Louisiana equivalent of Florida's Myakka or St. Joseph, or Alabama's Gulf State Park—much less a national park or seashore of the sort that this region really deserves. Motorized campers will usually have to find hookups at commercial campgrounds or motels, and canoeists and boaters are well advised to bring their own craft with them. Granted these minor drawbacks, southern Louisiana is a region you don't want to miss.

The state does have one brand-new little national park just south of New Orleans. This is the Barataria sector of **Jean Lafitte National Historical Park**. Small as it is, its 8600 acres offer a nice sample of the sort of country you will find in both the great marsh that composes most of Louisiana's coastline and the vast Atchafalaya Swamp, which lies not far to the west. If you cannot tear yourself away from New Orleans for more than an afternoon, Lafitte at least introduces the natural wonders you will otherwise miss. If, on the other hand, you do plan to investigate the hinterlands, the park makes a nice appetizer.

Jean Lafitte Historical Park has the distinction of being the only national park in the United States that is named after a certified, if colorful, crook. True, during the War of 1812, Lafitte apparently made a deal with General Andrew Jackson to help the Americans in their remarkable victory over the British at the Battle of New Orleans. (The battle, by the way, is commemorated at the Chalmette sector of the park on the eastern side of the city.) But most of the time, the enterprising Jean was occupied in less patriotic pursuits such as piracy and smuggling. Barataria Bay, south of the park, was his home base during the early nineteenth century.

If you don't get caught in commuter traffic, you can reach the park in less than an hour from New Orleans. Cross the Mississippi River Bridge to the West Bank and head upriver on the expressway. By the time this book is published, the overpass over the Harvey Canal will probably be completed; if not, take the Harvey Tunnel. Immediately beyond lies Barataria Boulevard. Follow it south for about seven miles, by which time it will have become Hwy 45. After the traffic and blear of New Orleans's West Bank suburbs, the switch to dense, enclosing forest will come as a sudden benediction. On the right, the spanking new Visitor Center and Museum should be completed. There you can get information about the local ecology and the hiking and canoeing trails. As of now, three walking trails, totaling about five miles, have been completed on the forested eastern side of the park. A planned trail on the west side will lead through the rich estuarine marshes bordering Lake Salvador. A lovely canoe trail—a leisurely five-to-six hour paddle—is already in place. It follows a bayou canal dredged more than a hundred years ago to facilitate the removal of cypress timber in the area.

The really important thing about this Barataria sector of Lafitte Park is that it allows you access to a small corner of the incredibly beautiful, if shrinking, world that lies behind the roads in Louisiana's coastal lowlands. Those lush, green canopies that you see elsewhere at an unapproachable distance, either across a canal or beyond acres of subdivisions, are here accessible without fuss or difficulty. A short walk and you are among vaulting corridors of live oaks, elms, and hickories shading a thick understory of palmettos—the latter advising you, as they did the early settlers, that this area is not flooded too often for too long. In southern Florida this relatively dry land would be called a hammock; and indeed, with the palms subtracted, the forests here resemble those at Myakka, except that in this fertile soil they grow twice as tall. Eventually, one of the paths leads you to a second-growth but nonetheless beautiful swamp of cypress and tupelo traversed by a boardwalk. As for the canoeist, he or she will drift between old spoil banks—the rim of dredged earth thrown up long ago—heavy with overhanging water oaks, black willow, sweet gum, and yaupon. Birding is terrific here and will be still better when the trail into the marshes is completed—though it's only fair to add that even in winter and spring, when it is at its excellent best, it doesn't quite match the incredible opportunities available further west in the great coastal refuges. Deer are present here, too, although the park is too small to protect them from the hunting roundabout; so they are apt to be skittish. On the other hand, mink, nutria, and even otters are quite often seen scooting across the trails.

Something else that you might see across the trails—literally across them—in late summer or fall is the huge web of the handsome but scarily large nephila spider. The nephila's web is one of the incidental hazards of strolling through the southern boondocks. If you are abstracted enough to collide with something so plainly visible—as I have done countless times—you'll get an unpleasant inkling of what the poor dragonflies and moths must go through when they do the same dumb thing. The nephila herself won't hurt you (though she might wish she could after you've messed up her nice web), but you'll be picking her filaments out of your hair for the next ten minutes. Viewed from an unsnared perspective, however, she and her web are something to marvel at.

No campgrounds are planned for this lovely but too-small park. I am told that canoe rentals will be available, but motorized boating will not be permitted. Boaters need not feel deprived, however. Immediately to the south of the park lies the town of Lafitte, the main gateway to Barataria Bay, where the fishing, when it's good, is very, very good indeed. (Jean Lafitte National Historical Park, Room 206, U.S. Custom House, 423 Canal Street, New Orleans, Louisiana 70130; 504/348–2923.)

An important note: By this time you will have become used to the idea that our progress around the Gulf Coast often involves alternate routes, each offering different pleasures, different aspects of the natural scene. Once aware of the options, you can make your own decisions, depending on your preferences. Or, if you have time enough, or a round-trip itinerary, you can usually have your cake and eat it too. The same principle applies in southern Louisiana, but there are special problems apart from the scarcity of public camping facilities and state parks mentioned above. West of New Orleans, the out-of-doors comes under two broad headings: the Great Marsh, which extends along the state's entire coastline, and the Great Swamp—the Atchafalaya—which lies athwart the coastal plain west of Baton Rouge. Although closely linked in the ecological sense, they are separate worlds as far as the traveler is concerned. There is no convenient way that you can sample, much less seriously explore, both worlds without doing a lot of zigging and zagging along the way. Hwys 90 and 82 give some access to the marsh, and I-10 and Hwy 70 or 75 enable you to approach the Atchafalaya; but the distances apart are considerable. In this travelogue, I propose to first introduce the Louisiana marshes and describe an east-to-west tour of them, and then back up and proceed in a sim-

ilar way with the Atchafalaya. Consulting your road map, you can decide how much of either or both routes you wish to explore, and
which roads suit your purposes if you plan to shuttle back and forth
between one itinerary and the other.

The Great Marsh

Rivers still shape the destinies of human cultures. But nowhere west
of the Nile is that obvious ecological fact more vividly illustrated than
in southern Louisiana. The physical existence of this part of the state
is due solely to the Mississippi River's fickle changefulness—its former
changefulness, that is. The mighty river and its tributaries drain half
of our nation's land surface. In doing so, the Mississippi carries not
only a stupendous volume of water in its lower reaches, but also an
enormous quantity of silt, or sediment—the washed-away topsoils of
places as far away as the Dakotas and Pennsylvania. In the past, and
this includes the quite recent past, these trillions of tons of sediment
were continuously deposited on the shallow coastal shelf of the Gulf
of Mexico, where they formed a vast, immensely fertile alluvial plain.
The Mississippi, like all alluvial rivers, was forever changing its route
across this abuilding delta, always trying to find a shorter, easier way
to the Gulf. Thanks to this temperamental indecisiveness, most of the
coast of Louisiana and southwestern Mississippi consists of the beds
of abandoned river routes along which the aforementioned sediment
was richly spread. This great delta is the river's masterpiece: a low, flat
landscape that has produced not only some of the world's richest agricultural lands, but the most productive marshlands in the world. In
our travels, we have been no strangers to marshes; but compared to
these of southern Louisiana, all the others are in the amateur class.
Because this is so, the Mississippi Delta is the capstone in the northern
Gulf's fertile crescent of fisheries.

   Coastal marshes are classified into scores of habitat types. But in
a general way, they come under the headings of freshwater, intermediate (low salinity), brackish (moderate salinity), and saltwater
marsh. Each hosts great numbers of dependent organisms, and all are
ecologically important—never more so than when they exist in an
elaborate sequence of overlapping zones. Scientists have repeatedly
demonstrated that an acre of healthy marsh will produce much more
protein than can be extracted from an acre of top-grade agricultural
land. Nearly all of the commercially valuable forms of marine life, including crabs, shrimp, oysters, clams, and most commercial fish species, are totally dependent on the marshes during at least part of their
life cycle. All of them depend on the alluvial marsh and its rich soup
of decaying vegetation and nutrient-rich water for their well-being. So
do countless other species, including millions of migrant waterfowl,
shorebirds, fur-bearers, amphibians and—last but not least—humans. Quite apart from what we put in our stomachs in the way of

seafood, the marshes enrich our fertilizers, fatten chickens and nour-ish our pets, supply assorted oils, and foster human vanities in the form of fur coats and perfumes. They buffer coastal communities against the full force of hurricanes. And they provide hundreds of thousands of people with jobs.

So—you would think that we would value this priceless resource, right? Wrong. Not to make a long story of it, but in the last half-cen-tury we have dredged, drained, polluted, and developed half of our marshes out of existence. Nowhere, not even in Chesapeake Bay or the Everglades, is the situation more calamitous than in Louisiana, a state that owes much of its economic and cultural vitality (not to men-tion its geographic existence), to the marsh ecology. In an epic reversal of the traditional land-building pattern of the delta, the state is now losing forty square miles of its coast—that's not a typo, folks; I mean *miles*, not acres—each year. Of course, the sea is always at war with the marsh, doing its best to erode and invade the coastline. So the marshes must continually receive transfusions of soil and freshwater from the river in order to rebuild and expand. This is where humans come in. The main problem is that the Army Corps of Engineers' lev-ees, which extend to the very mouth of the river, have prevented the Mississippi from dispensing its annual largesse to the surrounding del-ta. Since the present river mouth is now at the edge of the continental shelf, all those billions of tons of sediment are simply dumped into the deep, where they don't even do the fish much good. The problem has been compounded by the oil industry, which has made a killing in Louisiana's marshes. Thousands of miles of canals and channels have been gouged through the marshlands, thereby accelerating erosion. The real heartbreaker is that this ecological catastrophe could have been foreseen and, to some extent, offset decades ago. But Louisiana politicians don't argue with oil companies, and the Corps, unfortu-nately, rarely considers the ecological consequences of its actions. The good news is that during the last few years environmentalists and fish-ermen have forced the Corps to conduct studies of the problem, and the state legislature is finally getting nervous. But it will be the turn of the century before even a small measure of mitigation is achieved. Meantime, much of the rich land surface that is now indicated on your Louisiana map as lying south of New Orleans will have been replaced by the blue of the Gulf.

Ah, well. As southern Louisianans say with the tolerant, easy-going shrug that is part of their charm and also part of their problem, "There's plenty left." Certainly this is true, especially in the south-western part of the state where we are headed, and where the erosion problem is much less severe than it is further east.

Cajunland   Parts of Hwy 90 west of New Orleans have been converted into an expressway, but the West Bank stretch from the Mis-

sissippi Bridge to Des Allemands is often crowded with traffic—and it's an eyesore to boot. To get around all that, you may want to take I-10 on the East Bank as it heads north toward Baton Rouge. Although interstates are not usually the best way to see America, the stretch through here offers some interesting views, since much of it is elevated above the shores of Lake Pontchartrain and its adjoining swamps. It is also a convenient way to take in a few antebellum homes along the Mississippi without wandering too far from our southerly course. When you reach the Gonzales (Hwy 44) exit, head west to Burnside and then turn right on the River Road (Hwy 942). Almost at once you will be at Houmas House, a grand example of the Louisiana plantation style, standing almost in the shadow of one of the lower Mississippi's many petrochemical plants. Regular tours are available (of the plantation, not the plant). Right up the road are a couple of other lovelies: the charming little Boucage and, at a distance, L'Hermitage.

Unless you plan to use I-10 to reach the more northerly sections of the Atchafalaya, you should now head back south along the River Road for about ten miles until you reach the Sunshine Bridge, taking in more plantation homes and industrial development along the way. Cross the bridge and head west and south on Hwy 70 until you reach Morgan City. This road is more scenic than the easterly sections of Hwy 90, offering views of sugar-cane fields, levees, bayous, and bottomland hardwoods, as well as some not-so-beautiful residential development. Most important, it also provides access for canoeists to a lovely stretch of the Atchafalaya Basin along Little Bayou Sorrel—about which, more when we discuss the swamp.

At Morgan City, the direction you choose will depend on whether you wish to visit the Houma and Grand Isle area of Louisiana's eastern marshlands—perhaps completing a loop that will take you back to New Orleans—or whether you want to tour the heart of Cajunland and the great wildlife refuges further to the west. Although the general motto of this book is Westward Ho, at least on the northern Gulf, it would not do to bypass this interesting eastern part of Cajun country without at least a brief visit. You *are* deep in the land of the Cajuns at this point, just in case you hadn't realized it yet. The Cajuns, as every reader of Longfellow's "Evangeline" knows, are descendants of the French Acadians who were exiled from Nova Scotia in the latter part of the eighteenth century. They made the long trek to the bayou country because Louisiana was still a French territory, and many of the older residents still have a dialect form of French as their first language.

Houma to Grand Isle   Between Houma and Morgan City, Hwy 90 follows Bayou Black, one of the countless slow-moving rivers that were until quite recently the main waterways of southern Louisiana. Even now the larger bayous carry a lot of water traffic to and

from the Gulf. Along their banks the Cajun settlers built homes, and their descendants do the same. Bayou Black is pretty typical. Its black water is splashed with bright green duckweed, and its banks are lined with great oaks as well as an almost continuous line of habitations on either side, ranging from lovely old Acadian frame dwellings, to relatively modest plantation houses, to modern ranch homes, to trailer ready-mades. At Hwy 311, on the western outskirts of Houma, plantation buffs will want to drive north for several miles along Little Bayou Black, where several splendid antebellum homes, the legacy of the great days of the sugar plantations, can be seen—from grandiose Southdown to the exquisite Orange Grove with its Acadian structural contours. Contemporary buildings—industrial, commercial, and residential—impinge on all of these lovely dwellings without any concern for climate, regional tradition, or setting. But if you do some imaginative subtraction of the clutter surrounding them, these old homes still look great.

Houma is distinguished by its collection of navigable bayous and canals. Shrimp boats and oil-industry vessels are in evidence everywhere, and it is both odd and pleasant to see them matter-of-factly cruising past the town's backyards on their own special streets. At bridge crossings the nice, damp smell of the marshes, and of fresh shrimp and wet nets, comes wafting up at you. Houma has lost most of its one-time laid-back charm, but it is still unmistakably a bayou town. It is also the focal point for both swamp tours and plantation tours in the area. The former take visitors into a wild bayou world that can only be guessed at from the highways. Herons, egrets, gallinules, alligators, turtles, and snakes usually show themselves while your Cajun guide fills you in on local color. In spring, Bayou Annie Miller, the most famous of the local guides, will take you to Lake Hatch, deep in the marsh, to see a great rookery of nesting white ibis, spoonbills, herons, and egrets, as well as a friendly alligator who comes when Annie calls him. For those interested in fishing, commercial charter boats can be hired here or in nearby towns. Check with the local tourist commission for advice. (Houma-Terrebonne Tourist Commission, Box 2792, Houma, Louisiana 70361; 504/868–2732.)

To the south on Hwy 1, via Hwy 24, lie the great eastern marshes. For the next fifteen miles or so, you will be on the southernmost stretch of the "longest street in the world." This is a narrow belt of merged-together Cajun fishing communities that extends along both sides of Bayou LaFourche for seventy-five miles, from Napoleonville in the north to Golden Meadow. Stay on the west side of Bayou LaFourche and enjoy the parade of vessels going about their business in the famous bayou right beside you. (Warning: when you reach Golden Meadow, drive below the speed limit. The town is a notorious speed trap.) Ten miles further south, at Leeville, a high bridge crosses the bayou. Even though you can't stop, the view from this overpass is in itself worth the trouble of this longish detour. The mosaic of grass and water laid out below you is absolutely stunning in its shimmering immensity. Short of being airborne, this is one of the best opportunities you will have along the entire Louisiana Gulf Coast to take in a wide view of the marsh landscape in all its jigsaw complexity and beauty. The marsh here, by the way, is predominantly saline, its flooded "meadows" composed of oystergrass, black rush, and saltgrass. If you have some string, a few pieces of meat (preferably overripe chicken) to tie to it, and a landing net, you may want to try your luck catching crabs at a nearby inlet.

For birders, this area is a paradise, especially from September to March. Along with countless waders, shorebirds, gulls, and terns, the marshes teem with migrant waterfowl, especially the dabbling ducks: pintails, shovelers, gadwalls, widgeons, and—first to show up in fall— the blue-winged teal. But there is also an abundance of scaups, redheads, and goldeneyes in the more open bays. In the experienced view of local birders, Hwy 3090, the spur of road to Fourchon City, is the best of the best. But the fine birding throughout this entire area continues all the way to Grand Isle.

Most of the long sand pit that is Grand Isle has been given over to fishing camps. They have no business being on this exposed, eroding beach, which the state has been rebuilding recently. Like their predecessors, they will sooner or later be swatted into Barataria Bay by a hurricane. Yet somehow I don't get as stirred up about this ragtag jumble of boxes-on-piers as I do about the megadevelopments on the coasts of Florida and Alabama. There is a relaxed unpretentiousness to this community that gives it a homely charm.

In the background, there are bits and pieces of woodland where, during their spring migration, staggering numbers of songbirds load the branches like Christmas ornaments. On the beach—to which you have access at any of several boardwalk piers—you might even see a brown pelican or two coasting above the mild surf. Louisiana's state bird was exterminated almost overnight a couple of decades ago by pesticides. Embarrassed state officials have reintroduced the species to the eastern marshes, where they are making a gladdening comeback; but there is no chance that their numbers will ever return to the tens of thousands that once ornamented this coast, if only because so much of their coastal habitat is being washed out from under them. Still, they are around, so keep your eye open. Now that peninsular Florida is far behind us, we can no longer take the sight of pelicans for granted.

Grand Isle State Park lies at the eastern end of the island. As earlier noted, this is the only state park with public campgrounds along Louisiana's entire coast. It, and Grand Isle generally, also possess the only swimming beach fronting on the Gulf that is both accessible and well maintained. Recently, the park has undergone extensive renovation, including a major effort to rebuild the badly eroded beaches.

Besides campsites, bathhouses, a nature center, a new observation platform, and swimming, the place offers some good surf fishing and boating. (Grand Isle State Park, Box 741, Grand Isle, Louisiana 70358; 504/787–2559.)

Morgan City and the Bayou Teche Country

As you approach Morgan City on Hwy 90, note the stretch of tupelo and cypress swamp that you pass through just west of Gibson and the junction with Hwy 20. Though technically outside the Atchafalaya Basin, the green-gray-black interlace of this dense, flooded forest will give you some intimation of the nearby Great Swamp that we will visit later. All too quickly, this intimation yields to intimations of a quite different kind: immense construction cranes tower above the trees, and the frames of colossal offshore oil platforms lie on their sides along the bayous. Morgan City is a boom town, the center of Louisiana's offshore oil-drilling industry, and it looks exactly the way you would expect that sort of place to look. It is also an accident waiting to happen, since the flood-prone Atchafalaya Spillway is literally at its doorstep. If there was ever a place *not* to encourage industrial and residential development, this has got to be it. But the location is convenient for the oil companies, and that's what counts.

For our purposes, the important thing about Morgan City is that it has a pleasant municipal campground with hookups, ramp, etc., on the shore of Lake Palourde. The lake is a large one, decked out with cypress. Even prettier are the swampy bayous that feed into it. There are good opportunities for boating and fishing here, but the scenery gets pretty crowded in warm weather, especially on weekends when motorboats and water-skiers are much in evidence. Still, for a fee, you can camp here for as long as ten days, and it makes a handy base from which to explore the bayou country and the southern reaches of the Atchafalaya. (Morgan City Tourist Information Center, 725 Myrtle Street, Morgan City, Louisiana 70380; 504/384–3343.)

Incidentally, Morgan City has a tiny Swamp Park that the kids might enjoy. Disneyland it's not, but there are real deer and a bit of real swamp, as well as mannequins engaged in the sorts of activities that few of the local people engage in anymore, such as picking Spanish moss (for mattresses, etc.), poling pirogues, and camping on houseboats.

Just a few miles beyond Morgan City and the great, broad torrent of the Atchafalaya River lies the most scenic plantation road that survives in southern Louisiana or, for that matter, anywhere on the Gulf Coast circuit. This is Hwy 182 between Calumet and New Iberia. In an on-again, off-again way, the road follows the serpentine course of legendary Bayou Teche through the heart of sugar-cane country. To be honest, its beauties are also on-again, off-again; but they nevertheless come closer here than anywhere else to surviving as a *toute ensemble*.

Considering the toll that Union troops, neglect, and fire have exacted, an amazing number of plantation homes still survive in southeastern and south-central Louisiana. Some of those near Baton Rouge or Thibodaux are more perfect, in strict architectural terms, than anything you will see along Hwy 182; but in most cases they appear as isolated oases, rejecting, and rejected by, their contemporary surroundings. In contrast, on Hwy 182, enough of the homes remain to keep you looking out the car window rather than at your guidebook. There must be at least a couple of dozen antebellum houses along these few miles, interspersed with wide fields of sugar cane. But that isn't all. A considerable number of raised Acadian homeplaces and cottages, their steep roofs extending in an uninterrupted line over sturdy wood porches, are also still intact. You will even see a few of the little Cajun shotgun houses that were once commonplace along every road in bayou country. Since World War II, southern Louisiana's oil boom has lined all those other roads with mile after mile of suburbanite houses and brand-new mobile homes. Certainly, no one begrudges Cajunland its contemporary affluence, but it is sad that the character of its charming, everyday past has been thrown away so carelessly. (Ironically, the renovation of traditional Acadian dwellings, and modern adaptations of its style, would have provided housing that was more economical and more congenial to the climate and setting than the ready-made architecture that has displaced it.) A Cajun friend of mine once explained, "We wanted to look *Americanized*." Cultural pride, he said, had come to his home region too late to do much good.

Except, that is, along Hwy 182. Here even the little towns, such as Verdunville, Centerville, and Franklin, retain something of their distinctive regional character. Indeed, Franklin and its environs get my vote for the best concentration of fine regional dwellings in all of Louisiana. (It's interesting to contrast all that traditional architecture with the modern, totalitarian-looking courthouse that oppresses the town square.) Another favorite stopping place of mine is Jeanerette. Overall, this town is not exactly attention-getting, although there are some fine buildings in and near it. (In particular, do not miss Alice plantation house on the east side of Bayou Teche; it is an example of one of the earliest Louisiana plantation styles with its different yet harmonious sets of columns along the first- and second-floor galleries.) The main reason I like to stop here, especially if I'm feeling hungry, is to buy the fresh French bread baked in the hundred-year-old brick ovens at Le Jeune's Bakery. Man cannot live by bread alone, of course; so add liberal applications of tomatoes, cheese, ham, fried oysters, or whatever, and you will have created a "po-boy"—a delicious loaf sandwich that southern Louisianans require the way the Irishmen require their potatoes. (Speaking of food, by the way, this entire area is notable for its excellent, unfancy restaurants featuring Cajun cooking.

In general, stay away from the motel eateries, and ask the locals about where to get a good meal. Here in the Jeanerette area, Landry's and, especially, the Yellow Bowl are good bets.)

Architecture and food aside, there is another reason for paying special attention to Jeanerette. Nearby, on the eastern side of Bayou Teche, lies **Lake Fausse Point** and its attractive new campground with hookups. A nearby canal and ramp offer access to this lake, which is even prettier, more cypressy, and, thus far, less heavily used than Morgan City's Lake Palourde on the other side of the Atchafalaya Basin. There is also a guided nature tour available. (Jeanerette Chamber of Commerce, 500 Main Street, Jeanerette, Louisiana; 318/276–4293.)

Before we reach New Iberia, I should mention one other bonus that this winding road has to offer: the live oaks. Since we left the Everglades, they have never been out of sight for long, but their presence in this bayou country is something very special. The fertility of the soil, and the fact that they grow here in open pastures and at the approaches to antebellum mansions, allows them the space and energy they need to achieve majestic proportions. Add to those advantages the fact that their trailing mantles of Spanish moss, which everywhere in the Deep South have been diminished by a mysterious blight, are here still much in evidence, and you become suddenly aware that this most patriarchal tree in all the world is allowing itself to be really seen. If live oaks had a consciousness, they would choose to be solitary. In crowded forests they must compete and struggle like other trees; but notice in this bayou country how two or three of them standing together in a field will lean away from each other like tactful Ents. Live oaks ennoble any landscape of which they are a part. Here along Bayou Teche all other natural forms, and even the traditional architecture, seem to have been shaped by their commanding presence.

The bustling town of New Iberia has lost much of the charm that still lingers in the smaller communities along the Teche, but its East Main Street (which is what Hwy 182 becomes) is the showplace for a number of grand homes. The Shadows-on-the-Teche is the most famous of them, but do not miss Mintmere, a lovely raised cottage, and the Broussard House—a rare, perfectly preserved example of eighteenth-century Acadian architecture. Coming from the east on Hwy 182, you will pass both these latter homes (they can be toured) about a mile before reaching the Shadows and downtown New Iberia.

St. Martinville, another noted town in Cajunland, is not far away, and you may wish to visit it because of its pretty courthouse square, or because this is the locale of Longfellow's celebrated poem "Evangeline." Actually, the main attraction is the Longfellow-Evangeline Commemorative Park outside town, where an absolute gem of an early Acadian plantation house is preserved. Not to belabor the point, but when you see it, you will wonder, as I have, why modern builders in the area have not been instructed by its sensible, elegantly simple design.

As noted earlier, zigzagging is the rule in bayou country. You can't head toward one interesting place without heading away from another, which is what you will be doing if you head toward St. Martinville and away from Avery Island. For our outdoors purposes, Avery Island, reached via Hwy 329, is much the better bet. The island is one of three unique formations in the Louisiana marshes aptly known as salt domes. Millions of years ago when the southern part of the North American continent was being formed, huge subterranean flows of pure salt were pushed to the surface. There they formed domes that are higher by far than any other land for many miles inland. Indians used to collect brine from the tops of these hills; now large companies mine the interiors, creating a weird underground network of salt caverns and tunnels. Avery Island is the only one of these islands that is really accessible to the public, although it is possible to drive to Weeks Island a few miles to the east and observe from the car window a dense, hillside forest—including even pines—that is unlike any we have seen since leaving the northern shore of Lake Pontchartrain. (If you do choose that detour along Hwy 83, it will probably be because you wish to reach Cypremort Point at the edge of Vermilion Bay. There is a boat ramp there, as well as a small state park where you can picnic, swim, and launch sailboats, but not camp. The fishing in Vermilion Bay is renowned locally. Sadly, however, Cypremort Point—an oak ridge, or chenier, that would be beautiful in a natural state—is covered with fishing camps and a dismaying amount of litter.)

Back to Avery Island. The island is owned by descendants of the McIlhenny family, and apart from its salt mine and tactfully hidden oil wells, it boasts fields of pepper bushes and a picturesque old factory, made of brick and covered with ivy, that turns out the tasty Tabasco sauce that has an honored place in almost everyone's cupboard. The condiment was concocted in the 1840s by Edmund McIlhenny from peppers he had planted on the island, and the business has been a going concern for more than a hundred years. But we have better reasons for honoring Edmund McIlhenny. He was that nineteenth-century rarity: a conservationist. During the decades when egrets were being pushed to the edge of extinction by plume hunters, he made the island a refuge for the birds and worked hard to have the trade in their feathers outlawed. Another member of the family, the late E. A. McIlhenny, carried on the conservationist tradition. He was largely responsible for the establishment of nearby Rockefeller Refuge and continued the protection of wildlife species on Avery Island itself. He was a trained naturalist, and it was one of his pleasures to landscape much of the island. He imported many tropical trees and shrubs and, in general, created a botanical wonderland.

Although a visit to the picturesque Tabasco factory is fun, the birds and gardens are what most visitors come to see, particularly in the spring. Racks constructed over one of the ponds are gladly used by American, snowy, and cattle egrets as a rookery site. Unconcerned, they raise their young only a few yards from where you watch. As for the gardens, they are not only very lovely with their massed banks of azaleas, camellias, and you-name-it, as well as their pretty paths and gleaming lagoons, but they are full of beguiling incongruities. Where else do moon bridges, exotic blooms, and an authentic Buddha share the scene with alligators, cypress trees, deer, and Spanish moss? And nutria?

The nutria, a South American rodent that looks and acts like a muskrat that has taken growth hormones, has a special relationship with Avery Island. It was here that the animal got its start as an immigrant species, thanks to McIlhenny's penchant for importing exotics. In this case the experiment almost got out of hand. For a while after it was introduced to the Louisiana marshes, the prolific creature seemed hell-bent on gobbling up everything green in sight, not excluding rice and sugar cane. However, its numbers are now more in balance with the environment. Since there is a steady demand for its fur, it has displaced the muskrat as cornerstone of the state's multimillion-dollar fur industry. Nutrias can often be seen swimming in roadside canals or fastidiously grooming themselves on platforms of grass in freshwater marshes. With their buck teeth and beady eyes, they have much the same furry appeal as a beaver or a woodchuck, their rat tails notwithstanding.

The Marsh Refuges

Our journey now takes us to Abbeville and Kaplan along Hwy 14. Half of the route is a one-street subdivision that goes on for miles; the other half is sugar-cane fields. (Somewhere along here, it would be a good idea to fill up the gas tank, since there are only a couple of easy-to-miss gas stations between the Intracoastal Waterway and Oak Grove.) At Kaplan we head south on Hwy 35 and then connect with Hwy 82 on its way to Pecan Island. The minute the old Intracoastal Waterway is crossed, we have left the "mainland" behind. We are in the Great Marsh again. Be prepared to enjoy it, since we won't be leaving it for the next hundred miles. Suddenly there is the sense of limitless space, an uninterrupted prairie of waving grasses wider than the Everglades. If you can arrange it, drive this road on a spring or autumn evening. Long V's of waterfowl will be crossing skies stained the color that inspired the name of the nearby Vermilion Bay. But if vermilion doesn't suit you, you may have gold, lavender, orange, peach, puce—that's right, puce—or any of a few dozen other hues instead, depending on the moment and the patch of sky you're looking at.

These first miles, while we are heading directly south, pass through a great expanse of freshwater marsh. How can you be sure? Well, unless you're an expert, you can't always be. But generally, freshwater marshes have more bright greens in their coloring and more different kinds of plants than any other type of marsh. Look for water lilies and for free-floating rafts of water hyacinth with their pulpy, curled leaves and, in summer, lavender blooms. Also look for bull-tongue (sagittaria), which likes the margins of ponds. It has modest white flowers and narrow, tapered leaves that look somewhat like aspidistra except for the much louder green of their coloring. Another dead giveaway of a freshwater marsh is alligatorweed, which, like the water hyacinth, forms free-floating mats of plants with lance-shaped leaves and small, white flowers. (Like the water hyacinth, it is an import that has made itself too much at home in our wet places, oppressing the native flora. Nobody has nice things to say about it.) Actually, there is a simpler way of telling a freshwater marsh from any other: just notice if people are fishing in the roadside canals. If they are, they are trying to catch bass, bream, and catfish—freshwater fish all.

Pecan Island is a chenier, one of the narrow sand ridges that lie inland from the Coast, often separating freshwater or brackish marsh on their inland side from the saline marsh that lies between them and the Gulf. They are invariably mantled by storm-blasted live oaks, along with understories of palmetto, hackberry, hercules'-club, yaupon, and—looking out of place—prickly pear cactus. When hurricanes strike, they are sanctuary for all the creatures of the swamp that cannot swim or fly away, which in the old days included people as well as raccoons and deer. And in the spring, of course, they are the precious first landfall for tired songbirds that have survived the long, hard flight across the Gulf.

Twenty-five years ago there were only a couple of dozen dwellings on Pecan Island. Now fishing camps and trailers are all over the place. Sad to say, none of Louisiana's large cheniers have been protected as natural areas. However, a few small cheniers lying near the Coast are within the boundaries of Rockefeller Refuge.

As we head west along Hwy 82, the camps, veteran oaks, and Pecan Island itself peter out. We are entering a zone of intermediate and brackish marsh. Notice the thick, cornlike stands of roseau cane— always a sure sign that the ground is a bit elevated above the marsh— that crowd the dredged banks of the canal. With a breeze swaying them and a red-winged blackbird or a grackle clinging to their stems, they are a Japanese silk screen come to life. To the south lies the twenty-mile-long expanse of Rockefeller Refuge. You cannot see the Gulf, five miles away, but you can smell its briny presence. Before long, the road again edges a wooded ridge. We are at Grand Chenier, which, as its name implies, is the longest of them all. The weathered, welcoming oaks reappear, as well as a thin line of houses and camps.

The headquarters and research buildings for Louisiana state's **Rockefeller Refuge** are located at the western end of the tract. You can pick up information there about what to see when. Opportunities for motorists and pedestrians are limited to a single gravel track that begins about three-quarters of a mile beyond the headquarters buildings and heads out for several miles into the marsh. It is called a nature trail, but it isn't really, at least not like the one we will visit at Sabine National Wildlife Refuge further to the west. There are no informational markers or anything like that, and most users seem to be local people who come to catch crabs and shrimp. All too typically, they leave a lot of litter behind. Yet you should not let these drawbacks put you off. Most days, there are not many people about, especially after you reach the point where the road is blocked and you must proceed on foot. Nowhere else along the Coast can you walk as far into a brackish-to-saline marsh as you can here. This is not, in the ordinary sense, a "pretty" world. There are not the variegated patterns of a freshwater marsh, and once you leave Hwy 82, there are no trees in sight. During the first couple of miles, the roseau cane on either side of the narrow road blocks the view (although if you stop at one of the unoccupied pull-overs, you may spot an alligator in the canal on your left). Further out, the screen of cane disappears. You are left with a seemingly limitless expanse of wire grass, widgeon grass, and saltgrass, interspersed with mud flats and sheets of water so shallow that, when the tide is

Louisiana marsh. *Photo by Jim Grice.*

out, dowitchers and black-necked stilts appear to be literally standing on the surface even when they are yards from the nearest shore. This prospect is admittedly monotonous; but then, so are views of prairies, deserts, tundras, beaches, heaths, and assorted other natural landscapes that a lot of people seem to find irresistible.

The great thing about this particular lovely monotony is that, more than any of the others, it teems with life. Mosquitoes, I must admit, are part of all that teeming. We are back in their country, so you should be armed against them during the warm months. But consider all the other things that teem. Shrimp and crabs are here for the taking in summer and early fall if you take along the inexpensive equipment needed to catch them from the shore. If you have a boat, the refuge's many lakes and impoundments provide a bounty of speckled trout, redfish, and flounder. The mud banks are covered with the tracks of raccoons, mink, nutria, and muskrat. In the shallows and the reeds are egrets, herons—great blue, little blue, tricolored, green-backed, night—ibis, cormorants, bitterns, king rails, and on and on. As for the songbirds, we have already commented on them. Come here in late April or early May, ideally just after the passage of a frontal system, and the "fallout" of birds in the oaks along Hwy 82 will leave you with your jaw sagging in amazement.

It is the waterfowl, though, that make this part of the Coast in general, and this refuge in particular, so incredibly special. Twenty-five percent of all the ducks and geese in North America come down the Mississippi flyway and settle in these marshes for the winter. Nowhere else in the country can they be seen in such concentrations. Even if you are just driving along the Coast road, their morning and evening flights can astound the eye. Ideally, the way to experience these great flocks and their watery world is in a flat-bottomed john boat, coasting along the canals at dawn or dusk just as the birds are moving to or from their feeding grounds. At times they rise in clouds that actually darken the horizon. More often they are strung out in long pennants trailing across the sky. Sometimes they will fly overhead in the day's last light; you can even hear them talking quietly to each other as they pass. Around you the rushes are silhouetted black against the sky, the water turns to molten gold, and in the distance the ducks and geese descend to the impoundments.

If none of that turns you on, chances are that you are not a marshy sort of person.

Rockefeller is a state refuge, but set up under strict guidelines imposed by the Rockefeller Foundation. For that fortunate reason, no hunting is permitted here—in contrast to most federal "refuges." But as long as you get a permit at the headquarters, boating and noncommercial fishing, crabbing, crawfishing, oyster gathering and shrimping are allowed. There is an important proviso, however: although some canals and bayous are open year-round, most of the refuge is closed to the public from December 1 to the end of February. Write to the headquarters for regulations and other information. No camping or boat rentals are available. (Rockefeller Refuge, Route 1, Box 20-B, Grand Chenier, Louisiana 70643.)

The stretch of road from Oak Grove to Cameron is another of those one-street suburbs—several miles of single-file housing, with the marsh behind and the Coast, coming closer to the road, in front. Just west of Oak Grove an easy-to-miss road leads out to Rutherford Beach, the first beach that can be reached by car since we left Grand Isle. Adaptable young folk who are traveling on a shoestring budget may be interested in the spot because they can put up a tent on the beach at no cost; but I wouldn't exactly recommend it. Much of the time, the sand here is thinly filmed with muddy sediments from the nearby marshes. Also, the berm is littered with plastic junk tossed overboard by the thoughtful people on the oil rigs and shrimp boats offshore. Still, broke is broke, and I have camped in worse places myself. There is also a small lot here among the dozen or so fishing camps where hookups can be had at a modest fee. Most RV campers, however, will settle for hookups at the few motels in this area.

If you do drive the two miles to Rutherford Beach you will notice the splintered wrecks of a couple of buildings along the way. They are melancholy reminders of the scary vulnerability of this coastline. In 1957, Cameron was destroyed by Hurricane Audrey, probably the most deadly hurricane ever to come ashore in western Louisiana. High tides swamped the area hours before the full force of the winds arrived, and people were trapped in their attics and on their roofs. More than five hundred people perished, and the town was obliterated. Now, except for those few out-of-the way broken buildings, you would never guess that any of that had happened. The place is booming. Its supply depots, processing plants, and crowded ship channel service the offshore oil rigs in this part of the Gulf, as well as—no kidding—the nation's leading port in terms of fish and shellfish volume: an average harvest of 900 *million* pounds of menhaden, shrimp, and crabs annually! Despite—and because of—this evident prosperity, there is nothing attractive to look at here except the sky in the evenings, the egrets flying overhead, and the fleets of shrimp and menhaden boats lined up at docks along the Intracoastal Waterway. Yet I always enjoy being in Cameron, at least for a little while. A New England fishing village it is not. Concepts of Puritan orderliness and neatness have never inhibited its Cajun consciousness; and the influx of nonnative roustabouts and roughnecks attracted by the oil industry has not exactly toned up the local lifestyle. But the place still has the air of a small town, unlike Morgan City. Its people—as is almost always the case in Cajunland—are friendly, work hard, and know how to enjoy themselves. Speaking of which, there are a couple of restaurants here, Pat's and the Jetties, where you can go blind trying to eat all the delicious things piled on a seafood platter. On the other hand, if you want to catch your own seafood platter, it is best to have your own boat. If you don't, however, the town's rock jetties are a fine on-shore fishing site. There are no boat rentals.

In winter, Cameron hosts the Louisiana Ornithological Society for obvious reasons. The bird counts here are always near the top of the national lists. Like most other sizable Cajun towns, Cameron also holds annual festivals at one time or another featuring street dances, fish fries, and parades; duck-calling, oyster-shucking, and/or nutria-skinning contests; and so on. (Note: most of Cameron Parish is owned by a few corporations and individuals. Organized tourism, as distinguished from local and regional recreational use, seems not to be particularly promoted by the parish. For information, your best bet is: Lake Charles/Calcasieu Parish Convention and Tourist Commission, Box 1912, Lake Charles, Louisiana 70602.)

A free, round-the-clock ferry crosses the Intracoastal Waterway at Cameron. On the other side, the road quickly brings you to Holly Beach, a little community of fishing camps where you can find no-frills hookups at the local grocery store/filling station. I like this modest place, set out against a great golden expanse of brackish marsh, with the wide Gulf lapping at the creosote pilings of the front row of houses on the beach. Like the community at Grand Isle, only smaller, it is the antithesis of the resort towns on the Florida and Mississippi coasts. The beach is pretty littered, although during the summer months is does get cleaned up periodically. At that time, the camps are full of papas, mamas, and kids spending their days crabbing, boating, and fishing, and their nights playing cards, drinking beer, and visiting friends from the summer before—or, in the case of the oil-field workers who rent some of the camps, whooping it up in the local bar.

But it is during the off seasons, when the summer fishermen have gone back to the "mainland" and the duck hunters haven't yet descended, that Holly Beach has a special charm. The empty matchbox camps are lined up along five or six deserted lanes, and in the absence of human activity there is an air of impermanency and expectancy about the place. This perception need not be dismissed as an imaginative fancy: the entire coast hereabouts is eroding away pretty rapidly, and the days of Holly Beach are numbered. If you drive a few more miles along the shore to Constance Beach—identical to Holly Beach except that it is cleaner and quieter and has an especially nice little motel on the beach—you will see what I mean. The coastal road has been moved back in several places. The black rocks that have been thrown down on the narrow beach are no more successful as a bulwark against the tides than the piles of litter—more souvenirs of the offshore rigs and shrimping boats—that share the beach with them. At Constance Beach, a front row of fishing camps has already surrendered to the Gulf; a few of them still lean crazily on their piers. The folks who live here grumble about the failure of the politicians to do "something," but otherwise accept the situation with a fatalistic shrug. Part of the problem, it seems, goes back to the Mississippi River and its confining levees: the littoral drift that used to carry sediment even this far westward no longer has any sediment to carry; so now the Gulf takes away the land and doesn't put it back.

You can drive on to Texas from here, but our own course lies northward on Hwy 27. It would be a great pity to leave this region without visiting **Sabine National Wildlife Refuge**. Sabine is even larger than Rockefeller—142,000 acres. Like Rockefeller, it is intensively managed for waterfowl. There are enormous freshwater impoundments that attempt to mitigate the effects of saltwater intrusion created elsewhere in Louisiana's marshes by dredging activities. These pools are a magnet for hundreds of thousands of water birds, waders, and waterfowl as well as great numbers of fur-bearers and alligators. At one of them, the refuge is extending a nature trail that will be more than two miles long when it is completed. For walkers, it affords the best close look at a large freshwater marsh that can be found anywhere along the Gulf Coast this side of the Anhinga Trail in the Everglades. Indeed, those who have the chance to tour both these trails will enjoy comparing and contrasting them. Both share many of the same wildlife species, and both are exceedingly beautiful; but their appearance and ecology are very dissimilar due to the differences in climate and water regimen. I find that when I am in the Everglades, I like the Anhinga Trail better; when I am here at the Sabine, I prefer this one.

The trail begins at a small wooden bridge (a sign announces Big Croes Marais) where a parking lot is located. In most seasons, the pedestrian bridge that crosses the canal is aswarm with local people happily fishing, crabbing, and, in spring and early fall, casting their nets for brown or white shrimp. But once you get beyond all that activity, you will be in a different world. The marsh is a shining jigsaw puzzle of disparate patterns and textures, the vegetation shifting from one type to another according to intricate adjustments in water depth, soil content, and current that even the biologists haven't altogether figured out. Over to your right is a sizable expanse of lotus, its elephantine ears suspended above the surface like stranded water lilies. On your left, a series of smaller ponds are edged by water hyacinth and alligator-weed. Ahead are stands of pickerelweed and bright green bulltongue. And always in sight are clumps of bullwhip, tall and spiky like whips that have been starched. There are some shrubs along the path— marsh elder and groundsel—but once you get past a stretch of roseau cane, the view is wide and open. Everywhere, and especially from September through April, there are birds in view. The common moorhen is always on display, often leading its half-grown chicks on their oversized feet through the rushes right next to the path. Snowy and great egrets are also present, as well as ibis and an occasional spoon-bill. At all times of year there will be mottled ducks. The migrant waterfowl begin arriving in late August and September with the blue-winged teal leading the way. In September the first northern harriers also begin to show up. Before long, here as at Rockefeller, the skies and water are aswarm with birds. There is a viewing tower at one point on the trail from which the wildlife and the variegated surface of the marsh can be most beautifully seen. Try it at sunset. But, at whatever hour you are there, don't forget the mosquito repellent!

This trail has always been the best place in Louisiana to see large numbers of wild alligators. I was surprised, therefore, to find none at all here during a recent visit on a warm September day. When I spoke to refuge biologists later, they didn't discount the possibility that poachers might have made their own tour of the area. It is a fact that after two decades of lying low, during which time the alligators have made a spectacular recovery, poachers are at work again in Louisiana. The legal trade in hides is controlled by means of a tagging system, but state wildlife people have also been promoting alligator tail as a tasty delicacy (which it apparently is). Since there is no handy way to tag the "legal" meat, state officials have unwittingly encouraged black-marketeers to start poaching the reptile exclusively for the sake of its now in-demand tail. Maybe there is a less gruesome explanation for the absence of 'gators along the Sabine nature trail. But if they aren't back in place by the time you visit the trail, you'll know that something is seriously wrong.

Until recently, the Sabine was one of the last strongholds of the southern red wolf. Sadly, the species is now extinct in the wild. However, a cross between the wolf and the coyote is still said to survive in the refuge. If you happen to be out boating and see what looks like a supercoyote on a levee, it may be one of these hybrid wolves. On the other hand, it may be a supercoyote.

From March 1 to October 15, three ramps along Hwy 27 permit access to some of the impoundments in the refuge as well as the vast marshy expanses bordering Calcasieu Lake. There is great fishing in the freshwater impoundments for bass, perch, catfish, and carp. In the canals, along with the shrimp and crabs, there are redfish, flounder, striped bass, and croaker, just to name a few. For anglers, Sabine, like the rest of Cameron Parish, is the land of plenty. (A twelve-to-fourteen-foot flat-bottomed john boat with a twenty-five-horsepower motor, or less, is best in the impoundments.) As is usual in federal refuges, no camping is allowed. (Sabine National Wildlife Refuge, M.R.H. Box 107, Hackberry, Louisiana 70645; 318/762–4620.)

As you will have gathered from the above paragraphs, the pickings are slim for people in search of public campgrounds, or any sort of really scenic camping, here in Cameron Parish. There are privately operated camping sites in Hackberry, just north of Sabine Refuge, and boats can also be chartered there. But the nearest public camping site is just across the parish line in Calcasieu Parish. It is on the south bank of the intracoastal waterway within view of the Ellender Bridge. The place is no beauty spot, and there isn't much in the way of shade, but the premises are pretty well maintained by the parish. There are picnic shelters, barbecue pits, restrooms, and some electrical hookups, as well as a boat ramp.

For those of you who are in search of a really beautiful campground in a park setting, I'm afraid that the closest place is forty miles from Sabine and sixty miles from the town of Cameron. This is **Sam Houston Jones State Park**, located a few miles northwest of Lake Charles. Signs on I-10 and Hwy 378 will direct you to the gate. Though it's a long way from the marshes, the park is worth visiting in its own right. After so many miles of marshlands and bayous, you will probably be ready for a landscape that is more dry than wet, in which gentle hills and tall forests are the rule. Not that there is any lack of water, since the park is situated at the confluence of the West Fork of the Calcasieu and the Houston rivers. Shady campgrounds, with and without hookups, are located near the river and a pretty little lagoon full of young cypress and tupelo. The lagoon is also full of acrobatic turtles that balance atop steep cypress knees when they want to take a sunbath. Plump, red fox squirrels with white noses are also much in evidence, and nearby a herd of whitetail deer roam about in a large, wooded compound. It is a very nice scene. Nature trails wind through impressive forests of loblolly and longleaf pines, oaks, magnolia, sweet bay, and dogwood, at times following the beautiful banks of the river. Boaters and canoeists will like this place too. (The current is not strong, so upstream paddling is no problem.) There are boat rentals, a couple of docks, and a boat launch. If you have the boat for it, there is nothing to stop you from traveling down the Calcasieu to its namesake lake, and on to Cameron and the Gulf.

The only catch, apart from its distance from the Coast, is that this attractive park gets considerable use on warm-weather weekends. (Sam Houston Jones State Park, Route 4, Box 294, Lake Charles, Louisiana 70601; 318/855–7371.)

The Great Swamp

Let us back up now and turn to southern Louisiana's other great natural treasure, the Atchafalaya Basin Swamp. Only Georgia's Okefenokee outranks it in size, and among river overflow swamps, it is easily the largest in the nation. Its half-million acres account for that rather blank-looking space on your state map that extends from northwest of Baton Rouge down to Morgan City and the Gulf. Apparently, the Atchafalaya River was once the main riverbed of the Mississippi—the

Atchafalaya Swamp, Louisiana. *Photo by Jim Grice.*

once and future riverbed, if some theorists are correct. The two waterways are linked above Baton Rouge, and there is no doubt that the Mississippi yearns to change its course back to its old route. If it gets its way, as it almost did in the 1950s, the port of New Orleans will have to pack its bags and move to Morgan City. The Army Corps of Engineers has built an enormous control structure at Old River, the link between the two great waterways, to prevent that from happening. But some nervous people warn that the structure may not withstand the next superflood that comes rolling down the Mississippi.

The paradox in all this is that the Old River link must be maintained. Why? Because when that superflood does come along—as it has once or twice in recent decades—the Atchafalaya is needed as an escape valve for high waters that might otherwise swamp New Orleans, Baton Rouge, and the whole lower Mississippi Valley. In 1929, Ole Man River did just that, drowning nobody-knows-how-many people and turning New Orleans into a lake with houses in it. As a result of that catastrophe, the Corps leveed the Atchafalaya Basin and created a vast spillway—about seventeen miles wide and seventy miles long—that continues to divert excess flood water from the densely populated areas to the east.

Because of its floodway status, much of the Atchafalaya has remained wet and more or less wild. God knows, it has had a bumpy time of it. The Corps has repeatedly tried to dredge deeper the already dredged river, thus depriving the river bottomlands of the seasonal overflows they need to survive. And in leasing the spillway lands from basin landowners, the Corps did so at top dollar, but with few strings attached—so that in the northern part of the basin thousands of acres have been cleared for high-risk soybean farming. Amazingly, even permanent settlement has been permitted—in a flood spillway! There have been all sorts of other problems too: siltation that has choked out many fine lakes; artificial fluctuations of water that prevent the regeneration of the cypress forest; and sudden releases of flood water that have drowned thousands of the basin's wild creatures.

Yet, after a decades-long battle on the part of conservationists, finally the state, the Corps, and the feds have begun to come around. Further clearing for agriculture and development is now prohibited in most of the basin, and sizable tracts are being purchased as wildlife management areas. Not the least of the good news is that this great ecosystem is still expanding. Sediment carried down the river is building land in Atchafalaya Bay, the only place along Louisiana's shrinking coast where that is happening.

Despite the beating it has taken, this is still an incredibly wild, wet, and lovely world. You can get some sense of its scale simply by driving along I-10 between Baton Rouge and Lafayette. But it is necessary to actually enter its labyrinthian melange of shallow cypress lakes, bottomland hardwood forests, winding bayous, and miles and miles of willow swamps to really experience its haunting beauty. Getting into it, however, is more easily said than done. There are a number of boat ramps, including ones that are easily reached at the two I-10 exits within the swamp: Butte La Rose and Whiskey Bay. Among others are those at Sandy Cove (east of St. Martinville via Hwy 96 to a right on Hwy 679, then a left on Hwy 3038, then ten miles south on the levee road); at Flat Lake, a couple of miles north of Morgan City on Hwy 70; and at either Bayou Sorrel or Pigeon on the east side of the basin, via Hwy 75). There are even more places where you can put in in a canoe. (Most of the boat ramps just mentioned are near very pretty lake and bayou areas, although usually these are not visible from the ramps.) As long as you stay on the main channels and canals, you shouldn't have to worry about losing your way. Unfortunately, these manmade waterways are, by far, the least scenic places in the swamp. Before entering into the wilderness behind them, it is absolutely essential—*I can't emphasize this too strongly*—to have topographical maps, a compass, supplies, and advice about water levels and other matters relating to the particular area of the swamp that you plan to visit (no one can hope to explore it all). It is impossible to supply this type of detailed information here. In New Orleans, you can find all the necessary advice and supplies, as well as canoe rentals, at the Canoe and Trail Shop (624 Moss Street, New Orleans, Louisiana 70119; 504/488–8528), and, on the west side of the basin, at the Pack and Paddle Shop (601 Pinhook Road East, Lafayette, Louisiana 70501; 504/232–5854). For anyone planning to do extensive paddling or hiking not just in the Atchafalaya but anywhere in southern Louisiana or Mississippi, let me recommend again the *Trail Guide to the Delta Country*, listed in the bibliography.

Camping and hiking opportunities, especially the latter, are limited in the Atchafalaya. Actually, there are large areas of the basin that remain dry during all but the highest water years; but much of this land is private property, trespassing is frowned upon, and there are no walking trails. However, now that state management areas are being acquired, the situation may soon improve for hikers, especially at the newly purchased **Sherburne Wildlife Management Area** just east of Krotz Springs on Hwy 190. Information about this tract should be available by the time this book is published. (Louisiana Department of Wildlife and Fisheries, Box 585, Opelousas, Louisiana 70570; 318/942–7553.) As for camping, the availability of primitive sites depends largely on the area, time of year, and water level. During summer, fall, and early winter, dry ground is usually in good supply, although in the dense bottomlands of the Atchafalaya, where sunlight often doesn't reach the forest floor, the earth can be pretty damp; so come prepared. In late winter and spring of high-water years, the overnighter may have to resort to spoil banks. As you might expect, mosquitoes can be a warm-weather problem, although they are never as bad as in the marshes further south.

There are no developed public campgrounds in the vicinity of the Atchafalaya Basin except locally managed Lake Palourde at Morgan City (see the preceding "Great Marsh" section). Many commercial campgrounds of the KOA type are available in towns around the perimeter of the swamp. In my opinion, however, the best bet is **Frenchman's Wilderness** in the Henderson Swamp area. It is just south of I-10 at the Butte La Rose exit. The setting is pretty, and there are plenty of developed sites, boat rentals, and access to the Henderson Swamp area. Except during hunting season and on fine summer weekends, you can have the place almost to yourself. (Frenchman's Wilderness, Box 646, Henderson Station, Breaux Bridge, Louisiana 70517; 318/228–2616.)

If you are in this vicinity and would like a comfortable introduction to the Atchafalaya, consider the enjoyable ninety-minute boat tour into the basin that is available at McGee's Landing. It is just south of Henderson at I-10's exit 115 on the western edge of the swamp. (McGee's Landing, Henderson, Louisiana 70517; 318/228–8523.) You may also be interested in knowing that the short stretch of road from I-10 to Henderson boasts some of the best seafood restaurants in Cajunland.

In a book like this it is necessary and, I hope, useful to talk about the Atchafalaya's size, the ways to approach it, and the accommodations available. But that isn't the same as trying to explain what you should and shouldn't expect when you enter the Great Swamp. Strictly speaking, it isn't a wilderness. The logging companies took out all the virgin cypress more than half a century ago. Entering some of the lakes, you will find yourself surrounded by stumps that have a wider circumference than your dining-room table. On their buttressed roots you can still see the notches where loggers inserted splints to support the planks on which they balanced while hacking the giant trees down. Along the bayous, there are occasional plastic milk bottles marking trot lines and crawfish traps. And, if you paddle far enough, there will always be another canal, another spoil bank. But somehow, once you begin to move down the tall naves of second-growth cypress, or slip into the shadows of the whispering willow forests, strict definitions of virgin wilderness cease to matter much. This is a wilderness all right, a world so ancient-looking that it seems paradoxically to look young—not greatly changed since that lost time when the planet was still innocent of us. Impressions crowd the senses. Especially in spring, the high-water season, the Atchafalaya's landscapes seem adrift, anchored only to their reflections. There is no telling what you may see, though much depends on season, hour, and your own silence: a barred owl watching you bemusedly from a branch five feet above your head; a trio of unafraid baby minks casually sharing a log with an enormous cottonmouth while nibbling crawfish their mama brought them; a brace of bitterns or a cloud of ibis rising from the reeds as you turn a bend; a prothonotary warbler perched on a tree stump, gleaming like molten gold; an armada of lavender water hyacinth in the bayou ahead of you, so formidable that it may force motorboatists to turn back; the decayed gray shack of a Cajun trapper; a wolf spider larger than a basketball player's hand skipping across the water from one tree to another; the pawprint of a bobcat on a muddy bank; a pair of brilliant wood ducks feeding among cypress knees. I have seen all these things in the Atchafalaya and a thousand more. And anyone who has spent some time in the swamp could go on and on in the same vein. The place is a stream of consciousness waiting to happen to you.

But remember, I warned you: you can't just jump into the At-chafalaya on your own, anywhere, anyhow. If you do, you'll be disappointed. And you just might get lost. Do your homework first.

8
The Texas Coast

At a glance

Access   Houston and Corpus Christi are the major air terminals, but Port Arthur, Galveston, Victoria, Harlingen, and Brownsville are all served by regularly scheduled airline flights. Between Galveston and Corpus Christi, Hwys 35 and 521 come as close as we can get to the Coast without taking side roads to Gulf beaches and refuges. South of Corpus Christi, Hwy 72, far inland, is the closest thing to a north-south route.

Climate   The great difference between the western part of the Gulf and other Gulf regions is measured less in temperature than in rainfall—the relative lack of it. Average precipitation is about twenty-two inches, considerably less than half the average on the Florida Coast. As for temperature, winters are generally moderate, with many fine days, although even at the border freezes do occur occasionally. The long summers are very hot—sometimes getting above 100°F in southern Texas—but, as you might guess, the humidity isn't quite as bad as it is further east. Most outdoor activities go on year-round.

Topography and Landscape Features   North of Galveston, the coastal plain is relatively narrow. Here, extensive marshes are backed by low hills, a transitional zone where, in prehistoric times, seas reached their highest benchmarks and, alternately, ice-age glaciers reached their southernmost limits. Further south, the plain broadens out into the vast, flat, semiarid terrain of southern Texas. Most of the Coast is lined by a long chain of barrier islands with wide beaches and high dunes. The islands shield productive bays and inlets from the open Gulf. Mottes—the Texas equivalent of Louisiana's sand-ridge cheniers—edge the bayside marshes. At the border, the fertile Rio Grande Valley, now heavily irrigated, marks the southernmost boundary of this coastal stretch. The Rio Grande's delta features vast salt flats and high sand and clay dunes.

Attwater's prairie-chicken. *Photo by Luther Goldman, U. S. Fish and Wildlife Service.*

Flora and Fauna   For the most part, the flora of Gulf Coast Texas resembles that of the marshes and woodlands to the east. However, the Big Thicket country north of Beaumont is notable for its unusual combination of vegetation types normally found further to the west or north with those that might be expected in this region. In the southern sector of the coastal region, desert plant communities take over, including some species more typical of Mexico than the United States. Wildlife, particularly on the federal refuges, is even more remarkable. The most spectacular winter resident is the whooping crane, but there are many other species of special note, including Attwater's prairie-chicken, chachalaca, ocelot, and javelina. The entire Coast, but especially the Rockport-Aransas area, is a funnel for great numbers of migrant songbirds, waterfowl, and hawks.

Camping   Texas is almost a match for Florida when it comes to public campgrounds. Sea Rim, Galveston Island, Goose Island, and Mustang Island state parks, and Isla Blanca, Padre Balli, and South Padre Island county parks, all have hookups and other facilities for RV campers. Padre Island National Seashore doesn't have the hookups but is still a good bet. All have areas for tent camping. Long stretches of unspoiled beach at Sea Rim, North and South Padre islands, and the Matagorda Peninsula are available for primitive beach camping.

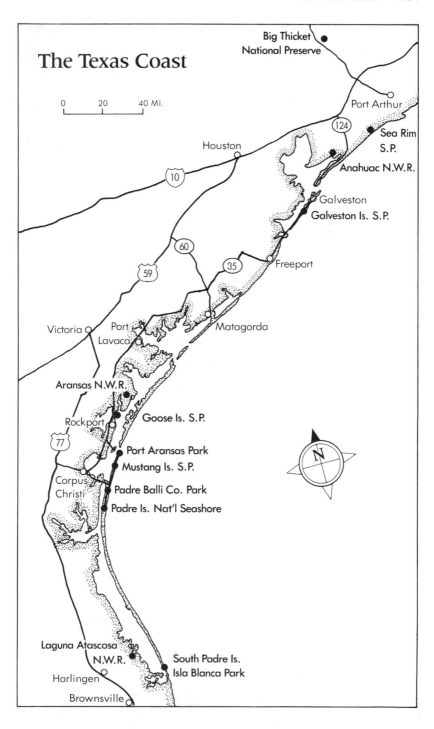

The Texas Coast

Big Thicket
National Preserve

Port Arthur

(124)

Sea Rim
S.P.

Houston

Anahuac N.W.R.

(10)

Galveston
Galveston Is. S.P.

(60)

(35)

Freeport

(59)

Victoria

Port
Lavaca

Matagorda

Aransas N.W.R.

Rockport

Goose Is. S.P.

(77)

Port Aransas Park
Mustang Is. S.P.

Corpus
Christi

Padre Balli Co. Park
Padre Is. Nat'l Seashore

Laguna Atascosa
N.W.R.

South Padre Is.
Isla Blanca Park

Harlingen

Brownsville

N

0   20   40 MI.

As of this writing, no camping is permitted in the Big Thicket National Preserve, but plans for a couple of sites are in the works.

Hiking, Canoeing, Boating, Etc.   There are nature walks at Padre Island National Seashore and nearly all the state parks, but most long hikes are of the beachcombing variety. However, Aransas has a fairly lengthy system of nature paths, and there are beautiful hiking trails in three units of the Big Thicket National Preserve (Turkey Creek, Hickory Creek Savannah, and Beech Creek). The Big Thicket area also offers varied opportunities for canoeing, including a 150-mile journey on the Neches River. In the central part of the state, the Colorado is reportedly a likely prospect. However, on most of this Coast, canoeing is limited to explorations of tidal creeks. Outboard boat owners, on the other hand, have their choice of hundreds of miles of bays and inlets to explore. Fishing is a way of life all along the Coast, and you don't have to have a boat. Texas has a number of excellent public fishing piers, causeways, and jetties where you can drop your line. For birders, the Rockport-Aransas area rivals Cameron, Louisiana, as a place to see migrant waterfowl and songbirds during winter and early spring, with the whoopers as a glorious bonus. A walking tour of Galveston is also worth your consideration.

Outdoors Highlights   Big Thicket National Preserve (especially Turkey Creek); Sea Rim and Mustang Island state parks; Anahuac, Laguna Atascosa, and, especially, Aransas national wildlife refuges; Padre Island National Seashore.

Whether you have been exploring Louisiana's marshes or the Atchafalaya, chances are that you will make your entrance into Texas on I–10. If that is indeed so, you may wish to head inland at Beaumont to investigate some part of the **Big Thicket National Preserve**. In theory, this would seem like a logical undertaking for any traveler who is in love with the outdoors. After all, the Big Thicket is one of the most remarkable ecosystems, or, more exactly, combination of ecosystems, that can be found anywhere in the nation. It is a biological crossroads in which plant and animal communities associated with the eastern forest, the Appalachians, the plains country, and the arid Southwest all exist cheek by jowl. Eastern bluebirds and roadrunners share the same neighborhoods; and Arctic reindeer moss, which moved here during the last ice age, finds a niche next to jungly palmetto on one side and cactus on the other. Sounds great, right? Well, it is. But you should know in advance what you can and cannot expect to see and do. This is *not* a national park. It is not even a preserve, but rather a fragmented collection of twelve preserves scattered over an enormous area, with usually a twenty- or thirty-mile drive between each of them. There are no park campgrounds (although "developed" primitive sites are in the works at this writing), no scenic drives, no vast wilderness stretches, and no hiking trails in most of the units. More of the latter are planned, as well as marked canoe trails and even a couple of access roads, but as of now, the opportunities for exploration are fairly limited unless you paddle your own canoe. In any case, since all of these tracts are ecological preserves, they should not, and probably will not, be heavily developed for recreation. (Ironically, however, most of them are available to hunters and trappers.)

The fact of the matter is that the Big Thicket has now become the Little Thickets. Judging from the uncomplimentary comments of early settlers, its original 3.5 million acres comprised some of the most impenetrable wilderness in the nation. But commercial lumbering and tree-growing operations, oil-drilling activities, rice farming, housing developments, etc., have reduced its scale to less than 300,000 acres—and of that pitiful remainder, only the 85,000 scattered acres in the federal preserve will probably be around at the turn of the next century. Compared to the Big Thicket, even the Big Cypress or the Atchafalaya Basin could be considered lucky. The sad thing is that the bulldozers came relatively late to this region. With better luck—that is, with a slightly earlier start at preservation—more of the area might

Big Thicket National Preserve, Texas. *Photo by National Park Service.*

have been rescued. As it turned out, the efforts to save a meaningful slice of the Big Thicket during the sixties and seventies were met by a truly exceptional display of greed, shortsightedness, and stupidity on the part of many big timber companies, state politicians, and local people. The joker is, that if a larger park and preserve had been established, it would probably have brought more long-term economic benefit to the region than most of the land uses now in effect. It might also have saved some of the rare species that made a last stand here, notably the Texas black bear and the Texas red wolf, which have both disappeared within the last decade. But, given the late hour at which this environmental battle was fought, the great miracle is that some of the tracts in the preserve have been saved at all. End of sermon.

In order to find out what the preserve has to offer, the best bet is to stop off at the headquarters in Beaumont. It is located at 8185 Eastex Freeway, in the Rosedale Shopping Mall near Hwy 105. There you can pick up information about the various units, their ecology, and the opportunities for exploration. Or, if you do not plan to do any serious canoeing or overnight hiking, you can simply take Hwy 69/287 north to the **Turkey Creek** unit of the preserve, located on a turnoff (Hwy 420) about twenty-five miles north of Beaumont. The preserve's main information center is here, as well as a very beautiful and fairly long nature trail—nearly two-and-a-half miles—that begins behind the center and leads you in turn through upland forests, bottomlands, wet "baygall" thickets (not much of the Big Thicket is really thickety), and a pretty slough lined with cypress and tupelo. If that only whets your appetite, there is an excellent nine-mile trail that parallels Turkey Creek through most of this unit, which is said to be the most botanically diverse part of the preserve. (The Hickory Creek and Beech Creek units also have trails.) In appearance, much of the terrain along the trail will remind you of the beautiful piney woods and riverine forests further to the east. In fact, these forests are reaching their western limit here in the Big Thicket country. There is a fair amount of wildlife on hand, but huntable species are wary. In this unit hunting is prohibited; but poaching is regarded as a fun pastime in eastern Texas, and preserve boundaries are not always respected.

No camping of any kind is allowed in the Turkey Creek unit. However, primitive backcountry camping is permitted in several of the other areas. Also, the opportunities for boaters and, especially, canoeists are varied and wonderful in some of these units. Indeed, half of them are simply narrow corridors protecting the shores of waterways in the area. Depending on your preference, you can choose upland creeks with sandy banks, or slow, swampy bayous, or a wide alluvial river (the Neches). In Beaumont or at Turkey Creek you can pick up information about the type of trip that would suit you best. (Big Thicket National Preserve, Box 7408, Beaumont, Texas 77706; 713/839–2689.)

Sabine to Galveston

For birders and marsh lovers, coastal Hwy 87 between Sabine Pass and Galveston is a fascinating stretch. There is only one tiny problem: the road may be closed north of the intersection with Hwy 124, as it has been the last couple of times I visited the area. The same problems of erosion that bedevil Hwy 82 in western Louisiana are at work here, and "moderate" Hurricane Allen a few years ago didn't help matters. Rumor has it that the Texas Department of Highways would just as soon forget the whole thing. For what it's worth, however, no one seems to pay attention to the Closed signs; and, if you are careful, it is possible to drive on the hard-packed sand beaches wherever the road gives out. If you do decide to try it, beware of dark patches of blue clay along the water's edge. For geologists, these gooey outcroppings of the Beaumont Clay Formation are of great interest because of the fossils they contain; for you and your car, they are very bad news, so steer clear of them! The main incentive for attempting this stretch, apart from avoiding the long, roundabout route, is simply the pleasure of having mile after mile of beautiful, undeveloped Gulf/beach/marsh mostly to yourself. But remember, I didn't recommend it.

In any case, **Sea Rim State Park** is still accessible from the eastern end of Hwy 87 via Port Arthur and Sabine Pass. This wonderful 15,000-acre park is a well-kept secret as far as outsiders are concerned because it is so out of the way. There is a large inland marsh unit, plus five miles of shoreline, most of it a pleasant, sandy beach with modest dunes, and the rest a tidal saltwater marsh. A day use area and campgrounds (including a few sites with electrical hookups) are located behind the dunes, about ten miles west of Sabine Pass. And primitive camping is allowed on the beach. East of the campground is a splendid three-quarter-mile nature trail that brings you out into the saltwater marsh on a raised boardwalk. This is cordgrass country, richly supplied with its own fauna. A careful examination will reveal all sorts of creatures, such as the gambusia fish, hermit and fiddler crabs, pulmonate snails, and marsh periwinkles, mucking around in the muck beneath you, while overhead gulls and terns, for more practical reasons, check out the same scene. The trail is named after the little gambusias, whose relatives we first met in Florida. Here as there, they are renowned for their consumption of mosquito larvae. But don't count on them to do the job; in warm weather you won't get far without your can of bug juice. Which reminds me: this is also a wonderful place to be when the weather isn't so warm. True, you'll have to come prepared. But in late winter, this windswept, eroding coast takes on a look of desolate grandeur that can be, for Byronic souls, or souls who simply want some privacy, very soul-satisfying.

About one-and-a-half miles to the east, on the northern side of Hwy 87, the park provides access to a vast expanse of brackish marsh.

There is a boat ramp, a noisy but interesting airboat tour, and canoe rentals (with trails you can follow, something that we sorely missed on the Louisiana Gulf Coast). The prospects for viewing wildlife are excellent in this protected area: on warm days, even in winter, alligators should be a sure thing; and there will probably be a nutria or muskrat loitering about. At dawn or dusk, raccoons or skunks sometimes show themselves. However, as always in the marshes, the birds are the stars. Wading birds, gallinules, and rails (at any season), and ducks, coots, and geese (in winter), are all over the place. And the fishing and crabbing are, with due respect for time and tide, first-rate. If by chance you are not in the mood to catch or grill your own dinner, Sartin's, the most renowned seafood reastaurant in this neck of the marsh, is just back up the road at Sabine Pass. Geneva's, right across the road, is said to be just about as good. Almost overlooking these excellent eateries—excellent, that is, if you like crabs and deep-fried fish—is a monument to a very Texas sort of hero: a Houston bartender named Dick Dowling. During the Civil War, he stopped a force of invading Yankees that had him and his minuscule band outnumbered one hundred to one. Put it all together—the sunny campgrounds, beaches, marshes, the good birding and boating, nice restaurants, and, for good measure, a touch of Texas-size history—and you have a very nice combination gracing this dead-end road. (Sea Rim State Park, Box 1066, Sabine Pass, Texas 77655; 409/971–2559.)

Our next major stop is **Anahuac National Wildlife Refuge**. Getting there involves a substantial detour from Hwy 124, but if you enjoy ogling wildlife, Anahuac is definitely worth the bother. As a bonus, there is the pleasure of exploring back roads that hardly anyone except local farmers and enterprising refuge visitors ever see. Take County Road 1985 (which is easy to miss) for six miles; then turn left at the refuge sign and continue for about thirteen more miles on gravel roads until you reach the ranger station. There you can pick up a map and bird list. Anahuac will remind you in some ways of a drive-through Sabine. The not-quite-10,000-acre tract is intensively managed for waterfowl, which means that it is divided into large impoundments. The most notable of these is a shallow, freshwater pond along Shoveler Road. Alligators will be lounging on the banks if it isn't too chilly, and the usual galaxy of in-season marsh birds will be on hand, including, in winter, incredible concentrations of ducks and geese. In spring, take heed of the wonderful variety of shorebirds: avocets, golden and black-bellied plovers, stilts, godwits, upland sandpipers, and, much rarer, Hudsonian godwits, and Baird's and white-rumped sandpipers. And at all seasons be on the lookout for mottled ducks and night herons. In summer, you may see wood storks, and in winter, along with the waterfowl hordes, a possible bald or golden eagle. Serious birders will be interested to know that the refuge's specialty is rails. Kings and clappers can be seen year-round, and, in spring, a grand slam of all six species is not impossible. Because rails are such secretive creatures, the refuge personnel offer marsh buggy trips during April that are especially dedicated to flushing these un-cooperative birds from their hiding places in the spartina grass. If you're interested, make reservations in advance.

Until recently, Anahuac had an even more fabulous specialty: the refuge and nearby marshes may have been the last place in the nation where a pure strain of red wolf survived, outlasting even those in the Big Thicket and at Sabine Refuge. A few of these animals were cap-tured some years ago and are now being raised in captivity in Wash-ington state; but in the wild, their genetic line has apparently been lost in miscegenetic coyote-wolf or dog-coyote-wolf combinations. Since a lot of Texans have a lot of money, and since the state is very big on monuments, it would be nice if someone erected a statue here-abouts commemorating the Red Wolf's Last Stand.

The usual ban on all camping in federal refuges is somewhat modified here: primitive camping is permitted on Galveston Bay at Anahuac for a maximum of three days. There are also several small, locally sponsored campgrounds with some hookups in the Anahuac area, notably Fort Anahuac and White Memorial parks. (Anahuac National Wildlife Refuge, Box 278, Anahuac, Texas 77514; 713/267–3131.)

When you cross the Intracoastal Waterway heading south on Hwy 124, take a quick look around and behind you. This is the best chance you will have had since crossing Bayou LaFourche (on the way to Grand Isle) to enjoy an unsullied overview of the Gulf's great salt marshes. To the south, you will notice a rare break in all that flatness: a small dome that supports the aptly named town of High Island. It also boasts two sizable patches of woodlands and dense underbrush, the Boy Scout Woods and the Smith Woods. Both parcels are privately owned, but birders are permitted to visit them if they behave. The mo-tivation for doing so is not hard to guess after you've been traveling in this country for a while: these tangled woodlots are the only signifi-cant stands of timber for miles and miles around. For thousands of tuckered-out songbirds caught by foul weather during spring migra-tion, they are Emerald City and the Grail Castle. The vine-covered trees and shrubs are literally showered with throngs of vireos, war-blers, thrushes, grosbeaks, tanagers, orioles, and so on, including no-table rarities from time to time. In short, when conditions are right for birders, if not the birds, this is the best spot on the north Texas Gulf Coast to fill in dozens of blanks on a Life List. Both patches of forest are east of Hwy 124, the Smith Woods on the north side of town and the Boy Scout Woods on the southern end near a ballpark. Townsfolk are used to birders and will direct you to these ornithological hot spots with only a mildly bemused look.

One final note about birding north of Galveston: if you haven't had enough of shorebirds at Anahuac Refuge, try the Bolivar Flats while heading for the free ferry to Galveston on Hwy 87. A few miles before you reach the ferry, turn toward the coast at the "Galveston Sanitary Landfill" sign, and when you get to the next right turn, head down to the beach and start walking toward the end of Bolivar Peninsula. Long mud-and-sand bars extend into the Gulf here, and at low tide they contain so many plovers, stilts, oystercatchers, etc., that it seems impossible that there can be any left over for anywhere else, Anahuac included.

Galveston

You will enjoy the free ferry to Galveston, partly because it is free, but also because you couldn't ask for a nicer ferry ride: a well-run operation, a pretty view of Galveston Bay, bracing salt air in the nostrils, and a continuous parade of boats swirling past, from fancy yachts to looming tankers.

Like several other cities on the Gulf of Mexico, Galveston started out as a hangout for pirates in the early 1800s. The man in charge of illicit operations was the most famous of buccaneers, Jean Lafitte, who certainly seems to have gotten around a lot. By the end of the century, however, Lafitte wouldn't have recognized his former stronghold. Galveston had become the largest and richest city in Texas, with a thriving port, an expanding economy, and a growing reputation as Fun City. Unfortunately, it also had the dubious distinction of being the most hurricane-prone community on the Gulf, with the possible exception of Key West. Instead of being situated behind a barrier island, it was built right on top of one. Given its location, the disaster that struck in 1900 seems, in retrospect at least, to have been inevitable. A powerful hurricane and its accompanying tidal waves wiped half the city off the map, killing more than six thousand of its citizens in the process. Photos taken soon after the storm reveal nothing but acres and acres of splintered wood. The catastrophe still ranks as one of the worst natural disasters in the nation's history. However, Galveston was just too big and economically important to pack its bags and move, as had other sizable Texas towns that had made the mistake of positioning themselves on barrier islands. Instead, the city battened down behind an imposing new ten-mile seawall and has stayed there ever since, despite subsequent batterings by hurricanes, some of them severe. In more recent times, Galveston has lost its ranking as the state's number one port to Houston—not because of the hurricane threat, but because a few wealthy people imposed a monopolistic stranglehold on the city's economy. Even so, Galveston remains a flourishing center of shipping and commerce. And it is still the most popular beach resort on the Texas Coast.

You will enjoy Galveston, I think. It differs from most of the Florida beach towns in that, like all interesting places (and people), it has a past that shows. When visiting here, by all means check out the older sections of the city that survived the catastrophe of 1900. Except for New Orleans, which is in a class by itself, there is no other city on the American Gulf that contains such a concentrated display of well-preserved nineteenth-century architecture. Almost all of it is very late nineteenth century, of course—"McKinley Victorian," often with Italianate, beaux-arts features. The most interesting residential areas are the East End Historic District, near the downtown area, and the much smaller but very handsome Silk Stocking District on 24th Street between Avenues L and N. Many of the homes in these districts are framed by the great effusions of oleanders in which Galvestonians take such pride, and a few of them have guest accommodations or are open for tours. On the Strand, once the "Wall Street of the Southwest" and still a busy commercial avenue, a number of restored old buildings with cast-iron facades lend distinction to an otherwise not very attractive business district.

Then there is the Seawall. This is Texas's answer to Fort Lauderdale Beach, although in fact the feel of the place reminds me of the old Atlantic City, only more tropical and more fun. The monolithic condos and new hotels have been kept back from the wide beach and its—for the Gulf—vigorous surf. The miles-long beachfront, the acres of beach umbrellas, the almost year-round abundance of tanned, shiny people and waxed, shiny cars cruising down the broad promenade with amorous radios in full cry, the gleaming Gulf and sky, the tacky souvenir shops and the older hotels (notably the Galvez) with their tile and stucco, the Toonerville Trolley tourist "trains," the coveys of adolescent roller-skaters—they all fit together in a daffy, good-natured way. The atmosphere is carny, but not so much so that it turns you off. And if you get bored looking at the oceans of skin and other distractions, you can fish at one of several public piers. Or you can park yourself at Seawolf Park and boat-watch. Along with the freighters, tankers, and shrimp boats, there is usually a parade of yachts going to or from the marinas in the bay. This is Texas, remember, where there's no fun in having money unless you flaunt it; and some of those floating pleasure palaces will make you wish you had a li'l ole oil well you could call your own. Maybe the nicest thing I can say about Galveston is that, again with the exception of New Orleans, it is the only sizable town on the American Gulf where just walking around is both feasible and a pleasure. (Galveston Convention and Visitors Bureau, 2106 Seawall Boulevard, Galveston, Texas 77550; 713/763–4311.)

Much of Galveston's West Beach is being increasingly given over to development. A hurricane a couple of years ago did a lot of damage to the new vacation homes in this area, even though they all had been dutifully built on piers. When I drove along Hwy 3005 in 1985, scores of these houses still looked like Christmas packages an impatient kid had opened. Yet the majority had been rebuilt and new ones were going up.

In the midst of this past and future devastation lies **Galveston Island State Park**. The beach side of the park is somewhat short on space, and what there is of it is pretty well covered by parking lots, bathhouses, and camping sites with little shelters that, in the absence of any vegetation higher than your knees, provide welcome shade. As long as you don't expect long vistas of virgin beach of the sort that can still be found at Sea Rim to the north or at Padre Island to the south, this little park makes a welcome stop. The sand is brownish and not overly fine, but it does very well for sunbathing and sand-castle construction; also, the berm, though it slopes pretty gradually, allows swimmers to reach deep water without wading themselves to death.

Nature lovers will be more interested in the much larger bayside sector of the park. Here a two-and-a-half-mile nature trail winds through the salt meadows and marshes, ending up at an observation platform that overlooks the intricate web of marshy grasslands, mud flats, oyster reefs, sloughs, and inlets that edge Galveston Bay. Further off, you will see the industrial complex that is Texas City, whether you want to look at it or not. The city is not on anyone's list of beauty spots, but its massive aluminum presence is a useful reminder of how vulnerable to pollution these surrounding wetlands are. Also, in fairness, all that petrochemical mishmash does look sort of dramatic at a safe distance. (Speaking of safe distances, if Galveston takes the prize for natural disasters, Texas City ranks high on the list of unnatural ones. In 1947 a ship carrying a cargo of combustible fertilizer blew up in the harbor, setting off a series of explosions at onshore chemical plants that turned a large section of the city into an inferno. By the time the nightmare was over, nearly six hundred people had died and thousands of others were seriously injured.)

For birders who don't have a boat at their disposal, this marshy section of Galveston Island State Park just may be even more promising than Anahuac or Sea Rim. It isn't that there are more birds here, but the excellent trail allows you to investigate a variety of marsh terrains. It also helps that the islands in Galveston Bay serve as rookeries for thousands of wading birds, cormorants, gulls, and terns. Finally, there are several observation platforms and blinds set up, where, suitably drenched with mosquito repellent, you can hang around for hours if you wish, waiting to see what turns up. (Actually, the blinds are most useful in winter, when there are lots of ducks on the premises and no bugs.) In any season, this is a good area for clapper rails and bitterns, and in the shallows hereabouts you will have the first really good chance of seeing reddish egrets since leaving southern Florida. Several freshwater ponds in the salt flats also add diversity to the habitat and the birdlife, and you can fish them if you have a Texas license.

(Galveston Island State Park, Route 1, Box 156A, Galveston, Texas 77550; 713/737–1222.)

Toward the southernmost end of Galveston Island the development thins out. From here on, at both ends of the toll bridge across San Luis Pass, there are several miles of lavender-gold-tawny marsh and beach, with dunes and wildflowers on the shoulders of the road. Keep an eye out for shorebirds and waders in the salt-marsh pastures along the way. Frigatebirds are quite often seen from the San Luis Bridge.

The Central Texas Coast

Once you reach Freeport, the best thing you can do is to get through the blur of big Dow Chemical, big subdivisions, and gruesome traffic between there and Brazoria as quickly as you can. Once you're on Hwy 521 west of Brazoria (careful; it's easy to miss the turnoff), you'll be in the clear again. Very much so. This section of the Coast is wonderful to explore for much the same reasons that apply to the across-the-Gulf part of the Florida Coast north of the Suwannee River. Both areas are at a considerable distance from major highways, and both are furnished with small agricultural communities and fishing towns that in some cases are cul-de-sacs reachable only by a single in-and-out road. Both are estuarine areas that teem with bird and marine life. Mercifully, the big developers have thus far passed them by (although some chichi condos are just beginning to go up at Matagorda Beach). They have in common a laid-back, salty atmosphere that attends all places where people would rather fish than fight, and where men are used to waiting, beer in hand, for the time and tide that waits for no man—if, that is, it means a chance to hit the reds or shrimp or flounder when they're running right. Finally, both areas defeat all purposeful itineraries. You have to go in and out and around if you really want to explore this country. And it helps at times to have a boat.

When you get right down to it, it is the human scene that accounts for the similarities between the two areas. There are big differences in the natural scene. In contrast to northern Florida, no piney flatwoods attend our journeys in coastal Texas. And, north of Brownsville, the only cabbage palms you'll see are those that have been planted along the streets of little towns. There are a lot more barrier islands than the Suwannee region, and therefore many more miles of beaches; and the southern part of this coast is a whole lot drier.

The drive from Brazoria to Wadsworth passes through an easy rolling, not-too-cultivated countryside in which shady pastures alternate with shady oak groves hung with Spanish moss. After the openness of the Coast and the spastic clutter north of Freeport, this sudden immersion in a bucolic Deep South landscape makes for a lulling change—so lulling, in fact, that you may feel the need for a dip and a seaside nap. In that case, take Hwy 60 and head for the brown, sandy beach and pleasant surf on the Matagorda Peninsula. The further up the beach you go, the more you'll have it to yourself.

You can pick up picnic supplies (or fresh fish if you have the means to cook it) and bait at the amiable little fishing town of Matagorda. A few weathered old buildings remind the visitor of the days when the community was a county seat and the port for Austin. If the drawbridge on the Intracoastal Waterway is up, it's no problem, since no one here is in a rush; and besides, it is very pleasurable to watch long barges and tall tugboats riding, as it seems, through fields of marsh grass. Just back of town, the Colorado flows to the Gulf. When the tide is in, fishing for redfish and sea trout is good.

The Colorado, incidentally, makes for a pretty easygoing canoe trip. It is one of the few floatable Texas rivers that reaches the Coast without having had most of its water siphoned from it and without having some large town or industrial complex sitting on its deltic plain. If you feel ambitious, you can paddle all the way down from Austin to the Gulf—nearly three hundred miles—past farmlands, oak and willow copses, gawking herds of cattle, and the occasional startled deer. This close to the Coast, though, the river is banked by thick, salt cedar scrub, marshlands, mud flats, and, in places, a lineup of fishing camps. For boaters, there are ramps on County Road 2031 that provide access to the river and the rich fishing grounds of Matagorda and Lavaca bays, as well as the opportunity to visit the wild bayside marshes and Gulfside dunes and beaches of (so far) unspoiled Matagorda Island. (Put in at the north end of the island.) Readers who keep up with conservation issues may already know that the island has been the subject of considerable controversy. A vital adjunct to Aransas National Wildlife Refuge on the nearby mainland, it has recently been turned over to the state of Texas for management. A lot of folks seem to feel, not without reason, that the state is interested in developing Matagorda Island as a place where people, rather than wildlife, come first. Since people also come first on most of the Texas Coast, that approach would be sadly shortsighted if it proves to be the case. Endangered peregrine falcons use the island during their migrations. Texas's rebuilding population of pelicans (almost wiped out, like Louisiana's, by pesticides) also need it. And whooping cranes, which only occasionally use its marshes now, will do so more and more as their numbers increase. But the issue isn't just a matter of protecting rare wildlife species, important as that is. On principle, there ought to be one sizable stretch of the wild Texas Coast where the public's four-wheel drives don't have the right-of-way.

Matagorda Island can be more handily reached from Port O'Conner, the only problem being that Port O'Conner itself is not so easily reached. After you pass through Port Lavaca (where anglers may want to try their luck on the old causeway, now a fishing pier), turn right on County Road 2433 and then follow the signs. Along the way, you may feel like taking the detour to Indianola if you have the time and are in the mood to contemplate the vanity of human ambitions. Indianola was the site of a once thriving nineteenth-century community of German immigrants that was done in by hurricanes. A sad little graveyard is about all that remains. Nearby is a statue that commemorates another, much earlier venture on this harsh coast. In 1684, the Sieur de La Salle discovered Matagorda Bay and claimed it for France. Unfortunately, this singularly disastrous expedition ended up with most of La Salle's followers dead of disease or devoured piecemeal, while still alive, by Karankawas Indians. You can think about these cheery bits of history while dining *al fresco* at the pleasant little picnic area that overlooks the bay.

As for Port O'Conner, it is a community that has also had its share of hurricanes and survived, though at times just barely. I like this untidy fishing town for the same reasons I like Steinhatchee or Suwannee, although I miss the almost tropical greenery that mutes the human motley of the latter places. As at all these untouristy coast towns, the same devoted people, most of them Texans, come back year after year. During summer and the autumn duck season, the scruffy collection of motels is often booked solid. The local cafe gets reviews that range from not so hot to pretty good. Birders, never at a loss even if they are boatless, may perhaps see a whooping crane, strayed from Aransas Refuge, exposing itself along Hwy 185 during the winter months. They will certainly see ducks, snow and greater white-fronted geese, hawks, and maybe sandhill cranes. And in spring there are godwits, golden plovers, and assorted sandpipers. Anyone interested in the natural scene should also take note of the landscape hereabouts: it is a coastal prairie that is in private hands and yet hasn't been altogether converted to agricultural uses.

Back on Hwy 35 en route to Aransas, there is nothing to take your breath away, but it is a pleasant drive all the same, as long as you don't try to hurry; sometimes there's quite a bit of farm traffic on the road. Here you begin to see what is meant by the "big sky" of Texas. Even the comfortably boring prospect of endless flat fields is enlivened by swooping crop dusters and, better, the occasional hawk. Although you've got the wrong state, you feel like bursting into a couple of choruses of "Oklahoma" anyway. Minuscule towns, bland but almost pretty, make you wonder whether—if you were someone else—you might not be quite happy living in them. Best of all, the small bays and inlets of the Guadalupe River come just when they are needed. Egrets and great blue herons wade beside dark green banks. You wish there were more of that. And then you remind yourself that, thanks mostly to Aransas, there is.

Aransas National Wildlife Refuge is perhaps the brightest gem in the priceless string of refuges along the U.S. Gulf Coast. Others can boast more of this or that wildlife species. Some are even prettier. A couple have more varied ecosystems. But even aside from its famous winter residents, the whooping cranes, this place seems—to the visitor's eye, at least—to have more of most of everything than any of the other refuges. There is, it is true, a self-serving side to this appraisal: Aransas is, by far, the most accessible of the Gulf refuges, more so even than St. Marks in Florida's Big Bend. Also, there is the setting itself: for mile after mile you have been driving through landscapes that have been utterly tamed by man—all those endless fields, the skyscraper elevators of stored grain, the networks of country roads, even a nuclear power plant looking surreal on the highway south of Wadsworth. Right up to the gates of Aransas that human dominance continues. The waves of corn and sorghum literally lap the refuge boundaries. Then, with no transition, you are suddenly in a sort of Eden—populated by mosquitoes, chiggers, and cottonmouths, it is true—but an Eden all the same. By all means, try to be here in early morning and/ or at evening, especially if you plan to see the refuge's mammalian population. The best months are from November through March, since not only the cranes but a host of other migrant birds are on hand.

Aransas is easily reached from Hwy 35 by means of County Road 239 just south of Tivoli or County Road 774 north of Rockport. For starters, take the sixteen-mile road that loops through the northern part of the refuge. Along the way, it parallels San Antonio Bay and its tidal marshes, crosses old sand dunes covered by windbent oaks (the Texas equivalent of Louisiana's cheniers), pauses at a high observation platform overlooking Mustang Bay, and then circles back through the interior of the refuge, passing a changeful landscape of marshy ponds, wild meadows, dense scrub thickets, and scattered clumps, or "mottes," of live oaks. Early and late in the day you are quite likely to count more whitetail deer along this road than you have ever seen anywhere else during an equivalent drive. Here, too, you will see for the first time along the Coast our continent's only native piglike mammal, the javelina, or peccary. This bristled, grunty little fellow is hard to spot in the scrub and tall grass, but then again, one just may cross the road in front of you or show up at the picnic ground. Other quite possible sightings could be opossums, armadillos, raccoons, or wild turkey—which I have seen here in flocks of up to twenty birds. If you come back often enough, you just may luck out with some of the more introverted species. There are coyotes and even a mountain lion or two here, as well as the very rare Attwater's prairie chicken. You might also see one of the feral hogs that prowl the refuge—the wildest, most boarlike that I've ever seen anywhere. There's no telling what will show up. I remember driving this loop one evening in summer—the season when the expectation of seeing wildlife is at its lowest—and spotting a largish, rather bulky-looking shape bounding across the road some distance ahead of me. I thought I knew what it was, but couldn't be sure. When I came abreast of the thicket where the animal had disappeared, I scanned it with my glasses—and there he was: a large bobcat, squatting on his haunches behind a bush, peering back at me. He looked for all the world like a streetwise but incorrigibly curious tabby cat!

In the end, it is the sheer abundance of such moments that overwhelms. To watch great drifts of egrets, herons, roseate spoonbills, wild ducks, gulls, terns, ibis, and pelicans lifting and settling at the edge of the bay in white-pink-blue waves tinged by the setting sun, while deer graze the headquarters lawn behind you *and* alligators and gallinules pose at your feet—it is almost more than you can take in!

Then, of course, there are the whooping cranes. Especially in midwinter there is a good chance of seeing at least a couple of them, as well as a visual feast of other birds, from the ramped tower overlooking the marshes of Mustang Bay. But the best bet by far is to pay the birds a visit aboard Captain "Brownie" Brown's famous boat, the *M. V. Whooping Crane.* The boat leaves from the marina at the Sea Gun Sports Inn, a highly visible pink motel on Hwy 35 near the north end of the bridge over Copano Bay. This just may be the best commercial wildlife boat tour in the States. On a par-for-the-course trip, you may see anywhere from half a dozen to thirty cranes, and once you have, you will not forget them. It is easy to understand why they have become the most glamorous and publicized creature on this nation's long list of endangered species. Although they have quadrupled their numbers since the 1940s, when only twenty were left, they retain the cachet that always attaches to extreme rarity. And they are aristocrats, elegantly beautiful by any standard. Most of all, though, they are big—I mean really big—a fact that doesn't fully hit home until you see them out here in the marshes of Aransas. (On this of all trips, don't forget to bring your binocs or scope!)

Captain Brown's tours are conducted Wednesday through Sunday, October 20 through April 10, and last from 1:30 P.M. to 5 P.M. The boat is pretty large, but reservations are advisable. (Sea Gun Sports Inn, Route 1, Box 85, Rockport, Texas 78382; 512/729–2341.)

Meanwhile, back at the refuge, there are other things to do. Several excellent nature trails take you into various refuge habitats. The winter and spring birding is, as you might expect, incredible. Three hundred fifty species, the highest record for any refuge, have been tallied here. Along with the songbird, waterfowl, and shorebird migrations, great numbers of hawks pass along this coast; in the fall, "kettles" of thousands of broad-tailed hawks are seen. A number of typically south-of-the-border species can also be viewed here: caracaras, the white-tailed hawk, Inca doves, and pauraques (a Mexican relative of the whip-poor-will). If you need to calm yourself after overexposure to these riches, or if you're tired of squinting through binoculars, you can always go fishing or crabbing in the bays. You can also contemplate what this entire coast must have been like one hundred years ago, if this one rescued peninsula can contain so much.

Except for special organized groups, there is no camping on the refuge, but a picnic area is available. Gates are open from dawn till dusk. (Aransas National Wildlife Refuge, Box 100, Austwell, Texas 77950; 512/286–3559).

Though Aransas doesn't have camping sites, there is a public campground just across the bay at **Goose Island State Recreation Area**. This is a small park with a big tree: the largest live oak in Texas. It must have been already quite sizable when the first Spanish explorer—more exactly, castaway—Cabeza de Vaca, staggered along these shores in the early sixteenth century. Earlier than that, it may have observed, with vegetarian distaste, the now-vanished Karankawas dining on human flesh. This one-tree forest is obviously in a class by itself, but there are a goodly number of less magisterial oaks on the premises, many of them shading the campground. There are restrooms, showers, and electrical hookups, as well as a swimming area on the bay and a long fishing pier. As at all small public-recreation areas, facilities take precedence over the natural world. But there are nice stretches of jungly red bay and yaupon favored by songbirds, the pier fishing is great, a boat ramp is available, and the dawn comes up like thunder out of Aransas across the bay. If there is room for you, this is a wonderful base of operations while you explore the refuge and the Rockport area. (Goose Island State Recreation Area, Route 1, Box 105, Rockport, Texas 78382; 512/729–2858.)

Although Aransas is the centerpiece of all outdoors experiences along the central Texas coast, the country around—and even in—Rockport deserves attention.

For one thing, this area is an ornithologist's dream. The Ghosts of Birders Past are known to haunt the mottes and marshes, and Birders Present often lose their jobs and families because they cannot tear themselves away. Almost any road is worth exploring; there is even a bayside sanctuary chock full of birds, the Hagar Refuge, within Rockport's city limits. The Chamber of Commerce will supply you with information sheets advising where to see what.

For another, even granting that there is no area along the Gulf where boaters and anglers cannot be happy, the bays around here more than hold their own. Charter boats, ramps, and, for the landlocked, fishing piers are in plentiful supply. (Probably the most notable of those last is the old Copana Bay Causeway, right next to the new one. Like the bridge at Port Lavaca, it is now entirely given over to rod-and-reel addicts.) And, regardless of whether they happen to be biting or not, there is no lack of fish.

Finally, there is no lack of easygoing local color and interesting sights, as long as you don't expect them to bunch up on you. On the beach drive between Rockport and Fulton, live oaks shade the road. They are very different from their patriarchal relatives in Louisiana's bayou country, but lovely all the same in their wind-whipped, spidery way. And at Fulton you can visit a local cattleman's hefty Victorian mansion that would have been perfect for *Giant* if it weren't for the trees roundabout. If you are in the mood for an inland expedition, especially if you can time it so that you are on County Road 774 close to sunset, try the drive to Refugio. Some nice, oil-rich people who own a lot of land in here have not turned it all into sorghum fields. As a result, you are practically guaranteed the pleasurable sight of nonrefuge deer along this road, and you may be happily obliged, as I have been, to stop your car while a large flock of wild turkeys crosses the road. Refugio itself is a pretty little town, decidedly Texan, yet with neat, turn-of-the-century frame houses that have a puritan Anglo-Saxon kinship with other neat, pleasant houses in New England and the Middle West.

There is only one restaurant around here that takes haute cuisine seriously, and that is Schrenkeisens (which is fairly expensive and dressy) in Fulton. But there's no shortage of places where you can get generous helpings of fresh fried seafood. The most popular of these is Charlotte Plummer's family-style restaurant (just down the street from Schrenkeisens on the Fulton waterfront), but you may have to wait in line.

One final comment about this central part of the Texas Coast. The people here are, for the most part, insular and yet genuinely hospitable, as they are in Cajunland. It is one more reason for lingering in these parts.

We, however, must move on.

Port Aransas to North Padre Island

When you reach Aransas Pass, take Hwy 361 and the Dale Miller Causeway to the free ferry landing where you can embark for Port Aransas. Along the causeway you should see swarms of plovers, oyster-catchers, sandpipers, and other shorebirds—also, maybe, reddish egrets. And in winter there will be lots of ducks. The small ferries that carry you across Aransas Pass are a treat. There may be dolphins riding their private roller-coasters in the pass, as well as immense freighters on their way to or from the docks at Corpus Christi. And gulls will make the passage with you. As for Port Aransas, you will enjoy it if you have a taste for unpremeditated funk and tackiness. If you don't, you won't. What with its swarm of blowsy motels, trailers-on-piers, and eccentric bars and eateries, Nantucket it is not. It isn't even Cedar Key. Personally, however, I think there is something—I'm not sure what—to be said for a place that has as its only architectural landmark the Tarpon Inn, a rambling, two-story box of a hotel built, or rather rebuilt, in 1924, with wide verandas and a rope fence out in front, and tarpon fish scales, as well as the fish themselves, on walls inside. As I've indicated more than once before, much can be forgiven in the way of funkiness as long as it hasn't come off the assembly line. The tarpon touches, by the way, are no joke. Port Aransas is a major locus for deep-sea fishing as well as commercial fishing on this part of the Coast. A lot of charter boats are for hire and, as such things go, the prices are reasonable. Port Aransas also boasts some good seafood restaurants, including the aforementioned Tarpon Inn and the Silver King Bar and Grill.

If you follow Cotter Avenue for one-and-a-half miles south of the ferry landing you will reach the South Jetty and the nearby **Port Aransas Park**. Campers can choose between this or the much larger **Mustang Island State Park**, about thirteen miles further south on Park Road 53, as a place to set up housekeeping while in the area. Both places have electrical hookups (although Port Aransas Park has considerably more than Mustang) as well as areas for tent camping. There are access roads to the beach all along the park road, so this entire eighteen-mile stretch of beach gets a great deal of heavy-duty use, with beaucoup car traffic heading up and down the beach. Still, eighteen miles is eighteen miles, and the further you get away from Port Aransas, the nicer the beach gets. When the tide is out, it is wider than a six-lane highway, and there are usually stretches where you can have a large chunk of the scenery to yourself. The scenery will remind you of some stretches of the Gulf Islands National Seashore in northern Florida, where all there is is the beach, the surf, and the dunes. Plus skies that are often mind-bogglingly gorgeous. There are a lot of shorebirds on the sandbars, and shellers reportedly find the pickings pretty good here. (Port Aransas Park, 10901 South Padre Island Drive, Cluster Box 3G, Corpus Christi, Texas 78418; 512/933—8121. Mustang Island State Park, Box 326, Port Aransas, Texas 78373; 512/749—5246.)

On the northern tip of North Padre Island, about three miles south of the junction of Park Roads 53 and 22, is yet another developed campground, Nueces County's **Padre Balli Park** with sixty-four hookup sites, a tent camp area, and the usual amenities, including a nice stretch of beach. (10901 South Padre Island Drive, Cluster Box 3G, Corpus Christi, Texas 78418; 512/933—8121.)

Campers who need electrical hookups will prefer the just-mentioned campgrounds. But those who are in the mood to get away from it all will much prefer to go on to **Padre Island National Seashore**, which begins twelve miles south of the bridge at Corpus Christi Pass. A mile below the ranger station is a forty-two-site campground with showers, restrooms, a small grocery store, and a Visitor Center. The four-and-a-half-mile stretch of beach in this area, Malaquite Beach, is

Padre Island, Texas. *Photo by National Park Service.*

off-limits to vehicles. South of it, the road behind the dunes leads to the shore.

And from there on, for about sixty-five miles, you are on your own. Below the South Beach access, you can do some primitive camping anywhere you wish as long as you stay on the Gulf side of the dunes, and you can drive as far as you dare along the beach if you have a four-wheel drive. Drivers of ordinary passenger cars are not permitted to go beyond the five-mile stretch known as South Beach, and, given the soft and often treacherous sand, they would be crazy if they wanted to. Even four-wheel drives do not always make it through the strands known as Big and Little Shell. Their drivers should check about conditions at the ranger station before they undertake the journey, and they should most definitely take along water, spare parts, and some kind of sun protection. Drive only on moist, firm sand, but keep at least twenty-five feet away from the water's edge, especially at low tide. Otherwise, if you do get stuck, your vehicle will need water wings.

So, what do you get for all these do's and don't's? For most of us semiordinary mortals, Malaquite Beach and South Beach offer about as much pristine coastline as we really need (once we distance ourselves from the occasional chemical toilets). But even for us, part of the joy of being here comes from knowing that there is this much and yet so much more. This is almost the only place on the U.S. Gulf Coast where there is an *excess* of solitude. And an excess of not much to do. The sand is exquisitely soft and white (much more so than it is further north), the surf is nice, and there are often lovely shells to discover and contemplate, as well as the sad but interesting carcasses of porpoises and fish. If you just happen to have a metal detector along, you can even search for gold. (Spanish treasure ships are known to have been wrecked along this coast, and coins and other relics have been found.) There are no sounds, other than those you provide, except the lap of the surf, the rustle of the breeze in the sea oats, and the mewling cries of the gulls.

Some people can't get enough of all this emptiness; others can. Padre is, after all, the meeting ground of two of the most featureless prospects this planet can afford us: the desert and the sea. For this really is a *desert* isle, not like the barrier islands along the northern and eastern rim of the Gulf of Mexico with their freshwater ponds and marshes and their backup brigades of oaks, palms, and pines. The rains are not generous here, whereas the scale is. The tall, sloping dunes drift on and on; Bedouins on camels would not be out of place. Even where a thin vegetation takes over in the interior swales—senna, evening primrose, and railroad vine—the look of things is still relentlessly dry; there is hardly a drop of shade for miles on end. Notwithstanding the ice chests and paperback novels we have lugged along with us, we become half-consciously aware that life is really hard here. Even given the riches of the sea, we wonder how the Karankawas Indians ever made it. After two or three days out here, the simple process of getting away from it all, or just getting a nice suntan, begins to take on the dimensions of a metaphysical experience. If we stray too far away from the campgrounds, we may find ourselves falling in love with existential solitude or whatever. After two weeks, we start thinking we're Lawrence of Arabia.

Boaters are not permitted to launch from the beach, but there is a ramp at Bird Island Basin on the bay side of the national seashore that provides access to Laguna Madre and the Intracoastal Waterway. Other launching sites are available under the Kennedy Causeway at the northern end of North Padre Island. A fishing pier is also located there, in the aforementioned Padre Balli Park. As for beach hiking, there is obviously as much of that as anyone could wish. But even the most ardent backpacker should think twice about taking on the whole length of the seashore. The sand is soft and makes for slow going. The interior's grasslands offer somewhat firmer footing, but there is less breeze and there are more insects than on the beach. Also, rattlesnakes are supposed to be quite numerous inland, although I've never seen one on my own brief forays. If you do plan a longish hike, check at the ranger station for information before starting out. (Padre Island National Seashore, 9405 South Padre Island Drive, Corpus Christi, Texas 78418; 512/933–8173.)

Corpus Christi

Corpus Christi is *the* city in southern Texas. It has its origins in a trading post set up in 1840 by one Captain Henry Lawrence Kinney, who dealt, among other things in contraband goods. Soon after Texas joined the Union in 1845, General Zachary Taylor prepared for the inevitable war with Mexico by using the high bluff here as an Army camp and supply depot. It still is an important military base, as well as one of the Coast's major deep-water ports. If you want to visit a nice, clean, up-to-date Sunbelt city, most of it built since World War II, Corpus Christi is just what the tour guide ordered. Like all "new" cities, it doesn't have a very distinctive character, and it spreads all over the place. But it is less intimidating and more cheerful than, say, Houston. It has a more moderate scale, pretty parks, excellent museums, good birding in and around the city, clean streets, friendly citizens, and, most attention-getting of all, an attention-getting bayfront boulevard with lots of ritzy homes and shiny, new highrises on one side and armadas of pretty boats on the other. It is pleasant to stroll along the wide sidewalk atop the imposing seawall, where you can take in fine views of the bay, the city itself, and the marinas with their long "T" and "L" ramps. At various points along the bayfront drive, little parks offer you the chance to rest your feet, and, at the north end of Shoreline Drive, you can visit the Bayfront Arts and Sciences Park and admire the view of the graceful Harbor Bridge. Another spot you might want to visit is Blucher Park, behind the business district, where the birding is excellent in spring. In general, though, this is not a town for walkers. (Corpus Christi Area Convention and Tourist Bureau, 1201 Shoreline Drive, Box 2664, Corpus Christi, Texas 78403; 512/882–5603.)

Laguna Atascosa and South Padre Island

South of Corpus Christi, or, more exactly, south of Kingsville, your map of Texas will reveal a large, white patch of what looks like terra incognita traversed by Hwy 77. This is the famous King Ranch—part of it, anyway. If you have time, you may want to take the twelve-mile scenic drive that circles a small corner of this vast domain. The Visitor Center at Kingsville will provide you with information and directions. In any case, be sure to check the fuel gauge in Kingsville or Riviera before heading for Harlingen; the stretch ahead is just as empty of towns and gas stations as it seems to be on your road map.

I like this lonesome cowboy country, not least of all because it is so empty. And in the early morning or evening, the sky looks the way a Berlioz or Brahms symphony sounds, depending on the weather's mood. But it is true that when you've seen one mile of rangeland and mesquite scrub (from a car window, that is), you've seen 'em all. It is instructive to reflect that this landscape did not always look this way. The accounts of early travelers indicate that, despite the dry climate, much of the region was blanketed by prairie grasslands. But as soon as the white man settled in, the blanket of grass gave way to a blanket of sheep. True to form, the animals reduced the land to semidesert. The plague of sheep has long since moved west, but the original vegetation has never recovered. Wildlife is still pretty abundant, however, and birders should definitely have their binoculars at the ready. This region is the northernmost range of several subtropical Mexican birds, among them the olive sparrow, long-billed and curve-billed thrashers, the black-crested titmouse, and the pretty green jay. The oak mottes at the rest areas are likely places to park and look around. This is also fabulous hawk country during the spring and fall migrations. And at any time you may see a resident white-tailed hawk, or a caracara, as well as the more common red-tailed hawk. Try to make the drive early in the morning if you want to see the smaller bird species.

You'll know when you've left the rangelands behind. There is no transitional stage. A line has been drawn across the desert at Raymondville, and south of it the irrigated sorghum fields take over suddenly and completely. If you are fascinated with aviation history, by all means check out the Confederate Air Force's Rebel Field at Harlingen, where dozens of old airplanes are on display, most of them dating from the World War II era. Otherwise, you would do well to bypass the town by turning east at Combes on Hwy 508. Follow it to Rio Hondo, where you will turn left on Hwy 106 and head south ten miles toward the Laguna Atascosa National Wildlife Refuge. If you are feeling lunchy along the way—and remember, Laguna Atascosa is not exactly handy to a grocery store—you may want to stop at Esther's Cafe a couple of miles beyond Rio Hondo at the intersection with farm road 2925. The place doesn't exactly service the carriage trade, but the hamburgers and simple Mexican fare are tasty and filling. When you hit the road again, take a good, hard look at the rich fields around you, the neatly comfortable farm homes, the decent-looking quarters for migrant workers, and the usually well-maintained farm roads. Keep this bland but prosperous landscape in mind for future reference when you cross into Mexico. The comparison will explain, more than a dozen articles ever could, why there is a tremendous problem of illegal immigration along our southern border.

Laguna Atascosa National Wildlife Refuge is the Rio Grande Valley's answer to Aransas. Like Aransas, it is an oasis of unspoiled wild country in a sea of sorghum. But this wild country is notably different from any other that you will visit in the United States (or, for that matter, any that you will find intact in Mexico). Like southern Florida, this Rio Grande area is subtropical. The great difference is that it is also very dry, averaging only twenty-six inches of rainfall a year. The result—influenced mightily by the Gulf and its estuarine bays—is a landscape that seems at first glance almost oppressively stark, yet teems with life. On the refuge's fifteen-mile bayside road, you will pass a large impoundment, then views of the open bay and cordgrass marshes, then miles of arid coastal grasslands and sand ridges where the omnipresent mesquite, yucca, and prickly pear cactus share the terrain with predominantly Mexican vegetation such as huisache, retama, and granjeno, much of it beautifully adorned with flowers in spring or summer. And you will pass large impoundments, lonely-looking salt flats, and cordgrass marshes, with views beyond them of Laguna Madre Bay. Along the way there is an overlook at Redhead Ridge where you can take in the whole panorama of marshes, brushlands, pools, and bays below. If you want to, you can also reflect upon the bad old days hereabouts (and be glad about the good new ones) by reminding yourself of how this ridge earned its name. Laguna Atascosa has been and still is the wintering ground for nearly all of the continent's population of redhead ducks. As far back as colonial times, this ridge was the favored spot of market hunters who slaughtered the birds by the tens of thousands, often for no other reason than to collect their fatty deposits as a saddle ointment. Now, happily, only binoculars are pointed at them as they and great numbers of other waterfowl fly above the lookout during the winter months. This is the southernmost point in the Central Flyway, and sometimes a million birds pass above this ridge. In winter the flocks sometimes darken the sky, providing spectacles that are even more awesome, in the opinion of some viewers, than the flights at Rockefeller and Sabine.

With notable exceptions, the wildlife species here are much the same as at Aransas. There are the same prodigious "fallouts" of migrating songbirds in the spring and the same large congregations of waders and shorebirds on the sand and mud flats along Laguna Madre and Atascosa bays. Deer, rattlesnakes, javelina, and quail—but not wild turkey—are also very common here and often seen. The same for coyotes and the rabbits and ground squirrels they hunt. But along with these more familiar creatures there are groove-billed anis, green jays, tropical kingbirds, the lovely but rare varied bunting, and the large, pheasantlike chachalaca. Also be on the lookout for the black-bellied whistling-duck, a long-legged Mexican bird whose only nesting ground in the United States is at this refuge.

Rarities are not just to be found among the feathered set. The refuge's most thrilling permanent resident is the spotted ocelot, an exquisitely beautiful wildcat that looks like a miniature version of a leopard. This shy creature was once rather common in the Rio Grande Valley but, except for the tiny population at Laguna Atascosa, it has all but vanished along with its scrub habitat. Even rarer, apparently, is another small species of tropical wildcat, the jaguarundi. If the ocelot looks like a small leopard, the jaguarundi resembles a diminutive mountain lion, only with a head too small for its long body. There is no likelihood that you will see either of these endangered felines; but, as with those southern panthers on the other side of the Gulf, there is a special joy in just being where they are.

Several walking trails are available in the refuge. The four-mile Whitetail Trail wanders through the Rio Grande scrub country, offering excellent opportunities for seeing desert wildlife if you walk it early or late in the day. Another trail follows the edge of a freshwater impoundment where there is a good chance of seeing black-bellied whistling-ducks. Near the Visitor Center are the Brushland and Paisano trails, both very short, but with much-needed labels that identify the area's unfamiliar plants and shrubs. Doves, rabbits, the madly energetic roadrunner, and even deer and javelina are often considerate enough to show themselves. Fishermen armed with a Texas license can try their luck in two designated places on the banks of the Harlingen Ship Channel at the northern end of the refuge, but there is no access to Laguna Atascosa Bay from the refuge. Camping is not permitted. (Laguna Atascosa National Wildlife Refuge, Box 450, Rio Hondo, Texas 78583; 512/748–2426.)

Our next stop is South Padre Island. From the refuge, take the road south until it meets Hwy 510. Turn east on 510 and follow it to Hwy 100, which takes you across the salt flats to Port Isabel and the South Padre Causeway. Port Isabel is another of those laid-back fishing towns that you begin, after a while, to collect and compare in your memory. This one claims that it is home to the largest shrimping fleet in the world, which may or may not be so; but certainly there are shrimp boats in abundance, as well as charter boats and private fishing boats of every conceivable size. Lined up along the docks and at the marinas in their harmonious multitudes, they make a more rewarding sight than the town itself. If you feel up to a steep, sixty-foot climb, you can have a look at both, not to mention a spectacular view of South Padre Island, the Gulf, and a sizable chunk of the Rio Grande Valley, from the top of the Port Isabel lighthouse. The structure, built in 1853, is a historic site, open to the public.

The lighthouse view also prepares you for the towering vision that looms ahead as you cross the causeway to South Padre Island. We have not seen anything quite like this since leaving Florida. Gulf Shores or the Mississippi Gulf Coast or Galveston can't compare. It is as though the condominium metropolis on San Marco Island, which we briefly visited when we were on Florida's west coast, had flown across the Gulf like Rodan just so it could lie in wait for us here. In its monolithic way, the place—it can't be called a town or a city—has a sleek, soulless beauty. This is narcissistic modern architecture at its best. It doesn't try to dominate its natural surroundings. It is simply unaware of them. One playfully imagines all these towers a century hence, poking out of the island's shifting sands at odd angles like the Statue of Liberty in *Planet of the Apes*.

Not that I am bad-mouthing South Padre. It is simply a Texas-size resort city with all the fixings—as distinguished from a Gulf fishing town or even Galveston (which, for all its resort facilities, has other lives to lead). At the island's southern tip is **Isla Blanca Park**, a half-mile-long, intensively developed public campground that includes, among other amenities, 400 sites with hookups, a motel, cabins, boat ramps, a marina, grocery, swimming pool, a beautiful white beach, and even a nondenominational chapel. Charter boats are available by the dozen nearby, and for good reason: even by the usual Gulf Coast standards, deep-sea fishing is big business on South Padre. Here as elsewhere, marlin, sometimes exceeding 400 pounds, are the Gulf sportsfisher's Holy Grail. But there are also kingfish, tuna, red snapper, bonito, barracuda, tarpon, shark, and monstrous groupers waiting offshore to test your skill, or your luck.

One of the park's best features, especially for those who want to get away from all the rest of it, is a long, sea-washed jetty that extends out into the pass between South Padre and the Boca Chica Peninsula. It is one of the very few places along the Coast where, without benefit of boat, you can actually transport yourself into the Gulf of Mexico beyond everything else there is—mainland, bays, even barrier is-lands—and experience the thing itself. When a baroque sunset is going on, you can sit there and feel like Toscanini conducting the Phil-harmonic in some particularly stirring symphony for the benefit of an audience of genuine sharks and gulls. The effect can be intoxicating. (Careful, though. The rocks are slippery.)

For boatless anglers, the place to be is the nearby Queen Isabella Fishing Pier on the bay side of the island. This is another of Texas's discarded causeways that has been sensibly turned over to the fishing public. This one is lighted at night, so you can fish twenty-four hours a day if that is your fancy. Depending on what's running when, trout, redfish, croaker, drum, flounder, or sheepshead may respond to your bait. Even if you don't have much luck, the causeway-pier is an ami-able place to be, with plenty of fellow fishing addicts on hand eager to commiserate and offer you advice. (Isla Blanca Park, Box 2106, South Padre Island, Texas 78597; 512/943–5493.)

The best thing about development on South Padre Island is that there is a limit to it. Six miles up the beach it comes to a dead stop, at least for now. This is the location of **Andy Bowie Park**. It is the an-tithesis of Isla Blanca in that there are no facilities here except for a fishing pier, although site development is in the works. Right now this is a fine place for primitive camping, swimming, surf fishing, shell col-lecting, sun worshipping, and long meditations on the Meaning of It All. It is also the departure point for excursions long or short, afoot or with four-wheel drive—or on a rented three-wheel motorbike—

along the twenty-eight miles of unspoiled coastline that extend north-ward to the Port Mansfield Channel. (Significantly, there is a towing service nearby.) The wild, splendid beach here is much the same as at the already described Padre Island National Seashore on the other side of the channel. (Andy Bowie Park has the same address and phone number as Isla Blanca Park, above.)

Sometime during your stay on South Padre you should visit and pay homage to the island's most famous character, Ila Loetscher, oth-erwise known as the Turtle Lady. This elderly, very endearing person-age has dedicated her life to saving the endangered Ridley sea turtle. Her novel approach is to put on fashion shows for delighted tourists that feature large turtles decked out in cute little dresses, undies, hats, and wigs. The effect is high camp; but when you're finished grinning, you discover that you care a lot more about the fate of these persecuted creatures than you did hitherto, and that you have contributed more than your best wishes to their survival. What the world needs is a mil-lion more people like Ila Loetscher. (Check with the tourist bureau or call 512/943–2544 to find out show hours.)

Back on the mainland, our road (Hwy 48) leads to Brownsville. Approaching the city, birders who don't plan to cross the border into Mexico should turn left on farm road 511, go one block, and then turn left again toward the Port of Brownsville and, more to the point, that famous scenic wonder, the Brownsville City Dump. Why? Because this dump affords just about your only north-of-the-border chance to add the Mexican crow to your Life List. Don't confuse it with the local grackles or the Chihuahuan ravens that visit here in winter.

511 also links up with Hwy 4, the only route to Boca Chica on the U.S. side of the Rio Grande's delta. The state eventually plans to develop the park site it owns near the mouth of the river. Meantime, however, people who want to do some primitive camping will love the wild loneliness of this area, with its high dunes and uncrowded beach-es. This whole section of the border has a very special ecological in-terest. Just a few miles upstream, the Audubon Society owns a small (174-acre) sanctuary that protects a jungly grove of Mexican sabal palms. At one time, dense stands of these trees were so commonplace along the lower Rio Grande that early explorers called the river the Rio de las Palmas. Now, the Audubon sanctuary is literally a palm oa-sis. The place is too small to be available to the general public, but it's comforting to know it's there. Closer to the river mouth, another sanc-tuary—the Loma Ecological Preserve—is being set up. "Lomas" are unusual clay dunes that are a specialty of this area. They have been described as "mini-Galapagos" because each shelters its own com-munity of small creatures that have evolved independently from those on neighboring dunes. The new preserve will ensure that these min-iature ecosystems are not left to the tender mercies of the dune buggies and pile drivers.

That's the good news. As usual, there is no lack of the other kind. The protection of the lomas is an environmental consolation prize for the imminent enlargement of the Brownsville Ship Channel. City officials have plans, apparently unstoppable, for the biggest, deepest (and, arguably, the least needed) port on the Gulf of Mexico. Like all such projects, it will cause great harm to the area's vital fisheries and, no doubt, its rich birdlife. The industrial development that accompanies the project will also further deplete the precious water supply of the Rio Grande. Not that there's much to deplete. The water is already so heavily siphoned off that hardly any of it reaches the Gulf. The aforementioned Loma Ecological Preserve may not seem much of a trade-off for the environmental havoc that the channel project will cause; but when you consider that 99 percent of the natural habitat in the Rio Grande Valley has already been wiped out, you realize that environmental beggars can't be choosers. Even now, the dry flats along Hwy 4 are beginning to sprout subdivisions the way they used to sprout yucca.

Speaking of subdivisions, we are now in Brownsville. Since we are about to cross the border, we should memorize this ultraordinary, medium-size American city as we did the prosperous farm country nearby. Brownsville has its distinctive features: a fine, small zoo, a couple of historic sites, and a heavily Hispanic population that influences local cuisine and lifestyle. But in terms of overall appearance, you could set the town down in almost any other state and no one would think it was out of place. Take note of the familiar suburbs, shopping centers, expressways, parking lots, boxy office buildings, and drive-in everythings that spread across mile after mile of the squandered landscape. Take note also of the relatively prosperous look of things. For better and worse, we are about to leave all that behind.

9
Mexico's North Coast

At a glance

Access   Brownsville, Matamoros, and Tampico are the major air terminals in this area, with Tampico served by Mexicana Airlines. Highway 101 from Matamoros (or Hwy 97 from Reynosa) takes you to San Fernando, and from there it's Hwy 180 all the way. Only a few paved roads give access to coastal beaches from the north-south highway.

Climate   The northern part of this stretch has temperatures comparable to those in southern Texas—in other words, averaging in the fifties during winter and often getting into the nineties between June and September. Rains can occur year-round, but fall mostly in summer, although even then periods of drought are not uncommon. However, as you move down this coast, approaching and then crossing the Tropic of Cancer, the tropical syndrome takes over completely, with more abundant summer rainfall and a decreasing range between winters, which are mostly warm, and summers (beginning in May), which are always hot.

Topography and Landscape Features   The wide, flat coastal plain just south of Matamoros was originally characterized by an estuarine lagoon and marsh complex backed by arid scrub country. However, impoundments in the lagoon, grazing in the marsh, and inland irrigation farming have completely altered the natural landscape. Further south the coastal plain is narrowed by a low range of mountains; inland the country is rolling and semiarid. Between Soto la Marina and Aldama, a relatively high range country of wide plateaus and gradual mountain slopes (Sierra José de las Rusias) is cut by a few river valleys. Here the coastal plain remains narrow. On much of this coast it fronts directly on the Gulf without intervening barrier islands and lagoons. South of Aldama the land gradually levels out into wide lowland valleys flanked by low hills.

F*lora and Fauna* In irrigated areas near the Rio Grande, natural vegetation has been almost totally displaced by sorghum. Further south, in hillier country, mesquite/yucca/cactus scrub is omnipresent. Steep mountain slopes retain considerable tracts of semitropical and tropical deciduous forest, including many species of acacias. In river valleys and on the coastal plain, palms and lowland tropical hardwoods are increasingly in evidence. Wildlife—especially birdlife—also becomes notably tropical, with many species present that are not

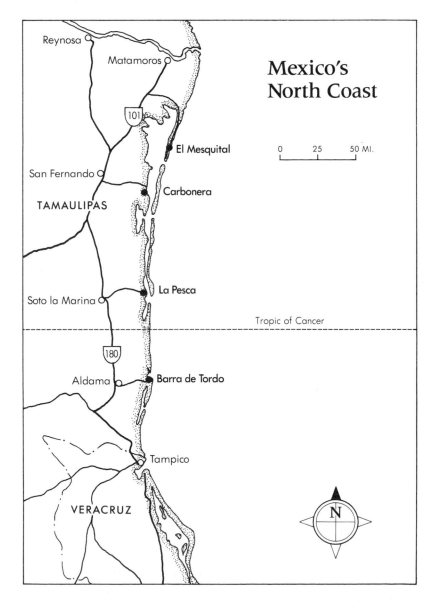

Mexico's North Coast

Reynosa
Matamoros
101
El Mesquital
San Fernando
Carbonera
TAMAULIPAS
La Pesca
Soto la Marina
Tropic of Cancer
180
Aldama
Barra de Tordo
Tampico
VERACRUZ

0   25   50 MI.

N

seen north of the border, including two or three parrot species, gray and roadside hawks, several tropical woodpeckers and doves, green parakeets, and motmots. Among mammals, coatimundi, coyotes, and ocelot can be found here, as well as whitetail deer and javelina; but game species are overhunted and hard to see. Only a few American alligators and crocodiles survive in coastal rivers. However, marine life is abundant and the fishing good.

Camping and Lodging   As noted in Chapter 1, there are no public or privately owned campgrounds of any kind on this part of the Gulf Coast. But there are many opportunities for unsupervised, on-your-own camping at or near small coastal fishing villages. The best prospects are beaches at La Pesca (east of Soto la Marina) and at La Barra del Tordo (east of Aldama). There is a nice small motel near La Pesca and very unfancy accommodations in small hotels at San Fernando, Soto la Marina, and Aldama. Really comfortable lodgings can be found only at Matamoros and Tampico.

Hiking, Canoeing, Boating, Etc.   The relatively modest mountain ranges that lie between Hwy 180 and the Coast along much of this stretch would undoubtedly make for interesting hiking. But here, as elsewhere in Mexico, you are on your own. Cross-country hiking should not be attempted without casing the area first. On the other hand, long walks along rural dirt roads and trails are available if you want to go native for a while. And there are endless miles of beach to explore afoot. Canoeing is not a very promising activity in most of this region, although Río Soto la Marina and, especially, Río Carrizal and its tributaries are interesting possibilities. In general, the area is much more suited for motorboating. El Mesquital, Carbonera, Barra del Tordo, and Soto la Marina are likely places to either launch your own boat or hire someone else's. Almost all of the bays and the few rivers on this Coast are great for fishing, but Río Soto la Marina and its lagoon are the most renowned. There are vast shallows, however, where it is easy to run aground. Surf fishing is excellent. For birders the possibilities are exciting anywhere you can find scrub or, especially, woodland—plus a place to park the car; but the areas around Aldama and Tampico are probably the best bets.

Outdoors Highlights   El Mesquital; La Pesca; Barra del Tordo; the rivers Soto la Marina and Carrizal; the coastal mountains near Soto la Marina and Aldama.

Now that we are crossing the border, you should note the introductory comments about Mexico in Chapter 1, keeping in mind that those comments are supplemental, not inclusive. They deal chiefly with Mexico's out-of-doors; the more general do's and don't's about travel in Mexico are summarized in brochures available at any Mexican consulate or in material supplied by Sanborn's Insurance or the Automobile Association of America.

At this point, however, a couple of comments about crossing the border at this particular point may come in handy—reaching it, for example. If you are coming from Harlingen, Hwy 77/83 will dead-end at International Boulevard, just a few blocks from U.S. Customs. If you've been following our itinerary and reach Brownsville from the Coast, just stay on Hwy 48 (Hwy 4 connects with it) and it will become International Boulevard.

It may also help to know that you can take care of all the red tape right at the border as long as you have a birth certificate (or voter's registration certificate) with you as proof of citizenship, plus evidence that you own the vehicle you're driving. Concerning exchange rates, the popular wisdom—understandably reinforced by the Mexican consulates—is that you can get the best rate at banks on the Mexican side of the border. Lately, however, the rates have been measurably better in Brownsville. There are a couple of exchange places on your right immediately after you turn onto International Boulevard from Hwy 77/83. As of now, they offer top value for your money. (You can, and should, also top off your gas tank nearby.)

As for insurance—indispensable in Mexico, where your regular car insurance does not apply—Sanborn's is still probably your best bet. There are two offices in Brownsville. One is on Hwy 77/83 as you are coming into town; it is just beyond the Holiday Inn on your right. The other is on Elizabeth Street a spit and a throw from U.S. Customs. If you don't need to stop and shop in Brownsville, the latter is the more convenient location. Elizabeth Street crosses directly in front of the Customs entrance. Just take a left and drive the short distance to the Best Western–Fort Brown Motor Hotel. Sanborn's is directly across the street from the hotel in a row of stores and offices.

U.S. Customs will probably just wave you through. On the Mexican side, officials will direct you to park behind the Customs building on your right. Go inside to the *Migración* desk to pick up a free Tourist Card or get the one you have validated. Then head for *Aduana*, where you pick up a vehicle permit, also free. The guards will check out your car, usually asking you to open some of your suitcases. Don't be surprised if one of them also asks you for a small gratuity because he's about to be married or he's contributing to the support of his ailing mother. "La Bite" is universal in Mexico. You won't be arrested if you refuse, but it simplifies life to have some small change—the current exchange equivalent of quarters or half-dollars—at the ready. In any case, be relaxed and amiable. Courteous behavior pays off in Mexico as everywhere else; yet you'd be surprised how many Americans, perhaps rubbed the wrong way by customs and attitudes not their own, forget that simple rule when traveling in a foreign country.

With any luck, all the red-tape rigamarole will be behind you in ten or fifteen minutes. Before leaving your parking place, though, read the detailed Sanborn directions about getting through Matamoros. That done, your Mexican adventure is under way!

Matamoros

Matamoros is a big city—much larger but more condensed than Brownsville. Instantly you'll be overwhelmed by the different feel of the place. For one thing, it really is a city in the traditional sense of the word. It teems with pedestrians; the streets are alive with the flow of humanity. For another, despite a lot of north-of-the-border touches, the layout and appearance of buildings and thoroughfares is unfamiliar. No inner-city expressways here, though for a while you will be driving on a wide, divided boulevard (Alvaro Obregon). More typically, the streets are narrow, and the buildings—the usual mix of colonial styles and zooty Mexican modern—are packed together and innocent of parking lots. Traffic tends to be noisily frenetic—so much so that American drivers new to Mexico are sometimes unnerved by all the vehicular hurly-burly, especially while trying to adjust to unfamiliar directional signs and not too clearly marked street names. Just don't get rattled by impatient horn blowers, and keep your eyes out for *Alto* (stop) signs and those signal lights that happen to be working. Head for *Centro*, the center of town. When you reach a large traffic circle (note the hotel El Presidente on your left), follow it partly around, crossing busy Boulevard Hidalgo. Then take a right onto the narrow Calle Cinco (5th Street), which leads through the center of town. Once you pass the town square—the Plaza Hidalgo, on your right—keep heading straight for the Coca-Cola sign in the distance. A block before you reach it, turn right on Calle Canales. After one block, turn left onto Avenida Sexta (6th Avenue), following the sign for Ciudad (Cd.) Victoria. From here on, you just keep going straight ahead.

Before leaving Matamoros, however, there are a few things you may want to know about this town. In my opinion it is, hands down, the best of the border towns, although it has its share of hokiness and sleaze. Connoisseurs of Mexican cities may not consider its architecture and ambiance anything to rave about, but first-time visitors will find the central city thrillingly foreign. If your arrival coincides with meal time, by all means stop to eat. Here at the border—and only here—restaurants eagerly accept American money, which apparently can then be exchanged at the same favorable rates that you enjoy. Because of this, you can make an absolute glutton of yourself at prices that are incredibly cheap. And the food is good! It is possible to work your way through a smorgasbord platter of meats, seafood (including excellent squid), and traditional Mexican dishes for five or six bucks at current rates. My favorite restaurant is the USA Bar and Grill at the corner of Plaza Hidalgo. The decor is motel-drear, but the chef knows what he's doing, and you get a Mexican organ recital of such Yankee favorites as "On Wisconsin" with your meal! If you want more atmosphere, and a slightly higher bill, you can dine upstairs at Garcia's (a short distance beyond Customs) or under the trees at Los Portales on Calle Sexto (6th Street) at the southern end of town.

You won't be interested in gift shopping on your way south, but since you may be coming back this way (and our tour won't), I should mention the market area that lies a couple of blocks west of Plaza Hidalgo. Shopping on the east coast of Mexico does not compare with the opportunities available on the Guadalajara–Mexico City–Acapulco circuit. But in contrast to most other border towns, where less costs more, Matamoros is about as good as the border, or the east coast, ever gets for shopping—at least, this side of the Yucatán. The shops and stalls have huge stocks of the usual trinkets—ceramic pigeons, shirts and blouses, costume jewelry (some of it quite pretty), and, horrifyingly, jillions of once-live, badly "stuffed" emerald toucanets, turtles, and horned toads. There is no decent pottery, woodwork, or fine silver at the market, but excellent handicrafts from all over Mexico are for sale at the government-sponsored Centro Artesenal, a large, unmarked building at Obregon and Avenida Quinta. Bárbara, on the Alvaro Obregon, is noted for fine jewelry and a lot of other quality items. Overall, though, Matamoros's strong suit is leather: well-tooled belts, wallets, handbags, and, for the walking-tall set, all the cowboy boots you would ever want to choose from.

Well, *vámanos*! Let's be on our way.

Heading South to Soto la Marina and La Pesca

If Mexico is your first Third World country, you will get your first close look at Third World poverty while heading out of town. Long rows of hovels line the road. Always, the poverty seems more abject in barrios on the outskirts of large cities than it does in rural settings. The litter, the lack of sanitation, the unsightliness of the thrown-together shanties are all more noticeable and grim. Yet this is not Handoutsville; the people here do not feel sorry for themselves. They don't want your useless pity; so don't offer it, even in your thoughts.

Before long, driving south on Hwy 101, you will pass the Matamoros Airport on your left. A couple of miles beyond, be on the lookout for the first paved road leading off to the left—that is, to the east. It is unmarked, but it will take you to a stretch of the Coast that tourists rarely visit. (If you reach the immigration check station, you will know you've overshot the turnoff by half a mile.) Before we take this interesting detour, however, those of you who like your creature comforts should be forewarned that there are no "U.S. standard" accommodations between Matamoros and Tampico—and reaching Tampico over not-so-hot roads is a full day's drive without any side trips thrown in. This particular detour is a pretty long haul—forty miles one way. Some of it is slow going, and there are no facilities. You can, however, camp on the beach here. Or, if you'd rather not, there are some clean, no-frills, Mexican-style accommodations further south along the main highway.

So, assuming you are not in a hurry and don't mind roughing it a bit, let us see what we can see. There are, after all, only three or four places along the entire northern Gulf Coast of Mexico where you can get to the Coast at all, and this is one of them.

The first part of the drive is not all that interesting: flat, open terrain with an occasional campesino's small *casucha* (hut) built of tin, wood, or stuccoed cement blocks. This was once productive marshland, but you'd never guess it now. Presently we will be stopped at a military training camp and asked to show our papers, and maybe have the luggage checked. That small hassle over, we embark on a different, more exciting stretch of road. We are in a landscape of wide, tidal salt flats and shallow water. Out in the middle of some of the sandy inlets are shrimp traps—the smell of dried shrimp is all-pervasive here— and close to the road there are low, rectangular pans edged with short stakes. In these, salt is trapped at low tide and collected by the local people in much the same way that it has been gathered for centuries.

The estuarine ecology in this arid region has been radically disturbed both by the destruction of inland marshes and by the operations of PESCA, Mexico's government-controlled marine-fisheries monopoly. The agency has turned the Laguna Madre (a different bay from the one in southern Texas) into a series of impoundments. Openings have been made in the barrier island to allow saltwater intrusion into these fish pens. The short-term intent is to improve local commercial fishing. For the long term, the effect has been to wreck the bay's ecological balance. One visible result is that the birdlife is not nearly as abundant as it once was. Even so, however, there are always some birds in view—egrets, great and little blue and tricolored herons, plus shorebirds, gulls, and terns. During migration, roseate spoonbills occasionally put in an appearance, and in spring keep an eye out for white pelicans, which are said to nest on nearby beaches. Roadrunners, living up to their name, are a likely sight at any time of year, and grackles and blackbirds are everywhere, as they will be throughout our Mexican tour.

Presently, the tiny hamlet of La Salinera (aptly named for the local salt industry) appears beside a shallow inlet: a few shanties, some of them vividly painted, and a dilapidated *restaurante* shimmering in the heat waves on the shadeless sand. The road becomes very narrow and shoulderless, easing across flats and sand ridges. This is the loveliest part of the drive: enormous beige dunes begin to close in, rolling along beside us for a while, then looming above us, encroaching on the road. The scene is not unlike that at Boca Rica on the American side, but we are much more exposed here. In this impoverished region—the most arid section of the Coast—the human presence may be tenacious, but it is plainly not in control. We have the uneasy feeling that if we do not keep moving, the dunes will try to bury us.

The road dead-ends at El Mesquital (with reference to the mosquito, another apt name!). This is a fishing community at an inlet to the bay, overlooked by a lighthouse, but how different it is from Port Isabel, not all that far away to the north. There are no yacht basins or trailer camps or condos here. Instead, you'll find a ragtag handful of huts surrounded by boards on which shrimp are drying. At the bay on which the lighthouse fronts, you may see the exceptionally shallow boats that are used by the local fishermen for drag-seining. Because of their impact on bay fisheries, the same boats have been outlawed in neighboring Texas.

Primitive camping is available here. However, be sure to carry everything you need with you, including water. Also, keep in mind that it's a bit chancy to take a vehicle across the soft sand between the road and the beach. Check out the stretch carefully before you try it, or ask the lighthouse-keeper for advice. With or without your wheels, you will discover that once you have put a little distance between yourself and the village with its aroma of drying shrimp, this entire peninsula is as beautifully wild and lonely as the most untrammeled stretches of Padre Island. The stretch of beach north of here can reportedly be negotiated by four-wheel drive. But remember that there are no park officials here to warn you about bad spots along the way. And El Mesquital doesn't have a towing service!

American fishermen in campers come here sometimes and set up on the beach. There is no need to have your own boat, although some southern Texans do. The lighthouse-keeper or local fishermen are usually available to take you out for a reasonable fee. Despite the drag-seining, the fishing is still good (in the short run, the impoundments probably help), and some of the deep Gulf species are said to come close to shore. But the real attraction of El Mesquital is that it offers much the same natural scene that you can find on the south Texas Coast without any of the cluttered trappings of "civilization." No hookups, no bikini-clad sun worshippers, no postcards, no motels with loud signs. This is emphatically not our world. People live close to the essentials here. If we are in the mood to shed the complications of our own lives, or at least put them into perspective, El Mesquital is a good place to be.

Back on Hwy 101, get ready to stop at the immigration checkpoint just a short distance down the road. This is the first of several such places on the road heading south. The inspectors are usually polite enough; but like minor officials everywhere, they sometimes like to throw their weight around a bit, poring over your papers and sizing you up before poking around a bit in your suitcases. The natural tendency of most of us to feel vaguely guilty when being scrutinized by law-enforcement types makes these sessions more uneasy-making than they need to be. Just be patient and polite. The same goes when, as usually happens at least once along the way, a squad of soldiers forms a temporary blockade on the road, checking for illegal contraband. The Army is a means of keeping a lot of people employed in Mexico, and a lot of other people intimidated. For the American traveler, it's a bit unnerving, but also just a touch exciting, to have to get out of your car and watch heavily armed men peering under the back seat. Mexico is not exactly a police state; but the felt presence of its Army makes you aware that the wherewithal is there if it ever decided to become one. As far as we law-abiding folks are concerned, however, the worst thing that will happen is that a soldier may ask you for a cigarette if you have some lying on the dashboard.

For the next many miles, brace yourself for a single-minded passage through sorghum country. Compared to soybeans or cotton, the crop looks cheerful, even colorful, if it has had enough water and is coming into flower. In winter, the flat, sometimes flooded fields are uniformly bleak, but the seed left at harvesting attracts waterfowl, as well as other water birds and shorebirds.

The Mexican government has been doing its best with its share of the Rio Grande's water to make the desert bloom in a desperate effort to keep Mexico's exploding population of country people—campesinos—down on the farm. Properties expropriated from large landowners have been set up as *ejidos*, which may consist of groups of individually leased farms or agricultural collectives. Each farmer operates his own holding, but officials determine how the land will be managed and can evict anyone who doesn't play ball. We Americans tend, understandably, to applaud land reform in Third World countries. However, in Mexico as in other nations, vast sections of the country are ill-suited for the kind of reform that is taking place. The land cannot be effectively managed in small parcels operated by subsistence farmers, even as parts of a cooperative. As their roadside hovels testify, most of these people are as poor as they have always been. The whole problem is compounded by mismanagement and corruption. Worst of all, immense areas that are unfit for agriculture are being given over to the plow in a hopeless effort to meet the demands of a fast-growing population. If our American West—deserts, mountains, national forests and parks, all of it—were divvied up into small parcels and distributed to government-sponsored sharecroppers, you would have a comparable situation. Most objective authorities believe that the system guarantees the worst possible abuse of natural resources. But such objections are met with the inevitable answer: people need to eat now. In the short term, the program is a crowd pleaser that helps to postpone social unrest. *Mañana* will just have to take care of itself.

Highway 101 between Matamoros and San Fernando is heavily patched, but you won't tear up your car as long as you drive at fifty-five miles per hour. And once you get past the not very attractive town of San Fernando, the road will improve for a while. While you're in San Fernando, be sure to check your fuel gauge; the next gas station is at Soto la Marina, eighty miles to the south. Also, you may be interested in taking another sortie to the Coast here, depending on how much time you can devote to exploration. The road east takes you to the fishing village of Carbonera. At one time, Carbonera tried to turn itself into a real tourist spot, but the idea never got off the ground. However, some Mexican tourists do come here, and so do a few American fishermen. There is a small area, used mostly by the local folks, where you can picnic. But the road does not reach the barrier island and the Gulf beach. The lagoon is so shallow that if you're determined enough you can wade to the barrier island. But it's a lot simpler to hire a boatman who will take you across. Once reached, the island offers the same long perspectives of high, rolling dunes, deserted beach, and shining Gulf waters that we encountered at Padre Island National Seashore and El Mesquital. There is often a pretty decent surf here, and porpoises ride the waves offshore. All things considered, though, if I had to limit the number of excursions I could take along the northern Mexican Coast, Carbonera would be the one I would most likely skip.

South of San Fernando, the road takes off into a landscape welcomely different from the one we have left behind. We are entering hill country—some of it rolling, much of it fairly steep and rugged, all of it much like our own Southwest. About thirty miles south of San Fernando we reach the junction with Hwy 180, the road that we will be following, give or take a number of side trips, for the rest of our long journey. As already noted, the surfacing on this eighty-mile stretch is in pretty good shape (as of this writing), and traffic is very light; but grades are steep by American standards, and the road is fairly narrow and winding. So take it easy. Since road shoulders are minimal, the landscape comes up close to you, severe, dry, lonely, but beautiful in its stark way: ravines, dense walls of scrub, cacti, occasional patches of undernourished sorghum on marginal slopes, circling buzzards, herds of ribby cattle half hidden in the mesquite, and a lot of spiky yuccas, often as tall as trees, looking like a form of plant life that has emigrated from another planet. Since human habitation is relatively sparse, there is still some wildlife hereabouts, including a few whitetail deer and javelina. You may even see a coyote—or the remains of one—on the road. This is great country (no political comment intended) for hawks and doves. If you take the time to look around, there is a chance of seeing white-winged, ground-, Inca, mourning, or (in woodsy swales) rare white-tipped doves, as well as the uncommon red-billed pigeon. Among the raptors, the likeliest possibilities are white-tails, red-tails, and dark Harris' hawks, the last often sitting on fence posts. The long-legged caracara is also present, usually sighted on the ground in the same sort of openings in the scrub where you might spot a roadrunner.

Soto la Marina and La Pesca

Another detour to the Coast presents itself at Soto la Marina. Before we take it, however, let us pause briefly at this little town, which most southbound tourists never even glance at. True, there are no notable churches here, no shops the traveler would be interested in (except one where equestrian types can buy beautiful western saddles for incredibly reasonable prices), and no decent restaurants. In short, there is nothing to do except look around at an ordinary Mexican town that is remarkable—to us—only because it is so unlike ordinary towns in the United States. The square is not worth a photograph; yet it is a real "people place," something that our own urban planners have a hard time trying to create. On the narrow side streets, all the shops and dwellings somehow come together as an integrated whole, including a few humble but picturesque thatched-roof huts that look like they predate Montezuma. And on the town's outskirts there are none of the usual American preliminaries—billboards, Dairy Queens, trailer parks, etc. It's true, of course, that at the drop of a sombrero the citizens of Soto la Marina would trade their tortillas and beans for our McDonald's, their wash lines for our washing machines, and, alas, their sense of community for our television sets and cars. But it's also true that, in spite of their relative poverty, the people here have a disconcerting way of seeming no more discontent with their lives than we are with ours. Communing with a town like this for an hour or so may make us "fortunate" folks more aware that we pay a price for our affluence and rampaging technology. Soto la Marina, and thousands of other Mexican towns like it, have a human scale and a harmony with place and time that most American towns have lost. It would be nice if we—and they—could have it all.

If you are road-weary and consider spending the night here, be advised that the two hotels on the square are spartan by our standards. There is no air-conditioning, and private bathrooms occupy partitioned corners of the bedrooms. Wake-up service is provided by roosters in neighboring yards. But the rooms are pretty clean and dirt-cheap.

The drive from Soto la Marina to La Pesca on the Coast is thirty miles one way on a narrow but adequate road. For a while the road sticks to a low valley where rangeland and sorghum fields alternate. Then it begins to climb through a small but steep mountain range with scrub-covered slopes and dense pockets of trees growing in deep ravines. Dry-looking though the prospect is, we are in the tropics now. For birders eager to see species that never come north to the border, these hillsides are a paradise. I still remember one late afternoon when I nearly drove off into empty space on this winding stretch. No, I wasn't speeding, and there was no motorized Pancho Villa coming around the bend in the wrong lane. What almost did me in was the first pair of wild parrots I'd ever seen. They were yellow-heads, feeding on the pods of some type of acacia just a few yards from the road. When they warily flew off as I slowed down, their brilliant yellow and green plumage all but extinguished the duller greens and yellows of the background hills. There are, of course, few guarantees when it comes to wildlife viewing, especially in Mexico. But even if you aren't lucky enough to see parrots—they are not all that common here— there are a number of other more or less tropical species on hand if you take the time to look around. Among the more likely prospects are squirrel cuckoo, brown jay, clay-colored robin, lineated woodpeckers, and sulphur-bellied flycatchers. Looking around, however, is easier said than done. In Chapter 1, I noted that Mexicans do not usually worry about trespassing the way we do as long as you aren't carrying a gun. But footpaths are hard to find hereabouts. So, for that matter, are roadside parking places. However, if you can find a safe spot to pull over (at least six or eight feet off the road), it should be okay to explore slopes and thickets close by, keeping in mind that this is tick heaven. You might also try your luck—if you can explain your intentions in Spanish—at the tiny mountaintop *aldea* (hamlet) of Villa Hermosa. The spot is well named for its beautiful view of the blue lowlands and the Coast far below. And there are trails leading down the steep slopes.

The approach to La Pesca is across marshy flats unpromisingly planted with the omnipresent sorghum. Several pretty villas and a very nice small motel line the bay at the mouth of the Río Soto la Marina. La Pesca itself is a sun-washed if somewhat untidy little town. The one wide street is lined by small dwellings whose once bright paint jobs have faded to dim pastels. Hogs and emaciated mutts doze in the street. (You will have to harden yourself to the sight of those wretched, skeletal dogs, I'm afraid. There is no place in Mexico where you can escape the sight of them.)

Beyond a last small stretch of marsh is the beach. A gleaming white lighthouse overlooks a rock breakwater and several small boats docked beside the blue bay. Nearby are rows of *sombreadores*—sun shelters—with thatched roofs. Don't be too put off if this pretty picture doesn't look quite so pretty close up. Mexicans are even more indifferent to litter than we are, and they take sanitation problems much less seriously (which is one of the main reasons why efforts to attract large numbers of U.S. tourists to these parts have always failed). Near the lighthouse, the lovely tawny beach is bestrewn with soft-drink bottles, and the little *sombreadores* shelter mosquitoes and flies. Not to worry, though. Once you head up the shore a ways, the litter thins out, and the blue purity of sky and water is all there is. The surf is almost as good here as at South Padre Island, and, in fact, American surfers occasionally come here. There are, of course, no campgrounds, but camping on the beach is free and, from all accounts, safe. Indeed, locals complain good-naturedly that we use the area but spend no money. In a way, given the limited supplies at Soto la Marina and the flies on the otherwise excellent fried shrimp you can buy, it's not hard to understand why. Nevertheless, you should spread a little *dinero* around while you are here, buying soft drinks, good Mexican beers, and so on. In particular, try hiring a local guide to take you out to fish and explore the long, narrow bay, Laguna de Morales, just to the south, or the Río Soto la Marina itself. Fishing is far and away the great attraction in this area. The bay, the inlet, and the tidal portion of the river (which reaches about ten miles inland) comprise a heaven for anglers in search of snook and tarpon. Old hands from the States bring their own boats down here, often putting in at Soto la Marina and heading downstream. But for the rest of us, the sensible thing is to hire a guide and boat. Or try the surf fishing, which is also very good.

Between Soto la Marina and Aldama the road surface is in pretty poor shape; but, considering the mountainous terrain, the grades and curves are surprisingly easy. This region gets somewhat more rain than the area to the north. In a natural state it supported extensive forests, but now the land is being rapidly cleared, often by means of brush fires. Yet despite the many signs of relentless and reckless exploitation, this is a pretty drive. There are large views. Mountains rise and fall in waves. In the swales, the remnants of palm forests cluster around green-looking homesteads. Along the roadside, our old friend from the Everglades, the gumbo limbo, has reappeared. Twenty-six miles below Soto la Marina, a spherical marker announces that you are crossing the Tropic of Cancer. You are officially in the tropics.

Aldama and La Barra del Tordo

Of all the few reasonably accessible places on the Coast north of Tampico, I suppose that La Barra del Tordo is my favorite, if only because, by the time I get to it, I'm ready for a bit more greenery than northern Mexico has to offer. The turnoff from Hwy 180 is at Aldama. This is the biggest town in the region, but that isn't saying much. It doesn't even get a cursory nod in the tour books, but I am fond of the place. It does that good urban Mexican thing: materializing suddenly and wholly like a walled medieval city without the walls. You turn off the highway onto a pleasant lane flanked by Australian pines, pass a colorful little cemetery with the usual political graffiti on its whitewashed flanks, and then, presto, you are suddenly on the main drag. The antispeeding bumps—*topes*—are a joke here. Without any help from them, the holes in the street will break the axle of your car if you drive faster than a burro walks. But aside from that little drawback, it's a nice town to say hello to. The usual melange of houses and shops presses right up against the narrow sidewalks, with doors and windows wide open and little kids playing on the sills. Even the poorest thatched-roof huts, walls sagging perilously outward, have their decent place here. And not all the homes are poor, by any means. Notice the small but comfortable villas tucked behind gates and walls on some streets. Their owners are somewhat insulated from their less prosperous neighbors, but at least they haven't fled to the suburbs.

There are no signs in Aldama directing you to the Coast. You have to take a dogleg to the right, then the left, to hit the road on the back side of town. The simplest thing is just to ask for La Barra del Tordo and anyone will point the way. Once past the garbage dump, the road passes through a moderate mountain range, some of it still forested. This is the eastern slope of the Sierra de Tamaulipas, otherwise known as the Sierra de las Rusias, one of the three places, all in Mexico, where mountains press close to the Gulf of Mexico. For birders, or anyone interested in the outdoors, the area is definitely worth a closer look. Ecologically, this is a transition zone, the meeting ground of flora and fauna peculiar not only to coastal and mountain environments, but to tropical and temperate climates. It is a terrific area for birding. Without even getting out of your car, you may see the gorgeous blue bunting, golden-browed warbler, hooded grosbeak, or red-crowned ant tanager flying across the road in front of you. Nearby woodlands and brush harbor partridgelike rufescent (thicket) tinamou, spotted wrens, and the demure singing quail, as well as the wary military macaw in his spectacular uniform of green, blue, and red. If you decide to do a bit of polite trespassing, it probably won't get you into trouble, although the local *vaqueros* (cowboys) may stop and question you. The best policy is to pull up at a campesino's homestead and ask for permission and advice. Offer him the equivalent of fifty cents or a dollar for minding your car while you prowl around promising-looking slopes nearby.

La Barra del Tordo looks like the set for a movie about some burned-out American expatriate who sits around drinking himself to death while waiting for a missionary's daughter or a revolution to come along. It smells of shrimp. There are only two possible reactions to the place: "You mean *this* is it?" or "I love it!" A couple of dozen houses in colors ranging from bright yellow and green to unpainted cinder block are strung along a single street that dead-ends in a mangrove swamp. In their backyards lies the lovely little bay of the Río Carrizal. And off in the distance is the *barra* for which the place is named: a wide break in the high coastal dunes where the surf and the waters of the bay meet in an impressive line of breakers. Myself, I am one of the "I love it" types. You can hire a boat and guide here and, for a couple of hours, travel up a beautiful river edged by tropical vegetation and, further inland, rocky ledges. Along with the more familiar species of waders, you may have the chance here of seeing the bittern-like bare-throated tiger heron at the northern end of its territory. Also keep an eye out for muscovy ducks and red-crowned parrots. In neighboring lagoons there are still caimans—a close relative of our alligator—and even crocodiles. Both, alas, are very rare, and no effort is being made to preserve them. When I was last in La Barra I saw a couple of "for sale" baby caimans competing with large turtles and fish for space in a laundry tank.

Fishing is excellent in the small bay and the river, as well as at the *barra* itself. And you can pick up delicious oysters just by wading in the shallows near the town. The splendid outer beaches are great fun to explore, but you don't have to get to them to do some sunbathing or set up camp. Just a quarter-mile before reaching town, a rock gravel road leads to the not-too-littered public beach with its wide berm and clear water. The terrain behind the beach is reminiscent of cattle country in central Florida: flat, with clumps of tall, broad-leafed trees in wide pastures. But in the background are the volcanic-looking mountains we drove through to get here. If you occupy one of the *sombreadores* for the afternoon, or overnight, you may or may not be asked to pay a pittance depending on whether anyone is around or not. In any event, if the breeze is keeping the mosquitoes at bay, this is usually a peaceful place to set up for a while. I say "usually" because during holidays seasons, especially Easter, the somnolent atmosphere of La Barra del Tordo is disrupted by the invasion of large numbers of Mexican vacationers.

The town, incidentally, has a couple of places where you can buy cold drinks and a few supplies, but that's about it. However, according to the townsfolk, a fancy tourist resort is being built nearby, accessible only by boat. Assuming that it ever materializes, you might want to check it out if you aren't doing Mexico on a shoestring budget. One way or another, this is a fascinating area to explore. Not the least of its attractions is the fact that few Americans have ventured beyond the town and the road.

Tampico

The closer you get to Tampico, the less pretty the drive becomes. The hills peter out, population densities increase, and clearing and development are evident everywhere. Also, there are more and more trucks on the road. From a sociological standpoint, though, it is interesting to take a look at "modern" Mexico. Outside the city, an expressway is being built that should enable you to get past the outlying strip of slums and other uglies pretty quickly. And Tampico can offer many of the amenities that you may or not have been missing. For starters, be aware that soon after you pass the airport, there is a big, modern supermarket–shopping center on your left where you can stock up on groceries or whatever. Not far beyond, also on the left are, first, a reasonably priced, air-conditioned motel, the San Antonio, and then, a mile further on, a fancier, more expensive one, the Camino Real. In between, on the right, is—are you ready?—a Kentucky Fried Chicken place that will comfort the hopelessly homesick. For those who want to eat well, if relatively expensively, the best bet is La Mansión, located on a side street (101 Fresno) across from the Camino Real. The food, including steaks, fish, and some local specialties, is very good and the setting pleasant. After La Pesca, Aldama, et al., this whole stretch along the Hidalgo Expressway will seem a little unreal to you—for better or worse.

If you plan to settle down in this area for a day or two, and you are interested in the local avifauna, you may want to take a side trip out along Hwy 70 (toward Ciudad Valles) for ten or twenty miles past the toll bridge. The road is a mess: lots of heavy trucks and industrial activity, and not too many places where you can safely pull over. However, it traverses many marshy areas, and there are some side roads or other suitable spots where you can get off the highway, beginning about five or six miles beyond the toll bridge. If you find a place that has both some scrubby brush and a view of the marshes, you're in business: you will have a good chance of seeing such south-of-the-border species as ochre (Fuertes') oriole, yellow-crowned (Altamira) yellowthroat, ringed and green kingfishers, and Aztec parakeet. The marshes harbor hard-to-see jacanas and red rails (ruddy crakes), and there will almost certainly be numbers of the more familiar shorebirds and waders—and perhaps even wood storks—in view. Large numbers of migrant waterfowl congregate here in winter, and in early spring the area is a funneling point for thousands of northbound hawks. Given the incredible industrial pollution to which these marshes are subjected, it seems a miracle that so many birds should thrive here; but as of now, they still do. If all of this simply whets your appetite, or if you are an angler in search of new horizons, you may want to find out about the possibilities of exploring the wide expanses of Laguna de Tamiahua south of the city. This is easier said than done, however. You will need a guide, probably someone in Tampico Alto. The best thing to do is to check with Tampico's tourist office. (Delegación Estatal de Turismo, Olmos 101 Sur, Despacho 1 y 2, Tampico, Tamaulipas, Mexico.)

Big as it is, Tampico barely gets a nod in most tour books beyond the notation that it is "Mexico's Houston"—that is, a major port for the nation's oil and petrochemical industry. Although the town was the setting for the Spaniards' last effort to reclaim their colony, it has limited historical or architectural interest. Cortés never slept here, and the new city overpowers the old. Interesting baroque and beaux-arts structures are crowded by Mexican modern, which runs to ornamental cinder-block facades. As is usual in Mexico, the newer buildings are coming apart faster than the older ones. Traffic is nervous-making, and in some of the poorer residential sections the streets are literally cratered. Still, the main plaza is attractive with its fine cathedral and elaborate bandstand, lots of benches, and shady trees sporting white-washed trunks. (And a very comfortable hotel, the Inglaterra, which is considerably cheaper than the Camino Real and only a few steps from the tourist office.) Also, in contrast to glossy, glassy, downtown Houston, where pedestrians are an oppressed minority, Tampico's central district is a vibrant, interesting area that remains alive and lively even after dark.

You may wish you never laid eyes on the place, however, by the time you've crossed the Río Panuco by ferry on your southward journey. This experience is the sort of thing that makes even the most un-ugly American start muttering about Mexican ineptitude. The problem is that there are two ferry depots at widely separated points. Sometimes the more accessible of these is reserved for truck traffic, sometimes not. If it is, you can wait in line for an hour and no one will tell you that you're wasting your time until you try to drive aboard. Then, when you ask how to get to the other ferry, the directions—even if they are correct—will be enough to make Theseus wish he were back in the labyrinth, especially since streets are poorly marked. If it's any consolation, even Mexican motorists get confused and lost. So, what do you do? If you're staying at a hotel, ask the manager which ferry is carrying passenger cars. He'll probably know. If he doesn't, just ask your way to the ferry *that is near the new bridge that is being built*. Keep asking someone else every few blocks, since quite a few zigs and zags are involved. And don't be surprised if the directions take you through some very pitted back streets. (Another option is to hire a taxi driver to lead the way.)

The above is a long paragraph to waste on a ferry crossing; but it's one of those hassles that can easily make you lose both your temper and a half-day's travel time if you aren't forewarned. Actually, though, there is a possibility that the forewarning will be unnecessary by the time you make your trip. For the last several years, a great vaulting bridge has been abuilding just below the ferry crossing. Some one of these days it will probably be completed. Meantime, console yourself with the thought that the return-trip crossing is almost always easier than the southbound one.

10
Mexico's
Central Coast

At a glance

Access   The only major air access points for this part of the Gulf that have regularly scheduled flights are Tampico in the northern sector and Veracruz in the south. Mexicana serves both cities from Mexico City. The only major coastal highway through this region is Hwy 180.

Climate   The hot, humid, wet summer season officially begins on this part of the Coast in mid-April, although I have traveled this region in late May on occasion, in an un-air-conditioned car, without much discomfort. Also, specific areas range pretty widely in temperatures and precipitation. Jalapa, in the mountains, is quite comfortable long after nearby Veracruz has begun to broil (but, on the other hand, it is drizzly in winter, when Veracruz is just right.) The mountainous Catemaco area is pretty livable at most seasons of the year, although it does get very heavy rains in summer. In ultrawet Tabasco, the Coast is not nearly as subject to deluges as the inland country. And to complicate matters further, even during the warm, beautiful winter months, *El Norte*—the harsh, cold wind from the northern Gulf—can keep everyone indoors for days on end. In general, though, this area is meant for winter and early spring travel. Summers define heat the way a Michigan blizzard defines cold.

Topography and Landscape Features   The range of visual prospects in this area is very varied. A summary can only suggest: volcanic mountains and conical foothills (the coastal outcroppings of the Sierra Madre Oriental) that dominate the foreground or the inland distance off and on again from the vicinity of Tuxpan to Veracruz, cropping up again in the Tuxtla Range on the Coast near Catemaco and once more in the Villahermosa-Palenque region; long stretches of coastal beach and grass savannah south of Tecolutla; beaches, high dunes, and wide lagoons south of Veracruz; marshes, vast river deltas, and coastal sand ridges in Tabasco.

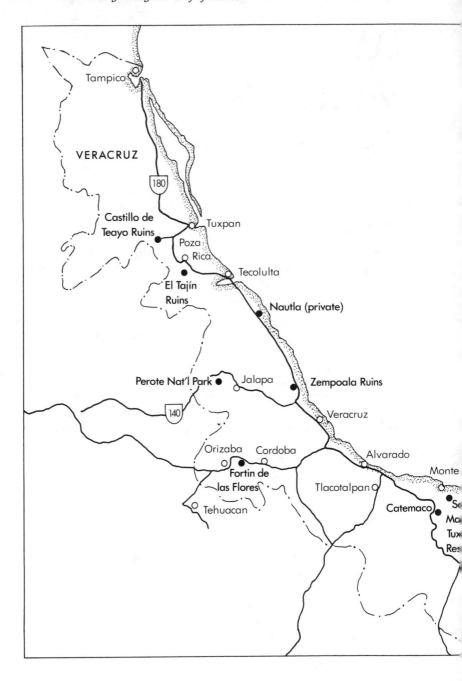

Tampico to Tabasco

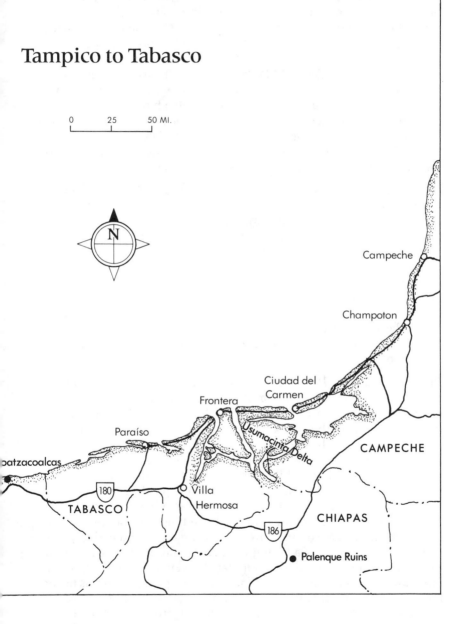

F*lora and Fauna* Although most of the luxuriant vegetation on this coast is now manmade—coconut and banana plantations, endless orchards of citrus and coffee trees, galaxies of imported or domesticated flowering trees and shrubs—there are still spectacular remnants of tropical rain forests and evergreen forests. And on the higher mountain slopes, temperate zone pine and oak woodlands give way to cloud forests saturated by abiding mists. Further south, one of the world's great mangrove jungles still blankets much of Tabasco's Usumacinta Delta. As for the native fauna, it matches the native vegetation both in variety and its threatened status. This is still a birder's tropical paradise, but those species that cannot adapt to the loss of rain forests are hard to find in many areas. All the larger mammals have been exterminated or are in desperate straits throughout the region, notwithstanding the outdated reports in most travel guides.

C*amping and Lodging* There are privately owned RV hookup facilities on this part of the Coast, just south of Tuxpan, near Nautla, and at Veracruz. In the Tabasco region, campgrounds can be found east of Coatzacoalcos and at Palenque. Plenty of potential off-the-road primitive camping sites are available for those who want to take their chances. For noncampers there are a wide variety of hotel accommodations to choose from, from luxurious to very inexpensive, at most of the sizable towns and beach places. Several away-from-it-all, on-the-beach motel/hotel facilities are available along the coastal stretch between Tecolutla and Villa Rica. And there is the wonderful Playa Escondida, mentioned in the travelogue, on the way to Montepio.

H*iking, Canoeing, Boating, Etc.* The general principles that apply to hiking in the northern sector of the Mexican Coast, as well as the relevant comments in Chapter 1, apply here as well. The special attraction of much of this region is the tropical beauty of the landscape. The mountain and hill regions mentioned above and described in more detail in the travelogue are truly lovely. As long as you do some on-the-scene preparation, hiking is feasible in a number of places, notably the rough tracks around Catemaco or Jalapa, the slopes of Perote, the forest reserve in the Sierra de los Tuxtlas, and the national park at Palenque—not to mention long beachcombing stretches on parts of the Coast. But you are on your own. There are tracks and paths aplenty, but no such thing as a hiking trail. Also, you need to realize that the state of Veracruz is densely populated. Even in seemingly remote mountain valleys and on empty beaches, the human presence is never far off. On the other hand, human conveniences and services—doctors, for example—are scarce. As for canoeing, this part of the Coast is relatively rich in streams and rivers, and some look very promising. Also, the Usumacinta Delta unquestionably has Everglades-like experiences to offer if you can find a place to put in. But only local people—some local people—know anything about these waterways. You must check them out as you go along. Boaters will have fewer problems, although, as noted in the travelogue, there isn't much point in towing an outboard this far when so many boats and guides are available on the scene, particularly at prime fishing areas such as Tuxpan, Tecolutla, Veracruz, and Ciudad del Carmen. Birding enthusiasts have hundreds of likely groves and forest edges to check out, and shell collectors should be happy almost anywhere on the southern Coast but especially at Isla del Carmen. Amateur archeologists, history buffs, and plain sightseers have a fine selection of ruins, historical sites, and picturesque towns to choose from. Finally, there is the pleasure of urban "hiking" in Veracruz. To sum up, this is an enchanting part of the Gulf Coast—but, for better or worse, most of its attractions have not been developed for the convenience of travelers. Some of the highlights listed below are not so easily reached and/or explored.

O*utdoors Highlights*   Tuxpan and nearby lagoons; El Tajín; Jalapa and nearby Perote; Veracruz; Lake Catemaco and the Tuxtla Forest Reserve; the Coastal Route from Paraíso to Isla del Carmen; the Usumacinta Delta; Palenque.

Tampico to Tuxpan

Once you get past a washboard stretch between the ferry and Tampico Alto, the drive to Tuxpan is really lovely. Don't try to hurry, though; the road surface isn't so hot, and gasping, rickety trucks will hold you up on the steep grades. Just remind yourself that if those steep grades weren't there, the scenery wouldn't be either. We are really in the tropics now. Even though most of the mountain forests have been obliterated, this is still a lush and green country. Royal and coconut palms are often in view. So are gumbo limbo, which here are used as living fence posts. In some small villages, cacti have been planted to form stockades. Neat little villas perch on the slopes, with verandas overlooking the valleys below. Chances are that these more prosperous establishments belong to former large landowners who have divided at least part of their former property among their kin as a means of escaping government expropriation. Such informal family "corporations" are almost always managed more efficiently than the usual *ejido* homesteads. But even poverty is softened here. Thatched-roof huts with cement block or stucco walls are often brightly painted and set among banana groves and brilliant red coral trees. Open-sided thatched shelters near the dwellings serve as *al fresco* dining rooms. Especially interesting are the homes walled vertically with poles, in contrast to the horizontally walled huts that were prevalent north of Tampico. These little homes are situated anywhere—right on top of small, steep mountains or in the bottom of equally steep gulleys where you would think they must wash away with a heavy rainfall. One suspects they sometimes do. But generally, life here wears a smiling face. On weekend evenings, groups of young rural people, immaculately dressed in white shirts and blouses, walk along the roadsides on their way to the open-sided hilltop pavilions where they will flirt and dance to the music of local bands.

One of the most magical effects is created by pale forests of what I have named, to my own satisfaction, the ghost tree. When you've seen it, you will know what I mean. It grows on the sides of steep hills, a gray-trunked tree covered with gray-lavender blooms in May and June, eerily superimposed on the tropical greens and beiges of the surrounding terrain like something that an artist had painted in. More often than not, however, the increasingly steep slopes of this region are given over to cattle pasture, citrus groves, and pineapple fields. By all means, if it's summer and the country folks are selling pineapples beside the road, buy one to eat as you drive along. They are delicious beyond belief. The women or kids who peddle them are experts with a machete and will skin and slice them for you in a twinkling. Paper plates and napkins don't come with this service, however, so have some newspaper or towels on hand to serve as bibs.

The closer we get to Tuxpan, the steeper and more majestic the mountains become. And the more volcanic. The blue peak that looks as though it should have smoke pouring out of it is named—what else?—Cerro Azul (Blue Peak). Many of these mountaintops look as though they've been subjected to a homemade haircut: the slopes are shaved almost to the top, but the crests are still crowned with a remnant of the stunningly beautiful tropical forests that once cascaded down their sides. Unlike temperate mountain forests, which tend to grow upright even when they are rooted on steep slopes, these ceiba, banyans, and gums lean outward into space, perpendicular to the tilted slope. The effect, when you drive under them, is dizzying. But you don't drive under them often anymore. Each year the forest crowns are cut back further. Already, most of the lower peaks are bald. Signs of erosion are often visible, and the effect on much of the local wildlife can be imagined. Monkeys, jaguar, and deer are finished in this region, although the habitat could still support a few whitetails if there were enforceable game laws. The beautiful birds of the tropical mountain forests are disappearing, too, but there are still some of them around. Recently I caught my northernmost glimpse of an emerald toucanet, its beak almost larger than all the rest of it put together, as it flew across this road late one afternoon.

Speaking of flying across the road: the manmade traffic bumps— *topes*—are really mean hereabouts. If you hit the one at Tempachi without slowing down, you and your car may both need a realignment on the spot. The special problem at Tempachi, apart from the badness of the bump, is that you may not notice the *tope* sign because the view is so glorious here, and also because this little town boasts a church, a very humble church, which is ancient even by Mexican standards. It looks as if it has grown there, like the rocks.

Tuxpan

What a pleasant little town—little city—Tuxpan is! The one sad note is the dreadful barrio on its hilly outskirts—the kind of ramshackle collection of tin huts, hardly bigger than doghouses, that bespeaks not just poverty but disease and real hunger.

Tuxpan lies in the delta valley carved by its namesake river just before it reaches the Gulf. It's a port city—not a very big one, but big enough. The esplanade along the river, as well as the main square that fronts on it, are bustling but thoroughly charming places to be. There are fountains, plenty of benches and steps to sit on, an attractive if rather plain church, pensive lovers strolling in the evening under rows of coral trees and palms with whitewashed trunks, and, of course, the ample presence of the river itself. There are a few modern office buildings built or being built. In the latter case, the process would give an American entrepreneur pause: offices are occupied as they are finished, even though the structure itself is nowhere near completed. Most of the architecture, though, is a pleasing mishmash of earlier styles and influences.

If you follow the riverfront drive (Avenida Hidalgo) several miles to the southeast, you will eventually reach the public beach, with its backup of Australian pines, palms, and suburban houses. (A surprising number of the latter look, not just unfinished, but deserted, possibly because Mexico's ongoing currency crisis has had a devastating effect on the country's middle class.) Though not too tidy, the beach is habitable, and, last I heard, you can camp here without incident. Compulsive fishermen, birders, or other venturesome souls may also inquire about boats and guides to take them out to the Laguna de Tampomachoco nearby, or the southern end of the Laguna de Tamiahua. The latter is a vast bay sheltered by the boomerang-shaped barrier island, Cabo Rojo, which is anchored off the mainland to a drowned coral reef. The bay side of the island is lined by extensive mangrove swamps and the outer coast by many miles of lonely, beautiful beach covered by fine quartz sand. The northern leg of the island, vulnerable to fierce storms—*nortes*—is backed by high sand ridges, much like North Padre Island, whereas the dunes on the southern leg are quite low. Cabo Rojo is familiar territory to a few local fishermen, but as far as most Americans are concerned, it is terra incognita.

For the less restless, Tuxpan has that rare Mexican convenience: a campground (María Bárbara) with water and electrical hookups for RVs. It is located just south of the city, about a mile beyond the bridge toll booths, on the right. This is a pleasant scene, shady and bucolic, with boating and even horsebacking opportunities. Make the most of it! There is also a big, fancy, modern hotel, the Tajín, to the left of the toll bridge, on the south side of the river. But if you're going to stay in Tuxpan overnight, it makes sense to stay in the city itself. There are a couple of very decent hotels just off the river on the Avenida Juarez: the Plaza and the Reforma. Both have comfortable rooms, air-conditioning, nice views, and even ice machines. There are also some good restaurants, including one at the Reforma, another at the Florida next door, and a third, Los Otates, just down the street. Sitting at a table by a window, you can watch the life of this provincial city swirl by outside—businesspeople, schoolchildren in uniform, street vendors, and Indians from the countryside in white, pajamalike native dress.

Tuxpan to Veracruz

About twenty-three miles south of Tuxpan, just beyond the not-very-progressive-looking village of Nuevo Progreso, is the marked turnoff to the Toltec ruin at **Castillo de Teayo**—our first archeological site! If you are not operating a four-wheel drive, however, you should consider very carefully whether you really want to make this detour. It's not quite forty miles round trip—but, at present, much of that distance is over some pretty bad roads, including occasional stretches that are nothing but lumpy rock. You *can* make it without hurting your car. The only question is whether you are prepared to average fifteen to twenty miles an hour or not. If you are, and you are interested in archeological sites, then by all means make the trip. Otherwise, don't. The much older and vastly more impressive ruins of El Tajín are not far to the south.

Those who are game for this expedition will wind in and out through a lovely landscape composed of smallish, conelike hills, which, in their general outline, might serve as models for the illustrations in a book of fairy tales. All they lack are little turreted castles perched on their crowns. Every last vestige of the tropical forest that once clothed these lilliputian mountains has been stripped away. Instead, they are mantled in banana or citrus orchards, pastures, or, most catastrophically, near-vertical fields of corn that are guaranteed to eliminate the topsoil in a handful of years. Yet only those who are tuned in to natural-resource issues will notice this terrific problem, and even they will have a hard time resisting the allure of this abused but charming, still verdant-looking countryside. Notice the bromeliads growing in the remaining groves of trees. If you have sharp eyes, you may also spot the stockinglike nests of the oropendola, a sort of "weaver" bird, hanging from branches. Given the condition of the road, of course, drivers may have less chance than they would wish to take it all in. On the other hand, there are many places to pull over, and the surrounding countryside offers an inviting scene through which to stroll.

The pyramid at Castillo de Teayo, about seventy feet high, is the northernmost of all the monumental ruins discovered in coastal Mexico. Compared to the great congregations of pyramids further to the south and west, this lone structure seems relatively modest in scale (not that it is likely to strike you that way if this is your first sample of Mexico's lost civilizations). But it poses a great mystery to archeologists. Its structural and decorative features indicate that it was built by a Toltec culture. The Toltecs were a warlike people from northern Mexico who gained control of much of Mesoamerica, from the Valley of Mexico to the Yucatán, during the tenth to twelfth centuries A.D. Mayan influences in the construction suggest that the people who built this pyramid derived from the Yucatán Peninsula during the period of Toltec dominance. The great riddle, of course, is what these people were doing here, so far from the furthest reaches of the Mayan empire. Anyway, there it is, impressive and also somewhat oppressive, dwarfing the little town that surrounds it. While you are scrambling to the top of it, you will discover that, as with all Mesoamerican pyramids, the steps have been deliberately designed to make ascent difficult. Scholars point out that, in contrast to the medieval cathedrals that were being built in Europe during this period, these temples were never intended for congregational worship. Ordinary folk had no part as participants or even witnesses in the rituals conducted on the platform high above their heads.

The view from the top may not be all that different from the one that greeted those long-ago priests and their sacrificial victims. There was probably a larger community in those days, but the general scale of streets and houses must have been about the same. And there was, no doubt, the same burning and clearing of vegetation on surrounding hills. The one thing that no self-respecting Toltec could possibly have anticipated was the hideous, spiky-looking bandstand in the square below—Mexican modern at its out-of-place worst.

Interesting as this site is, it cannot compare with the one that lies waiting for us not much further down the road. This is the great citadel of the Totonacs at **El Tajín**, about ten miles west of Poza Rica. In a morbid sort of way, it is instructive to pass through Poza Rica, and then, immediately afterward, to behold the ruins at El Tajín. Poza Rica is a major center of Pemex, Mexico's nationalized oil industry, and presumably a place where a lot of money is in circulation. But much of it is a living ruin—ugly, polluted, and depressing—incapable of even beginning to deal with its own uncontrolled growth. Many of the not-very-picturesque streets and buildings are disintegrating before your eyes. In the middle of it all, an immense petrochemical complex dominates its surroundings more absolutely than any ancient pyramid. But maybe, in a way, things were not so different in the ninth century, when the great civilizations of Mesoamerica's Classic Period began to fall apart. Even while the temples and rituals were becoming more and more complex (and more imitative), populations were outgrowing their food supplies, and natural resources were being overused and mismanaged. With the onset of an extended period of drought, the whole fabric of society disintegrated and Mesoamerican culture entered upon a dark age. Granted that these analogies are ultra-amateur, two observations seem to me inarguable: if oil-rich Poza Rica is a vision of Mexico's future, that future will not work; and if the place ever becomes a dead ruin, instead of the living one it is now, its remains are going to look pitiful compared to those of El Tajín.

To reach El Tajín, take a right just after passing the aforementioned Pemex refinery and stick with the main road. About three miles out of town, bear left when you come to a fork. Then keep going for about seven more miles until a sign indicates a left turn down a country lane. When you reach the gate at the site, park, get a cold drink, and prepare yourself for a fairly lengthy walk. Also, prepare yourself to be impressed.

El Tajín flourished during the period when Europe was experiencing its own post-Roman Dark Age. The Totonac peoples who built it were one of several subcultures of the Veracruz region. Apparently they had contact with, and were influenced by, the advanced culture of Teotihuacán in the Valley of Mexico to the west. (Some scholars think the influence might have worked both ways.) Anyway, this incredible city was their religious center, devoted to their rain god. It is a truly awesome place: dozens of pyramids—many of them uncovered and restored, most still buried under mounds of earth—overlook plazas, ball courts, and avenues, the whole complex covering an area of four square miles. Not just size and scope, but the decorative detail, are absolutely astonishing. On a typical hot day, as you climb up and around the Pyramid of the Niches or some of the other temples being wrested from the scrubby jungle, you may well wonder what it must have been like to actually build these edifices without benefit of machines or even beasts of burden.

Aside from the ruins themselves, there are a couple of other reasons for visiting El Tajín. This is a good place for birding at any time, especially weekdays, when it isn't crowded; and a great place for people watching on weekends, when it sometimes is. The recreational facility outside the gates of the site is often aswarm with Mexican families on outings or coveys of enchanting schoolchildren learning about their cultural past. And, on Saturdays, the voladores—the birdmen—perform their traditional, heart-stopping feat: climbing to the top of a high pole and then spiraling downward at the end of unwinding ropes. The faces and pantaloon costumes of the voladores, as well as those of many in the crowd, make one vividly aware that this is Indian

Mexico. In the high cheeks and aquiline noses of some of these people, centuries-old sculptures and bas-reliefs spring to life.

The mix of scrub and woodland surrounding the ruins is great habitat for many small Mexican songbirds, although they aren't always cooperative about allowing themselves to be seen. If you get here pretty early in the day, however, there is a good chance of seeing such species as ruddy or blue ground-doves, blue-gray and yellow-winged tanagers, grayish and buff-throated saltators, blue-crowned motmots, fork-tailed emerald hummingbirds, and enough other birds to keep an ardent birder searching for days. You can wander quite a distance in the area behind the restored ruins, although the paths tend to peter out. No camping is permitted at the site.

Back at Poza Rica, our road leads southward again. The highway between here and Papantla makes its way along the green coastal slopes of extinct volcanoes, and the views are lovely—although you will no doubt find yourself cussing from time to time when you get stuck behind some exhausted Mexican truck as it tries to make the top of yet another steep grade. Papantla, once the "vanilla capital of the world," is a picturesque town crowded into the ups and downs of a mountain valley. If you have a choice of spending the night here or in Poza Rica, by all means choose the clean, reasonably comfortable Hotel El Tajín here.

You can detour from Hwy 180 about ten miles south of Papantla to the resort of Tecolutla on the coast. Actually, this is another of those coastal towns that never made it as a tourist mecca, which is too bad for its promoters but not necessarily for tourists who do find their way here. The town itself is not notably picturesque, but there are a couple of faded hotels, notably the Balneario Tecolutla, which you might enjoy if you have, as I do, a taste for resorts that are always out of season. The beach is pretty, peaceful, and lined with palms; but the sand is taking on the volcanic texture that it will keep from here to Tabasco, which means that it tends to stick to your wet feet. No big problem. The lowland reaches of the Río Tecolutla (about twelve miles) might be interesting to explore by boat; such an expedition would probably be easy to arrange at Tecolutla, although I know of no one who has tried it. I have seen red-crowned parrots flying across the fields from the riverine forest, and the view of the river from the toll bridge on Hwy 180 is very pretty.

RV drivers take note: there is a camping facility with all hookups and other comforts (including ice!) at the Hotel Playa Paraíso on Hwy 180 just eighteen miles south of the Río Tecolutla. The place is right on the beach and makes a very pleasant stop if it's getting on in the day and you don't want to make the final push to reach Veracruz or Jalapa by nightfall.

Hwy 180 sticks close to the coastal plain from here on. There are some hilly stretches, but most of the terrain is flat. The road surface is in good shape in some places, but much of it (especially between Nautla and Villa Rica) is pretty beat up. Think positively about covering long stretches at fifty miles per hour. You will have more time to take in the passing countryside, and all of this drive to Veracruz is interesting and very scenic. In some areas the landscape looks superficially like the American Deep South. Spanish moss hangs from isolated groves of banyans and other trees—all that remains of the tropical evergreen forests that once grew here. Rangeland, sometimes fenced with cacti, and coastal prairie alternate with banana groves, coconut palms, and fields of sugar cane. The road crosses a number of intriguing-looking streams and rivers bordered by marsh or mangrove. To the east, the tall mountain ranges are in some places no more than a distant blue shadow. Elsewhere, they come right up to the road. In particular, there is an extraordinary volcanic outcropping a few miles north of Palma Sola that juts out from the chain behind it like a vertical monolith. If I were a mountain-climbing type, I would want to tackle it; and I suppose it would be okay to do so as long as you didn't run into some marijuana grower along the way. It is a great pity that the government has not claimed this stunning area as a national park. If it were seriously protected and its fauna and flora allowed to return, it would surely attract not only naturalists but money-spending tourists from north of the border. As it is, some of the most perpendicular slopes are being burned and cleared, though even goats need shorter legs on one side than the other to make it on such tilted pastures.

For a considerable stretch you drive right along the Gulf, its dunes and beaches lined by palms and Australian pines, villas, and small resorts. There are several spots where you can conveniently get to the beach and swim. But check out the surf first; there is a considerable undertow at some places on this coast. (Also, check out the scene carefully before thinking of camping along here. Reportedly, some drug smuggling goes on in this area north of Veracruz.) Below Palma Sola is the impressive passage across the river of that name, and then the grand view of an enchanting bay, Laguna Verde, overlooked by the tallest cliffs on the Gulf of Mexico. Regrettably the effect is somewhat spoiled by the hard-to-ignore presence of a thermonuclear power plant (Mexico's only one) perched on a high headland.

Archeology enthusiasts may be interested in two Totonac sites in the vicinity. Both places were still inhabited in the sixteenth century and offer clues to the condition of Totonac culture at the time of the Spanish conquest. One site is **Quiahuiztlan**, where a few pyramidical tombs indicate the one-time presence of a Totonac village that was visited by Cortés. It is located off to the right of the highway about four miles south of the nuclear plant. The site is undeveloped, and you have to take a footpath up a hill to reach it. The other, **Zempoala**, is about seventeen miles further south and requires a two-mile detour inland on the road to the village of Zempoala. The city that once stood on the

Headland north of Veracruz. *Photo by Jonathon Sauer.*

site of the present-day *poblado* was the first major Amerindian community that Cortés and his followers encountered after setting up camp at Veracruz. At a distance, their wishful eyes convinced them that the city's gleaming white walls were made of silver. But even after they discovered otherwise, the size of the place impressed them. They were less thrilled, however, with the human sacrifices that were performed daily and soon put a stop to the practice. Cortés, with typical wiliness and nerve, also managed to trick the Totonacs into becoming his first Indian allies. He seized several Aztec emissaries who had just arrived at Zempoala to collect a tribute of sacrificial victims for Montezuma's altars. The Totonacs were horrified by this audacity; but, convinced that Montezuma would blame them for the deed, they threw in their lot with the Spaniards. Both this site and Quiahuiztlan, especially the latter, are good spots to look for tropical songbirds, hummingbirds, and butterflies.

A Detour to Jalapa

At Cardel, Hwy 140 heads for the mountains and Jalapa, and so shall we. If you have the time, this inland journey is definitely worth making. For one thing, it enables travelers who have never been to south-central Mexico to experience one of the beautiful provincial cities of the interior. For another, it offers the best opportunity we will have to take a close look at the rugged mountain world we've been skirting without digressing very much from the coastal route.

The ascent to Jalapa is a passage through an ecological layer cake. By turns, we move through the humid lowlands, once covered with jungly forest and now with mango and papaya plantations; the dry, brittle-looking foothills, much like those of our Southwest except for the out-of-place-looking plantations of coconut palms; then the sharply drawn shoulders of the mountain range (at the ugly truck-stop town of Rinconada); and finally the mountain slope (on a not-bad road) with its fine views of deep valleys, some of them still wooded. At last we enter the "cloud shadow" zone in which Jalapa lies. Here the high mountain ridges catch clouds from the Gulf and, like highwaymen, relieve them of their rain. In general outline, these layered life zones resemble those, say, along the coast of California. But because we are in the tropics, the details are very different. Variety was the spice of life here. For every kind of tree, bird, flower, or bug that California has to offer, there were twenty or more hereabouts. Note the tense. Although we will find bits and pieces of that intact world a little later, much of the original vegetation has been cleared away along the road. Nevertheless, this is still a beautiful drive.

Jalapa is the capital of the state of Veracruz. Early on, it became a refuge for Spanish colonists eager to escape the malaria and miasma of the steamy coast. In exchange for that benefit, residents put up with drizzly, sometimes chilly winters, a fact of life with which local heating systems are ill-prepared to cope. Most of the year, however, the climate is wonderful. And the city itself is altogether charming. The main city planner has been the mountainside. In obedience to its topography, cobbled streets twist, plunge, level out, and dead-end. Houses seem to grow from the hillsides. Below the shady terraces of the central plaza, or *zocolo*, a cascade of rooftops descends to a narrow plateau on which much of the city finds a footing; and far in the distance the snowy peak of Orizaba hovers in the sky. The plaza itself is one of the most pleasant in eastern Mexico, and the cathedral that presides over it is a beauty, with a great main nave that slopes like a ramp. Altogether, this is a delightful city to prowl around in, provided you have the wind for it.

There are hotels in Jalapa to suit any budget. The ritziest—that is, the one that most resembles U.S. motel-modern in its amenities and interior decor—is the María Victoria. Its main attraction, though, is its location on busy Calle Zaragoza. At one end of the block is the plaza, with cars swarming out of a tunnel that runs beneath it, and at the other, a helpful tourist-bureau office. In between are two delightful eating places, one fancy and the other not. The former is the beautiful Canzones de los Beatidos, with its glassed patio, high ceilings, and tasteful decor (including interesting old photographs of the city). The latter is the cafe next door where unbusy government office workers and businesspeople gather during coffee breaks, brunch, or lunch hour to exchange gossip and discuss the headlines. If you can live with the fact that the clientele is almost exclusively male, this is a pleasant place to relax for an hour and absorb the local atmosphere. The food is okay, and the *café con leche*, made from the renowned local coffee beans, is poured with great flair.

Outdoors lovers will be even more interested in the surrounding countryside than in Jalapa itself. For starters, by all means visit the Botanical Gardens on the city's outskirts and the Biological Institute (Instituto de Biología) next door. The former encompasses a small mountain slope still furnished with its native vegetation, and many of the species are helpfully labeled. Among all the exotics it is surprising to find our old friend from the U.S. river bottomlands, the sweet gum, so well represented. A lovely trail climbs up and down the incline, tunneling through a damp, ferny lattice of broad-leafed greenery. (If you have seen the popular film *Romancing the Stone*, you will already have some ideas of the forest's appearance, since several scenes in the movie were shot here.) Because the slope is an ecological oasis, it attracts much of the region's avifauna. If you spend a little time here, you may hope to see masked tityra, golden-olive or pale-billed woodpeckers, violaceous and possibly mountain trogons, one or more species of exquisite tropical hummingbirds, and, in winter, some American migrant songbirds.

At the Biological Institute, above the trail, you can also pick up some advice about other places in the vicinity that are suitable for exploration. Among the possibilities are two impressive waterfalls. One is a few miles to the northeast at Naolinco; the other is south of Jalapa near the hamlet of Teocelo (which is reached via a narrow, stone-paved turnoff road just as you approach Xico). The Naolinco waterfall offers only a distant view, since the approach to the falls is precipitous and slippery, but it is certainly worth seeing—and besides, the expedition makes for a pleasant outing. You can have a good lunch in Naolinco and get a spectacular view of the *cascada* from an overlook. (The town, by the way, is famous for its fine made-to-order boots.) The Teocelo falls, both at top and bottom, allow for a much closer approach; you can sit on the rocks and get wet from the spray if that's your pleasure. The cliffs and woods nearby, though a bit littered, are fun to explore and offer excellent prospects for birding. (A power plant is located at the falls, but it isn't the eyesore you'd expect it to be.) Incidentally, in traveling to both of these locations, you will pass mountain slopes that seem to be covered with a dense, shrubby forest. Actually, these "forests" are almost certain to be coffee-tree plantations. In spring, the hillsides are brilliant with their blossoming. In winter, armies of pickers harvest the beans by hand, which is hard, miserable work, not at all like the cheery visions conjured up in television coffee commercials. As already noted, the coffee in these parts is one of the finest in Mexico, and at the National Coffee Institute in Jalapa you can see the way it is processed. But from our point of view, perhaps the most interesting thing about these plantations is the fact that they are often rather unkempt, which is good news for many of the interesting native birds associated with forest edges and hedgerows. In contrast to birds that require tropical evergreen forests for their survival (various creepers and tropical wrens, jungle tanagers, etc.), these more fortunate species are still fairly numerous, and the more overgrown coffee plantations are good places to look for them.

The main natural attraction of this area should be the national park, **Cofre de Perote** on the high slopes of the like-named mountain. And in some respects it is. But, as noted in Chapter 1, Americans must get used to the idea that in Mexico the national park system is in a sad state (although there are faint hints that the present administration may take steps to improve the situation). The park on the high slopes of Perote is no exception to the general rule: within its boundaries, local campesinos cut timber, graze their goats, plant potatoes, and set up their little houses. Yet despite these abuses, the park is well worth your time. For backpackers, it offers real adventure. It is reached via the road to Perote, a little town whose inhabitants boast of being of pure Spanish stock. Certainly, they make an excellent Spanish sausage hereabouts. Also, if you happen to be already satiated on mangos, pineapples, and papaya and have a hankering for the fruits of more temperate climes—apples, peaches, or plums—you can find them at this high altitude. The road to the town winds steeply through an interesting mountainous terrain in which forests of pine (four kinds) gradually give way to mixed stands of oaks and pines. About halfway to Perote, a major lava flow, fairly recent, appears as a black cascade on a slope in view of the road. Pines grow from the dark ash, and, in a weird combination, bromeliads cluster on their branches.

The drive makes for slow going, since this highway carries quite a bit of traffic. And in the late afternoon there is sometimes fog. After you reach Perote and head for the top of the mountain, you will really need to take your time, especially if you don't have four-wheel drive. You will probably have to tackle the last short stretch to the crest on foot. For those who persist, however, the panoramic view from the top should be its own reward. The entire mountain range lies below you in dun and green folds, with the volcanic peak of Orizaba, about 19,000 feet above sea level, looming in the blue distance. Near at hand—although not visible from the road—are bits of alpine meadow and an alpine coniferous forest. You can camp up here—no facilities, of course—but, as you might expect, temperatures can get very low at night. Intrepid backpackers may also wish to consider the possibility of descending the southeastern slope of Perote, aiming for the little town of Xico. This side of the mountain is the steepest and therefore the wildest, with much of its natural flora and fauna still present. You can reverse the route, of course, starting at Xico and climbing up the mountain; but even heading downhill, this is a fairly rugged expedition that can take about three days. It is definitely not for amateurs. Even experienced mountain hikers should visit or call the Biological Institute in Jalapa and get some detailed advice before taking off.

Veracruz

If you have decided to skip Jalapa and are approaching Veracruz on Hwy 180, turn onto the *cuota*—the coastal toll road—south of Cardel. Aside from being a good road, it offers a short detour to La Antigua, the place where Cortés made his historic landing in 1519. This is a pretty spot, a green and shady village with cobbled streets, and there is a nice little restaurant where you eat on the terrace under the trees. The town is so untouristy that there are not even signs directing you to the remnants of Spanish fortifications or the tiny, white chapel, surrounded by a white stucco wall, that is one of the first two churches built in the New World.

We, however, are aiming for Veracruz from Jalapa. We will take the scenic "old route," the lower segment of Hwy 140 that branches south below Rinconada and approaches the city from the rear. This southern leg of Hwy 140 begins with a crossing over a tempestuous if shallow mountain river and then passes for a while through rolling foothills. Here there are tall, branched cacti, flowering trees, rangeland, and hillside citrus orchards that look like chenille bedspreads on an unmade bed. In the ravines, remnants of tropical forest survive, including tall, strangling ficus that encircle their host trees or, more often, the empty space where those trees once grew. Before long, however, we are in the tropical lowlands. One small *pablado* after another nestles in a thick, jungly-looking setting of ficus trees, mango orchards, bananas, and coconut palms. All along the road, goats and burros are tethered so that they can graze to within an inch of the busy highway's edge. Most of the local people live in humble little houses with thatched roofs, doorless doors, and glassless windows. Chickens, dogs, hogs, and children are everywhere. Yet the tropical luxuriance of the narrow coastal plain—the generous abundance of fruits, corn, and sugar cane—greatly modifies the pervasive poverty. No one looks hungry, and most people are cleanly, decently dressed. This is for the most part a green and smiling landscape, even though the increasingly heavy traffic as you approach Veracruz can be a bother.

Only New Orleans can rival Veracruz as the Gulf's most beautiful, historic—and lively—city. The two have much in common: both are major ports; both have a European rhythm and a rich inheritance of Spanish and Spanish-French architecture; both have a taste for Carnival in particular and good times in general; and both have a decently human scale that is very pleasing to the spirit as well as the eye.

Veracruz was founded by the clever Cortés as a legal maneuver designed to make him technically responsible to the distant king of Spain rather than the too-nearby Spanish governor of Cuba (who tried mightily to take credit for the explorer's conquests). The first place on Mexican soil to bear the imprint of a Spanish boot, it was also the last stronghold of the Spaniards when, three hundred years later, they were driven from the country. In 1833 the French Navy bombarded the city and landed troops here. In 1847, during the Mexican-American War, U.S. General Winfield Scott, with a staff of young officers that included Ulysses S. Grant and Robert E. Lee, began his daring march on Mexico City from here. In 1861 the French invaded again. And during a revolution in 1914, as the result of a diplomatic hassle that almost started a second Mexican-American War, Woodrow Wilson sent the U.S. Marines to the city. For true, Veracruz has seen 'em come and seen 'em go. And it still does, although nowadays the invading hordes are more peacefully composed of crews from foreign ships and thousands of tourists, foreign and domestic—especially the latter. During Mardi Gras (in February or early March) and the Easter season, the town is packed with people from all over central Mexico who come to enjoy the festivities and the beach.

There are many sights to see in and near Veracruz—among them the old cathedral, the museum, the aforementioned hamlet of La Antigua with its historic church, and the equally ancient fortress of Castillo San Juan de Ulua, which can boast some of the finest dungeons in the New World. If you are in the mood for fishing, there are many small charter boats available at the harbor (check at the tourist bureau on the plaza for information) at reasonable rates. There is also the extensive public beach with its volcanic sand, holiday crowds, shark net, and backdrop of hotels and modern villas. In fact, the Gulfside drive along the Boulevard Avila Camacho offers a prospect that is fairly rare in east-coast Mexico: a sizable stretch of affluent middle-class suburb, well-maintained, up-to-date, and furnished with all the conveniences, including shopping centers and spacious parking lots.

But interesting as these attractions are, it is the city as a city that makes Veracruz such a pleasant place to be. It is a feast for the senses. Details matter as much as whole compositions: the exquisite tile facades on some of the old colonial buildings; the aromas of coffee, cigar tobacco, fried shrimp, and fresh fruits and vegetables emanating from shops and stalls at the market; the unsonorous clank of the cathedral bell; the Fellini-esque look of old stucco buildings whose finely molded sills and cornices are melting under the sandblasting pressure of *El Norte* winds and the carbon monoxide fumes from thousands of battered tailpipes.

Clearly, this is a city where you will want to spend hours just strolling or sitting around. The square and all the teeming streets in its vicinity are fine for the former occupation, but the real revelation is the walk along the quay that extends out into the harbor. Veracruz makes a virtue of its waterfront location. Huge tankers and freighters lie moored only a short distance across the water, and next to the lighthouse looms the futuristic but already peeling tower of the Banco de México, an intimidating structure that looks as though it might house Darth Vader and a battery of laser guns. Across the street, the sidewalk is lined with modernistic cubicles whose tenants sell some of the most enchantingly tacky trinkets imaginable, including heaps of loud jewelry, shell boxes, and all possible versions of Christ Crucified in plastic. Nowhere else will you find so many perfect gifts for snooty acquaintances whose faces you might enjoy watching as they try to say thank you while gagging at the same time.

During the day, sitting is best accomplished at the famous Café de la Parroquia on a corner of the square. (Don't confuse this establishment with the much less interesting cafe of the same name located across from the quay.) If you can get a table outside, this is a fine vantage point for people watching. This is a real coffee house, with espresso and cappuccino available; and the *café con leche* is delicious and thrillingly poured. Good food too. At night, the arcades of the Prendes and Colonial hotels are the perfect places to park yourself. These open-air establishments are the Mexican equivalent of Mediterranean cafes—crowded, bustling, and sociable. Waiters carrying beer or coffee and peddlers (but not too many of them) selling lottery tickets and good cigars weave among the tables. Groups of musicians equipped with guitars and xylophones compete with each other, and you can pleasantly fluster your girlfriend by hiring some guitar-toting kid to serenade her while onlookers at neighboring tables applaud. From the center of the square, there is the plash of the fountain. Overhead the palms and acacias break up the loud strings of lightbulbs outlining government buildings across the way. It is quite wonderful to see how all of this busyness works together. This is not the sort of scene you can hope for in cities where the climate and the collective psychology are more temperate. Even the neon tubing running along the groined arches of the arcade, splashing garish light on the chatting swarm below, seems in place here.

Veracruz is so easy to like that it is possible to overpraise it. In truth, it is a microcosm of what is best and worst about Mexico. There is much here that is cheap and even vulgar; much that is untidy and falling apart. Certainly there is breathtaking poverty. But there is also so much else that is charming or beautiful. In a single block, you can see lovely colonial buildings with grand doorways and balustraded windows standing cheek by jowl with Mexican modern, either spiffy, or decayed, or never finished. Prosperous shops and apartment buildings alternate with tenements that look as though they may collapse at any minute.

When you add up all of these impressions, chances are that you will remember Veracruz affectionately. Warts and all, the city conquers you in a way that most American cities don't. It is alive and lively, and it has an amiable soul.

The best time to visit is the fall or winter. In summer it is either very hot, or *El Norte* is blowing sand, followed by heavy rain, into the city. Since this is a resort town—a thriving one—there are plenty of hotels and motels in every price range. The fanciest and most expensive (Hyatt Exelaris, Hostal de Cortés, etc.), as well as some of the moderately priced ones, are along the beach. Downtown, the Colonial and the Veracruz are comfortable, reasonably priced, and have pools. For those who are looking for a very nice El Cheapo, my favorite is the Hotel Prendes, located in a beautiful colonial building. It's a bit run-down but clean, and if you get one of the (sort of) air-conditioned rooms facing the plaza, the view from the balconies is grand. For RVers, there are several places with hookups. The nearest to town is at the Villa del Mar Hotel on the Boulevard Avila Camacho. Two larger RV parks, the Fiesta and the Parador los Arcos, are located a few miles south of the central city on Hwy 180. The Fiesta is located at the suburban community of Mocambo, and the Parador los Arcos a mile beyond, both on your right, heading south.

There are also some very good restaurants in Veracruz, of which Los Cedros on the waterfront is probably the most renowned and expensive. Some of these places like Submarino Amarillo do nice things with beef; but, as in most port cities, the seafood is generally the best bet. I like the Villa del Mar Olympico. As for quality shopping, Veracruz is pretty disappointing, unless you or someone you know is into fine cigars.

A Detour East to the Land of Beer and Flowers

Although our route south from Veracruz will be along the coast, many travelers consider the winding inland route (Hwy 150) to Córdoba, Fortín de las Flores, Orizaba, and Tehuacán a very interesting detour. The drive up from the Coast to Córdoba is not nearly as dramatic as the ascent to Jalapa; but the towns themselves are interesting, and beyond Córdoba the road becomes more scenic, with views of the nearby mountains, including (especially at Fortín) the mighty Pico de Orizaba. Temperatures are cooler than in the lowlands, and the environment is remarkably diverse, ranging from lush mango, banana, and papaya orchards in some of the valleys, to dry, desertlike plateaus, to coffee plantations and remnants of cutover natural forest on steep slopes. Many of the country people speak an Indian dialect as well as Spanish, and in some areas the women wear an especially attractive version of the native blouse, or *huipil* (which can be purchased in Córdoba and probably the other nearby towns). Córdoba, though not as architecturally impressive or as vertical-looking as Jalapa, is a pleasant place once you get away from the dull-looking *zocolo* and into the nearby streets. There, old colonial houses come equipped with flowering patios, wooden balconies, and facades broken by massive doors and grilled windows.

Tehuacán and Fortín are noted resorts, the former famous for its mineral waters and the latter for its year-round displays of flowering vegetation—orchids, lemon trees, roses, camellias, fragrant cuatismilla, gardenias, you name it. Orizaba, a much larger town, boasts an early mural by Orozco and the brewery that makes Moctezuma XX and XXX, the best of Mexico's many good beers. The birding opportunities in the suburbs of these towns, on surrounding hillsides, and at resort locations are good, encompassing both highland and lowland tropical species. For that matter, you can have amazing luck just sitting in the enchantingly beautiful double square at Fortín de las Flores. But the remaining wild areas cannot be reached by car, and do-it-yourself campsites are pretty hard to find.

The great outdoors challenge in these parts is 18,851-foot Pico de Orizaba. Aztec legend has it that the god Quetzalcoatl's body was consumed here by divine fire when he died, and even now, the mountain is reportedly held sacred by some Indians in the area. Snow-capped throughout the year, it is emphatically not designed for amateur alpinists. (Besides, it doesn't really lie within the territorial range of this book, since serious climbers almost always approach it from the western slope. It is possible, however, to hike some of the lower pine forests surviving on the eastern slopes from the hamlet of La Perla, which can be reached from Orizaba by rough road.)

Back on the Coast

If you don't feel like driving up and down mountains at the moment, don't worry about it. The coastal route offers more than enough interesting sights to keep you busy. For starters, there is Mandinga, a small fishing village just five miles beyond the less appealing, much more built-up resort town of Boca del Rico. To reach it, cross the bridge just south of Boca del Rico and turn left on the dead-end spur road leading to the Naval Academy at Antón Lizardo. After four miles, take a right for another mile. Here there are several thatched-roof open-air restaurants (the best is Casa Uscanga) where you can stuff yourself with the bounty of both the deep and the shallows: clams, oysters, squid, fried shrimp, and fish. While you're eating, you can feast your eyes on Laguna Mandinga, a beautiful brackish bay framed by a green tropical setting. There are small boats for hire, and the lagoon is well worth exploring. Water birds patrol the shores, snail kites are sometimes overhead, and tropical songbirds flicker in the trees.

Weekends, when Veracruzanos descend upon this little place, the human scene is also very lively, with lots of marimba music and conviviality. On your way to or from Mandinga, you may also want to drive the few miles further to the Naval Academy at Antón Lizardo. The site is pretty, and cadets give you tours if you're interested in that kind of thing.

Once back on Hwy 180 and past the turnoff to Córdoba, the road (in good condition throughout this stretch) passes across miles of rolling, rather arid savannah alternating with cactus-covered sand dunes. In the insatiable effort to turn every possible acre of this unfertile country into marginal grazing land, brush fires eat away at the last vestiges of native vegetation on already eroding slopes. Presently, on your right, the blue expanse of a large lagoon will parallel the road, with mangroves in the distance. Birding is interesting through here, especially at water edges. Waders and cormorants are pretty common, and there is a good chance of spotting black-shouldered and/or snail kites, ringed and Amazon kingfishers, mangrove swallows, and fork-tailed flycatchers. Also, take a good look at any buzzards flying overhead. Although they will probably turn out to be the common black and turkey vultures, the lesser yellow-headed vulture is also sometimes seen on these coastal savannahs.

In some places along the Coast, the cactus hedges—planted in an effort to keep the dunes and the road from disappearing—are impenetrable, but there are a number of spots where you can park and take a stroll along the deserted Coast. Frigatebirds are sometimes in view overhead, and collared plovers may be among the shorebirds on the beach. At a couple of breaks in the dunes you will notice *sombreadores* that might be okay places to camp (although I'm not recommending them, and you may have to pay a small fee if a caretaker happens to be around). Before venturing out too far into the surf, swimmers should keep in mind that sharks are reportedly sighted quite often along this entire stretch of the coast.

Alvarado and Tlacotalpan

The small port of Alvarado is another one of those Mexican towns that have nothing much in the way of "sights" to recommend them but are pleasant just to be in for a little while. Without trying to be picturesque, it nevertheless is. The crowded waterfront market, the busy wharf with its fishing boats and small freighters, and the narrow side streets lined with bright tile-roofed dwellings and high sidewalk ledges all fit together into a colorful harmony that is a pleasure to behold. The inhabitants are pretty colorful too. Aside from the fact that many of them still wear native dress, they are famous throughout

Mexico for their picaresque lifestyle and their flair for cussing brilliantly. Closer to home, they are noted for their good taste in food. The
Port Authority's restaurant is something of a culinary landmark in the
area, serving excellent fare to sailors, port employees, and travelers-
in-the-know at very reasonable prices. To get to it, turn right at the
Puerto Piloto sign as soon as you enter town and keep going until you
reach the Port Authority building. If a sentry stops you, just tell him
you're going to the restaurant. One other thing about Alvarado: you
can hire a river launch here, either to go fishing in the lagoon, Lago
Camaronero, or to make the two-hour trip up the Río Papaloapan to
the beautiful little town of Tlacotalpan, which until fairly recently
could not be reached by road.

Just south of Alvarado, a high bridge crosses the bay, offering a
fine view of the town, the Gulf, and the mangrove-fringed lagoon.
Soon after, you will approach the mouth of one of Mexico's most imposing waterways, Río Papaloapan, the River of Butterflies. If you are
not in a hurry, by all means take the road (via a new toll bridge) that
leads inland along the north side of the river. Follow this road far
enough and you will reach the charming riverside town of Cosama-
loapan. But even if you aren't up to that much of a detour, by all means
visit Tlacotalpan, just twelve miles from the coast. En route, the alluvial landscape suggests the Mississippi Delta country, only here there
are no levees to bar the view of the powerful river. At high water it
comes up almost to the road. Small fishing boats drift on its surface,
and so do flotillas of water hyacinth being washed out to sea from
inland lakes and streams. Banana groves and coconut palms cluster
around metal-roofed *chozas* (huts), and on the opposite bank an occasional little hacienda, pretty but forlorn-looking, stands at a river
bend. Closer at hand, gallinules and egrets frequent the roadside
ditches. At intervals along the smooth but narrow road, mysterious-
looking pits appear. These are homemade reservoirs built to catch rain
run-off. In this estuarine world, with water everywhere, there's not a
brackish drop of it that's fit to drink.

Interesting as they are, these sights will not prepare you for Tlacotalpan. The town's chief claim to fame is that it is the birthplace of
Agustín Lara, Mexico's most famous composer of popular music. But
the American traveler will probably be more impressed by the fact that
it is one of the prettiest and oldest communities on the eastern coast
of Mexico. The architecture is almost pure colonial. It is clean, neat,
and prosperous-looking, with nearly every building wearing a bright
coat of whitewash or pastel paint. In the not very distant past, when
the town could only be reached by boat, the streets themselves were
covered with bright green grass. They aren't anymore, but not too
much else has changed. The small, drowsy waterfront offers a fine
view of the river, a restaurant that looks like a wooden trolley car, a

hotel, and several stores. A block away are two linked plazas, each fronted by a marvelous church. The more ancient of these is a white stucco structure, with a well-maintained but plain colonial facade. Inside, however, it is ablaze with teeming murals painted in raw, brilliant native hues. As though self-consciously intent on contrast, the other church offers the world an exterior that is provincially baroque—a cheerful wedding cake of a building with a white curved dome and steeple outlined in loud blue. Whereas inside, its walls are unadorned—the better to set off the magnificent wooden altars and rows of glass cases that house statues of the saints.

The square in front of this latter church boasts a cast-iron bandstand that looks as though it was made of sugar icing. It is surrounded by handsome cast-iron benches and tall palms with whitewashed trunks. (Mexicans wainscot everything with paint—as, to some extent, Americans also did generations ago. Trees in the plazas, the exterior and interior walls of public buildings and tiny huts, and even an occasional citrus orange orchard get the two-tone treatment.) Until recently, when a great dam was built upriver, periodic floods used to inundate the town and leave their own muddy wainscoting on trees and buildings, but apparently without any lasting ill effect.

For all the charm of its little squares and churches, the best thing about Tlacotalpan is the ordinary appearance of its ordinary streets—

Public square, Tlacotalpan.

of which there aren't many. In terms of colonial architecture, we have entered the tropical zone of the arcaded hacienda. Residences and shops are linked by columned galleries, usually very simple in design, soundly practical in purpose. Together, they present to the street a perfectly beautiful colonnaded front that is at once uniform yet various, simple yet elegant. From now on in our travels, we will meet many of these colonial (and ultimately Mediterranean) structures, standing singly in the countryside or in rows on city streets; but nowhere will we find them more handsomely intact than here.

Tlacotalpan is so small that you can walk its length and breadth in an hour. Aside from hiring a boat and going fishing or sightseeing on the beautiful river at the town's doorstep, there isn't a thing in the world to do here except loaf and feel peaceful. Unless, that is, you arrive here during the local fiesta, January 31 to February 10. It is exceptionally lively, even by Mexican fiesta standards, with regional dancing, music, and bunches of bulls occasionally turned loose in the streets so local *bravos* can play matador.

The town has a couple of good seafood restaurants and a decent hotel. It is a perfect place to take an overnight break. But even if you can only spare Tlacotalpan a couple of hours, this pretty place deserves a visit. It is the Mexican Gulf Coast's equivalent of an ideal New England village.

Once back on Hwy 180, you will pass the small town of Lerdo de Tejada about twelve miles down the road. This was the birthplace of Sebastian Lerdo de Tejada, an arrogant nineteenth-century revolutionary whose land "reforms" deprived Indians of their communal holdings. He succeeded the great Juárez as president of Mexico but was soon ousted by the long-reigning dictator Porfirio Díaz. Apart from this historical association, the town is morbidly interesting to the traveler because its ugliness offers such a contrast to Tlacotalpan and, in its different way, Alvarado.

After a stretch of sugar-cane country, the impressive Sierra de los Tuxtlas, with its climactic volcanic peak, looms ahead. Before the road begins to climb into this mountain range, you may want to take a break at the waterfall just beyond the town of Tula. Look for the homemade sign announcing the *Cascada* and turn right along a rutted rural street for a couple of hundred yards. There is a cafe terrace overlooking the falls, built next to the ruin of a sugar factory. On Sunday afternoons, when it becomes a gathering place for local people and a band is playing, the place is very lively; the rest of the time you'll have it to yourself. The terrace is a nice place to cool off with a cold drink or a beer while admiring the bromeliads on the cliffs and watching swallows zip in and out of the cave behind the *cascada*. But don't expect too much. The waterfall is only about thirty feet high, and, except during the rainy season, when you're not likely to be down here, the volume of water is not impressive.

Catemaco and the Sierra de los Tuxtlas

On our way again, the road is often banked with hibiscus, oleanders, and a pretty, white-flowered shrub called *cruz de malta*. As the road climbs, spectacular views begin to open up: steep slopes quilt-patterned with pastures and patches of sugar cane; remnant woodlands perched like toupees on mountain peaks; the great dead volcano, San Martín, reappearing from new and unexpected angles. Gumbo limbo fences line the twisting road, but human habitations are relatively few. This region gets a lot of rain—an average eighty-three inches per year—so it still manages to look verdant in spite of the loss of so much of the original forest. If you can find a place to park along one of the steep dirt roads that depart the highway here and there, you should have a good chance of seeing such birds as ruddy ground-doves, squirrel cuckoos, barred antshrikes, and clay-colored robins in hedgerows and groves of trees. But, as we shall discover, there are better opportunities for enjoying a wilder version of this same terrain east of Catemaco. Santiago Tuxtla and the much larger San Andrés Tuxtla are both pleasant mountain towns. The *zocolo* of the latter has been partly ruined by the ugly presence of out-of-scale modern buildings (one of them a pretty good hotel); but to compensate, a couple of the older buildings are being rehabilitated. And the steep, winding side streets, often graced by handsome galleried dwellings, are thoroughly charming. The market behind the square is the usual medley of ripe color and aromas, but there isn't much in the way of touristy stuff for sale. However, nearby shops sell the excellent cigars that are manufactured here.

From San Andrés Tuxtla, the road descends the eight miles to Catemaco. It's sort of a heresy to say this, but this resort town would be no big deal if it were not for its location on the loveliest lake in Mexico. Not that the place is unattractive; just less charming than some of the other towns we've visited, including San Andrés. The main negative is the shadeless central plaza with its exceptionally ugly bandstand and rather characterless buildings. Even the El Carmen church, pretty at a distance with its shining silvery dome, is sort of terrazzo-glitzy-looking close up. But once you've settled in and found your way to the lakeside, none of that matters. There, under shady acacias and flame trees that are crowded with egrets at morning and evening, you can relax at one of several pleasant open-air restaurants and contemplate the dreamy spectacle of the lake itself: a turquoise expanse drifting off into the shimmering distance, in which rounded islands and headlands, some still wearing their original mantle of tropical jungle, seem to float above their own reflections. An exploratory cruise on the lake is an essential part of being here. The little launches can be hired at a reasonable fee and will take you wherever you wish to go. You can take along a picnic lunch and put ashore at any place that takes your fancy. Among the possibilities: the still-forested Isla de los Changos, where a more or less tame troop of howler monkeys is in residence; the lovely Teoteapan waterfall just outside the town; or the shady little village of Coyame on the northwestern edge of the lake, the site of a mineral-water bottling plant that features naturally carbonated water of surpassing excellence. Although I know of no one who has tried it, it would not be difficult to arrange a primitive camping setup on one of the islands if you can manage to explain to a boatman that that is what you, you crazy gringo, really want to do—even though there are perfectly good hotels right at hand.

Speaking of hotels, there are a number of pleasant accommodations in Catemaco. The fanciest are the new Hotel La Finca on the lakefront just south of town and the attractive motel, Playa Azul, also on the lakefront, but a couple of miles north of the city on a dirt road that we shall be following shortly. In town, either on the square or on the lakefront directly below, there are several hotels ranging from moderate to dirt-cheap. The Berthangel is a good compromise. There is also a basics-only but nicely situated camper facility just beyond Playa Azul on the dirt road leading north along the lake. As for restaurants, La Ola on the square and especially La Luna on the lake are very pleasant, although the local specialty, *mojarra*, a type of rather bony lake perch that is supposed to be bass, is nothing to rave about.

Although access is difficult, Catemaco offers us a gateway to what is left of the verdant tropical forests that once covered this mountainous region. Tragically, most of that native vegetation—even on the islands in the lake—is being cleared at a rapid rate to make way for ever more pastureland and government-owned coffee plantations. Those who come here expecting the jungle paradise of even ten or twenty years ago, with wild monkeys swinging from the trees and jaguars lurking in the forests, will be sadly disappointed. Guidebooks that blithely mention the "wildness" of the region, and cheerfully cite as evidence the fact that *changocon*—monkey meat—is served at Catemaco's restaurants, are writing of a world that no longer exists, except, as we shall see, in the backcountry of the Sierra de los Tuxtlas. (*Changocon* is still advertised on menus, but it's actually pork.) As of now, almost all the larger mammalian wildlife in this coastal area is extinct or nearly so. Even the adaptable whitetail deer has vanished under the double pressure of habitat loss and uncontrolled hunting. Lest all this sound too grim, however, be assured that the aspect of the countryside is still generally green and lush, even where it has been tamed. And this is still an ornithologist's paradise. From the window or balcony of your hotel room, you can see blue-gray or yellow-winged tanagers flitting among the Australian pines.

But much more exciting is the prospect of exploring the Sierra de los Tuxtlas lying just to the north of Catemaco. Here, at last, there is a chance to experience a sizable remnant of bona fide tropical rain forest—at its northernmost limit in the Americas. The reason it survives at all is that this region has only recently been opened up. In Mexico, of course, "opening up" is accomplished by the presence of even the most miserable sort of road, and a miserable road is what you get on the way to Montepio, our destination. If you don't have a four-wheel drive, you may seriously want to consider taking a taxi—that's right, a taxi—from Catemaco. As of this writing, it only costs about fifteen dollars to cover the twenty-odd miles one way, which is a bargain, especially if there are three or four of you, compared to the wear and tear on your car. I don't want to exaggerate the difficulty of the trip— after all, the cabbies make it often—but if you do decide to drive it in your own passenger car, be prepared to cover much of the distance at less than ten miles an hour.

Given that forewarning, you won't be sorry if you decide to undertake this expedition. For a while you will drive north along the lake, past the aforementioned motel Playa Azul and, several miles further on, Coyame. This stretch of the road is not that bad. Once you get beyond Coyame, however, your route follows an up-and-down course along the slope of the Sierra, which plunges precipitously toward the Gulf. The scenery along the way is both heartbreaking and breathtaking. Heartbreaking, because you will see the rain forest disappearing before your eyes—great swaths of it being cut down or burned at the perimeters of pastures that reach higher and higher up the steep slopes. Breathtaking, because as long as your aesthetic, rather than ecological, perceptions are in charge, your eye will delight in a dramatic, shifting landscape wherein broad vistas of high hills, deep valleys, distant inlets alternate with passages through the local equivalent of country lane or, further on, swatches of surviving rain forest. Along the road, *vaqueros* on sturdy horses, campesinos equipped with their indispensable machetes, and boys driving bullocks or zebu cattle will glance at you with only mild curiosity. They have become used to seeing townsfolk and even the occasional *turista* in their once isolated hinterlands. But even now, much of the volcanic slope above you holds considerable interest for the anthropologist. The predominant Indian dialect in this region is Nahuatal, but there are also isolated villages—unseen from the road—where Popoluca Indians speak an entirely different dialect and practice customs, including sorcery, that are as yet not much affected by the recent intrusion of the twentieth century.

During this drive, the road climbs, but not all that much. For the most part it stays parallel to the unseen Gulf. However, a few miles beyond Coyame, at the only crossroads on the route, a narrow side road does ascend the side of the mountain toward the 5,650-foot peak of San Martín, offering spectacular views of the rugged mountain range and some superb close looks at what remains of its rain forest. Ultimately, it peters out at the minute, thatched-roof Indian settlement of El Vigía at the base of the volcano itself. As far as vehicles are concerned, this rocky ascent is strictly for four-wheel drives—unless, of course, you don't mind subtracting a year or two from the life of your car. However, if you decide to settle in the area for a couple of days (more about that in a minute), and you like to hike, you should keep this interesting trail in mind.

On the less precipitous but still bumpy route to Montepio you will presently pass through the one-street village of La Palma. A little way beyond, after traversing a harrowingly small bridge of four beams laid across a streamlet, the road will ascend again. Soon after, you will encounter a small homemade sign on the right announcing Playa Escondida—Hidden Beach. A rocky track that looks like, and is, a farmer's passage to his back forty, drops toward the Gulf. (Actually, the first couple of hundred yards are the roughest.) If you follow it, you will arrive, about a mile later, at one of the most enchanting spots on the entire Gulf Coast—hidden, indeed! This is the "resort" of Playa Escondida, located on a headland that overlooks a view worthy of the northern California coast—if, that is, the northern California coast were translated to the tropics. This bluff is one of those rare spots where the Gulf's coastline is significantly elevated and relatively pristine. It juts out between two beautifully balanced concave beaches. The one to the south is occupied by an isolated little fishing village backed by a coastal plain; the one to the north is fronted by a continuation of the high, wooded bluff on which the resort is located. A wide strand of volcanic sand separates the blue Gulf from the green land.

It is at moments like this that one really appreciates Mexico. In the United States, a coastal landscape like this would be guaranteed a coastal highway—to see that it didn't go to waste. But here, "Hidden Beach" is not the name of a condominium development. Playa Escondida means what it means. The spot from which you can view the scene just described is marked by a dirt path, a crude board bench, and nothing more. The joker, ironically, is that probably nothing here except the Gulf itself will stay the way it is unless this area receives more attention from tourists, the Mexican government, or both. As of now, all the land around this promontory could be cleared at any time.

The term "resort" must be used loosely in describing the establishment at Playa Escondida. A luxury hotel it is not. Mostly it is patronized by Mexican middle-class professionals who have developed a taste—very rare, south of the border—for getting away from it all. What they get, at modest rates, are plain rooms with baths in a couple of whitewashed cement-block buildings, plus good but simple meals on a small, covered dining terrace with a little kitchen alongside. And that's about it. No frills. Except, of course, for the glorious setting, which includes the fine grove of tropical trees that surrounds the buildings, a breathtaking view, an unspoiled beach with a decent surf, and the beautiful wooded path (more literally breathtaking than the view) winding steeply down the bluff. Also, an impressive display of indigenous birds, the possibility of hearing at evening the last troop of howler monkeys in the woods to the north living up to their name, and the option of walking the peaceful entrance lane through small woodlands and across green, hilly pastures. And—perhaps best of all—the opportunity to have a nifty headquarters from which to venture into the surrounding area. (Intrepid tent campers may want to try their luck on their own. But, as is usually the case in backcountry Mexico, the landscape is not as empty of people as it looks. There are secluded places away from the road, but you'll have to scout around a bit.)

Just a short distance up the road is another rare thing in Mexico: an ecological research station, **Los Tuxtlas**, with an accompanying biological reserve, run by the Instituto de Biología. Here the species composition of a high evergreen rain forest is being studied. The institute's property is small, but it adjoins a much larger state-owned reserve of nearly 25,000 acres on the flank of the San Martín volcano. Most of the reserve is virgin wilderness. Not surprisingly, it is subject to a lot of pressure. Indeed, poaching and wood cutting are par for the course. And state politics, rather than ecological considerations, may decide its fate. Nevertheless, as of now, it is the largest, most northerly tract of rain forest surviving on the Mexican Gulf Coast and one of only three sizable tracts that remain in all of Mexico between Veracruz and Chiapas. For us, it offers the best chance to experience this extraordinary ecosystem this side of Palenque, nearly three hundred road miles away.

The research station is a tiny, inconspicuous affair, tucked into the jungle on the right side of the road a couple of miles beyond the detour to Playa Escondida. The minimal staff, chiefly consisting of the husband-and-wife team of Drs. Alejandro and Rosamond Estrada, do a good job of trying to educate the local populace to the importance of preserving the rain forest environment. A miniature zoo and a nature path on the premises are part of this program. And the station welcomes tourist visitors; they may help, after all, to convince the state of the reserve's economic importance. You may pick up useful information about good birding areas and ways of entering the forest without getting lost. But remember that this is a biological reserve, not a state park in the United States; there are no elaborate information services, no marked hiking trails, and no campgrounds, primitive or otherwise. The station does maintain a trail system for patrols and research, and you can walk some part of it. But ask permission first.

In the station's entranceway, you may be greeted by a delightful, uncaged spider monkey. It would be pleasant to assume that he is simply an extroverted member of some wild troop living in the nearby jungle; but, in fact, he is alone. His species, which is highly specialized in its feeding habits, has been exterminated in Los Tuxtlas in recent years. Other species—*el tigre* (the mighty jaguar), Baird's tapir, the Mexican whitetail deer—are also gone. But an amazing diversity of wildlife still remains: the diminutive brocket deer, black howler monkeys, ocelot, jaguarundi, kinkajous, coatis, and numerous other mammals, as well as ninety-two species of reptiles, fifty of amphibians, thousands of kinds of insects (including enough butterflies to make a lepidopterist think he or she was in heaven), and some three hundred species of birds! In botanical terms, the rain forest is even more diverse and complex. Compared to the incredible variety of plant life that flourishes in this tropical ecosystem, even the subtropical woodlands of the southeastern United States seem impoverished. We can only hope that this biological treasure house will still be here ten, twenty, one hundred years from now.

There are several different zones in this mountain rain forest, each with its own ecological features. In general, though, the effect is not unlike that of a southern bottomland forest in the United States, if such a forest were transferred to a mountainside where it was always summer. There is the same damp, ferny stillness, the same brown scent of vegetable decay. But here the pervasive dampness is the direct result of floods of rain, not the overflow of rivers. The whole reserve is like a vast, steamy greenhouse. It may occur to you that if you stand in the same place too long, *Something* might start growing on you. This deliciously spooky feeling only adds, however, to the forest's magical effect. Here, indeed, are the green mansions you have always heard about. At any moment you might expect Rima the Bird Girl to appear, perching on the looped root of some enormous ficus, or swinging on a liana as thick as cargo rope, with a freshly picked orchid in her hair. The sense of mystery that this world inspires is not just the figment of an impressionable sensibility. Forests such as this really are still a mystery, even in a coldly scientific sense. In spite of the best efforts of a handful of scientists, their intricate biological rhythms are little understood; and at the rate they are disappearing, they will take most of their secrets with them to the ecological boneyard.

Meanwhile, however, enjoy this enchanted place. As in any other wild area, early morning and evening are the best times to see the forest's inhabitants. Although birdlife in particular is terrifically rich, most species are rather secretive, or at any rate hard to see. But with patience and luck you can hope to add the likes of the keel-billed toucan, black-shouldered kite, golden-crowned warbler, red-throated ant-tanager, white-throated robin, plain-breasted brush-finch, red-lored parrot, ivory-billed woodcreeper, or the staggeringly beautiful white hawk to your Life List.

Some of these birds, as well as a lot of lovely scenery, might be observed by just walking along the road between Playa Escondida and Montepio. (Or riding. In this country, where anyone who can afford it has a horse, you shouldn't have much trouble renting a mount.) Montepio, incidentally, is an isolated little thatched-roof fishing village on the beach. You can walk from it to Playa Escondida along the coast, as well as on the road, if you have time and energy enough.

One final comment before we leave the Sierra de los Tuxtlas: this area on the eastern slope gets as much as a hundred inches of rain a year, which is a *lot* of rain. Summer is the wettest season, and early spring (March through May) is the driest. So plan your trip accordingly.

Catemaco to Tabasco

This section will be brief. Once you've left Catemaco and the mountains south of it behind (at Acayucan), the drive to the border of the state of Tabasco is not exactly a scenic treat. The countryside is mildly hilly for a while, but brutally overburned and overgrazed. And getting through the ugly industrial city of Minatitlán is a mess. Fortunately, a new highway is being built that will help matters whenever it is completed. The stretch between Minatitlán and the outskirts of Coatzacoalcos is more interesting, since you pass through some really serious delta marshland, of which we haven't seen much—at least not from the road—since leaving the United States. There are wading birds out there, as well as black-shouldered and snail kites, migrant waterfowl in winter, and interesting-looking palm hammocks in the distance. But truck traffic is heavy, and there aren't many places to pull over and look around. Besides, nowadays most of this once-rich delta system has become, to speak frankly, an environmental pigsty. Along the road, especially at the mouth of the Río Coatzacoalcos, you will see marshy edges inches deep in oil.

Old-timers who traveled Mexico's east coast twenty or twenty-five years ago fondly remember Coatzacoalcos in those days—an easygoing fishing town of 20,000 or so, fronting on the river and the beach. Since then its population has been multiplied by twenty due to the spectacular growth of the sulphur and petroleum industries in the region. Some people hereabouts have been making big money, one way or another, but not much of it is reflected in civic pride. The main plaza is an attractive place, and so is the beach section. But much of the area compares unfavorably with the Jersey flats. If you need a place to spend the night, there is a pretty good selection of hotels, ranging from the rather fancy motor hotel Terranova (off Hwy 180 before it turns east to skirt the city) to several less expensive but comfortable hotels (Margon, Valgrande, Coatzacoalcos) located downtown and east of the central plaza. There is also a quite nice RV campground, Rancho Graham, on the left side of Hwy 180 about twenty-four miles east of the bridge over the Río Coatzacoalcos. Hookups, showers, and other amenities are available, including a lake that sometimes offers good birding opportunities. However, those twenty-odd miles between the river and the campground can try your patience, since they pass through a petrochemical wasteland along the route that is often packed with fume-belching trucks. Perhaps by the time you travel this route, an expressway that is presently being built will have relieved much of the congestion. If not, you can take your mind off the traffic by noting that, from a topographical point of view, the surrounding hills over which the road passes have a certain interest: for those of you who intend to stick to the coast between here and the Yucatán, these are the last bits of vertical terrain you will see until you approach Champotón.

The Río Tonalá marks the boundary between the states of Veracruz and Tabasco, as well as the boundary between two very different worlds. Most guidebooks badmouth this stretch of the road, ironically for all the wrong reasons—at least from a nature lover's point of view. They complain that, aside from a shortage of tourist sights—especially near the Coast—Tabasco is flat, hot, humid, buggy, and, above all, wet. They are right, of course; but they might as well be complaining about the Everglades or Louisiana's marshlands. The comparison with those areas is more than superficial, as we shall see when we get to Paraíso and the Coast. For now, it is enough to note that much of Tabasco, as well as a large chunk of eastern Campeche, consists of a vast delta plain built by the sedimentary deposits of several large rivers, of which the rivers Usumacinta and Grijalva are the most important. Tropical lowland forests, large and small bays, immense marshes, mangrove swamps, and a labyrinthian maze of flood-prone waterways are pervasive elements in the natural scene here; and together they compose one of the richest, if also one of the most inhospitable, ecosystems that survives in Mexico. Be advised, however, that not much of that mazy world is visible from the relatively few roads that penetrate this region. The roads, after all, traverse the highest elevations; and wherever they exist, the land around them, no matter how marginal in terms of human development, is apt to be inhabited and cleared. The discovery of a vast oil field in western Tabasco has not exactly helped matters either. Wherever the drillers have penetrated, the natural scene has ceased to exist. Yet, for all that, even many stretches along Hwy 180 in Tabasco are very exciting, including the first twenty or thirty miles that you will cover when you enter the state.

Soon after you cross the Río Tonalá, a side road leads north to **La Venta**, one of the most important archeological sites in North America. There is nothing much to see there now since most of the important artifacts have been removed to an impressive setting at Villahermosa. Still, it is somehow exhilarating simply to be passing close to the place that many archeologists believe was the fountainhead of all of Mexico's ancient civilizations. This Olmec site, occupied for 3000 years, was discovered in 1925. A religious precinct, it contained an astounding number of monolithic basalt figures, altars, and intriguing heads, one of which has markedly Negroid features, and another, just as markedly, the features of a Caucasian. Quite apart from the sophisticated rendering of some of these sculptures, there is the mind-boggling fact that several of the pieces weigh between twenty and thirty tons—and *all* of them had to be dragged about a hundred miles, through jungle and swamp, from the nearest possible quarry to this improbable location, guided, most likely, by the visions of some god-inspired priest-king.

Even without this sense of being close to the origins of civilization in the New World, the road through here—straight and in good condition—has much the same appeal that the Tamiami Trail has in southern Florida. Wide, grassy savannahs are broken by stands of palms and jungly groves. The Indian huts have steeper thatched roofs than any we have seen thus far, a sensible feature in a land where dwellings must either shed the prodigious rains in a hurry or risk saturation. Habitations are relatively few until you begin to near Cárdenas. Because of this, you may be lucky enough to see a scarlet macaw or a pair of red-lored parrots flying across the road.

If you have come from the States by car, you presumably plan to get back that way, too, in which case you have the rare and pleasant choice here in Tabasco of taking one route on your outward journey and another when you're heading home. One of these routes lies along the coast, the other inland. Both have important, very dissimilar attractions. There is no great difference in mileage. However, the coastal trip takes quite a bit more time, especially if you make the journey via Paraíso—as we shall—rather than by way of the less scenic but also less ferry-prone route from Villahermosa to the crossing at Frontera. For the purposes of this travelogue, the only coastal route we will discuss is the one via Paraíso. After all, if you're going to make this trip at all, you might as well go all the way.

Okay. First the coastal journey; then the inland one.

The Route Along Tabasco's Coast

The drive from Cárdenas to Paraíso is the equivalent of a drive along one of the main highways in Louisiana's Cajun country: you are never out of sight of human habitations strung out along the road. In Cajunland I grouched a bit about this sort of one-street suburbia; so it seems only fair that I should do the same here. But I can't! I love this road. Instead of yellow-brick ranch houses, billboards, and zillions of mobile homes, there are here, one after another, hundreds of those lovely columned little villas that we first began to notice in Tlacotal-pan. Only here they stand separate from each other, often with ver-andas front and back on which the ubiquitous gray turkeys of Tabasco strut and preen like peacocks. The visual effect of the tropical setting—palms, coconut groves, lemon, mango, and flowering flame trees—doesn't hurt either. Neither does the general impression of relative prosperity. Interestingly, the fundamentalist Protestant sects—which have made large inroads everywhere in Catholic Mexico and Central America—have really become entrenched in this area. Every mile or so there is another tiny Adventist church.

Twenty-five miles north of Cárdenas, at **Comalcalco**, lies a site that will interest archeology buffs. It consists of a few uncovered or partially uncovered pyramids and walls, a couple of them very im-pressive, that mark the westernmost reach of Mayan civilization. Here, in 1925, a tomb chamber was discovered that contained finely sculpted, red-painted relief figures. But perhaps the most notable fea-ture of this site is the thin, gray bricks that were used as building ma-terials. Aesthetically, they have the unfortunate effect of making the ruins look more like abandoned factories than temples, but they are one more evidence of Mayan ingenuity and adaptability. This place is certainly worth a short visit. Just don't expect it to be as beautiful or impressive as Palenque or some of the sites in the Yucatán. The sur-rounding woodlands have been cleared, by the way, and the birding is not as good as it usually is at archeological sites; but you may spot a few forest-edge species in nearby hedgerows.

After you've left the site, if you're short on food supplies, you should keep your eye out for a well-stocked little supermarket just up the road a way on your right.

Paraíso is a really nice little town. You will like the charming church with its delicate baroque cupolas atop tall, slender bell towers and the busy, palm-lined square surrounded by (usually) quiet streets. There is the all-right little Restaurante Señorial on the square, where you can have your favorite fruit juice squeezed while you wait and meantime perhaps chat with the gregarious ship crews and officers that service the offshore oil industry. (Their accounts of oil pollution in the Gulf and Pemex's mismanagement and waste are informative, if depressing.) There are also a couple of seedy but pleasant open-air cafes at the ferry crossing at Puerto Ceiba, a couple of miles east of town, where you can get good fresh fish and shrimp. There, too, you can hire a launch to take you into the western sector of the Usuma-cinta Delta, about which, more presently.

Paraíso has only a couple of small hotels—cheap, clean, and plain. The best is Hotel Sabina on the square. Whitewashed bunga-lows, some with air-conditioning, are available on the beach at El Li-món, three miles away. The natural setting here is idyllic—a wide strand of coconut palms overlooking the Gulf beach and its soft (if sticky when wet) volcanic sand. The human scene is less ravishing—notably the awful-looking pavilion with its folded-paper contours and, on weekends, the clutches of drunk oil workers and their equally smashed girlfriends. During the week, however, you will have the place almost to yourself, and if you keep away from the dreary pavilion, this is a lovely place to be. During daylight hours the mosquitoes are usually not a problem. Walk down the beach a few hundred yards, keeping your eyes peeled for movement among the palms, and you may see three-foot-long iguanas hustling away. The poor things are wary, though. Here, as elsewhere in Mexico, they are a staple in native diets.

The Ferries on the Coastal Route   It is only about

140 miles—which doesn't sound like much of a distance—from Paraíso to Ciudad del Carmen, the "queen city" on Tabasco's coast. However, five ferry crossings currently mark the journey, and if your timing isn't lucky, this little junket will take you most of a day. Even if you are lucky, you would be wise to cultivate in advance the Mexican gift of patience (or decide to forget Paraíso and take the less ferry-prone route from Villahermosa). Ah, but if you do convince yourself that you are in no hurry, and if you have a cultivated taste for the tropics at their most laid-back and colorfully funky—and if you bring along a novel or two by Joseph Conrad or Graham Greene to hone that taste while you while away an hour or so waiting at a ferry landing—*then* you will have a wonderful time doing the sort of Mexican thing that tourists in Mexico rarely get a chance to do: you will experience a residual bit of the way that life in this country was lived in days of yore. That is, ten or twenty years ago.

The ferry at Puerto Ceiba is quickly reached from Paraíso. At the landing, if you have to wait, you can spend the time in one of the thatched-roof open-air cafes drinking limeade. But there should not be too great a delay here since the crossing is very narrow, and quickly made. The only worry is if the line is long, since the ferry, a small barge, can only take a few vehicles at a time; and just a couple of trucks can hog most of the space.

The few miles to the next ferry traverse the sand ridge right along the coast. The road passes through a setting worthy of Gauguin: an unbroken grove of coconut palms, tiny thatched huts sitting underneath, and machete-carrying natives (many with markedly Asiatic features) walking at roadside. Near most huts you will notice piles of split coconut shells, some of them burning. The thick smoke from these fires is the only defense most local people have against the clouds of mosquitoes spawned in the mangrove jungles just south of the coastal ridge. For you, the trick is not to become so fascinated with the passing scene that you forget to slow down for the jarring *topes* bracketing numerous clinics and schools along the way.

Ferry crossing to Frontera.

The ferry landing at the imperceptible community of Aquiles Ser-
dán—my favorite of the lot—would do nicely as a set for *Lord Jim*. The
ramp is cantilevered by two large chunks of cement suspended by
chains. And the ferry itself, when it finally materializes, is little more
than a motorized raft, onto which you are harrowingly squeezed
along with, say, a truck and another vehicle or two—the maximum
load. Yet the wonderful part of all this is that it makes you part of the
scene. And what an excitingly different scene it is! The sizable river,
thickly banked with water hyacinth, flows past a solid wall of graceful
palms. From upstream, a small launch may approach the landing, carrying not just a group of dark country people loaded with bags and
baskets, but also a sense of the unseen country behind the coast, a
green, uncatalogued world where small boats like this one are the
only means of getting around.

That impression of being at the edge of the tropical outback is intensified at the crossing to Frontera, a city that, even now, seems rightly named. A bridge is being built across the mighty Río Grijalva here.
No doubt its completion will be the occasion of much celebration
among those who make this journey often. (I remember watching a
truck's cargo of ice progress from melting trickle to pouring cascade
in the hot sun, while the driver fumed and the ferry did its usual dis-
organized, unhurried thing.) Viva progress and all that. But all the
same, it is a little sad that this untidy crossing will be abolished. The
thatched-roof stands and vendors will disappear. There will be no
chance to notice the wood storks and lesser yellow-headed vultures
wheeling overhead, or to gaze across the river at the distant waterfront
of Frontera, looking grungy but picaresque, as a frontier town or pi-

rates' lair (it has been both) ought to look. Above all, there will be no chance to contemplate the river itself—a sort of Mexican Amazon, still redolent of the wild, jungly country from which it comes, carrying fishing boats and silt and huge rafts of hyacinths on this final passage to the Gulf. When the bridge is completed, man will have once again vanquished nature and his own past. I don't blame the driver of that ice truck for being delighted by the prospect, but I also don't blame myself for being a little sad.

As of now, Frontera has only frontier accommodations for travelers. Unless dusk is coming on, an overnight stay is not recommended.

Beyond the town, the coastal sand ridge is notably less settled than the stretches already traversed, with pasturelands, mangroves in tidal pools, and occasional clumps of palms. And birds! Hard to believe, but dozens of bright-legged snail kites—so rare in Florida—sit on fence posts just a few feet from the road. In wet places, scores, sometimes hundreds, of egrets and ibis gather. Often they are accompanied by wood storks.

The next-to-last ferry is at Campechito, a sorry little settlement of huts and shacks that squat in their own garbage. Even so, it is interesting to take in the local scene while the little ferry takes its time. This might be a trading settlement on some tributary of the Amazon: the usual hogs, barefooted children, mangy dogs, and—the community's social center—a little open shed right by the landing where local youths roll dice in the presence of an antique nickelodeon, and where mercifully cool soft drinks or beer can be bought while you wait in the hot sun. Here, as at the other landings, an occasional small launch arrives from the isolated outposts within the wilderness fastness of the Usumacinta Delta. To the disembarking native passengers the untidy hamlet of Campechito must seem a thriving metropolis.

The last lap of the journey to Ciudad del Carmen is much like the preceding stretch, except that for several kilometers the road, studded with *topes*, borders a beautiful inland lagoon, passing narrowly between lines of small houses and under the deep shade of flowering trees.

Birders—all wildlife lovers—should take special note of this area. To the north of the highway, a mile or two across the savannah, lies one of the most spectacular wading-bird rookeries on the Gulf of Mexico. A lagoon parallels the shoreline between the sand ridge you have been traveling and the coastal dunes; it is bordered by a mangrove jungle eighty feet high. Atop the mangrove canopy, relatively safe from human intruders, a vast breeding colony of egrets, herons (including boat-billed, chestnut-bellied, and bare-throated tiger-heron), ibis, spoonbills, wood storks, and jacana assemble to hatch and rear their young each spring. The angle of vision and the intervening foliage make for imperfect viewing; but you can still get an eyeful from more or less dry land by following one of the occasional tracks that turn northward from the coastal road after you have traveled about thirty miles beyond the Campechito ferry crossing at the Río San Pedro y San Pablo. Since the mangrove forest and its bird rookery extend for a considerable distance, there is no one vantage point from which to see it. In any case, if and when you do behold this stirring springtime spectacle, remind yourself that it is only the most visible of the Usumacinta Delta's many ecological treasures.

The Usumacinta Delta   In the foregoing paragraphs I have referred more than once to the wilderness character of the Usumacinta River drainage system. The area involved is enormous—about 3600 square miles. Even now, when almost every accessible acre of relatively dry land has been cleared, the core wilderness that remains is still vast: a tract roughly equivalent to Everglades National Park and the Big Cypress Preserve combined. The comparison does not stop there, however. Although the geology of the Usumacinta in many ways resembles that of the Mississippi Delta—that is, it has been formed by the changeful patterns of a large river system flowing across flat, alluvial wetlands—it looks like southern Florida, if southern Florida were even more tropical than it is. As in the Everglades ecosystem, there are vast marshes—seas of grass—punctuated with island hammocks and small ponds and lakes, as well as with strands of jungly forest along the rivers and creeks, and a seemingly endless mangrove labyrinth bordering the Laguna de Términos and other large coastal lagoons. But there are important differences too. Although the familiar sabal palm is much in evidence, no slash pines or cypress flourish here. Instead, along the rivers, there are gallery forests of mahogany, ficus, ceiba, logwood, macayo, cochun, and jobo. As for the hundreds of square miles of mangrove forest, its outer periphery along Laguna Términos will look familiar enough to anyone who has visited the Everglades. But in the depths of the Usumacinta, it assumes the character of a true jungle, rising to a height of seventy or eighty feet above the literally impenetrable maze of its vaulting roots.

Also in contrast to the Everglades, the Usumacinta Delta ecosystem still functions in a natural, healthy state—a fact that is all the more remarkable when you consider the sorry fate of nearly every other natural ecosystem in eastern Mexico, not to mention our own despoiled Gulf wetlands. Indeed, acre for acre, this is the most pristine, unpolluted estuarine system of any size that remains in North America south of Canada. Luckily, no major oil fields have been discovered thus far in the delta, in contrast to the area immediately to the west. And although human habitation along some of the higher river bluffs probably dates back to Mayan times, even now the native population has not been able to find a permanent foothold in much of this wet world. Whether this continues to be the case will depend a great deal on developments that occur in the next few years. A proposal has been put forward by American research scientists to organize a cooperative international study of the area, and steps are being taken to give the delta recognition as an ecological reserve of international significance.

It is amazing how little is known about the Usumacinta Delta. In a world where it sometimes seems that everything has been discovered twice over, this wilderness area remains a mystery. Airplanes fly over it, and boats ply its navigable waterways; but the interior expanses of its marshes and mangrove jungles remain virtually unexplored. Compared to the Usumacinta, even the wild Everglades seems downright tame. In terms of wildlife, it is already apparent that the delta is a naturalist's El Dorado, even though only a few superficial studies have been made thus far. On the basis of aerial transects, scientists estimate that this area contains the highest concentration of breeding wading birds on the Gulf (and therefore in all of North America). A conservative estimate suggests that more than a quarter of a million waders are in residence between the Grijalva River and Laguna de Términos during winter and spring, including tens of thousands of breeding pairs. All the major U.S. species are present, including a large population of wood storks. In striking contrast to their diminishing Florida counterparts, these Usumacinta storks seem to be thriving— a clear indication of the delta's ecological health. Moreover, a breeding population of the heavy-beaked jabiru stork has been recently discovered, the first evidence that this rare Central American bird is more than a transient in Mexico. Mexico's other native waders, the bare-throated tiger, chestnut-bellied, and boat-billed herons (all uncommon and little studied) are also to be found here. So are fifteen types of hawks and kites, four kinds of vultures, and the rare ocellated turkey. Large flocks of black-bellied tree ducks inhabit the marshes, and parrots and scarlet macaws are still sometimes seen in rain forests along the waterways.

Among mammals, the ocelot, Central American tapir, manatee, and jaguar are still in residence. Indeed, for those latter three, the Usumacinta may be their final stronghold in Mexico, if stronghold it proves to be. Jaguars are still killed occasionally not far from Ciudad del Carmen, but the animal's ability to oudistance dogs when moving across the stilt roots of the mangrove jungles has thus far ensured its survival. The inaccessible mangroves are also the saving mercy for the black howler monkey, although its numbers here, as everywhere, are declining. In traveling the highways that encircle the delta you are apt to see a group of boys at the roadside selling one of these pathetic baby creatures—as it lives up to its name by howling for its murdered mother.

An impressive variety of amphibians and reptiles are known to be present in the Usumacinta, although they, too, have thus far not been studied. Three crocodilians—the Morelet's crocodile, the American crocodile, and the Central American caiman—still survive here, although overhunting has made all of them scarce. A biologist who ventured on foot for a short distance into the gallery rain forest near Palizada has observed boa constrictors of awesome size. And sea turtles, often caught by fishermen in nets just off the coast, are thought to nest on delta beaches. Like everything else about the Usumacinta, the importance of its estuary to the Mexican fishing industry—particularly the pink shrimp—has not been measured; but there can be no doubt of its vital importance. We can only hope that the Mexican government will recognize the importance of this ecological treasure chest and takes steps to protect it from the encroachment of civilization. Wisely managed, it would make one of the great national reserves on the North American continent, with a real potential for attracting money-spending tourists to the area.

As of now, however, if you are the adventurous sort and would like to explore some part of the Usumacinta, be aware that you are on your own. There are no equivalents of the Everglades' marked canoe trails, campgrounds, and nature walks, nor any helpful brochures or detailed maps. Suitable high ground that is not already occupied by native villages is hard to reach. On the northern side of the delta, you can hire a guide and motorized skiff at Frontera, Ciudad del Carmen, or, probably, Campechito on the Río San Pedro y San Pablo. But you should check carefully with any potential guide to determine his familiarity with terrain that is somewhat off the main waterways. Also at Ciudad del Carmen, it may be possible to get yourself taken on as a passenger on the small boat that makes the trip up the Río Palizada to the community of Palizada on the periphery of the great mangrove jungle. Palizada can also be reached by car from the southern side of the delta on a road that branches off Hwy 186, the Palenque route. But be forewarned that the road, unless it has been recently resurfaced, is often in terrible shape. If you do make this trip, you can hope to observe many wading birds, hawks, and, in roadside ditches, the gallinulelike jacana with its beautiful yellow wings. However, do not expect to see much of the wild delta from the car window, since most of the savannah along the route is given over to *ejidos* and cattle ranching.

One final comment about the Usumacinta Delta concerns the Río Candelaria, which empties into the eastern corner of the Laguna de Términos. The Candelaria is reportedly one of the wildest and most beautiful of the delta's rivers, bordered by still-impressive jungles of mangrove and gallery rain forest. Launches can be hired at Ciudad del Carmen that will take you up the river. Inland, Hwy 186 crosses it about sixty miles east of the turnoff to Palenque. Though it looks like a promising waterway for enterprising canoeists, you should not try to make this trip without a guide and/or plenty of on-the-scene advice. There is, after all, no take-out at the mouth of the river, and the mangrove labyrinth is intimidating and thick with mosquitoes. Another possibility is to take the rough road that turns south about ten miles east of the river and drive to the little upstream town of Candelaria, putting in there and taking out at Hwy 186. Human populations have been growing rapidly along this stretch, however; so it is uncertain how wild it will still be when and if you consider making this trip. Again, it is vital to check locally about the condition of the river before you even think about tackling it.

Ciudad del Carmen and Campeche   The strait between Laguna de Términos and the Gulf is very wide, and it takes the ferry a long time to cross to Ciudad del Carmen. If you just miss it, you're in for a ninety-minute wait without much to do except gulp soft drinks at the nearby grungy *sombreadores*, or watch porpoises, pelicans, and frigatebirds from the jetty. Once you do make the crossing, you may or may not decide that you like Ciudad del Carmen. In contrast to Frontera, the town looks very pretty and tidy from the ferry, with its steeples and low, tiled roofs framed by palm trees. Two hundred fifty years ago, however, this was the pirate capital of the southern Gulf. For decades, its inhabitants terrorized the Coast from Veracruz to the Yucatán and were even successful in driving the Spaniards out of Tabasco for a time. Between those long-ago days and the past of ten or fifteen years ago, the town remained a sleepy fishing village. Some of that ambiance still remains. The waterfront is pleasant to stroll along, with its open-air cafes and the largest fleet of shrimp boats in Mexico. And a couple of nights a week there are bands and sometimes dance groups performing in the main plaza. Nearby beaches are also attractive.

But although Ciudad del Carmen still has much to recommend it, and is still described with admiration by most guidebook writers, it has lost much of its one-time picturesqueness. A lot of oil-field workers have invaded the city in recent years, and there seems to be a considerable military presence too. Trucks with blaring horns and impatient drivers pack the narrow streets, and the influx of money has inspired a lot of tacky modern facades around the central square. In general, the atmosphere is much like that of a "liberty" town located near a large military base. (There is a naval station here.) There are no fine restaurants, although you can get a good fish dinner at a few places, notably Los Flamboyanes. As for lodgings, by far the best places to stay at the moment are Lli-re and Isla del Carmen. Out on the east end of town is Lino's Motel, which has become a bit seedy but is still okay. The same goes for the Jet on the northwestern tip of the island. But the budget-conscious traveler should think twice about staying in Carmen's downtown "economy" hotels. They take a beating from their hard-living clients and are pretty cruddy.

Sports fishermen, however, will rightly protest that this less-than-rapturous description of Ciudad del Carmen does not take into account the town's strongest suit: it is home base to some of the finest freshwater and saltwater fishing you can find anywhere. This just may be the best area on the Gulf for tarpon, and there are many other species available for the taking in the rich waters of the Laguna de Términos and the Gulf. Fishing boats are readily available and can be hired at reasonable rates. Here, too, you can arrange for an expedition into the Usumacinta wilderness. The hotels mentioned above will provide the necessary contacts.

The road from Ciudad del Carmen to the final crossing at Puerto Real—where a causeway is already in place—passes close to the Gulf and is sparsely inhabited. Coconut palm plantations flank the inland side of the road, mangroves and sea grape the Gulf side. For a long stretch, the narrow beach presses right against the road, with wooden barricades erected to keep storm-driven waves from devouring the tarmac. Pelicans are abundant, and shell collectors reportedly do well here. In some places there are private cabanas, but much of this coast is open to anyone who wants to beachcomb or camp. In particular, campers should be on the lookout for the road leading off to the left just a half-mile before you reach the causeway. (There is a large sign indicating that you should take the right fork to reach the bridge, the Puente de Unidad.) This left fork leads to the abandoned ferry landing. More to the point, it offers access to a lovely stretch of coastline. The somewhat sticky lava sands in the state of Veracruz have long since been left behind. Here a finely ground shell beach alternates with slabs of porous volcanic rock that descend like steps into the surf. Gray iguanas, looking much like their close relatives on the Galapagos Islands, hustle across the rocky shelf. The dunes behind the beach are anchored by cacti and an interesting fragment of the gnarled, semideciduous tropical scrub that once lined much of this coast. There are a couple of minor drawbacks to this spot, however. Weekend picnickers from Isla de Aguada across the causeway (where there is a more developed beach) leave their litter behind them, so you have to walk up the beach a considerable distance to get away from it. Also, when a breeze isn't blowing, the mosquitoes get bad.

Isla de Aguada is a small but growing town. There is a fishing resort here, El Tarpon Tropical, for those anglers who prefer a less well-known base of operations than Ciudad del Carmen. Also, Aguada is directly across the Laguna de Términos from the mouth of the Río Candelaria, so you may prefer to hire a guide and boat here rather than at Carmen for a day's expedition up the river. Furthermore, sun and sand lovers who are not satisfied with the aforementioned beach on the western end of the causeway may wish to take a dip in a beautiful, more palmy setting about twenty miles up the road at the turnoff to Sabancuy. (Note, however, that the beach here is too close to the highway to be suitable for camping.) Finally, make a point of checking your gas gauge at Isla de Aguada. Whether you are taking the long, desolate road up the coast to Campeche or turning inland, this is the last orthodox place to get gas for the next many miles. I say "orthodox" because homemade "gas stations" still flourish in the outback areas of Mexico, and one of them is located just south of Sabancuy. Getting your tank filled at such a place is an interesting, if unnerving, experience. The gas is mouth-siphoned into your car from open drums, after being measured out in quart cans. The proprietor would presumably turn into a flame thrower if he ever lit a cigarette. But he seems to accept the condition of his fume-filled lungs—as well as the fact that his thatched-roof establishment is an explosion waiting to happen—with the fatalism typical of rural Mexicans.

The Inland Route: Villahermosa to Palenque

Villahermosa   For those who choose the inland route, the first major stop is Villahermosa. The city has several decent hotels if you need lodgings for the night. Other than that, there is only one reason to take time out in this booming, fairly neat, but generally uninteresting capital city of Tabasco. That reason, however, is a compelling one for any person interested in Mexico's ancient civilizations. The city offers a spectacular display—two of them, actually—of the region's archeological treasures. The more renowned of the two is the Museo de La Venta, on the road to the airport. This is where the earlier-mentioned treasures from the ancient Olmec site at La Venta are exhibited in a jungle landscape that is much like their original setting. Strolling along the paths here, confronting those enormous sculpted heads and finely carved stone altars, it is possible to imagine something of what the archeologist Franz Bloom must have felt when, only a half-century ago, he discovered these monolithic pieces buried in the gloom of the rain forest. (Their arrangement, however, is not the same as that in which they were found.) To add interest to the exhibit, deer wander about freely, and there are other native animals in enclosures. Birders should carry their binoculars with them. The trees in the park harbor a variety of tropical birds, including clay-colored robins, Aztec parakeets, and golden-fronted woodpeckers. Also, take along repellent to deal with the mosquitoes that this authentic setting harbors. The other museum, more conventionally arranged indoors, is the excellent Museo de Tabasco on the central plaza. Although it also displays Olmec treasures, it is much more eclectic than the Museo de La Venta. Here are exhibits of Mayan, Totonac, Aztec, and Zapoteca artifacts, among others, all of them attractively displayed.

The best thing that can be said of the sixty-mile trip from Villahermosa to Palenque is that Hwy 186 is, as of this writing, in good shape. The road skirts the foothills of the Chiapas Range. For as far to the south as one can see, these steep, camel-hump hills are being subjected with a vengeance to the grisly syndrome of slash-and-burn agriculture. Rows of corn try to grow on newly cleared slopes that are already eroding. On the north side of the road, gaunt Brahma cattle overgraze the rolling savannahs. Before long, much of this land will be a tropical badlands.

Palenque The Maya ruins at **Palenque** are considered by many people, this writer among them, the most beautiful in Mexico. Though very grand, they do not match the colossal size and authoritarian power of those at Chichén Itzá or Uxmal. But for that very reason, they strike the eye as being more delicately molded, more various in form, more humanistic in scale. Even so, it is the natural setting— or rather, the perfect harmony between the ruins and their natural setting—that more than anything else creates the surpassing loveliness of this site. For Palenque is situated on rising ground—the foothills of the Tumbala Mountains—in the midst of a magnificent rain forest. The canopy of that forest seems to cascade down the mountainside in a green billowing avalanche, intent on once again burying this site which for nearly eight hundred years it had concealed. This impression is not entirely fanciful. It requires a considerable maintenance effort to keep the relatively few ruins that have been excavated free of the forest's embrace. But there is an implicit irony in this perception of the encroaching jungle. Just over the hills, this same jungle is being destroyed by hordes of subsistence farmers. It is quite likely that the rain forest at Palenque will seem as rare and precious to future generations as its Maya ruins are to us.

Much more has been learned about this site than archeologists would have thought possible even a few decades ago, thanks to advances in research, including the considerable headway made in deciphering hieroglyphic texts. The city became prominent fairly late in the Classic Period of Maya culture. Its greatest ruler, Pacal, came to power in A.D. 615 and died in A.D. 683. Most of the imposing buildings—the Palace and the Temples of the Sun, the Cross, the Foliated Cross, and the Inscriptions—are associated with his reign. Indeed, the Temple of the Inscriptions was built over this god-king's tomb, a discovery that rattled the long-held assumption that temple pyramids in Mexico were never used as mausoleums. When Pacal's remains were exhumed from the elaborate crypt, he was wearing a jade face mask, another unprecedented discovery. There are many such marvels to be contemplated at Palenque. Among them are the magnificent Palace with its unusual number of rooms, its marvelously elaborate stucco reliefs, and its observatory tower; the exceptionally well-planned design of the civic precinct; the ingenious underground aqueduct; and the elaborate panels on the Temple of the Cross depicting the succession of Pacal's son, Chan Bahlum, which are so arranged that just once a year, on the day of the winter solstice, sunlight shining through a notch behind the the Temple of the Inscriptions symbolically spotlights them.

Impressive as the site is, it barely suggests the scope and grandeur of the city that once stood here. Sometime during your stay, walk for a couple of hundred yards along the little track that leads off across the flat pastureland directly below the ruins. Then turn and look up at them. Picture the entire slope before you literally covered—for more than five miles—with the hundreds of temples and palaces that are still buried in the jungle on either side of the excavated site. Imagine all of those buildings covered by brilliantly painted stucco, emblazoned with bas-reliefs, crowned by roof combs of lacy stone. Only then will you have some sense of the Ozymandian grandeur that once existed here. How awed ancient pilgrims must have been when, passing across the the then-jungle-covered plain, they beheld this jewel-like city from many miles away!

Sic transit gloria mundi. By the late eighth century, Palenque, like most of the other great cities of the Maya, was in decline. A century later, the jungle had moved in.

The jungle: For travelers in eastern Mexico who have not had a chance to visit the reserve in the Sierra de los Tuxtlas, Palenque offers the best—and almost the only—remaining opportunity to experience a montane rain forest in all its pristine magnificence. The Mexican government has designated a substantial area around the ruins as a national park, including large tracts that have already been cleared. Whether these good intentions actually come to anything will depend on the willingness of officials to follow through. Agricultural holdings will have to be purchased, reforestation programs established, and protective measures enforced. Wistfully, officials at Palenque even mention the possible reintroduction of wildlife species that have vanished. The skeptics, of course, will shrug and say, "*Mañana.*" And it is true that Mexico's current fiscal problems make "*mañana*" seem, more than ever, a long way off. But the country's economic planners must eventually become aware that Palenque, which already attracts a couple of hundred thousand visitors a year, could be an even greater tourist gold mine if it were to combine its archeological attractions with those of a Mexican version of Yellowstone National Park.

Even now, although access is very limited, the rain forest at Palenque is an enchanting place. One steep path climbs the slope behind the Temple of the Cross. If you climb high enough, you can enjoy a stunning view of the coastal plain—now a plain, indeed, though it was once covered end to end by jungle. My favorite short hike, however, is along the path that leads up the mountainside from the slope behind the Temple of the Inscriptions. It is not very noticeable, and few people venture along it for more than a short distance. In fact, it allows for a considerable climb through a magically beautiful if sweaty world of massive trees where convoluted roots sprawl, in the best Jungle Jim tradition, across the forest floor like pythons. A plashing streamlet (which once watered Palenque via the underground aqueduct) courses down the mountainside nearby. Still buried in the slope you are ascending is the Temple of the Jaguars. Other temples, discernible only as wooded mounds, crown the ridge above. The air is green. Your fellow tourists, struggling up the radical pyramid steps below, their voices crushed by the forest's heaviness, are psychologically and literally left behind just a few dozen yards within the perimeter of the forest. The mind takes odd turns: you imagine what it must have been like when this entire region was shrouded in forests such as this. How exhausting and thrilling and unnerving it must have been for travelers who, not all that long ago, risked malaria, dysentery, and heat prostration to visit this splendid place.

Anyone with the soul of a naturalist will be happy here. There are so many varieties of plants and trees that, by comparison, temperate forests seem impoverished. As for birds, no handy lists are available, but something like four hundred species have been identified in this area, including numerous winter migrants from the United States. Many birds are difficult to see in the high canopies; but if you arrive early in the morning or hang around late in the afternoon, you should add a good many species to your Life List. There are, for example, half a dozen kinds of tropical tanagers, each more gorgeous than the last; trogons (citreoline, collared, and violaceous); the brilliantly blue (red-legged) honeycreeper; motmots; and golden-olive, golden-fronted, and smoky-brown woodpeckers. While sitting atop the ruins at evening, it is commonplace to see a couple of collared araçari or keel-billed toucans, or perhaps a parrot, flying by. If it is quiet, you may also hear black howler monkeys noisily settling down for the night on a nearby hillside. Park officials say that spider monkeys also survive in the park, as well as ocelots and both whitetail and brocket deer.

If you have time while you are at Palenque, you might enjoy a morning's drive south on the road to Ocosingo, with the waterfall at Mizola as your destination. The falls, about a hundred feet high and framed by a fragment of rain forest, are very beautiful. Magnificent trees grip boulders with their naked roots, tropical birds and butterflies flit about, and slippery, somewhat littered stone steps lead down to the pool at the base of the falls. At the entrance to the area, you will be asked to pay a small toll.

The round trip is roughly twenty-five miles—long enough to get a close look at the Tumbala Mountains. The road is winding and steep but more or less paved, at least as far as the turnoff to the falls. (Be on the lookout for the handmade sign on your right.) The mountains on every side are still hauntingly beautiful; but what is happening to them is hauntingly grim. One moment you will be driving through what looks like a formidable stretch of montane rain forest. Then, at the next curve, a whole mountainside will be stripped raw; at the next, forest groves will be burning; and at a third, a vista of corn fields planted madly on sixty-degree slopes will come into view. You will have seen much of this sort of thing before now, but never on mountainsides more precipitous than these. This is "milpa" farming: the slashing and burning of woodlands every two or three years to create new cropland. That is how long it takes for the acres cleared to become infertile—first, because the soils that support rain-forest ecosystems are very thin (the trees thrive on their own fast-decaying loam) and second, because in this region of torrential rains and vertical terrain, what little topsoil there is washes away in no time at all. So the farmer must soon abandon the fields he has cleared and slash and burn new acres higher up the mountainside. This is the way the Maya have been farming since long before the temples at Palenque were built. You will occasionally see their little huts sitting high up on bald, cone-shaped peaks. You will also see the Maya themselves walking along the road, the men toting machetes and the women and girls sometimes loaded down with large baskets or babies carried on their backs with the aid of headbands. Seeing these wide, expressionless faces can be startling if you are visiting this region of Mexico for the first time. It suddenly dawns on you that although the great age of Maya civilization was done for long before the Europeans set foot on this land, the Maya themselves are still very much around, more numerous by far than they ever were. You have just been gazing at these same faces on Palenque's stones and terra-cotta plaques.

Your thoughts are apt to turn back to Palenque. No one will ever know the exact sequence of events that brought about its decline, but most authorities now agree that, here as elsewhere in the Maya empire, the ruinous equation mentioned in Chapter 1 (too many people + too great an abuse of natural resources + extended drought = cultural disaster) was the root cause. As Maya population centers grew, the milpa farming techniques could no longer keep up with the demand for food. The slash-and-burn cycles were shortened; even short dry spells had disastrous effects; social tensions grew; and the delicate fabric of alliances within and between Maya provinces swiftly came apart. One doesn't need to be a professional Cassandra to be dismayed, traveling through this region now, to see a similar pattern unfolding. After so many centuries of enduring a dark age imposed by the loss of their own cultural heritage and the imposition of various foreign dominations—Toltec, Aztec, Spanish, and Mexican—these Indian peoples are once again acting out the fateful formula of overpopulating and overexploiting their ancient land. Only this time, some of the long-term effects will probably be different. Many of the pyramid temples of their ancestors may stand in the middle of a desert rather than a jungle. Certainly these people will not be able to turn back the clock. Perhaps they do not think much of what has been lost, any more than we do. But will they be happier in that desert future? Will they be better off? Are they happier or better off even now than they were a mere generation or so ago, when most of these steep mountainsides were green?

Well, enough of such speculations—for a while at least—except to note that at the turnoff where the hand-painted sign points to the Cascada Mizola, there is another, more official-looking sign, put up by Mexico's Forestry Department. It declares in Spanish: "Forest fires cause misery and poverty." It is a hopeful thing, this rare evidence of the nation's ecological concern. But just down the road, in plain view as I read this message, a fire was burning on the hillside.

The modern town of Palenque is a lot less attractive than the nearby ruins that have made its name famous. The restaurant at the corner of the square where the local folks meet to eat is a pleasant scene and very reasonable. It reminds me of some of the small-town restaurants in Louisiana's Cajun country. But that's about it for the town itself. Until fairly recently, visitors to the ruins had to make do with some pretty basic lodgings there. But all that's changed now: there are several very nice places on the way to the ruins. Among the comfortable possibilities are: Chan-Kah, which was the best for a while but now gets mixed reviews; the attractive Motel de las Ruinas, which is actually within the boundaries of the planned park; La Cana-da, near town, with its rustic, thatched-roof cottages; and the Nutu-tum, a short way down the Ocosingo highway. La Canada's annex, Tulipanes, and the Nututum have camping areas for RVs. A luxury establishment, Hotel Misión, is supposed to be open by the time this book is published. At the other end of the budget, tent campers can set up in a field near the ruins for a small fee. All of the new places on the road to the ruins have decent to good restaurants.

One final note about Palenque: during the winter season the place crowds up, and on weekends especially it is sometimes hard to see the ruins for the people climbing them. In summer the area catch-es more rainfall than any other part of Mexico. So try to time your visit for late fall or early spring.

11
The Yucatán Peninsula

At a glance

Access   Mérida and Cancún, especially the latter, can be reached by direct or connecting flights from most major U.S. cities. Both cities are also served by Mexicana and Aeromexico airlines. You can even get to Cozumel by direct flight from several U.S. cities. Mexicana has daily flights to Campeche and Ciudad del Carmen. For those on wheels, Hwys 180 and 261 are the main north and south coastal routes between Tabasco and Mérida, while Hwys 180 and 176 cross the northern end of the peninsula east and west. However, as indicated in the travelogue, there are many interesting side routes. Because the Yucatán is such a long haul from the U.S. border, many people fly in and then rent cars at Cancún or Mérida, or else travel by local bus. (If you rent a car, try it out before you put your money down, and make sure that you understand what the total costs will be, including insurance, which is essential.)

Climate   The Yucatán Peninsula is much more tolerable than the rest of Mexico's tropical Gulf during the summer, particularly on the beaches. Cancún, for example, is a year-round resort. But inland, especially, July and August get awfully hot and humid. Rainfall is notably heavier on the Caribbean side of the peninsula than the Gulf side, and even there it falls more often down around Cozumel than at Cancún. It can also fall at any time of year, although summer has the lion's share. Then, even western Yucatán can experience heavy downpours, although they usually don't last very long. Winters are generally fine, although the weather can turn surprisingly cold and unpleasant when one of the *nortes* hits the coast.

Topography and Landscape Features   The Yucatán Peninsula is very similar to southern Florida in its geological evolution. Its land mass is composed of an ancient carbonate reef transformed by chemical processes into limestone. Like peninsular Florida, the Yucatán has been periodically submerged in, or left high and dry by, ancient seas. Although the Puuc Hills provide some elevation in the west-central part of the peninsula, most of the surface is relatively flat. Topsoils are so thin that mechanized cultivation is impossible in most areas. Yucatán's limestone core is typically riddled by subterranean caverns and sink-holes (*cenotes*) created by the erosive action of water. Underground springs well to the surface on some parts of the Coast, creating productive estuarine ecosystems. However, because the Yucatán's limestone platform is relatively high—higher than southern Florida's—water drains down into the porous rock. As a result, surface waterways are very few.

Flora and Fauna   By way of introducing this section, it should be acknowledged that many visitors to the western Yucatán find the pervasive tropical scrub—dense, dry-looking, thorny, with limestone rock all over the place—a monotonously unlovely prospect. I'll agree with all the adjectives except unlovely. But there's no use arguing the point. Either you like this harsh, challenging environment or you don't. At any rate, one good thing can't be denied: although people are scattered throughout this country, they are less numerous than in most other parts of coastal Mexico, and their presence is understated. Anyway, the vegetation is far more diverse than it looks, with a wide variety of acacias, caleandra, mimosa, albizia, ceiba, gumbo limbo, various endemic palms, agave, cacti, and now-rare logwood. A great many of these not very tall trees are deciduous, and some of them are usually covered with blossoms at any time of year. In Quintana Roo, there are still surviving belts of genuine lowland rain forest, complete with banyans, strangler figs, and mahogany. Along much of the coast, both on the Gulf and the Caribbean, mangroves are the predominant vegetation. As for the fauna, the flamingos at Celestún and particularly Río Lagartos are the premier wildlife show, but there are countless other tropical birds to be seen, including keel-billed toucans (in Quintana Roo), boat-billed herons, parakeets, and a number of songbirds endemic only to the Yucatán. The mammalian fauna is much less visible, but jaguars and ocelots still survive in Quintana Roo, as do black howler monkeys, anteaters, and coati. Deer, though greatly reduced in numbers, are still common enough in some areas to be featured on hotel menus. Rattlesnakes are also rather common in the thorn scrub.

Camping   There are a couple of good RV campgrounds at Mérida, and that's about it. For rough-and-ready primitive campers, however, there are any number of likely (but, of course, unsupervised) spots along the less heavily populated inland roads and on the beaches throughout the peninsula, especially on the western and northern coasts. Some promising areas are mentioned in the travelogue. Hotels range from the superdeluxe to the very cheap, although there are none in the latter category between Isla Cancún and Tulum. There are some excellent accommodations at reasonable prices in Valladolid and Mérida, and even in Cancún City (outside the tourist zone).

H*iking, Canoeing, Boating, Etc.*   The best places to penetrate the inhospitable thorn forests of the Yucatán on foot are at the small archeological sites south of Kabáh. At Cobá there is an opportunity to experience what is left of Quintana Roo's jungles during a lengthy

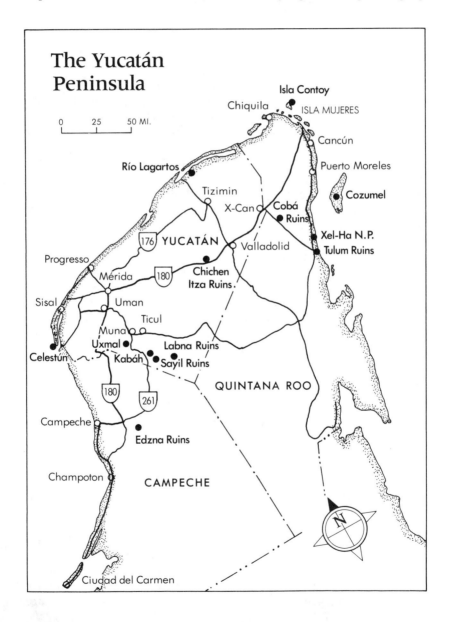

The Yucatán Peninsula

0   25   50 MI.

Isla Contoy
Chiquila
ISLA MUJERES
Cancún
Río Lagartos
Puerto Moreles
Tizimin
Cozumel
X-Can
Cobá
Ruins
Xel-Ha N.P.
176   YUCATÁN
Valladolid
Tulum Ruins
Progresso
Chichen
Mérida   180   Itza Ruins
Sisal
Uman
Ticul
Muna
Uxmal
Labna Ruins
Celestún
Kabáh   Sayil Ruins
QUINTANA ROO
180   261
Campeche
Edzna Ruins
Champoton   CAMPECHE
N
Ciudad del Carmen

walk. But in general, this thorny country is just not designed for cross-country hiking unless you know how to use a machete. On the other hand, there are narrow dirt roads and tracks leading deep into the scrub or up into the Puuc Hills that would be interesting to explore on foot, although they invariably lead to isolated *ejidos* and other small settlements. Some part of the track along the sand ridge that links Celestún, Sisal, and Chuburna Puerto would also make a fine hiking trail. As for canoeing, forget it. The last river that counts is the Champotón in Campeche. There are some beautiful lagoons on the peninsula, and a few lovely lakes in the vicinity of Cobá, but a hired native dugout, complete with native, is the way to go. Open-water boating and fishing are great at Champotón, Campeche, and the whole Caribbean stretch around Cancún, and these places are set up for chartered trips. At Celestún or Río Lagartos you can hire guides to take you into the beautiful flamingo-haunted lagoons. Snorkeling off Cozumel is the best the Western Hemisphere has to offer. Birding everywhere is terrific. And everywhere you go, there are ruins and more ruins, waiting for you to clamber to the top of them. The old colonial cities are lovely too.

Outdoors Highlights   The beaches and lagoons at Celestún and Río Lagartos; all of the many archeological sites, but with special emphasis on El Sayil and Cobá for those who are interested in natural, as well as human, history; the caves at Bolonchén; Campeche, Mérida, and Valladolid; the reefs at Cozumel; Xel-Ha; Isla Contoy.

There are so many parts of Mexico's Gulf Coast to like, from the austere desert lagoons of the north, to the fragment of rain forest in the Sierra de los Tuxtlas, to the tantalizing, hard-to-get-into wilderness of the Usumacinta Delta, that it seems pointless to try to rank them. Still, if I were allowed only one stretch of that Coast to see again, I would probably have to choose the Yucatán Peninsula. As far as this text goes, it's a case of saving the best for last. Not the least of its attractions are its people. They are among the most courteous and friendly in all of Mexico.

Most visitors reach the peninsula by plane to Mérida or Cancún. If they want to explore the region beyond the limited itineraries offered by the tour buses, they must either make do with crowded public buses (a lot of young people with limited budgets take this option, but it often involves hours of standing in the aisle) or they can rent a car, which is pretty expensive even at bargain rates of fifty or sixty dollars a day (including insurance and tax).

As for us, we will continue our counterclockwise odyssey along the Campeche coast in our own trusty vehicle. It may be the long way, but it is also the best way to go for anyone who has the time and really wants to see the country. This entire eastern corner of Mexico, by the way, has the most consistently good roads that we will have found on the Mexican part of our journey; and since truck traffic in this region is relatively light, they should stay that way for a while. Of course, they are fairly narrow and innocent of shoulders; so if you have a flat, you have to fix it on the road—one more good reason for not driving after dark.

On to Campeche

If you have crossed Tabasco via Ciudad del Carmen, you will automatically keep going on Hwy 180. If you're coming from Palenque, you can cut across on the road to Sabancuy, which skirts the edge of the great mangrove jungle at the northern edge of the Usumacinta Delta. Either way, check your gas gauge before starting out. You won't be missing much by bypassing the cattle town of Escárcega. Until only a few years ago, Hwy 186, cutting across the base of the Yucatán Peninsula, held tremendous interest, since it bisected the largest jungle in Mexico, the haunt of tapir, spider monkeys, and jaguar. Now, however, although the entire region is unsuited for intensive agriculture, the Mexican government has handed over the north side of the road to refugee settlers from Guatemala, who are fast destroying not only the forest but the thin soils in which it was rooted. The area south of the road has been set aside as an ecological reserve; but how long it, and the government's resolve, will withstand growing population pressures remains to be seen.

Hwy 180 along the Coast makes for a lovely drive. The road passes through coconut plantations and offers wide views of the Gulf, which on this long, gracefully concave stretch is more properly called the Bay of Campeche. The little fishing town of Champotón has its important page in all histories of the Conquest of Mexico: Hernandez de Córdoba, the daring, if not notably successful explorer who first set foot on Mexican soil, landed here in 1517 after being repulsed by Toltec-Mayas further up the peninsula. He and his crew made the mistake of spending the night ashore. They were overwhelmed by a large Indian force; Córdoba was mortally wounded, and fifty of his men were killed. The spot is still known as the "Bay of the Bad Fight."

Champotón's location is idyllic: a small headland juts out into the Gulf, with the narrow, palm-fringed delta of the Río Champotón emptying out beside it. But the town doesn't quite live up to its setting. There is a nice remnant of Spanish fort to climb up on, a view of pelicans, gulls, vultures, and small fishing boats at rest on sandbars, and, at the back end of town, a pleasantly homely old church. But most everything else is cement block, and the bandstand in the bleak square

Limestone beach at Chompotón, near Campeche. *Photo by Jonathon Sauer.*

looks like a futuristic gibbet. Another little drawback is that Champotón swarms with heavily armed police, apparently because a garrison or academy is located there. On the other hand, the nearby waters swarm with pompano, snapper, and tarpon, making this a notable spot for fishermen. On the waterfront is a small, not-bad hotel with air-conditioning, the Snook Inn, that caters to a fishing and hunting clientele. The proprietor, José Sansores, arranges both fishing trips and expeditions into what is left of the jungles of Campeche.

Just behind the town, the Río Champotón's narrow lagoon is lined with mangroves and rich in birdlife. If you wish to do some local exploring, a guide and skiff can usually be hired at the aforementioned hotel. In any case, all river lovers should take special note of this waterway, if only when you cross the bridge heading out of town. This is the last real river that you will see on the entire western side of the peninsula. I don't know of anyone who has traveled the Río Champotón upriver beyond its delta lagoon. There has got to be white water in the hills, but at least part of the inland stretch is said to be navigable. I suspect the river would be thrilling to explore via canoe, since so much of it passes through still wild country. But I'm not recommending it.

By the time we leave Champotón, the Puuc Hills are pressing close to the Coast. North of the town there are some sandy beaches, but more often the shore is lined by wave-eaten limestone rock. Shallows extend out a long way into the Bay of Campeche, and for this reason the coast here is better suited for sunbathing than for swimming. But beautiful it is, what with the lovely mix of coconut groves, rocky bluffs, and crescent sand flats prettily cluttered with fishing boats. Egrets, great and little blue herons, shorebirds, and gulls are frequently in sight; and there are a few places where you can pull off the road or find tracks leading to the beach. If you can find a secluded spot, this could make a nice area for on-your-own camping.

Once you reach the turnoff to Cayal and the Ruinas Edzna, you must make the difficult choice of which way to go—difficult because both routes are a pleasure to the eye. My own advice is to take the long coastal way 'round to Cayal via Campeche, a city you really should visit, and then backtrack to the Edzna Ruins if you have the time to spare. You will miss some very attractive wooded, rolling landscape on Hwy 261 between Hwy 180 and Edzna, but very similar country still lies ahead on the road to Uxmal.

So then, on to Campeche. Not far above the intersection with Hwy 261, about fifteen miles north of Champotón, you will hit a charming little beach rightly called Costa Blanca. On the headland at the northern end of its crescent is a very nice resort hotel, Si Ho Playa, for those who like their creature comforts while sunning, fishing, and so forth. Not far beyond, the road swings inland through the Puuc Hills for a few miles. These really are hills, not mountains, but driving through them is a bit like riding on a roller-coaster. When you emerge on the other side, there are several more miles right along the Coast, passing through the one-street fishing town that forms the suburb of Campeche. About three miles south of downtown Campeche is a high hill with a steep road detouring up the side of it. Crouching massively at the top is the Baluarte San Miguel, the largest and most self-contained of Campeche's several Spanish forts. And what a perfect gem it is! A little kid's dream of exactly what a fort should be, complete with moat (once furnished with crocodiles, so the local story has it), cannons, turret towers at the corners, and a magnificent view of the cerulean bay and the rooftops of Campeche. Like the fortifications that surrounded—and, to a considerable degree, still surround—the old city, this sturdy bastion was built in the late seventeenth century as protection against the incessant raids of pirates. Presumably San Miguel served as a fallback position when and if the city was taken. The stone rooms in the fortress walls, which once housed Spanish soldiers, now offer a very nice display of Mesoamerican artifacts from many parts of Mexico.

Because it involves a considerable detour for travelers intent on getting to Uxmal or Mérida by the shortest route, Campeche receives relatively few tourist visitors. This is a great pity, since a good case could be made that, along with Veracruz and the older sections of New

Orleans, it is one of the three most beautiful cities on the Gulf. Although no single building stands out in terms of exceptional architectural importance—other than the wonderfully preserved forts—all of the old sector of the city, excepting a few jazzy public buildings and new hotels on the waterfront, is composed of a beautifully intact collection of colonial buildings complete with massive doors, narrow balconies, and elegant grilled windows. (A special mention should be made of the artful, and more recent, stone paving of streets near the waterfront.) Some people might miss the diversity of styles found in the French Quarter or Veracruz; but in its relatively homogeneous way, the overall effect of downtown Campeche is very satisfying.

All the older cities of the Gulf have their tales of woe to tell: rebellions, hurricanes, fires, military invasions and occupations, economic disasters. But Campeche would probably win the dubious prize in the Hard Times category. Founded in 1540 by the ambitious Francisco de Montejo, "the younger," it became in the sixteenth century one of the most flourishing colonial ports, thanks in large part to the export of logwood, or *palo de tinte*, a tree whose precious resin dye was (and still is) used in everything from the coloring of fabrics to vintage wines. But the city's wealth—and its isolation—made it a favored target of pirates on the Spanish Main. Most of us think of that swashbuckling time, if we think of it at all, in terms of the relatively modest operations of Jean Lafitte, or late-night movies starring Errol Flynn and Maureen O'Sullivan. It takes a bit of imaginative effort to realize that piracy was the most persistent economic threat to the Gulf, especially the southern Gulf, for centuries. Campeche was pillaged and burned, its inhabitants massacred and otherwise abused, by almost all the elite of the pirate world, including the likes of Diego the Mulatto, the Englishman William Parker, L'Olonois, and the outrageous Lorencillo (who ended up on the menu of Caribe cannibals). Only after the system of walls and forts was completed at the end of the seventeenth century was the city made safe from these depredations. (There is still a remarkable network of blocked-off tunnels in the limestone rock under the city, where frightened citizens used to hide.) Luckily, Campeche kept its walls in good repair even after effective naval actions made piracy unfashionable. During the War of the Castes—the uprising of the peninsula's Maya peasantry that began in the 1840s—Campeche, along with Mérida, became a besieged island of refuge for the region's people of Spanish or mixed blood, who were elsewhere massacred by the thousands.

Nowadays, although this provincial city is a busy port and boasts a thriving fishing industry, it would like to be besieged again—this time by money-spending tourists. For sure, it has a lot to offer even apart from its architectural *tout ensemble*. Like New Orleans's French Quarter, the old section makes for easy strolling, and in the evening you can sit at the breakwater and watch the sun make its baroque exit.

Excellent handicrafts and examples of contemporary art, plus replicas of Mayan pieces, are very reasonably priced at the converted Church of San José. There are small but interesting museums, a lively Carnival before Lent, and a helpful tourist center on the waterfront. A couple of pretty fancy hotels overlook the bay, and a nice colonial one, Lopez, is on Calle 12. Several cheaper but adequate places can be found on Calle 10 or around the corner on Calle 57. The town has several good restaurants, of which the Mirarmar, serving excellent seafood and an interestingly unsweet margarita, is my favorite.

Finally, for adventurous souls with about a thousand dollars to spend and a hankering to see ordinarily inaccessible ruins and what is left of the jungles on the Mexico-Guatemala border, Campeche is the departure point for ten-day expeditions, via the upper reaches of the Usumacinta, to a world that is still virgin wilderness. (Contact: Sr. Marco Tulio Gomez, Tour Guide, Calle José A. Torres No. 31, Campeche, Campeche, Mexico.)

The Road to Uxmal

When you leave Campeche, you can head north for Mérida either on Hwy 180 or Hwy 261. The former is the shorter route, which will take you through low hills, scrub forest, and, further on, henequen plantations, to Becal, where you can buy one of the Panama hats—not made in Panama—for which the town and the region are famous. Also on this road there is a nice-looking camping facility about forty miles north of Becal.

But Highway 261 is much the more interesting route. As already suggested, if you have taken the Campeche detour, you can head south a few miles at Cayal and take the recently paved spur road to **Ruinas Edzna**. The fine central pyramid and plaza here date from the late Classic Period (seventh century A.D.). The site is dominated by a grand, five-tiered pyramid surmounted by a large temple somewhat defaced by time and graffiti-writing vandals. From the top you can look down on the handsomely designed quadrangle below, flanked by palaces and smaller shrines. You can also see, less than a mile away, a very high hill blanketed in scrub, obviously an unrestored pyramid that is as tall as the one you're standing on. To the south, a still impressive expanse of forest extends toward the horizon. If you have your binocs with you, you may be able to make out some of the birdlife in nearby trees; but the impenetrable scrub surrounding the site makes a close look impossible—unless you've brought a machete along. One of the great attractions of this place is that it is not much visited. You and the resident iguanas may have this high, lonely ruin all to yourselves. It is lovely to sit up here in the late afternoon and think about the Mayas, who must have thought their world would last forever.

The road north is a pleasure to drive. The country is gently rolling, with flatlands interspersed among the hilly ranges. Until recently, all of this was wild country. Now, much of the lowlands has been cleared. The soil is brick red like the Georgia Piedmont and also brick hard when it is dry. Fields are planted to maize, sorghum, and new mango orchards. But although there is evidence of the slash-and-burn techniques of milpa farming on many of the slopes, the hills in general are still forested, at least by tall scrub; and there are some stretches where trees—among them, ceiba, jabin, ciricote, and the iron-hard zapote or sapodilla (which produces the chicle in old-fashioned chewing gum)—still grow pretty tall. Although there are plenty of people around, their presence is not much felt for long stretches. Grasses and wildflowers crowd the shoulders, growing tall enough to obscure highway signs. A plain chacalaca, which looks like a pheasant that wants to be a turkey, may fly across the road, and every once in a while a roadrunner will court suicide by zapping out in front of you. The country people in this area swear that a few *tigres*—jaguars—still roam these hills, and since the region has been opened up to settlement only recently, they may be right. There are many new *ejidos* hereabouts, some of them populated by refugee Guatemalans, whom the natives concede are hard workers. Surprisingly, however, in view of Mexico's socialistic land-reform policies, some of the largest spreads are owned by individual *patrones*.

Bolonchén lies not far south of the Campeche-Yucatán border. The town itself is not too interesting, but nearby is one of the largest cave systems in eastern Mexico. At last count, the discovered caverns extended more than five hundred feet below the surface. Although the descent has been made less harrowing than it used to be, you should take a guide along if you plan to go that far down. This is not the Carlsbad Caverns, with elevators and tidy ramps. You'll love the place, though, with its stalactites, dank stairway, spooky caverns, and especially its series of "bottomless" wells (actually underground *cenotes*, or limestone sinks, like those in southern Florida). Each of the wells has its own distinctive features—differences in temperature, color, and so on. Some local people still call the caverns La Gruta de Xtucumbil-Xunan, or Cave of the Hidden Woman, to commemorate the young maid who, the story has it, withdrew to this dark world after suffering a broken heart in the one above.

An enormous archway, looming across the straight-as-an-arrow road in the middle of nowhere, marks our entrance into the state of Yucatán. While we have been traveling north, you will have observed that the forest has become increasingly lower, drier, and more scrubby-looking. Note the abundance of drought-resistant species that belong to the legume family of trees: various acacias, albizias, the widespread gumbo limbo (which is known hereabouts as the "naked Indian lady"), and the ceiba. Ceibas, when allowed to reach a substantial height, are a strange but handsome-looking tree, with smooth, grayish trunks somewhat swollen in the midsection, like the leg of an elephant. The ceibas, like most of the other trees hereabouts, are deciduous, but in this tropical climate they seem to shed their leaves when they feel like it. Usually some trees are in flower. Large pods hang from branches that often bristle with fierce thorns. The general aspect of this landscape bears a closer resemblance to African bush country than anything we see in the United States, even in the western states. Excepting the occasional *norte*, rain comes to the Yucatán Peninsula from the Caribbean, not the Gulf, and the state of Yucatán gets less of it than neighboring Quintana Roo. Still, many scientists now believe that centuries ago this region was covered by tall jungles rather than scrub. During extended drought in the seventeenth century, epic fires are said to have swept the peninsula. But a more probable explanation for the present thickety woodlands is the ubiquitous practice of milpa agriculture, employed by the Maya long before the birth of Christ and more prevalent than ever today.

At any rate, get used to this landscape: there are subtle variations in these plant communities from area to area, depending on climate and human factors; but in general aspect, this tough, knotted vegetation will look the same throughout much of the Yucatán.

Seeing these dense, virtually impenetrable walls of brushy woodland, anyone familiar with the preferred habitat of most deer species will not be surprised that the Yucatán Peninsula contained, until recently, one of the largest concentrations of deer (whitetails and brocket) on the planet. Until the last decade, venison—*venado*—was available at any restaurant at any season, and it was a staple in the poorest homes. You can still get it, unfortunately, in many hotels. However, it is now one of the most expensive items on the menu—for the obvious reason: throughout much of the peninsula, deer have been totally wiped out by market hunting and expanding settlement. Despite the seeming abundance of protective scrub habitat, a general scarcity of surface water in the Yucatán forces deer and other wildlife to seek out the few *cenotes* and small ponds available to them. There they are easily ambushed. Protective laws have been enacted but are openly ignored. So please, dear reader, don't contribute to the problem by ordering *venado* at a restaurant.

Incidentally, if it's getting dark as you travel along this road, and you are set up for primitive camping, you should be able to find occasional spots, not too near habitations, where you can pull off the main road and spend the night. Just make sure that you aren't blocking the entrance track to someone's homestead.

Soon after crossing the state border, we reach the recently surfaced turnoff to the ruins at **El Sayil**, **X-La'Pak**, and **Labna**. By all means, visit these fascinating sites if you can manage it! They are part of the incredible network of Maya cities that extended throughout this region, and each has its special personality. They belong to the late Classic Period and feature Puuc elements such as clusters of columns as a decorative motif and halls of round columns that once supported temple roofs. These places are still out of the way enough not to be crowded with tourists, and only a limited amount of restoration has occurred. They have a more intimate and much less intimidating appearance than Kabáh and Uxmal to the north. El Sayil is my favorite, in large part because of its beautiful, sprawling palace embellished with the stylized "elephant" faces of the rain god, Chac. The place has a hundred rooms and looks like a cross between a Babylonian ziggurat and the palazzos of Renaissance Italy. Labna has a fine palace, too, but it is less intact-looking. Its main feature is a relatively small but lovely quadrangle overlooked by a temple with a wonderfully preserved comb. One enters the precinct through an elaborate corbel arch, inevitably imagining the processions of gorgeously feathered priests and nobles that once passed under it.

Interesting though they are, the ruins are not the only reason for being here. As already noted, the Yucatán scrub forest is all but impenetrable without benefit of a machete or a tank. I know of no other places in the western Yucatán where you can so painlessly gain access to this fascinating but hostile environment as at El Sayil or X-La'Pak. At the former site there are two long trails, one leading to Temple 2 deep in the forest and the other (across the road from the parking lot) climbing to another temple that is perched on a high, very steep hill. The former trail is the more ecologically diverse, passing through fairly recent milpa clearings, dense thickets, and quite tall forest glades. All along the narrow path, which roughly follows what once must have been a notable avenue, lie mounds of overgrown rubble, the remains of one-time Maya dwellings and small temples. The birding here can be truly wonderful. The stocking nests of the Montezuma oropendola hang from boughs, and the birds themselves are often visible, along with such stunning fellows as the orange oriole, Yucatán jay, and the turquoise-browed motmot with its pendant tailfeathers. The second trail requires a lot more stamina, especially if you've already been knocking yourself out all day climbing pyramids. The ascent through dense scrub is very steep, and both soil and rock are crumbly. If you're not careful, it's quite easy to bust your butt. However, the climb is worth the effort: you are very likely to see spotted wood-quail or the blue-black grassquit fluttering off during your ascent. And when you reach the top, the temple, crowded by surrounding vegetation, offers a superb vantage point from which to view a vast chunk of southern Yucatán. Take along a drink and a snack, and rest up here a spell.

Both the paths at El Sayil are pretty long, but serious hikers will opt for the trail at the X-La'Pak site. This is the old jeep road, the only way that archeologists could get to any of these sites until fairly recently. Now much overgrown, it affords a chance for extended exploration of the stony Yucatán boondocks. The birding is terrific. And local people say that javalina, deer, anteaters, or the ocellated turkey, weirdly beautiful with its carbuncular red crown, are occasionally sighted only a kilometer or two from the ruins. If you have an overnight pack with you, the trail affords one of the rare opportunities hereabouts to camp out in the heart of the "big scrub." Bugs are usually not too bad during winter months, but there are ticks about. Before starting out on an overnight hike, tell the attendant at X-La'Pak that you plan to leave your car in the parking lot and give him a tip.

Kabáh is just up the road a few miles—indeed, the highway goes right through the middle of the site—and **Uxmal** is only about twelve miles further on. Both are spectacularly impressive and also, perhaps, a bit daunting in their massive, heartless splendor. Particularly when Kabáh comes into view, I always feel I should get out of my car and genuflect or something. The huge temple complex on the east side of the highway, dominated by Codz-Pop, or Temple of the Masks, has been largely restored. On the west side, although the group of immense pyramids has been cleared of vegetation, they remain in a rubbled state. For some reason, the looming effect of these unreconstructed piles is more awesome than the assembled structures across the way. The whole area has been extensively cleared, as has the site at Uxmal, so neither affords the opportunity to experience the scrub woodlands that you can find at El Sayil and X-La'Pak. But there is good birding along the edges of the precincts, and at Kabáh a path on the west side of the road (just as you approach an immense, recently restored arch) takes you a considerable distance into the woods.

Uxmal is more put back together and developed than Kabáh. It's a huge site—you can easily spend most of a day poking around—yet, typically, only a part of the original precinct has been reclaimed. The ruins here are among the grandest in the ancient world—*any* ancient world—which is all the more remarkable since, even by the standards of this water-starved country, Uxmal is located in an exceptionally dry zone and must have suffered from a chronic water shortage. The wonder is not that it was periodically abandoned but that it was periodically rebuilt, bigger and grander than ever. As at many another ancient city, the history of these reoccupations is written (though none too clearly) in stone. The ruins encompass a series of cultural stages layered one upon another. Such layering is most visible in the enormous Temple of the Magician. This unusual elliptical pyramid was completed in the late ninth or tenth century, at the end of the Classic Period, when the assimilation of Toltec peoples from central Mexico caused a renaissance of Maya cities in this area. It incorporates in its bulk several earlier stages of construction that date as far back as the sixth century. Uxmal architecture features many Toltec elements, but the style is essentially that of the Puuc (western Yucatecan) Maya: there are spacious plazas and courts, an abundant use of freestanding and clustered pillars, and a studied contrast between plain walls and the elaborate stone mosaic lattice that crowns them. In terms of proportion, the so-called Nunnery Quadrangle and especially the Governor's Palace are considered to be among the finest expressions of Maya architecture to be found anywhere. Evenings, during a sound-and-light show, the structures are glamorously illuminated, their stone fretwork set out in bold relief. Not exactly what the builders had in mind, of course; but given their own flair for dramatic effect, Maya priests probably would have loved to use spotlights if they had been available.

Despite my own squeamishness about the totalitarian heaviness of the place, Uxmal is a must if you are anywhere near it. You may miss the human dimension of Greco-Roman ruins, but there is enough grandeur and magnificence here to make your eyes, and your feet, tired. When it all becomes too overwhelming, you can restfully watch cave swallows swirling above the stone cornices or common and ruddy ground-doves nervously scooting along thicket edges. In terms of setting, however, the grounds of the Uxmal Gardens Hotel, just across the road from the archeological zone, are far more lovely than those of the ruins themselves. The hotel is the only one right at the site, and it just may be the most tastefully furnished and best maintained in eastern Mexico. It's relatively expensive, but a grand place to take it easy for a day or two. The restaurant's food and service are not the greatest, but conservation-minded guests will be pleased to note that the management has conscientiously banished venison from the menu. Even more, visitors will be enchanted with the gardens that earn the hotel its name. Much of the landscaping is manicured, but a wide variety of native trees and plants are present. At the roadside, groves grow to an impressive height, raising questions about whether they more truly represent the original vegetation of the area than the surrounding thicket woodlands. In any event, these bowery places are perfect for checking out the local avifauna. Tropical mockingbirds, Yucatán jays, Altamira orioles, exquisite hummingbirds, the turquoise-browed motmot, golden-fronted woodpeckers, and all sorts of tropical wrens and flycatchers are on the premises. Here you can see many such species without budging from your lounge chair.

Travelers who can't afford the luxuries of Uxmal Gardens should not despair. If you're willing to rough it a bit, there is always the Hacienda San José Tib-ceh. It appears in no guidebooks, but in its own way is more aesthetically charming than most swank hotels. To reach it you must head north the few miles to Muna and then east toward Ticul and Felipe Carrillo Puerto. About five miles outside Muna is the tiny hamlet of San José and, on its western edge, the Hacienda. It is just that: a jewel of a hacienda with a graceful, colonnaded gallery—even a little chapel—one of the few such places in the whole region that is, if somewhat run-down, still intact. Apparently, it is used mainly by the Maya equivalent of traveling salesmen, since the room part of room and board seems to consist mostly of chambers in which you can hang your own hammocks on the hooks provided. At one time, more grandiose accommodations must have been planned. There are sizable washrooms and a waterless swimming pool at one end of the main house. But even without these luxuries (or any others), what a lovely place this is! The Yucatán equivalent of a Deep South plantation that has seen better days. For next to nothing you can park your van or set up your tent on the untended lawn, imagine the life of a henequen planter in the quite recent past, be served a simple but filling home-cooked meal, and make yourself at home.

While you're on this road, you may be interested in knowing that there is a great place to buy reproductions of Maya sculptures and pottery a bit further inland at Ticul. It offers a wider variety and much more reasonable prices than you'll find in Mérida or anywhere else in the Yucatán. You can't miss the place; it's on the left side of the road as you are about to enter the town.

The Area Around Mérida

You can keep heading north from Muna to Mérida, less than an hour's drive away, and use the city as headquarters while exploring the nearby coast. Or you can turn west on the adequate if somewhat frayed road (not shown on most maps) to Kinchil and, from there, proceed directly to the fishing town of Celestún. We will choose this latter route to save some mileage.

This entire area surrounding Mérida was, and still is, the heartland of the henequen, or sisal, industry. You will have seen fields of the crop ere now, perhaps the most ferocious-looking plant ever raised. It belongs to the agave family, related at various removes to the century plant, yucca, and maguey. Of the whole lot, there isn't one that is more rigidly spiky and hostile-looking. Just the thought of walking through a field of the stuff is enough to make you cringe. Yet until a half-century ago, henequen fiber was the raw material out of which the strongest, most durable rope in the world was made. In the Yucatán, it was the equivalent of the Deep South's King Cotton and perpetuated a society that, in its Spanish-Creole way, was remarkably analogous to our own antebellum culture, complete with a landed aristocracy (substitute their haciendas for Greek-revival mansions) and—in all but name—slaves (substitute Indians for blacks). In the early decades of our own century, Mérida—the New Orleans of this planter society—is said to have had more millionaires per capita than any other city in the world. More recently, as with cotton, substitute materials have greatly reduced the market; but a lot of henequen is still grown. Also until recently, many of the plantations survived as going concerns, and the haciendas, though run-down, were still owned by the original families. In the last two decades, however, the combination of government expropriation and the centralization of henequen manufacturing in the hands of a government monopoly, plus the greater mobility of the campesinos, plus the inability of the henequen *patrones* to adapt, have pretty much spelled Gone With the Wind for the old system. In no time at all, the haciendas have fallen into ruin. You will see many of their crumbling walls and sagging gateways along the roads around Mérida, including some on our route to Celestún. Their abandonment seems a pity, if only because, like the more durable Maya ruins nearby, they are an important architectural and cultural legacy that could eventually add much to the tourist attractions of the area.

Kinchil is a more picturesque little town than Muna: its people very Maya-looking, the older women all dressed in spotless white *huipils*, the kids carrying baskets on their heads, the streets lined with neat limestone rock walls, and the ancient, lichen-blackened church looking as though it had been scorched. The thirty-six-mile drive from here to Celestún (check your gas gauge) covers some ecologically interesting ground, even though you may not be too aware of the fact just driving along the road. The limestone terrace that is the Yucatán flattens out as you approach the coast. If you were in a plane, you would notice that the vast scrub forest phases into wetlands and, presently, mangrove swamps. In this transitional area, natural springs (not *cenotes*, which are, in effect, natural wells) carry water to the surface from the peninsula's underground aquifer. Seen from above, these *petenes* appear as round, blue pools, each ringed by tall, green vegetation. Only once, when you are a couple of miles outside Celestún, does the road skirt one of these springs. The change in vegetation is sudden and striking: a great tangle of mangrove jungle rises on the left. You can just make out the snaky network of stilt roots winding upward through the foliage. The trees are five times taller than the mangroves you can see in the Everglades and almost a match for those found more extensively in the Usumacinta Delta. It is a hammock in reverse—an island of vegetation built upon a welling-up of water. Passing in a car, you have just a glimpse of this impenetrable world, gone in a minute.

Celestún is a sleepy, rather disheveled little fishing village, with a half-dozen streets lined with thatched huts and a few one-story colonial dwellings. The wide, dusty square boasts a small church and a row of graceless cement-block stores. The stores are limited in their merchandise, so you had better carry your own wine and other little luxuries with you. Except between December 8 and 12, when there is a quaint fiesta in honor of the Virgin, there is nothing whatever to do here. The point, of course, is that doing nothing is what Celestún is supremely good for. There is a perfectly beautiful sandy beach lined with groves of coconut palms where you can bake or swim while doing nothing. And at the north end of town is a little pavilion restaurant, El Torero, where you can get a tasty lunch or dinner of fresh seafood and beer while gazing out at the Gulf, still doing nothing. Or you can do nothing by wandering along the main street, smiling at the villagers and the handful of other do-nothings who have discovered this place. (The townsfolk are kindly—as almost everywhere in the Yucatán—and tolerant of foreigners; but visitors, particularly women, should be considerate enough of local sensibilities to wear slacks or a wraparound skirt over their bikinis when they leave the beach.)

The above paragraph is not meant to suggest that doing nothing must be an altogether aimless activity at Celestún. You can, for example, walk back up the road a quarter of a mile to the area's greatest attraction, the lagoon that you will have crossed to reach the village. Even from the bridge, it is a pleasure to behold—no wider than a good-size river, banked with tall trees, very shallow, and, usually, bedecked with egrets, great blue herons, cormorants, perhaps a roseate spoonbill, and, most exciting of all, small groups of wood storks.

Even this, however, is not the best part. Celestún is one of the two places in Mexico (both in the Yucatán) and one of the four or five locations in the Western Hemisphere, where you can dependably see colonies of *Phoenicopterus ruber*, otherwise known as the greater (American) flamingo. The opportunity should not be taken lightly. For sheer flamboyance, few wildlife spectacles can match the sight of a large flock of these creatures gathered in the shallows of a tropical estuary. Occasionally a couple of birds show themselves near the Celestún bridge, but ordinarily you must hire a guide—at a modest cost— to take you further up the lagoon to the broad shallows where they usually hang out. It is a fine trip, with many other birds, including winter waterfowl, along the way; and the sudden appearance of what seems a vivid red-pink mist at the water's edge is like nothing else in the natural world. The flamingos have a lot to say to each other, and you will hear their gooselike voices at a considerable distance. Most, if not all, of these birds are a winter spin-off from the larger concentration of birds at Río Lagartos (which we will presently visit), on the northern edge of the peninsula. At any rate, you should see hundreds, even thousands, of flamingos using their bent bills to sift mud and sand for the tiny marine organisms that form their diet. You can get fairly close to them, and, until the tourist traffic becomes heavier than it presently is, it probably won't hurt if some of them become a touch nervous and take off. In which case you are in for a stunning sight, indeed—long necks and frames unfurled like pennants, and great, stroking wings unexpectedly edged with black. But please keep in mind that there is no surveillance or management of these flocks. If you encourage the guide to charge them with his boat, he will probably oblige. The birds are already under considerable pressure, their numbers gradually decreasing. They don't need any more harassment than they already get.

On the other hand, visiting and admiring them—and paying for the privilege—will encourage the people of Celestún to value their rare and lovely neighbors. Such considerations are all the more vital because PESCA, the government's marine-fisheries agency, plans to break the sand ridge that shelters this lagoon *and* the one at Río Lagartos in order to create the same sort of fish pens that have been constructed elsewhere along the Coast. If these ecologically disruptive plans are realized, both of the flamingos' vital sanctuaries will be threatened. One optimistic note is that the Mexican division of Ducks Unlimited will have built a research station at Celestún by the time you read this; so perhaps its presence and influence may help to modify the damage.

Accommodations at Celestún are limited to a small, no-frills hotel on the town's beachfront and a couple of rooms above the aforementioned El Torero restaurant. For primitive campers, there is the opportunity to settle at an abandoned bathhouse-cabana about a half-mile north of town on the sandy washboard track that parallels the Coast. A fading sign announces Balneario Los Flamingos. The place is apparently someone's ambitious failed effort to make Celestún more touristy. It still looks pretty nice; but there is no water, so the bathhouse facilities, needless to say, don't work. Still, the thatched *palapas* are in good repair (as of this writing), and the splendid beach goes on for miles to the north, pristine and usually empty of people.

Speaking of miles to the north, the sand track narrows to a single lane just beyond the bathhouse, but it continues along the coast to Sisal and then to Chuburna Puerto (not usually shown on maps, but fifteen miles beyond Sisal) where the tarmac begins again. Some of the scenery along this "road" is wildly beautiful and beautifully wild, well worth a daylong hike. Also, there are many opportunities for improvised camping. But I can't recommend the trip to motorists who do not have four-wheel drive, even though some local people in regular beat-up old cars take this shortcut frequently—which is why their cars are beat-up. If you do want to experience part of this stretch, I suggest that you back up to Kinchil, cross over to Hunucmá (another nice little colonial town), drive to Sisal, and pick up the trail from there. You will miss some grand views of the Gulf by skipping the southern stretch of this coastal route, but for the most part the scenery between Sisal and Chuburna Puerto is just as great, and—more to the point—the road is both a little less bad and not so long.

Before we embark on it, however, take a look at Sisal. This was once the major port of the Yucatán from which henequen fiber, otherwise known as sisal, was exported to the world; but you'd never guess it now. It is less than half the size of tiny Celestún and looks as forsaken as it is—the sort of place where even a taste for doing nothing can be carried too far. The mangrove swamp at the entrance to the town is strewn with garbage, accommodations are nil, and the most impressive building, apart from the lighthouse, is a ruin. Still, I like Sisal. Just where the road dead-ends at the beach there is a sign with a slogan that we all might adopt: "Keep the beach as clean as your conscience."

Just before the sign is reached, we turn right. The track quickly leaves pavement behind, and from then on it alternates between rutted mud and corrugated sand, mostly the latter. As long as you take your time, it really isn't that bad. (Just hope that you don't meet another vehicle on one of the many stretches where passing is impossible.) At times, the road knifes through vegetation so dense that it walls the wayside exactly like a high boxwood hedge on a country estate in Sussex. More typically, however, the view is pretty open, and what a view it is! You are traveling on a narrow sand ridge separating the Gulf from a vast mangrove swamp. At intervals, on the beach side, there are coconut plantations reminiscent of some South Seas island, but for the most part the track travels through a fierce, low dune scrub— cacti, yucca, sea grape, and stunted acacia—with alternating vistas of Gulf and swamp.

After the first few miles, there are several places where you can pull off on one side or the other to see what can be seen. (On no account, however, should you try to penetrate this burry scrub without benefit of a path; you'll feel like a pincushion before you've gone three steps.) The mangrove swamp varies in its mood from spot to spot. Sometimes small, low islands crouch in a plain of water barely a foot deep; elsewhere, tall hammocks of raw jungle would suggest pure wilderness if it weren't for the occasional shotgun shell in the mud flat at your feet. Birding here can be magnificent if you hit it lucky: in the shallows, rafts of white ibis intermingle with white-faced ibis and egrets, and the secretive bare-throated tiger-heron or the even harder to see boat-billed heron may be startled from its roost. In the scrub, there are vermilion flycatchers, mangrove warblers and vireos, yellow-faced grassquits, white-lored gnatcatchers, Yucatán quail, and assorted other birds that make a birdwatcher's life worthwhile. On the beach side, pelicans, shorebirds, terns, and gulls rest on sandbars, and frigatebirds often soar overhead. The beach itself still looks as it must have looked before Grijalva, Cortés, et al. ever landed on these shores. But access points are relatively few, even when you can see the Gulf only a dozen yards away. If you want to camp, and you see a turnoff that looks suitable, take it. (One further word of caution: this is the tropics, and this is mangrove country; so even in winter take along mosquito repellent.)

Once you reach Chuburna Puerto and the paved road, you will see why there is a lot to be said for not making all road surfaces hard.

From here on, the Coast looks like a Mexican version of Naples, Florida: you will drive past an endless row of wall-to-wall bungalows, the retreats of well-to-do citizens from Progreso and Mérida. When, as I fear it shall, the paved road advances south, the world described in the previous paragraphs will disappear. So if you have nerve and car enough, make the most of it while it's still there.

You swerve inland from Chemel through a last stretch of mangrove swamp to catch the Mérida-Progreso expressway. Frankly, I wouldn't bother visiting the port city of Progreso. The best that can be said for it is that it isn't as bad as almost everyone says it is. Along with a lot of grunginess, there is a pleasant beachside esplanade with a nice old-fashioned balustrade atop the seawall. If it were your first Mexican city—like Matamoros, for example—it would seem thrillingly foreign. But since it isn't, head inland here for Mérida. If you have time, take the brief detour to the east, about midway between Progreso and Mérida, and visit the ruins at **Dzibilchaltún**. The most interesting features are a temple that is unique because it has windows as well as doors and a sacred *cenote* of exceptional depth in which a great many sacrificial victims lost their lives. But the real archeological importance of the site lies in its longevity as a continuously occupied Maya city—from 2000 B.C. until after the Spanish Conquest. The part that is being restored only hints at the extent of the original precinct, which covered twenty-five square miles.

Mérida

This old city was founded in 1542 by the like-named son of Francisco de Montejo, the derring-do Spaniard who, royal grant in hand, had set out to conquer the Yucatán fifteen years earlier. The cathedral and other old buildings around the oft-renamed central plaza were built with stones from the Maya city of T'ho, which the younger Montejo razed after he had conquered it. Like New Orleans, Mérida has always been both insular and cosmopolitan, with closer ties to Europe than to Mexico City. This isn't surprising when you consider that the first highway connecting the Yucatán Peninsula with the rest of Mexico was completed only in the 1960s. Henequen made Mérida rich in the nineteenth century, but long before that, when dyewood, beef, woven cotton, and salt were the main exports, it was, more than Campeche and Valladolid, the administrative and social center for the peninsula's Creole aristocracy. Though isolation allowed the city to escape some of the turmoil that the rest of Mexico endured in the century following independence, it suffered its own home-grown horrors, most notably during the War of the Castes, when it was besieged and almost taken by tens of thousands of rebelling Maya Indians.

Overall, Mérida is a less well preserved colonial city than Campeche, but the central plaza, shaded by ancient imported laurels (reputedly rescued from a shipwreck) and flanked on two sides by arcades, is the most charming public space this side of Veracruz and Jalapa; and the surrounding buildings, though somewhat mutilated in the post-Independence period, are still extremely handsome in their withdrawn Spanish-Moorish way. A standard guidebook to the city will give you a run-down of all the sights to see. Indeed, given the outdoors theme of this book, I've probably spent too much time talking about architectural elements and the like. But I can't resist a brief mention of three indoor landscapes here: those belonging to the palace of the Montejos, the cathedral, and the governor's palace.

The Montejos family seat boasts an astonishing doorway crowned with a type of bas-relief called plateresque. Along with the family coat of arms, it unabashedly depicts a pair of armored Spaniards standing on the heads of anguished-looking Indians. But the real fascination lies within: high rooms crowded with massively ornate furniture and patios crowded with untended plants and trees. The dining room, in particular, is a study in tropical gothic: it opens at either end onto separate patios, and the juxtaposition between the heavy grandeur of the room and the uncontrolled, twining vegetation from the patios—which was literally crawling through the open doors when I last saw it—creates an unforgettably eerie yet beautiful effect, a paradigm of civilization in the tropics. Until recently the building was occupied by a descendant of the Montejos, but it has now been taken over by the government. Reportedly it has been nicely restored and tidied up. But not too much, I hope. That spooky dining room should be left alone.

Although most experts would not agree, I think the interior of Mérida's cathedral is one of the most beautiful in Mexico. The place was looted during the 1917 revolution, but even before that it must have been unusually spartan looking for a Mexican church. The usual Mexican version of baroque whoop-de-doo is often a feast for the eye, but this church is an effective reminder of how much the elements of simplicity, harmony, and balance have to do with beauty. The immense but elegantly proportioned columns and the majestic romanesque sense of space belong more to the twelfth century than to the sixteenth, when this edifice was built.

Finally, a mention should be made of the Palacio de Gobernador. It is a nineteenth-century beaux-arts version of earlier colonial architecture—and, I think, a wonderfully successful adaptation of traditional styles, even if the critics tend to brush it off, presumably because it's derivative or whatever. Anyway, the main attraction lies within: the enormous Pacheco paintings that cover the walls of the courtyard and the gilded reception hall upstairs. They are superb examples of what in our own country might be called the WPA 1930s school of art. The propagandistic themes are about as subtle as an editorial cartoon, and the representational style has been out of fashion for ages.

Yet what a delight these quasimurals are! Full of sneering oppressors and heroic *indios*, crammed with brilliant color, and pulled together by a melodramatic but vigorous sense of composition, they are as entertaining, and in their way well done, as a flashy folkloric ballet.

Mérida is a pleasant place for walking even though, as in all Mexican towns, the narrow downtown sidewalks get crowded late in the morning and late in the afternoon. Don't miss the immense and gaudy *mercado* (market); and if you can't afford one of the horse-drawn carriages, you can always walk the eight blocks to where the Paseo de Montejo, a wide, handsome avenue lined with turn-of-the-century mansions, begins.

The city has an abundance of accommodations, from plush to very reasonable. The Reforma, clean, with a fine tropical ambiance, is probably the best bet in the latter category. The Gran Hotel, with its sweetly naive ceiling frescoes, is also nice in its faded colonial way, even though the entrance is sometimes a bit obstructed by long lines of people—a common scene in Mexican cities—waiting to get into the cinema next door. For campers, Mérida offers two trailer parks with hookups and other amenities: the Mayan Trailer Paradise, very near the airport, and the Quinta Loreta, quite a way west of the main plaza on Calle 59. As for restaurants, there are many in the city, some with a pleasant continental atmosphere. Another nice continental touch is the practice of displaying menus at restaurant entrances, so that you are able to shop around for your dinner. Either chicken or pork wrapped in a banana leaf and cooked with regional spices (*pibil*) is usually a good bet here and throughout the Yucatán.

Tizimín and Río Lagartos

When you are ready to leave Mérida, you can either head directly toward Chichén Itzá and Valladolid on our old standby, Hwy 180, which passes through the peninsula's now-familiar scrub woodlands, or you can aim north and then east toward Tizimín on Hwy 176. The latter route is scenically more various, passing first through the heart of the old henequen plantation country and then, beyond Temax, shading into cattle country. The run-down colonial towns and ruined haciendas along the way have seen a lot of history, much high living, and much bloodshed. Tiny, half-abandoned San Antonio Camera, east of Temax, and the more or less intact Hacienda Kambul, near Motul, are very photogenic. As long as you don't barge through someone's front yard or garden, you can prowl around such places and get a feel for a world that has only recently breathed its last breath.

Beyond Buctzotz there are still a few stretches of fairly tall, deciduous tropical woodlands left. At a distance these stands look like the hardwood forests of Mississippi or Alabama, but instead of oaks and maples they are composed of ceiba, cedro, and gumbo limbo. There are lots of songbirds through here, including blue buntings, the pretty little red-capped manakin, and the tropical mockingbird. In a tall tree you may spot the large, handsome gray hawk. If so, wish him luck; like all roads in the Yucatán, this one is patrolled by cycling campesinos with guns slung across their shoulders, ready to blast away at any wild thing that shows itself.

Although you will see considerable swatches of stony pasture as you approach Tizimín, most of the cattle land is out of sight. Like the milpa operations throughout the peninsula, the cleared ranchlands here are often shut away from the road by a wide band of scrub. You think you are surrounded by unbroken miles of low forest when in fact you are often passing through what are, in effect, hedgerows concealing large expanses of cleared land. Old tires or plastic bags on poles mark the easy-to-miss entrances to unseen ranches and homesteads.

Tizimín is a big cattle town, with narrow streets that dip and rise on modest hills. Though it boasts little in the way of colonial architecture except a blackened church and crumbling monastery, and has nothing like the charm of Mérida to the west or Valladolid to the south, it is nevertheless a pleasant, peaceful place—except, that is, during the days before and after the Feast of the Epiphany on January 6. Then it is still pleasant but hardly peaceful. All the country people from miles around pour in and the place is packed. Acres of makeshift stalls covered by tents and awnings display everything from trinkets and clothing to vegetables and sticky sweets. There are fairs, dances, bands, and cattle shows (where some of the most magnificent Brahmas I've ever seen are on display). It is a major local event—a part of the "real" Mexico rarely seen by tourists. While it's going on, you may have trouble finding lodgings here, but at any other time those who are on their way to Río Lagartos to see the flamingos can get very comfortable rooms at the Hotel San Carlos on a side street near the square. On the square itself is a cheaper but very adequate hotel, as well as a little corner restaurant where food is both reasonable and good. Best of all, just a couple of blocks away is that rare thing in Mexico, an excellent bakery with delicious pastries and a banana bread that tastes like good pound cake.

As you leave Tizimín, a large billboard—still, happily, an uncommon phenomenon in eastern Mexico—luridly advertises a brand of chemical herbicide. And sure enough, the scrub diminishes and the landscape really opens out between Tizimín and Río Lagartos. However, the presence of scattered palms in many of the wide pastures suggests that machetes and fire, not herbicides, still do most of the clearing. This country, though subdued, is easy to look at. The terrain is gently rolling, and the pastures are broken by scrub hedgerows and occasional patches of taller forest. As you approach the Coast, the

Cast net fisherman, Río Lagartos. *Photo by C. C. Lockwood.*

country becomes thornier, drier, bonier. You can smell the sea. Suddenly, you are passing through a mangrove marsh. A mile or so further and you ease over the inevitable *topes* and into Río Lagartos.

If you didn't like flaky little Celestún, you won't like this town either. If you did, you will. Not that the two places are all that much alike when it comes to details. There are no palm plantations at Río Lagartos, and in general it looks more bleached and arid. The community is on the inland side of a lagoon (actually a wide, shallow river not unlike a southern Florida slough), so the beach is not in its front yard as it is at Celestún. And—an unusual sight in this land of pole and thatch huts—many of the little houses (the tropical equivalents of Nantucket cabins) are walled with planks of wood. But, in general, there is the same feel to this place that you find at Celestún: a laid-back sense of being off everyone's beaten track. Plus an easy, unself-conscious mix of the picturesque and the tacky. No doubt the mix was always here. Although it is now a peaceful place, and its inhabitants wonderfully courteous and friendly, Río Lagartos was once a capital of the pirate world. Evidently, quite a few of those long-ago buccaneers were Anglo-Saxon types who took their duties as founding fathers seriously: while they weren't making life miserable for Spanish ships and towns, they found time to immortalize themselves in the blond hair and blue eyes of many of the town's present-day citizens.

Unlike most Mexican villages, Río Lagartos is not dominated by the village church, which here is a low, modern thing sadly reminiscent of the prefabricated religious architecture we see along some of our own highways. No, the only lofty edifice in sight is the Hotel Nefertiti, which, except for being five stories high, looks exactly like a movie theater from the 1930s. I can't honestly recommend it to the comfort-conscious. The rooms, though large and clean, are spartan; and the top two floors have never been finished. Built to accommodate a tourist boom that never happened, the Nefertiti is yet another example of the Mexican tendency to conceive ambitious plans without much attention to reality. But for what it's worth, I have nothing but happy memories of this place. Behind the hotel there is a thatched pavilion overlooking the shallow blue bay and the little town. Among the fleet of moored fishing skiffs, brown pelicans, cormorants, gulls, and terns hustle after schools of fish. Further off, a wall of mangroves conceals the beautiful barrier beach. At evening, while having a drink from the (pretty limited) bar, or a good, simple meal of fresh fish or shrimp, you can immerse yourself in the spectacular sunsets that bloom and die just where the Gulf of Mexico ends and the Caribbean begins. If you are lucky, a flock of flamingos will fly over the bay, catching the last light with their wings.

The time may come, God forbid, when Río Lagartos will be an extension of Cancún. Meantime, however, it remains another of those slightly scruffy, gloriously untouristy places along the Coast where you can forget the job and the mortgage (and the plastic luxuries) back home and pretend that you are the Outcast of the Islands. In fact, the hotel management is taking an enlightened attitude toward the prospects of future development. There is an awareness that both the ecology of the bay and the lifestyle of the town's good-natured people are seriously threatened, and that they can best be protected if Río Lagartos becomes a biological research center where both American and Mexican students can study the elaborate tropical estuarine system along Yucatán's northern coast. Steps have already been taken to accomplish that good end, and perhaps the first University-level summer sessions will have begun by the time this book is published.

But whether or not all that comes to pass, Río Lagartos deserves the attention of anyone who is interested in the natural world. The river/lagoon on which the town is situated is fifty miles long and varies greatly in width from place to place. It is sheltered from the sea by one of the most beautiful barrier islands on the Gulf Coast. True, it doesn't have the lovely bayside forests of some of the islands on the northern Gulf nor the high dunes and wide beaches of Padre Island or Cabo Rojo. Instead, it offers an almost abstract landscape that doesn't quite seem to belong to our planet at all—a stark world populated by jagged wild agave and dainty miniature palms. Luckily for the bay, the low dunes are tightly carpeted with sand shrubs and plants, including, in places, an extraordinary vine that looks exactly like a brilliant orange wire mesh.

On the mainland side of the lagoon lies a mangrove swamp, only a mile or two wide, broken by small open marshes and beautiful jungle hammocks that will remind you of parts of Big Cypress or the Everglades. As at Celestún, there are limestone springs here—*ojas de agua* (eyes of water)—that are vital in keeping the lagoon supplied with a measure of freshwater. Indeed, this balance between saltwater and freshwater has become a critical issue lately, since the health of the entire estuarine system depends on it. The government has officially recognized this priceless ecosystem by declaring it a national reserve. But that designation may not mean much when it gets in the way of special interests. Río Lagartos's lagoon produces some of the finest salt in the world, a fact well known to the ancient Maya who built settlements here more than two thousand years ago. Presently, the large operation at Los Colorados mines the salt from a series of leveed pans that cover thousands of acres of the bay's surface. If the expansion of these pans continues, the bay may become a briny sink. As though that were not enough of a problem, PESCA, the government's fisheries agency, plans to break the fragile barrier ridge here, as well as at Celestún, and build its own levees in the lagoon as a means of increasing fish production. The projects, if they are completed without adequate safeguards, are bound to have a traumatic effect on Río Lagartos's crowning glory, its extraordinary congregation of greater

Greater flamingos, Río Lagartos. *Photo by C. C. Lockwood.*

(American) flamingos. The birds are still about 20,000 strong, but for years their numbers have been slowly declining. One can only hope that a more enlightened management program can be worked out before it is too late. It would be a great tragedy if the proposed research center at Río Lagartos were to be launched just in time to record the disappearance of the region's most spectacular attraction.

You can drive to the upper reaches of the lagoon via the interesting road to Los Colorados. For a while it sticks to the mainland, passing along the interface between the mangrove swamp and a dry, thorny scrubland full of cacti, yucca, and various acacias. Then it turns to the Coast through jungly wetlands where herons, egrets, coots, and perhaps a roadside hawk can be seen. At a narrow point the road crosses the lagoon on a wooden bridge and for the next many miles travels through the dune landscape described above, where iguanas or possibly a little gray dune fox may scoot across your path. Though unpaved, the road is in good condition. Los Colorados is a neat little settlement shaded by coconut palms; when you reach it you will see the first of the endless salt pans in the bay, varying in hue from blue to heliotrope purple depending on their salinity. If you continue beyond Colorados for about four or five miles and then venture onto the network of levees, you may get a view of the flamingos out on the shallow bay.

However, as at Celestún, the best way to approach them is by boat, an expedition that can be arranged at the Hotel Nefertiti. At reasonable cost, the likable Luis, who conducts most of these tours, offers a short or long excursion. The former involves making the trip just described in your car and then taking a boat from one of the salt-pan levees. But if you have three hours to spare, by all means take the longer trip through the lagoon from the hotel wharf. The Río Lagartos widens, narrows, then widens again as you travel east, skirting sandbars and lapping mangrove roots. The fishing is often excellent, and so is the birding, even if you don't count the flamingos. There are many shorebirds and waders on hand, and some people are lucky enough to see a bare-throated tiger-heron or, even more fortunately, the nocturnal boat-billed heron lurking in the mangroves. Sadly, the alligatorlike caimans from which the lagoon takes its name are very rare now, and the chances of seeing one almost nil.

As for the flamingos, you are certain to see, at the least, two or three thousand of them in this very specialized estuarine habitat. With their long legs, coat-hanger necks, and impossibly gorgeous coloration, they look for all the world like a mass of stalky, animated flowers drifting on the shallow water. I promise you that, once seen, the flamingos of Río Lagartos will remain a cherished memory for the rest of your life.

Primitive campers should be happy on this totally unspoiled coast. The best bet is to find a place a mile or two beyond Los Colorados (which, by the way, you can reach by bus from Río Lagartos). The only problem is that the road is scraped to a level well below the surrounding dunes, so there are very few places where an ordinary passenger car can pull over on the beachside. Bayside, there are a number of side roads leading to the salt-pan levees. You can always park beside one of these and walk the short distance to the narrow but beautiful beach. As of this writing, people in this area still don't seem to know what crime is, so your vehicle should be safe.

In any event, contrive to visit Río Lagartos with its fine bay and glorious flamingos if you are traveling in northern Yucatán. As long as you don't expect the wrong things—Cancún comforts, for instance—you'll love this out-of-the-way place.

Moving Inland to Chichén Itzá, Valladolid, and Cobá

Luckily for the environment, if not for us, there is as yet no highway that follows the coast around the horn of the peninsula to Cancún. Even if there were, you would want to back up and visit Valladolid and Chichén Itzá. As you head south toward Valladolid, note how much more populous the route is below Tizimín compared to the stretch between that city and Río Lagartos. You can always tell the few older roads in the Yucatán from the many that have recently been built by the number of established-looking towns and villages that border them. In the old days, Tizimín was on the frontier, whereas the area south of it was heavily settled. Probably the scenery through here hasn't changed all that much since the War of the Castes was suppressed (in this region) more than a century ago. Same neat little villages of pole-and-thatch huts, with flowering shrubs blooming in the yards and, occasionally, acacia trees touching branches overhead.

Of the peninsula's three largest colonial cities—Mérida, Campeche, and Valladolid—the last suffered most heavily during the great uprising of the Maya peasantry in 1848. The town prided itself on the high percentage of its citizens that were of pure Spanish descent. These Creoles tended to be conservative, scorning the more mercantile mood of nineteenth-century Mérida and Campeche in favor of the traditional cattle ranching that had made their fathers rich. It is difficult now, visiting this charming, sleepy town, to imagine the time when the streets were filled with rampaging Maya, when the grilled windows of burning houses were gruesomely adorned with the bodies of raped women, and the city's survivors were marshaling for a slow, bloody retreat to the uncertain sanctuary of Mérida. In any event, a charming, sleepy town it now is, with even its rebuilt sections much resembling the colonial town that was. The main tourist attraction is the Cenote Zaci, a short walk to the east from the main plaza. This deep underground pool, reached by a precipitous stairway, is located in a small park where a little restaurant serves good food. On the plaza itself, the sixteenth-century church, which survived the War of the Castes, looks as impressively old as it is. Across the square is another architectural survivor, the Mesón del Marquez. This beautiful building, once one of the city's grander private residences, is still owned by a descendant of the original builder. It now houses a very pleasant hotel as well as a gift shop that is better than any you will find in Mérida, much less Cancún. Apart from these sights, though, the city is just a very congenial place in which to stroll around. The northern sector, with its pleasing combination of old stuccoed huts and new villas, and its flowering gardens behind walls of rock or crushed limestone, is particularly worth a stroll.

Besides my favorite, the Mesón del Marquez, there are two or three other nice hotels. The most up-to-date and expensive is the San Clemente, which has a good restaurant with regional dishes. But the María de la Luz and the Hotel Zaci are also very pleasant. Prices at any of these places are cheaper than at their equivalents in the hotel zone at nearby Chichén Itzá. However, as you should have learned long before now while traveling in Mexico, you must be a bit patient with the service, which is sometimes pretty haphazard.

Chichén Itzá is probably the most visited of all the great pre-Columbian Maya cities—which is not surprising since it lies within easy reach of tour-bus expeditions from either Cancún or Mérida and since so many superlatives apply to its architecture. Even more than Uxmal, it is an overwhelmingly impressive place. Although the city dates from the Mid-Classic Period (fifth century A.D.), its mightiest structures were built in the tenth and eleventh centuries after northern Yucatán had undergone a series of immigrations and invasions, still not clearly worked out, which brought to the region the cultural influences of Maya from the Gulf Coast, then the Itzá, and, finally and most emphatically, the warlike Toltec-Mexicans of central Mexico. The many sculptured representations of the Toltec's plumed serpent god, Quetzalcoatl, signify the rise of a new Toltec-Maya dynasty, apparently founded by a great Toltec leader, Kukulcan, who was identified with Quetzalcoatl in a later period. Under this new dynasty, Chichén Itzá became the center of power in the peninsula during the Post-Classic Period. In its heyday it was one of the world's great cities. Even in ruins its grandeur persists. There is plenty to look at—and to climb, if you have the legs for it. The temple atop the towering El Castillo is still furnished with its jaguar throne and once blood-soaked *chacmool*, a small altar on which still-warm human hearts were piled. At the spring and autumn equinoxes, the ingeniously designed northern stairway seems to writhe with the snakelike shadows cast by the feathered serpents on its balustrades. The ball court, the largest in Mesoamerica, has superb acoustics and high-up ball rings. The Temple of the Warriors is guarded by finely carved columns and another *chacmool*. And then there is the huge Sacred Cenote into which large numbers of little bells and little children were thrown in order to placate the rain god.

Yet, you know, for all its monumental splendors, the central precinct at Chichén Itzá, even more than the ruins of Uxmal and Kabáh, provokes more awe than aesthetic delight. Then, too, there are peculiarly modern drawbacks that diminish even awe. The area is usually aswarm with your fellow tourists, and the pathway to the Sacred Cenote, once a proud boulevard, is inexcusably littered. For me, the southern sector of the site is far and away the most attractive part of Chichén Itzá. This is the quadrangle dominated by the Caracol and the Nunnery. The Caracol is a truly extraordinary building. Even without benefit of a guidebook, you would instantly, and correctly, identify this handsome structure as an observatory. The dome and rounded walls are rare in Maya architecture, and the interior layout, with a circular stairwell that gives the building its name (*caracol* means "snail"), is very sophisticated in its design.

If you can get a little bit away from the littered paths—not too far or you may get lost—the woods at the site are full of rubbled ruins that have barely been cleared, as well as many spiny plants. Some of the larger trees are decked with bromeliads and a parasitic cactus that hangs from the branches in segmented loops. Many of the typical songbirds of the region—gray-breasted martins, Altamira orioles, Yucatán jays, singing blackbirds—frequent the scrub forest, especially at the Sacred Cenote and the Xtoloc Cenote on the southern side of the precinct. Occasionally, flocks of Aztec parakeets show themselves.

The nearby hotel zone with its gardens and tall trees is also a good place for birds. Accommodations here are very comfortable but, predictably, more expensive than at Valladolid. If you have your own vehicle, you may want to consider the attractive little Hotel Dolores Alba as a place to stay. It lies between Chichén Itzá and a truly unique archeological site that many travelers in the region never even hear about, namely the **Balankanche Caves**. This large network of caverns has been known to local people for centuries, but in 1959 a tour guide made an amazing discovery: a sealed passageway, hidden for centuries, led to an underground chamber containing a Maya shrine. There he found a *cenote* and a remarkable stalagmite "tree" with a crown of stalactite "leaves." Assembled around the base was a large collection of pots, incense burners, carvings, and other offerings that had lain in total darkness all these hundreds of years. They are still there. It's hard to explain but, notwithstanding the electric lighting and all that, you can feel the living presence of the ancient Maya more vividly in this chilly cavern than in the mighty ruins nearby. Check at the Chichén Itzá gatehouse for information about when the cave is open.

Cobá and the Tulum Area

By any geographer's definition, we have left the Gulf Coast behind us. But since we could hardly call a halt to our journey in the middle of north-central Yucatán, it makes sense to continue, with at least a few brief comments along the way, to the more logical destination of Cancún.

Besides, I really want to at least mention **Cobá**, which lies about fifty-five miles southeast of Valladolid. For anyone who wants to see what is left of the peninsula's eastern wilderness *and* visit a particularly beautiful archeological site, this out-of-the-way place should not be passed up. The turnoff to Cobá is at Xcan. There is no sign; so be on the lookout for the paved road that heads south from the middle of this little town.

Almost as soon as you leave Xcan behind, you will notice that the forest along this road is greener, lusher, and generally taller than the thorny woodlands to the west. We are now in the state of Quintana Roo, which is more generously blessed with rains and freshwater lakes than the dry western part of the peninsula. Until only a couple of decades ago, this entire vast region was a true wilderness, inhabited, as the tour books had it, with deer, monkeys, tapirs, jaguars, and isolated tribes of Indians that white men rarely encountered. Indeed, until the beginning of this century much of the area remained the stronghold of Maya rebels who remained unconquered, and still dangerously hostile, long after the bloody War of the Castes petered out in western Yucatán. To this day, many of the people here speak only Maya; but, far from being hostile, they are almost invariably friendly and courteous. However, civilization has arrived overnight, and both their traditional way of life and their wilderness world are vanishing with incredible swiftness. Even the dense woodland along the newly paved road to Cobá and Tulum is no longer the forest primeval. Still, a lot of the old wildness is left. At the tiny settlement of Punta Laguna, between Xcan and Cobá, the insatiably curious may want to take a right turn (west) and drive the short distance to the beautiful lake for which the place is named. Along its shores, the jungle towers impressively. Little Maya boys will follow you down to the water's edge, and if it is late afternoon, and you are adequately dressed in sturdy Levis and boots of some sort, they may be able to lead you to the evening roosts of a troop of black howler monkeys that still frequents the area.

At Cobá itself, a large swath of the jungle has thus far been spared the advance of the milpa farmers. Somewhat ironically, this wilderness flourishes on a site that rivals Dzidzantún as one of the largest and most continuously occupied cities in the Maya world (from the seventh century A.D. until after the Spanish Conquest). More than seven thousand platform structures of varying heights were built here, including many temple complexes and sprawling palaces. Thanks to the four lovely lakes that surround it, the city was endowed with a generous water supply, which it used to establish an elaborate irrigation system. From its broad avenues, limestone roads once led to Chichén Itzá, Tulum, and other Maya centers. It also maintained close ties with Tikal in faraway Guatemala. The aristocracies of these two great cities often intermarried, and stelae at Cobá indicate that noblewomen from the south had exceptional status and authority here.

Excavation has scarcely begun at the site, but even in its present condition the scale of this once-great metropolis is not hard to grasp. If you make the precipitous climb to the top of the tall pyramid near the entrance gate, you will see, besides two of the blue lakes, the towering Nohoch Mul pyramid, even taller than the Castillo at Chichén Itzá, looming above the forest canopy more than a mile away. It is a moving sight, especially when you reflect that the priests who once stood where you are standing looked down upon busy avenues and rooftops where now the jungle grows. As it is, the setting at Cobá makes it the most beautiful archeological site this side of Palenque. The considerable walk to the Castillo through a magnificent tropical forest would be thrilling even without the presence of the ruins themselves. Although monkeys and other wild animals that were common in the area just a few years ago have been driven away by the growing human presence, the birding is terrific. If you can arrange to be perched atop Nohoch Mul early in the morning or late in the afternoon, you may have the rare opportunity to observe all three species of Mexican toucans—collared araçari, emerald toucanet, and the spectacular keel-billed—at one sitting.

There is a very nice little hotel on the lakeshore near the entrance to the archeological zone, as well as a couple of modest restaurants in the village. If you want to camp, you should not have much trouble finding a place to park for the night near the lake, although you may be bothered by curious kids. Ask advice at the gate first.

Although our own journey will not progress further south, you may very possibly want to push on to the ruins at **Tulum**, a sort of subdivision of a larger Maya city that was still flourishing here when the Spaniards first sailed this coast. In fact, the local citizens scared the would-be explorers off. The architectural scale is modest compared to that of most other sites; but the ruins have been extensively restored, and the setting, on cliffs overlooking the Caribbean, is stunning.

If you take this route and then head north along Hwy 307, you will be paralleling, but not seeing, one of the prettiest coasts in the world. Stretches of palmy, white-sand beach alternate with craggy but not too towering limestone rocks at the edge of an ink blue sea. The only fault with this tropical paradise is that it has been discovered with a vengeance. Almost the only access to the coast between Tulum and Cancún is via roads leading to new resort hotels or to fishing towns that are also becoming resort centers. The towns, however, have public beaches where you can sun and take a dip. (One of them, Puerto Morelos, has a certain melancholy ecological interest because, like Louisiana's Holly Beach, it is washing away.) The beautiful island of Cozumel has also become a much-visited tourist haven, easily reached by ferry or plane from Playa del Carmen. Cozumel is an El Dorado for anglers and especially divers: the Palancar Reef offshore is second only to Australia's Great Barrier Reef in size. And in terms of the variety of marine life and coral formations, even the reefs off the Florida Keys can't compare. Back on the mainland, however, the out-of-doors is in pell-mell retreat: between the tourist developments on the beach and the milpa operations springing up along the highway, the whole area is becoming like southern Florida in the 1960s. But it isn't that bad yet.

First-class accommodations between Tulum and Cancún are the most expensive in eastern Mexico, excepting Cancún itself. Still, they are a relative bargain compared to beach resorts in the United States. For the budget-conscious, the adequate Cruceros de las Ruinas Motel at Tulum (right at the turnoff to the ruins) is fairly reasonable, and there are basic facilities for campers. The pleasant, thatched-roof restaurant draws an interesting mix of customers ranging from well-heeled types to international hitchhikers, and the food is surprisingly good. While you're in this area, by all means visit the stunning marine park at Xel-Ha, just a few miles north of Tulum. Even by the standards of this always magnificent coastline, Xel-Ha is something special: a meandering bay carved into the limestone rock; water clearer and bluer than a Beverly Hills swimming pool; and schools of large, brilliantly colored fish with which you can fraternize with or without the aid of a rented snorkel.

Cobá to Cancún

There is a lot more to say about this *región turística*, but for us, the last lap of the journey lies along Hwy 180. A few miles beyond Xcan, at the inspection station at Nuevo Xcan, a recently paved road leads north to the little fishing village of Chiquila on Laguna Yalahano, a mangrove-edged bay much wider and more open than nearby Río Lagartos. There are no amenities at Chiquila, and only the occasional itinerant flamingo shows itself. But the northbound road passes through country that is relatively untamed. An occasional ocelot skin is still stretched out to dry in the barely noticed villages along the way, and the first wild (live) anteater I ever saw ambled across this road in broad daylight, as oblivious to danger as a tortoise or an armadillo. If a fisherman-guide is available, you can visit the lonely, empty beaches

Windward coast of Isla Mujeres. *Photo by Jonathon Sauer.*

of Isla Holbox. For Americans, this is almost virgin territory, with all the joys and inconveniences thereto appertaining. If you are interested in wild estuarine areas, in birding or fishing, or in exploring places not many tourists see, you will be happy here. Otherwise, forget this considerable detour, especially since you must backtrack in order to reach Cancún.

Twenty years ago, Cancún was an isolated, lovely Nowhere frequented by nesting sea turtles, mosquitoes, troops of monkeys, and a few fishermen. Now it is the ultimate in planned resorts, the sort of place people either love or hate, depending on what they're looking for. One thing is for certain: it has nothing whatever to do with the real Yucatán. But it does very well what it is meant to do—namely, provide a snazzy, up-to-date Xanadu where gringos—whether millionaires or secretaries who have saved their pennies—can exchange the sleet and snow of home for a few days of sun-and-sea worship. It's all here: the bright sand and palm trees, the bluest sea imaginable, the hotels ranging from very comfortable to ultraluxurious, the boat tours, scuba diving, wind surfing, deep-sea fishing, you name it. There are quickie bus tours to Chichén Itzá and ferry trips to the now very much discovered but still pretty Isla Mujeres. Some of the same sort of corruption and crime that you would find in places like Acapulco has sprung up here, but there are few hassles if you stay on the beaten track. The tap water is safe to drink, restaurant menus are printed in English, and your credit card is welcome almost everywhere.

Compared to swank resorts on the U.S. Gulf Coast, Cancún is a relative bargain if you don't count the air fare; but still, it costs to stay here. As a rule of thumb, the further away a hotel is from Punta Cancún (the elbow in the long barrier island on which the resort city is built), the less expensive the rates will be (though they will still run you fifty or sixty dollars for a single during the winter season). But even at these less pricey places, accommodations are pretty plush, and some of the grander hotels are a real show. Take a peek at the Fiesta Americana even if you can't afford to stay there (or wouldn't want to). With its pastel balconies, its meandering swimming pool where bands play night and day on islanded *palapas*, its hamburgers made to order, and its rows of lounging guests wearing expensive bikinis, nose shields, and varying degrees of tan or burn, it is a Cecil B. DeMille vision of what a holiday resort should look like.

Lest this outdoors-oriented travelogue end on too tame a note, I had better add that there are still some wild and unspoiled places near Cancún, though they are not easy to explore. The wide Laguna Nichupte, which Isla Cancún protects, is ringed by an impressive mangrove maze, and the bay is still vital to an important local fishery. About twenty miles north of Cancún lies the most remote of the area's islands, Contoy, which has been declared a national park. It is a more sun-baked and windswept version of what Isla Mujeres used to be; in short, everything that Cancún is not. There is a tiny community and lighthouse here, but few tourists get this far. Miles of snowy white beach and lovely little tidal lagoons invite you to play Robinson Crusoe to your heart's content. Although Cozumel has more specialty species, notably the Cozumel vireo and thrasher, Isla Contoy is an important breeding ground for the area's coastal birds. In spring it is also land's end for many migrant songbirds.

For us, too, Contoy is land's end—a fittingly wild and unspoiled place at which to end our journey and this book.

Directory of U.S. Campgrounds

Columns: *RV Camping · **Primitive Camping · Showers/Rest Rooms · Swimming · Boating · Canoeing · Nature Trails · ***Hiking Trails

The Florida Keys

	*RV Camping	**Primitive Camping	Showers/Rest Rooms	Swimming	Boating	Canoeing	Nature Trails	***Hiking Trails
Bahia Honda 305/872–2353	x		x	x	x		x	
Long Key 305/664–4415	x		x	x	x		x	
John Pennekamp Coral Reef 305/451–1202	x		x	x	x	x	x	

The Everglades and the Big Cypress Country

	*RV Camping	**Primitive Camping	Showers/Rest Rooms	Swimming	Boating	Canoeing	Nature Trails	***Hiking Trails
Everglades National Park								
Long Pine Key 305/247–6211	x	x	x				x	x
Flamingo (same)	x	x	x		x	x	x	x
Chekika 305/253–0950	x		x	x			x	
Big Cypress National Preserve 813/262–1066		x						x

Florida's South-Central Coast

	*RV Camping	**Primitive Camping	Showers/Rest Rooms	Swimming	Boating	Canoeing	Nature Trails	***Hiking Trails
Collier-Seminole 813/394–3397	x		x		x	x	x	
Koreshan 813/992–0311	x		x		x	x	x	
Cayo Costa 813/332–0808		x		x	x		x	
Oscar Scherer 813/966–3154	x		x	x	x	x	x	
Lykes Fisheating Creek 813/675–1852	x	x	x	x	x	x	x	x
Myakka River 813/924–1027	x	x	x		x	x	x	x
Fort DeSoto 813/866–2662	x		x	x	x		x	

Florida's North-Central Coast and the Big Bend Country

	*RV Camping	**Primitive Camping	Showers/Rest Rooms	Swimming	Boating	Canoeing	Nature Trails	***Hiking Trails
Hillsborough River 813/986–1020	x		x	x	x	x	x	
Withlacoochee State Forest								
Richloam 904/796–4958		x						x
Croom (same)	x	x	x	x	x	x	x	x
Citrus (same)	x	x	x	x				x
Manatee Springs 904/493–4288	x		x	x	x	x	x	x
Apalachicola National Forest								
East 904/926–3561	x	x	x	x	x	x	x	x
West 904/643–2477	x	x	x	x	x	x	x	x
Ochlockonee River 904/962–2711	x		x	x	x	x	x	
St. George Island 904/670–2111		x	x	x			x	
St. Joseph Peninsula 904/227–1327	x	x	x	x	x	x	x	x
Dead Lakes 904/639–2702	x		x		x	x	x	
Torreya 904/643–2674	x	x					x	

From Florida's Panhandle to New Orleans

	*RV Camping	**Primitive Camping	Showers/Rest Rooms	Swimming	Boating	Canoeing	Nature Trails	***Hiking Trails
St. Andrews 904/234–2522	x		x	x	x		x	
Grayton Beach 904/231–4210	x		x	x	x		x	
Basin Bayou 904/835–3761	x		x	x	x		x	
Rocky Bayou 904/897–3222	x		x	x	x		x	
Blackwater State Forest 904/957–4111	x	x	x	x	x	x	x	
Gulf Islands National Seashore								
Ft. Pickens (Fla.) 904/932–5302	x		x	x	x		x	
Perdido Key (Fla.) (same)		x			x			
Big Lagoon 904/492–1595	x		x	x	x		x	
Gulf 205/968–6353	x		x	x	x	x	x	
Pascagoula Wild. Mngt. Area	x	x		x	x	x	x	x
De Soto National Forest								
Northern Unit 601/928–4422	x	x			x	x	x	x
Southern Unit 601/928–5291	x	x			x	x	x	x
Gulf Islands National Seashore (Miss.)								
Davis Bayou 601/875–3962	x			x		x	x	
Petit Bois/Horn/Ship (same)		x			x	x		
Buccaneer 601/467–3822	x		x	x				
McLeod 601/467–1894	x		x			x	x	x
Fountainbleau 504/626–8052	x		x	x	x		x	
Fairview 504/845–3318	x		x		x			

*   Most of the parks listed have some sites with electrical hookups, but not all. Among the notable exceptions are Everglades Nat. Pk. and Padre Island Nat. Seashore.

**   Virtually all parks have areas where you can pitch a tent. This listing is reserved for relatively isolated, secluded sites.

***   Hiking trails are distinguished from nature trails here in that they involve distances of more—usually much more—than one or two miles. Beach hiking is not indicated. Also note that a number of the refuges (not listed here) have excellent trails although camping is not permitted.

	*RV Camping	**Primitive Camping	Showers/Rest Rooms	Swimming	Boating	Canoeing	Nature Trails	***Hiking Trails
New Orleans and the Louisiana Coast								
Grand Isle 504/787–2559	x		x	x	x	x		
Morgan City Lake Palourde 504/385–2160 or 504/384–3343	x		x	x	x	x		
Jeanerette Lake Fausse Pt. 318/276–4293	x		x		x	x		
Frenchman's Wilderness 318/228–2616	x		x	x	x	x		
Sam Houston Jones 318/855–7371	x	x	x			x	x	x
The Texas Coast								
Big Thicket National Preserve 713/839–2689		x			x	x	x	x
Sea Rim 713/971–2559	x	x	x	x	x	x	x	
Galveston Island 713/737–1222	x		x	x			x	
Goose Island 512/729–2858	x		x	x	x		x	
Port Aransas 512/933–8121	x		x	x				
Mustang Island 512/749–5246	x		x	x				
Padre Balli 512/933–8121	x		x	x	x			
Padre Island National Seashore 512/933–8173	x	x	x	x	x		x	
South Padre Island								
Isla Blanca 512/943–5493	x		x	x	x			
Andy Bowie (same)		x		x				

A Glossary
of Spanish Words and Phrases

above, atop arriba, encina de, obre de

address dirección

afternoon tarde

agreement, bargain trato

to arrive llegar

ask for pedir

assistance, help ayuda

below abajo

boat/small boat barco/lancha, bote, chalupa

book libro

bookstore librería

boy niño, muchacho

bridge puente

broken roto, quebrado

bump (road bump) tope

to burn encinder, quemar

to carry carga, llevar

caution cuidado

cold frio

cool fresca

day día

to depart salir, partir

to do hacer

to drink beber

dry seco

to eat comer

the end/to end fin, limite/ terminar

entrance entrada

exit salida

far lejos

few pocos

forbidden, prohibited se prohibe

garden jardín, huerta

gasoline gasolina

gas station gasolinera

girl niña

to go ir

good bueno

high alto

highway, road carretera, camino

hot caliente

house casa

hut palapa, choza

kill matar

to know saber

lady la señora, dama

light luz

to look mirar

lost perdido

man hombre

money dinero

more más

name nombre

new nuevo

night noche

old viejo

owner dueño

pass/to pass paso/pasar

to pay pagar

permission permiso

place lugar, sitio

pretty bonito

quick rápido, pronto

rain lluvia

to rest descansar

rock piedra, roca

route rumbo, trayecto

ruin ruina

to be sad estar triste

school escuela

sea mar

see ver

sick enfermo, malo

to sleep dormirse

to stop   detenerse, pararse
storm   tempestad, norte
street/avenue   calle/avenida
sun   sol
sweet   dulce
thick   grueso
thin   delgado
toll   cuota, cobro
tourist   turista
travel   viajar
traveller   viajero
trip   viaje
trouble   trabajo
turn/to turn   vuelta/voltear
up   arriba
vehicle   vehiculo
very   muy
village   pueblo
to walk   caminar
water   agua
welcome   bienvenido
wet   majado
with   con
without   sin
woman   mujer
work/to work   trabajo/trabajar

Words Relating to the Outdoors

animal   animal, creatura
bait   carnada
bay   bahia
bird   ave, pájaro
boat/small boat   barco/lancha,
     bote, chalupa
to camp/camping   acampar/cam-
     pismo
campfire   fogata, lumbre
campground   campamento
canoe   canoa
coast   costa
countryside (or field)   campo
fishing/to fish   pesca/pescar
flashlight   foco
flower   flor

forest   bosque, monte
to hike   caminar, marchar
hill   loma, cerro, colina
jungle   selva, jungla, monte
lagoon   laguna, estero
lake   lago, laguna
mangrove swamp   manglar
map   mapa
mosquito   mosco, mosquito
motorboat   motonauta
mountain   montaña
oar   remo
to paddle   remar
point (of land)   punta
rapids   rápidos, raudas
river   rio
river mouth   boca
shallows   los bajos
shore   orilla, litoral
snake/poisonous   culebra/vibora
     snake
stream   arroyo
to swim   nadar, banar
tent   casita de campaña
thicket   matorral
trail   vereda, camino, sendero
trailer park   parque de traylers
tree   árbol
valley   valle
wild   silvestre
wilderness   desierto, yermo

Getting Started

Hello   ¡Hola!
Good day/Good   Buenos días/
  afternoon   Buenas
                        tardes
Good night   Buenas noches
Goodbye   Adios
Pardon me   Perdon
Please   Por favor
Thank you   Muchas gracias
You're welcome   De nada
Pleased to meet you   Mucho gusto

man señor
married woman señora
young woman señorita

At the Hotel

I'd like a single room.	Quisiera una habitación sencilla.
We'd like a double room	Quisiéramos una habitación doble
with two beds.	con dos camas.
with a double bed.	con una cama matrimonial.
with a private bath.	con baño privado.
Is there hot water?	¿Hay agua caliente?
Is there laundry service?	¿Hay servicio de lavanderia?
What is the price per night?	¿Cuál es el precio por noche?
Could I see the room?	¿Puedo ver la habitación?
The room is too noisy/dark.	El habitación es demasiado ruidosa/oscura.

Small Talk

What's happening?	¿Qué pasa?
What time is it?	¿Qué hora es?
It is hot/cold.	Hace calor/frio.
Do you speak English?	¿Habla inglés?
I don't understand.	No entiendo.
I don't know.	No sé.
What?	¿Cómo?
How do you say . . . in Spanish?	¿Como se dice . . . en español?
Why?	¿Porqué?
Could you help me?	¿Puede usted ayudarme?

I need	Necesito
I want	Quiero
No	No

In Town

Address	la dirección
Where is the post office?	¿Dónde está el correo?
bank?	el banco?
beach?	la playa?
airport?	el aeropuerto?
church?	la iglesia?
drug store?	la farmacia?
marketplace?	el mercado?
Which way?	¿Por dónde?
How far?	¿Hasta dónde?
near/far	cerca/lejos
to the right/to the left	a la derecha/a la izquierda
straight ahead	derecho
open/closed	abierto/cerrado

Eating

I'm hungry.	Tengo hambre.
Is there a restaurant nearby?	¿Hay un restaurante cerca de aqui?
Is there a menu?	¿Hay una lista (*also* carta *or* menu)?
Do you have?	¿Tiene usted?
I'd like	Quisiera
waiter	el mesero
a table for	una mesa para
menu	la lista *or* la carta
food	la comida
beverages	las bebidas
drinking water	un vaso de agua purificada
beer	una cerveza
soft drink	un refresco
Where is the ladies' rest room?/men's rest room?	¿Dónde está el lavabo de damas?/de señores?
the check	la cuenta

breakfast   el desayuno
lunch   la comida
dinner   la sena

Driving

I would like to rent a car.	Quisiera alquilar un automóvil.
gas station	una estacion de gasolina
Fill the tank.	Llene el tangue.
oil el aciete	
road el camino	
map el mapa	
brakes los frenos	
tires las llantas	

Leaving Town

Is there a plane to?	¿Hay un avión a?
What time does the flight leave?	¿A qué hora sale el vuelo?
Where is the train station?	¿Dónde está el estación ferroviaria?
Is this the train to?	¿Es éste el tren a?
I'd like a ticket to	Quiero un boleto a
When is the next bus to?	¿A qué hora es el próximo autobús a?
Does this truck go to?	¿Va este camion a?
How long does the trip last?	¿Cuánto dura el viaje?
What is the fare?	¿Cuánto es la tarifa?

On the Trail

Where is the trail to?	¿Dónde está el camino a?
Where does this trail go?	¿Adonde va está camino?
How many kilometers is it to?	¿Cuántos kilometros hay a?

How far is the next village?	¿A que distancia está el proximo pueblo?
I'm lost. Me he perdido.	
Where is the nearest water?	¿Dónde está el proximo agua?
What is the cost per day?	¿Cuál es la cuesta por día?
How long is the journey?	¿Cuánto dura el viaje?
May we camp here?	¿Podemos acampar aqui?

Other Useful Phrases

Can I cash a traveler's check?	¿Puedo cambiar un cheque de viajero?
What is this called?	Cómo se llama esto?
I don't understand.	No comprendo.
Speak more slowly, please.	Habla más despacio, por favor.
May I leave this baggage here?	¿Puedo dejar esta equipaje aqui?
What's the price?	¿Cuál es la cuesta?
Where is my luggage?	¿Dónde está mi equipaje?
Where is there a doctor who speaks English?	¿Dónde hay un médico que hable inglés?

Emergency

doctor   un médico
police   la policía
hospital   el hospital
ambulance   una ambulancí

Bibliography of Special Interest Books

Florida

Gerald Grow *Florida Parks: A Guide to Camping in Nature*, Long Leaf Publications, Tallahassee, Fl., 1981. A useful handbook covering all of Florida's parks.

John M. Keller, ed. *Walking the Florida Trail*, Florida Trail Assoc., Box 13708, Gainesville, Fl. 32604. Looseleaf booklet with maps, data, on all trail segments. You may have to join the Association to get it.

Florida Canoe Trails, Florida Dept. of Natural Resources, Crown Bldg., Tallahassee, Fl. 32304. Pamphlet listing some of the state's more notable canoeing rivers.

Elizabeth F. Carter *Downriver Canoeing in the Big Bend*, obtainable through Dalton Books, 1500 Apalachee Pkwy., Tallahassee, Fl. 32301. A small but valuable pamphlet describing several north Florida rivers.

Louisiana and Eastern Mississippi

John P. Sevenair, ed. *Trail Guide to the Delta Country*, obtainable through New Orleans Sierra Club, 111 S. Hennessey St., New Orleans, La. 70119 or Canoe Shop, 624 Moss St., New Orleans, La. 70119. An invaluable guide to canoeing and hiking in the area of southern La. and Miss.

Texas

Mildred Little *Camper's Guide to Texas Parks, Lakes, Forests*, Lone Star Books, Division of Gulf Publishing, Houston, Texas. Brief rundowns of facilities and attractions at all Texas parks. Maps.

—— *Hiking and Backpacking Trails of Texas*, Lone Star Books, Division of Gulf Publishing, Houston, Texas. Brief descriptions of parks and trails. Maps.

Mexico

Carl Franz *People's Guide to Backpacking, Boating, and Camping in Mexico*, John Muir Publications, Santa Fe, N.M. Although this is not a guide to specific areas, I have included it here because it is the only book on camping in Mexico. Information is general but helpful and entertainingly presented.

Note: For a magnificent visual introduction to the beauty of the United States Gulf Coast, C. C. Lockwood's book of photographs, *The Gulf Coast* (Baton Rouge: Louisiana State University Press, 1984), is highly recommended.

Index

A *Note to the Reader* Readers are invited to send updated information and corrections for any title in the Sierra Club Adventure Travel Guide series to the author, c/o Travel Editor, Sierra Club Books, 730 Polk Street, San Francisco CA 94109.